DATE DUE

A Cause Greater than Self

NUMBER 139
Williams-Ford Texas A&M University Military History Series

A CAUSE GREATER
THAN SELF

The Journey of Captain Michael J. Daly,
World War II Medal of Honor Recipient

STEPHEN J. OCHS

Texas A&M University Press *College Station*

Library of Congress Cataloging-in-Publication Data

Ochs, Stephen J.
  A cause greater than self : the journey of Captain Michael J. Daly, World War II
Medal of Honor recipient / Stephen J. Ochs.—1st ed.
    p. cm. — (Williams-Ford Texas A&M University military history series ; no. 139)
Includes bibliographical references and index.
ISBN 978-1-60344-783-6 (cloth : alk. paper)—ISBN 1-60344-783-0 (cloth : alk.
paper)—ISBN 978-1-60344-803-1 (e-book)—ISBN 1-60344-803-9 (e-book)
    1. Daly, Michael J., 1924–2008. 2. United States. Army—Officers—Biography.
3. World War, 1939–1945—Campaigns—Western Front. 4. Medal of Honor—
Biography. 5. Soldiers—United States—Biography I. Title. II. Series: Williams-Ford
Texas A&M University military history series ; no. 139.
  U53.D35O24 2012
  940.54'1273092—dc23
  [B]
                                        2012003945

Frontispiece: Michael J. Daly's Medal of Honor. Courtesy W. Sanford Miller Jr.

Dedicated to the memory of Theodore C. Ochs, Dorice J. Ouellette,
Aloysius C. Galvin, S.J., and Michael J. Daly, veterans of World War II:
father, father-in-law, colleague, and friend—members of the "greatest generation"

Contents

Illustrations

A new mission   185
Exorcising ghosts   189
"From a grateful nation"   200

"Roland is fierce, and Oliver is wise / And both for valor may bear away the prize."
—from *The Song of Roland*

"Heroism is not about skull-cracking. It is, first of all, about profound moral conviction. . . . The hero must also be the possessor of ability and be conscious of that ability without any self-flattering hubris . . . must possess perseverance . . . must always be ready to move forward."
—Allen C. Guelzo

Preface

In February 2002, Robert C. Barry, one of my longtime colleagues at Georgetown Preparatory School, in North Bethesda, Maryland, walked into the faculty office and asked me whether Prep had any graduates who had received the Medal of Honor. Bob uses such facts as extra-credit questions on his English vocabulary quizzes, questions that run the gamut from school history to geography to sports. He asked me because in 1989 I had written a history of the school for its bicentennial celebration. My book, however, covered only the period from 1789 to 1927, at the end of which Georgetown Prep legally separated from Georgetown University. Since I had not written about the WWII era, I turned to a short history of Prep from 1919 to 1969 written by William S. Abell, a Prep alumnus. When I consulted it for Medal of Honor recipients, I found the name of Michael Joseph Daly, class of 1941. Bob and I then went to the Internet and found the citation that accompanied his medal on the website of the Medal of Honor Society. Its description of his actions at Nuremberg, Germany, on April 18, 1945, astounded us. Bob included the question in his quiz, and I remained intrigued.

The next day I asked Brian Ray, who handled alumni relations, if he had any current information on Mr. Daly. (I gained such respect for Michael Daly that I could never bring myself to address him other than as "Mr. Daly.") It turned out that he did. Daly was alive and well and, at age seventy-seven, still living in his hometown of Fairfield, Connecticut. He had remained in contact with the school, and Brian had spoken with him by phone not long before. Buoyed by the news, I phoned Daly to ask if he would talk with me about his wartime experiences so that I could share them with my students and the rest of the Prep community. At first he seemed embarrassed, protesting that he was no hero, that the real heroes were the men who gave their lives during the war. But he kindly consented, especially when I pleaded the benefit that students in my US history classes at his alma mater would derive from learning and reflecting on his story. He insisted, however, that I tell the story "warts and all."

Thus began my association with a man whom I came to know mostly over the telephone. As I learned more about him, I became convinced that his story deserved a book. Over the course of six years—I could work on the book only during summer vacation—Mr. Daly and I spent hours on the phone discussing aspects of his life in both war and peace. We also debated current religious, political, and military issues, and I enjoyed sparring good-naturedly with him. He loved words—poetry, history, epigrams—and wrote, often eloquently, in an elegant longhand. Diagnosed with cancer in the late spring of 2008, he died, surrounded by family, at his home in Fairfield on July 25. He was a gentleman in the truest sense of that word, among the most gracious, humble, kind, generous, and intelligent people I have ever had the privilege of knowing and loving. And, of course, he was a warrior-hero—one of the bravest of a generation that went off to war and saved the world.

Abbreviations

3rd Battalion Unit Journal Unit Journal, June 2, 1944, 3rd Battalion,
  18th Infantry
88 German 88-mm antiaircraft and antitank gun
ADC Army Depository Copy
Americal Americans in New Caledonia
B-17 ("Flying Fortress") and B-24 ("Liberator") US heavy bombers
BAR Browning Automatic Rifle
CT Regimental Combat Team
DFP Daly Family Papers
FDMC First Division Museum, Cantigny
GPSA Georgetown Preparatory School Archives
JU-88 German dive-bomber
IRTC Infantry Replacement Training Center
LCI(L) US Landing Craft Infantry, Large
LCT US Landing Craft, Tank
LCVP US Landing Craft, Vehicle, Personnel (Higgins Boat)
M1 US Carbine, Caliber .30, M1
MG 42 German machine gun
MP 40 German machine pistol (Schmeisser, or burp gun)
NARA II National Archives and Records Administration II,
  College Park, MD
NCO noncommissioned officer
NPRC National Personnel Records Center, St. Louis, MO
PUA Princeton University Archives
SHAEF Supreme Headquarters Allied Expeditionary Force
TD tank destroyer
TIC telephone interview with Troy D. Cox
TID telephone interview with Michael Daly
USMAL United States Military Academy Library
USMASCA United States Military Academy Special Collections
  and Archives

Introduction

World War II, the so-called good war, continues to fascinate the public even as the "greatest generation" fades from the scene before our very eyes. Certainly the torrent of books, articles, films, museum exhibits, conferences, and oral-history projects over the last twenty-five years has added immensely to our understanding of America's armed forces during that titanic struggle. The Army History and Education Center proudly proclaims as its goal "Telling the Army's Story . . . One Soldier at a Time." This book attempts to do just that by recounting the story of Medal of Honor recipient Michael J. Daly, one of the bravest of the greatest generation. In doing so it explores, in the life of one man, the questions many of us have about the members of that storied fraternity who have received the Medal of Honor—those men and one woman whose actions seem to define bravery: What factors shaped them? What motivated them? What was the nature of their courage? What happened to them after their feats of heroism? What, if anything, did they have in common? What do their stories teach us? The book also uses the prism of Daly's experiences on the platoon and company level, where battles were fought and won, to highlight key aspects of the war in Western Europe, especially the challenges faced by American troops, not only in well-known battles such as Omaha Beach but also in lesser-known and often-ignored campaigns in the Colmar Pocket, in Eastern France, and in central and southern Germany. In the closing months of the war, a defeated yet still dogged and resourceful foe tried to spill as much Allied blood as possible. Men such as Daly helped make possible the final destruction of the Third Reich.

Michael Daly was raised in privilege, but his father, Paul G. Daly, a highly decorated veteran of World War I, set him on the path to selfless heroism. Paul expected much from his son, but as a teenager, Michael frequently disappointed him. Failing to live up to expectations led Mike into the infantry in late 1943. In the cauldron of war during 1944 and 1945, serving first as an enlisted man and then as an officer in two of the most storied infantry divisions (the 1st and the 3rd) in the US Army, Daly redeemed himself from the irresponsibility and failures that had plagued his teenage years. He proved himself on the battlefield, forging an identity separate from that of his larger-than-life father even as he traveled much the same path and drew upon the values and skills that the older man had imparted to him. Michael Daly found a sense of purpose and mission in a socially and ethnically diverse citizen army. Seemingly afraid to show fear, he proved himself a brave, fierce, and skillful warrior-leader, receiving numerous decorations for gallantry, including three Silver Stars, a Bronze Star with *V* device for Valor, two Purple Hearts, and finally the Medal of Honor. Many men in his company described him as the best officer and bravest person they had ever encountered. By the tender age of twenty he had become a captain and company commander. In the process he discovered his best self: a man for others, a "protector-rescuer" devoted to his men both on and off the battlefield. He ardently believed in the justness of the Allied cause, possessed an intuitive ability to adapt to conditions on the battlefield, and displayed a mastery of fighting skills and small-unit tactics. He modeled the infantry motto, "Follow Me!" and embodied a quality absolutely crucial to ultimate Allied victory: the initiative to close with and aggressively engage the enemy. All the while, in addition to accomplishing his unit's mission, Daly made the welfare of his men a top priority and sought to bring home as many as possible. To that end he repeatedly placed himself in harm's way. He believed that aggressively pressuring the enemy by setting him back on his heels would ultimately save men by bringing the war to a speedier end.

Like so many veterans returning home from war, Daly faced the challenges of readjustment, a task made trickier by his war-hero status at such a young age. For a while he reverted to the irresponsibility that characterized his pre-army years. Eventually, however, he found new direction and meaning in his life, starting his own business, marrying and raising a family, and serving for forty years as a board member of St. Vincent's Hospital in Bridgeport, Connecticut. There he became known as "the conscience of the hospital" for his work on behalf of the poor and the terminally ill. Over the course of forty years he raised millions of dollars on its behalf. Michael Daly's devotion to causes greater than himself should inspire and reassure Americans as they face a war on terror today. The generation fighting this battle is heir to the legacy of soldiers such as Michael Daly: a man willing to risk his life and reluctantly do violence so that good people could sleep safely in their beds at night.[1]

Note on Sources

This book is based on archival research in military and school records and on personal interviews with Michael J. Daly's family, friends, and associates and with some of the men whom Daly commanded or with whom he served. During several trips to Europe, I retraced the route Daly had followed between his landing at Omaha Beach on June 6, 1944, and his near-mortal wounding in Nuremberg on April 19, 1945. In the course of those trips, I was able to interview some of those whom Daly helped both to liberate and to defeat. Unfortunately, by the time I began my research, many of Daly's contemporaries had passed away or were too ill to be interviewed.

Between 2002 and 2008, however, I was fortunate to share many hours of conversation—most over the telephone—with Michael Daly, who was seventy-seven years of age when we first began to correspond and converse. He remembered many things vividly, others only vaguely, some not at all. Initially I was stunned when he could recall very little about the specific actions that resulted in his three Silver Stars and the Medal of Honor. He explained that in the heat of combat, with adrenaline pumping, he seemed to fuse with the moment. And because combat was so similar from day to day, it tended to "run together" in his mind—an unintended acknowledgement, by the way, of how the heroic can become ordinary. He also explained that the bullet that struck him in the face on April 19, 1945, "scrambled" his memories of the engagement that led to his receiving the Medal of Honor. Luckily, army procedures for the awarding of medals require sworn descriptions from third-party witnesses. This was particularly true of the Medal of Honor.

In using the Daly interviews in this book, I have attempted, when possible, to verify Daly's recollections by consulting unit action reports and other military records as well as interviews, memoirs, and secondary accounts. Throughout the book I quote from the transcripts of our conversations, placing Daly's statements in quotation marks. Sometimes I quote him looking back on events. At other times, I quote his best recollections of what he heard or said years before.

A Cause Greater than Self

Prologue

August 23, 1945: the gilded, chandeliered East Room of the White House. President Harry Truman held the gold, five-pointed star[1] slightly away from the chest of Michael J. Daly, the tall, young infantry captain who stood at attention before him in his tan service dress uniform. Truman had just draped the medal around Daly's neck and now reached back with his left hand to adjust the broad, silky, light-blue ribbon from which the gleaming medal dangled. At age twenty, Daly was the youngest of the twenty-eight recipients gathered that day to receive the Medal of Honor from the president's hand.[2] As had become Truman's custom when bestowing the decoration, the former World War I artillery officer told Daly he would rather have the Medal—the nation's highest military award—than be president. At that moment, Daly, still bearing facial scars from his brush with death three months earlier, briefly closed his eyes. The images and feelings all ran together—numbing fatigue, rubble everywhere, enemy snipers, shots, explosions, men falling, carnage, adrenalin pumping, running, firing, bobbing and weaving, maneuvering, firing again and again, fifteen dead Germans in his wake, and later a wall, a leap, a shot, blood surging into his throat, gasping for air. His eyes opened. Then, in keeping with tradition governing the ceremony, the commander in chief, in a departure from normal military protocol, saluted the captain first rather than wait for him to render the courtesy. Daly solemnly returned the salute, feeling a mixture of pride, humility, and grief, vowing silently to try to live a life that would reflect honor on those who, he believed, truly deserved the medal: "the guys who didn't come home."[3]

The medal Daly received from Truman's hands on that rainy summer day in 1945 originated in an act of Congress passed on July 12, 1862, during the Civil War. (Because the medal was bestowed in the name of Congress, it is often referred to as the "Congressional Medal of Honor," but its correct name is Medal of Honor.) On July 9, 1918, Congress amended the law in order to clarify the criteria for the honor. It stipulated that the president or his designated representative should bestow the medal in the name of Congress upon a member of the army—enlistee or officer—who distinguished himself

August 23, 1945—the White House: President Truman awards Capt.
Michael J. Daly the Medal of Honor. *Courtesy Daly Family Photos (original
in National Archives)* "I would rather have this Medal than be President,"
Truman said. Paul Daly told his son that he had never met a Medal of Honor
recipient who was a "gentleman."

conspicuously "by gallantry and intrepidity" in battle with an enemy "at the
risk of his life *above and beyond the call of duty*" (author's emphasis). Indeed, a member of the army could not receive the Medal of Honor for simply
acting under orders, no matter how bravely he executed them. The deed had
to be such that, had the soldier not performed it, he could not later have been
justifiably criticized for having failed to act. To distinguish between "gallantry above and beyond the call of duty," and estimable but lesser forms of
bravery, Congress also established a new "pyramid of Honor" providing for
the Distinguished Service Cross, the Silver Star, and the Distinguished Service
Medal. Congress authorized their presentation by the president but not in the
name of Congress.

The army established rules and procedures for determining whether a soldier should receive the Medal of Honor. These required two eyewitnesses of the deed, a recommendation within two years of the date of the deed, and the conferring of the Medal within three years of the deed. Normally a soldier's immediate commander would nominate him, and then the nomination would proceed for review up through the serviceman's chain of command. The review process included a Decorations Board, which could recommend the Medal of Honor, a lesser decoration, or no award at all. The army chief of staff, the secretary of the army, the secretary of war, and finally the president all had to sign off on the award.

During World War II approximately fourteen million served in the armed forces of the United States. Of these, four hundred and sixty-four received the Medal of Honor, more than one-half posthumously.[4] These recipients constitute one of the most illustrious warrior fraternities in the world. Michael J. Daly belonged to that select and very diverse company. Truman probably noticed the colorful bar of ribbons pinned just below Daly's silver-and-blue Infantry Combat Badge and just above the left breast pocket of his uniform—evidence that Daly's heroism at Nuremburg was not a flash in the pan. Rather, it was the culmination of eleven months of consistently brave actions in the European Theater of Operations. During that time, Daly, who had entered the army as an eighteen-year-old enlisted man, earned an officer's commission and advanced to the rank of captain commanding an infantry company. Prior to receiving the Medal of Honor and his second Purple Heart, he had received three Silver Stars, for gallantry in combat, and a Bronze Star with an attached combat V device for valor. All this happened within two years of his being dismissed from Portsmouth Priory School in 1942 and from the United States Military Academy in 1943.

Sitting proudly in the audience during the White House ceremony were Mike's six brothers and sisters and his mother and father, Mary Madeleine Mulqueen and Paul G. Daly. His father, a highly decorated officer of both World Wars who himself had been nominated for the Medal of Honor in 1918 and who only recently had returned from service in France after sustaining a serious leg wound, had found himself repeatedly angered, embarrassed, and disappointed by his son's behavior in the not-so-distant past. Indeed, at times he probably despaired of his oldest son's becoming the gentleman he wanted him to be. But the colonel never lost his faith that Michael could lead men in combat. After all, he had prepared Michael his whole life for the events that culminated in Nuremberg and led them to the White House on this dreary, humid August day. In matters of courage, honor, duty, leadership, selflessness, and heroism, Michael could have had no better teacher than his father. Proud though he was of his son's war-time exploits, Paul both cautioned and challenged him: "I never knew anyone who won the Medal of Honor," he said, "that was a gentleman."

1   Hero-Father

April, 1918.

As an officer, Paul Daly was far better at soldiering than attending to administrative details. He had come to France to fight, not to do paperwork! This became apparent to Major Joseph Dorst Patch in late April 1918, when he assumed command of the 1st Battalion, 18th Infantry Regiment, 1st Division on the Picardy Front near Cantigny. Inspecting the records of the company commanders of the battalion before visiting them at the front, he noticed that the paperwork from Daly's Company D had more deficiencies than any other. He decided to raise this issue with Daly when he inspected Company D in the field. When he arrived at the company's command post, which lay north of the Bois de Saint-Eloi, he found "a tall, athletic-looking gentleman who greeted me courteously." Daly's men had burrowed into the sides of the ridge but were at that moment taking advantage of a brief lull in what had been relentless, nerve-shattering, and deadly German artillery barrages. The doughboys sat in the sunshine picking lice from their clothes. Patch was about to mention the missing paperwork when the conversation somehow turned to Daly's passion: horses. As Daly told Patch about an Irish hunter with great jumping ability, heavy shelling commenced. The men of Company D immediately took cover, but Daly did not pause in his story, recounting how the horse could jump five feet or better. Patch recalled that it was all he could do not to yell, "To hell with the horse! Don't you know we are being shelled?" They finally did take cover, but when the shelling ceased, Patch found himself listening to Daly's sequel to the story. When he returned to the command post, Dorst instructed the adjutant, who was an old regular and a stickler for adhering to regulations, to take care of the paperwork at battalion headquarters and not to bother the commander of Company D with clerical details. Years later, in his memoir, Dorst explained, "I thought I had met a real front line officer, and future events proved I was not far wrong,"[1]

Because Medal of Honor recipients come from such varied backgrounds and experiences, generalizing about common factors that shape them is difficult. Michael "Mike" Daly's path to heroism began at his father's knee listening to stories about knights and military figures, courage and valor. To the boy the stories had added credibility because they were told by a man who was a genuine hero in his own right. Michael's father, Paul G. Daly, was a successful New York City lawyer, real-estate investor, horse breeder, and highly decorated soldier who had risen to the rank of major in the 18th Infantry Regiment during World War I. Known for great integrity, intelligence, courtesy, and courage, Paul Daly had distinguished himself in combat, receiving the Distinguished Service Cross, a Division citation for valor (later converted to the Silver Star), the Croix de Guerre with Palm, the Legion of Honor, and three Purple Hearts. As a boy, Mike loved, admired, and respected his stern, warrior-hero father, whom he viewed as the very embodiment of patriotic gentlemanliness.

Paul Daly was the grandson of Timothy Daly, an Irish immigrant who in 1848, during the calamitous potato famine, had left the town of Muntevary, in County Cork, for New York City. Daly married Ellen Maria Flynn, and the couple had seven children. Daniel, their youngest, later became a successful lawyer in New York City specializing in real estate. The *New York Times* identified Daniel as "a conspicuous Tammany man" of the 28th Assembly District, an identification that no doubt proved lucrative for him. Daniel and his wife Anna raised four children. Their oldest son, Paul, was born in 1891. After attending the Jesuits' Loyola School in Manhattan,[2] sixteen-year-old Paul entered Princeton University in 1907, certainly a badge of respectability for an ambitious and upwardly mobile "lace curtain" Irish family.

Paul, however, proved a poor student, failing all but one course and leaving the university at the end of the first semester. Despite his brief stint, he nonetheless got on well with his classmates, who dubbed him "Pete" and made it a point over the years to invite him to their class reunions and to report on his doings in the *Princeton Alumni Weekly*.[3]

In June 1912, Paul entered the United States Military Academy as a member of the class of 1916. The class immediately above his, the class of 1915, later became known as "the class that the stars fell on," with 59 of its 164 members earning the rank of general, the most for a single class in the history of the Academy. Its ranks included two future five-star generals, Omar N. Bradley and Dwight David Eisenhower. But Daly would not remain long at the Academy. Although he once more proved popular with his classmates, he again struggled with math, and also with West Point discipline. In June 1914, for example, he finished 3rd class mathematics with a deficiency and was, in Academy parlance, "turned back" to the next lower class to repeat the year. At the end of the following year he was dismissed from the Academy for having accumulated 104 disciplinary demerits—4 above the maximum allowed—between December 1 and May 31. At the time of his departure he stood 120th out of 145 in class rank. With his strong, chiseled facial features, the tall, dapper young man looked as if he had stepped out of a newspaper advertisement for Arrow shirts. He went to work at Charles Broadway Rouse, a clothing store on Broadway.[4]

Several years later, in April 1917, Paul, along with many of the business and social elite on the East Coast, answered President Woodrow Wilson's crusading call to "make the world safe for Democracy" by enrolling in Officer Candidate School at the Plattsburg Training Camp outside Plattsburg, New York. Believing strongly that "gentlemen" made the best officers, and motivated by a strong sense of patriotism and noblesse oblige, Daly earned a commission as a second lieutenant in the United States Army in August 1917. He was one of 341 "ninety-day wonders" graduated from the first group of the Officer Candidate Schools established by Congress. Assigned to the 1st Infantry Division (later known as "the Big Red One" for its distinctive patch featuring a red "1" on a shield of khaki), he sailed for France on September 11, 1917. After some additional training in France, on November 20, 1917, he was assigned to the 18th Infantry Regiment of the 1st Division, the unit with which he served throughout the war.[5]

Intelligent, fearless, and unflappable in battle, Daly made an excellent combat officer. Gen. Frank Parker, who commanded the 18th, later characterized Daly's conduct as "courageous at all times," noting that on numerous occasions he volunteered for hazardous night patrols and raids across "no man's land" into enemy lines. Returning from one such raid in March 1918, Daly and a fellow soldier became disoriented, unable to find the designated path through barbed wire. Both embarrassed and nervous, Daly nevertheless remained outwardly calm, all the while praying to the Virgin Mary for help. "A group of stars, low over the . . . lines suddenly shone for me with an intense brilliance," he later recalled. "The preparation fire from our artillery lifted, and I went for the stars and right to a gap in the . . . wire you could have driven a load of hay through."[6] On May 5, 1918, General Pierre Georges DuPort, commanding the French 6th Corps, commended Daly for his great courage, energy, and skill in conducting reconnaissance patrols. As a result, Daly received a Division Citation (converted to a Citation Star on July 9, 1918, when Congress established that medal) for the "great and splendid gallantry" that he had displayed in leading patrols.[7]

Paul Daly continued his heroism as "a real frontline officer" during the Battle of Soissons, July 18–23, 1918, which marked the beginning of the Allied counteroffensive that four months later culminated in the Germans' suing for an armistice. Three divisions, the 1st and 2nd American and the 1st Moroccan (which contained the Foreign Legion), received orders to counterattack the northwest end of the salient that the Germans, during their great spring offensives, had driven into Allied lines as far as the Marne River at Château-Thierry. The Allies intended to cut two roads and a railroad at Soissons that served as supply arteries for German troops in the salient. The loss of those transportation lines would force the Germans to withdraw.[8]

The 1st Division went into battle under difficult and trying circumstances. The men were thoroughly exhausted after having struggled through rain, mud, and darkness along miles of roads clogged by artillery, tanks, and transport. Some troops reached the departure line just as the Allied artillery opened fire for the first barrage and thus had had no time to rest before 5:20 a.m., when they received the word to attack. Nevertheless, both American divisions made remarkable progress, advancing more than three miles on the first day. On the second they renewed their attack, but because the Germans had been heavily reinforced with machine guns and artillery the previous night, the going was slower and more costly.[9]

At the outset of the battle, Lieutenant Daly served as the scout officer of the 3rd Battalion, which would follow the 1st Battalion in the order of battle. On the morning of July 19, during a lull in the action, Daly went out to inspect the ground ahead and to the left. There he came across the 1st Battalion, which had been decimated during some of the heaviest fighting the Americans had yet encountered. Finding all but one of the officers dead or wounded, Daly took command of the shrunken battalion, now numbering only ninety men. He led them on a road that ran through rough and thickly wooded heights to the Château de Buzancy, where, in a lightning-quick attack, they captured 210 German soldiers. Then, with his fifty remaining men, Daly organized an ambush, repelling a counterattack by a slightly larger German force. Daly's much-diminished battalion had reached and held the line of the final objective of the division before any others. Although wounded on both July 21 and 22, Daly refused evacuation for treatment until the regimental commander ordered him to the rear.[10] The advances of October 1918 proved costly to the 1st Division as the Germans fought tenaciously, skillfully taking advantage of the hilly, heavily forested terrain. During that month the 1st Division suffered 7,169 men wounded or killed and 1,713 missing.[11]

Following Soissons, the commanding general of the French 10th Army awarded Daly the Legion of Honor—the highest decoration in France—with the Croix de Guerre with Palm for heroism. In addition the US Army awarded him two Purple Heart medals and the Distinguished Service Cross, the army's second highest military award. Dorst Patch said later, "I really believe his performance at Buzancy was one of the outstanding feats in all of the Division's battles." Others apparently shared his opinion. Daly was twice nominated for the Medal of Honor. The second time, after the war, General Parker

Major Paul G. Daly. Courtesy Daly Family Photos. During World War I, Paul G. Daly, the son of prominent Irish-Catholic parents with ties to Tammany Hall in New York City, served with the 18th Infantry Regiment of the First Infantry Division. A highly decorated war hero, Daly advanced to the rank of major, receiving three Purple Heart medals, a Commendation for Valor (later changed to a Silver Star), and the Distinguished Service Cross—the nation's second-highest military honor. Of Daly, General Frank Parker, commander of the 18th Regiment, later said, "With such men . . . we take our objectives."

appeared personally before the Board of the War Department to make the case that Daly's Distinguished Service Cross should be upgraded to the Medal of Honor. "We have here," he said, "a case of genuine practical heroism, accountable for most important results." The opposition of General R. C. "Corky" Davis in the War Department, however, blocked the award. Within twelve days of the action at Buzancy, Daly was promoted first to the rank of captain and then to major. When asked later why his promotions had come so quickly, he quipped "because, I could speak French and ride a horse."[12]

Soon after the Armistice ending the Great War on November 11, 1918, Daly found himself mounted on a handsome horse—he always loved the cavalry—acknowledging with a salute the welcoming cheers of a crowd as he led the 3rd Battalion of the 18th Infantry Regiment into Luxembourg, where the residents greeted the Americans as liberators. Along with the rest of the 1st Division, Daly's battalion then moved into Germany and eventually took up occupation duties northeast of Koblenz.[13]

On January 25, 1919, in a letter to Daly relieving him of command of his battalion in preparation for his return to the United States, General Parker included a written testimonial of Daly's service with the 1st Division. "You have been three times wounded and have, from the commencement of your service at the front and consistently thereafter throughout the war been conspicuous for your intelligence, personal gallantry, and leadership. . . . In my opinion, no member of this Division has done his duty in a more efficient, courageous, and soldierly manner than yourself." When Maj. Gen. Joseph Dorst Patch (ret.) wrote his memoir of the 1st Division, he dedicated it to Paul Daly, taking care to quote words that Parker had once offered in response to a general officer's complaint about "such men as Daly." "With such men as Daly," Parker replied pointedly, "we take our objectives."[14]

In late March 1919, Daly returned to a hero's welcome in New York City as a crowd of fifty thousand filled Central Park and cheered the 27th Infantry (to which he had been attached) and watched as thirty-one men received decorations: twenty-eight the Distinguished Service Cross of the United States Army and three the Croix de Guerre of France. The March 30 edition of the *New York Times* prominently displayed a photograph of Maj. Gen. John F. O'Ryan of the 27th Division pinning the Distinguished Service Cross on Paul Daly's tunic. Declining French General Weygand's offer of command of a brigade fighting for Polish independence, Daly opted for the life of a civilian.[15]

On December 28, 1920, the twenty-seven-year-old war hero married debutante Mary Madeleine Mulqueen in a wedding held at Saint Patrick's Cathedral in New York City and reported in the society pages of the *New York Times*. Archbishop Patrick Joseph Hayes celebrated the nuptial mass. The wedding illustrated how successfully the American Irish had pursued social mobility, wealth, and respectability through their skillful fusing of ethnicity, religion, and politics. The bride's father, Michael J. Mulqueen, was a successful New York City attorney and a prominent Catholic layman: president of the Catholic Club and, by appointment of Pope Benedict XV, a Knight of the Order of Saint Gregory. Madeleine's maternal grandfather, Thomas F. Gilroy, had served as a former Grand Sachem of Tammany Hall and as mayor of New York City from 1893 to 1894. The red-haired bride was witty and high-spirited but also deeply pious. In the words of one close family friend, Madeleine was straightforward, kind-hearted, and possessed of a sharp "New York sense of humor." She was quick to notice the humorous aspects of life. "She always had a different take on things, very original," and often expressed it with a straight-faced, deadpan delivery that delighted her friends and acquaintances.[16]

After a honeymoon in Europe that lasted several months, the newlyweds took up residence at 21 East 55th Street in New York City. After attending Columbia Law School between 1921 and 1924, Daly opened a law practice in the city.[17] In 1924, Paul and Madeleine Daly moved to a large, two-story colonial house on a farm in the Connecticut countryside off Hull's Farm Road in Fairfield. Residents of the town called it "Daley's Chateau," probably an admiring reference to his exploits at the Château of Bouzancy. They also addressed and spoke about him as "Major Daly" ("Colonel Daly" after

World War II), such were his military bearing and reputation and his commanding personality and physical stature.[18]

By occupation Paul Daly was a lawyer, but his great passions were military history and horses. One author described him as "a civilian soldier horseman." He raised and trained steeplechase horses on his farm, and in 1940 one of them, "Mansfield Park," won both the Pennsylvania Hunt Cup and the Meadow Brook Cup. From 1937 until he reentered the army in 1942, Daly practiced law and invested in real estate, but he much preferred going to the track and riding to the hounds with the Fairfield County Hunt Club. He purchased seemingly incorrigible horses and transformed them into mounts suited for fox hunting. The dark, sprawling, paneled living room of the Daly house was filled with easy chairs and lined with bookshelves. Two mounted grimacing fox heads stood sentinel on either side of the oak mantelpiece that framed the oversized country fireplace and bore the stains of burned remnants of Paul and Madeleine Daly's cigarettes.

Paul Daly had become a gentleman—a country squire—a role he relished. He named his place Belle Assis ("Well Seated"), as if it were an Irish manor. The names of Paul and Madeleine appeared in the New York City Social Register, and they won general acceptance from the WASP elite that dominated Fairfield, becoming two of the earliest Catholic members of the Fairfield Country Club. One acquaintance described Madeleine as "tremendously entertaining." Another remembered Paul as "extremely genteel" in a "Chesterfieldian sense." He could "rip your lungs out, but do it in a most polite manner after which he would assume the most courteous, respectful, and courtly demeanor toward you, as if it were all a joust."

Ever the gracious host, Paul Daly paid attention to the needs of his guests, making sure that they felt comfortable. Although normally self-possessed and reserved, among friends Paul Daly displayed a winning sense of humor. Alcohol and the camaraderie of drinking were central to the Dalys' socializing. They were famous for mixing incredibly strong drinks for guests, disappearing into the pantry to pour straight Scotch or Bourbon "to hand you still another one that you didn't need." They liked their guests to stand in front of the roaring fireplace and hold forth on whatever topic the Dalys had chosen for discussion—usually a topic they knew better than anyone else present. The combination of liquor and heat loosened up most visitors and led to "terrific sparring" in the words of one who attended such gatherings.

In the bucolic upper-class setting of southeastern Connecticut, Paul and Madeleine raised a family that would grow to six children. Their second child and oldest son, Michael, was born there on September 15, 1924.[19]

2   Born with a Silver Spoon — "Slightly Bent"

"Belle Assis," Fairfield, Connecticut, 1925–37.

Ever the didact, "Major" Paul Daly sought to inculcate what he regarded as the "manly" virtues of patriotism, duty, courage, persistence, and selflessness in his son Mike. Horsemanship thus became an arena for moral instruction and character development. Michael later recalled: "We always had temperamental horses throwing us off. We weren't supposed to cry. We weren't supposed to show fear. We were supposed to get right back up on the horse again." "Listen," Paul Daly would say. "I'll tell you what bravery is. Bravery is being brought up in such a way that you are more afraid of letting anyone know you are afraid than you are of what you are afraid of." The senior Daly would later say that the best training for a new army officer was for him to take a horse on a difficult jump because it took nerve to keep oneself and the horse steady and in control. Mike took naturally to horses and, when he was six or seven years old, displaced his older sister Madeleine ("Madge") for the honor of competing at Madison Square Garden in the horsemanship contest of the American Society for the Prevention of Cruelty to Animals (ASPCA), an honor open only to first-prize winners in the ASPCA horsemanship competitions at accredited summer horse shows. His boyhood dream was to win the Grand National Steeplechase. He thought not at all about entering the army. Meanwhile he proved adept at stealing apples and galloping through neighboring farmers' hay fields.[1]

Mike also learned rudimentary military tactics during playtime with his dad. The major had a large collection of Napoleonic-era toy soldiers that he arranged in battle formations, sometimes in the back yard. During Mike's formative years, Paul would take him into the fields to play war games. Paul situated himself on a knoll as an "observer," and Mike had the task of sneaking up on him using concealment and stealth. Although Mike never succeeded in surprising his father, he did become adept at sneaking up on woodchucks. He learned his lessons well and later would develop a reputation among his men in the army for his uncanny and instinctive ability to use terrain to his advantage.

"Only afraid to show fear." *Courtesy Daly Family Photos.* The Daly children learned to ride at a young age. Faced with temperamental horses that often threw them off, they were not supposed to cry or to show fear. Paul Daly expected them to get right back up on the horse again." "Listen," he would say to Mike, "I'll tell you what bravery is. Bravery is being brought up in such a way that you are more afraid of letting anyone know you are afraid than you are of what actually frightens you."

Mike's father also shared with his boy his own fascination with military history and adventure, reading stories to Mike about Napoleon and Alexander the Great and King Arthur and the Knights of the Round Table. But the tale that father and son returned to most often as they sat together reading in the living room was the *Song of Roland.* A medieval epic poem set in the time of Emperor Charlemagne's campaigns against the Saracens in France, it recounts the story of Roland, Charlemagne's brave but impetuous nephew, and Roland's best friend, the equally courageous but far wiser Oliver. Failing to heed Oliver's advice, Roland bravely but unnecessarily sacrifices not only his own life, but also those of Oliver and his men. Clearly, in his rendering of the epic, Paul considered Oliver the more admirable of the two, for he possessed not only bravery, but also wisdom. When young Mike learned to read on his own, the first passage he read to his father came from the *Song of Roland,* which began, "Roland is fierce, and Oliver is wise, And both for valor may bear away the prize." Eventually he committed the entire poem to memory. Its moral helped shape the officer he became.[2]

Michael Daly grew up in the shadow of his strict, reserved, larger-than-life father, who sought to mold his son into a brave, patriotic, honorable

Daly Family ca.1937. *Courtesy Daly Family Photos.* Seated left to right: Bevin, Alison, Madeleine, Gilroy, Daniel, Paul G. Daly, Mrs. Madeleine Daly, and twelve-year-old Michael. Returning from World War I, Paul Daly married Madeleine Mulqueen. Paul and Madeleine reared six children on their farm near Fairfield, Connecticut, where Paul raised steeplechase horses. Paul Daly also practiced law and looked after his real-estate interests in New York City. He often read to young Michael from the medieval epic poem *The Song of Roland:* "Roland is fierce and Oliver is wise / And both for valor may bear away the prize." Major Daly emphasized the need for wisdom as well as boldness in a leader.

gentleman. Mike loved and respected his father. Paul Daly was indeed an admirable role model who provided Mike with unshakable core values. But he could also be somewhat austere and distant, even when the two engaged in activities together.

Paul shared his passion for horses and things military with his son. He and Mike took long horseback rides together through the fields, which sometimes included "scouting" forays into the woods "searching" for Indians. They both pretended that smoke rising from stacks in the town constituted proof that Indians were burning nearby villages. On one occasion, Paul shipped two horses up to the Green Mountains, in Vermont, where he and his son spent two weeks exploring the scenic area. Sometimes he took Mike with him when he drove up to the racetrack at Saratoga Springs, New York. On one such excursion, Mike came to the stark realization that, as regards automobiles, his father had feet of clay. When the car engine began to sputter, Paul pulled the vehicle over to the side of the road and asked Mike to raise the hood. Mike did so and stared aghast as his father poked a stick around the engine trying to figure out how to check the oil! In many respects, Paul was a man of an earlier era: the turn of the century. But although automobiles challenged him, character formation certainly did not.[3]

Patriotism permeated the Daly family. A large American flag flew from a tall pole in front of the house. Astride a horse, Paul Daly customarily led the Fairfield Memorial Day parade, and on Independence Day, which also was his birthday, he always hosted a daylong party complete with a great fireworks display. Michael later recalled that as a youngster he believed that all the celebration and hoopla on July 4 was to celebrate his father's birthday!

Paul and Madeleine Daly were also devout Catholics. During October and May they gathered their children after dinner for the recitation of the Rosary. Paul and Madeleine participated in the spiritual and social life of their parish, faithfully attending Sunday Mass at Saint Thomas Aquinas church with their lively brood of children in tow. They usually arrived late, and to Mike's keen embarrassment, his father insisted on parading up to the front pew. One morning, driving home after Mass, Mike and his sister complained about the long, boring sermon that the priest had delivered. His father reminded them that they were there not for the priest but for God.

Sometimes during the family's religious rituals, Mike's impish high spirits added a note of levity. One evening one of Mike's uncles joined the family for the Rosary. As usual, they knelt in a circle facing away from the center of the living room. With mischievous purpose in mind, Mike decided to give his uncle a "hot foot." He was crawling toward his uncle with matches in hand when one of his sisters noticed and warned the uncle. Everyone had a good laugh, and after Paul Daly good-naturedly rebuked his son, the family resumed its prayers.

In addition to his involvement with his church, Paul Daly also became active in local government and politics. For many years he served as finance chairman of the Fairfield Board of Finance and as a member of the Fairfield Democratic town committee. (Neither Paul nor Madeleine had a very high regard for President Franklin D. Roosevelt.) Many of Paul's friends in Fairfield were Republicans, but despite their sometimes differing political affiliations, they shared one deep bond: the memory of their service as officers during World War I. Generally a laconic man, Paul Daly nevertheless possessed a unique charisma that drew others to him. One fellow veteran, who lived a couple of miles away, would come by early every Sunday afternoon. He and Paul would sit in the living room saying little while drinking a couple of martinis. The neighbor would then stand up, say, "Good, Paul. I'll see you next week," and leave.

Throughout his life, Paul remained close to the Patch brothers, Alexander ("Sandy") and Joseph ("Dorst"), and also to Jeremiah Evarts, all 1st Division men. In their company, Paul loosened up, especially when talking about the war, when they each had given their all. These were not the disillusioned former soldiers of the "Lost Generation" described by authors of the 1920s. They were "true believers." They possessed a sense of noblesse oblige and remained convinced that they had fought in a noble endeavor on behalf of their country and the world. As a boy, Mike could not understand or appreciate the power of that experience. Only later would he come to know it for himself.[4]

Mike's major interests as a youngster were sports, horses, and any outdoor activity. He learned to shoot a rifle—a gentleman's activity—but did so because he enjoyed marksmanship, not hunting animals. At this point in his life, he did not much like to read, but when he did, he tended to read historical fiction such as G. A. Henty's *With Clive in India*. Unlike his father, who had little use for team sports, he was also an avid fan of the Boston Red Sox and the Army football team.

Paul Daly suffered some real-estate losses in New York City during the early years of the Great Depression, partly as a result of his alcoholic brother-in-law's mismanagement. But he and his family weathered the economic hard times much better than most. Paul Daly told his children, "We're not rich, but we're privileged." During the summers, Mike worked for his father and for neighbors pitching hay and picking potatoes. Many years later, Michael wryly observed, "I was born with a silver spoon in my mouth—slightly bent." The family had domestic help, including a cook and a man named John O'Brien who, along with his wife, lived in a small house on the property and looked after the horses. Mrs. O'Brien had been one of Ireland's first female jockeys, and everyone called her "the Duchess." After working for the Dalys, John became the fire chief in Weston, Connecticut, and remained very close to Michael until he died. Mike also enjoyed a warm relationship with the family nanny, an Irish girl named Mary Martin, who functioned in his life as an emotionally supportive surrogate mother.

The parents of some of Mike's friends dressed formally for dinner each evening, but Mike's parents did so only on special occasions. Nightly dinners featured wide-ranging conversation. The parents, seated at opposite ends of the table, talked back and forth about many topics, including current events, and often solicited their children's views. Richard ("Dick") Joyce Smith, a prominent and politically well-connected utilities lawyer, and his wife, Sheila ("Sheda"), became close friends of Paul and Madeleine. The Smiths and the Dalys were the two most prominent Irish Catholic families in a town dominated by wealthy Protestant businessmen. Every Sunday the adults got together for drinks while their large broods of children played together. Andrew, one of the Smith siblings, remembers the Daly family as "a different breed: tall, elegant, dressed in tweeds, rangy and crazy, living up in that rabbit warren of a house, surrounded by animals. . . . They all had a funny accent that wasn't Irish. . . . [I]t was some sort of Mid-Atlantic vaguely British thing." Looking back many years later on those days in Fairfield as a Catholic minority, Mike would joke with one of the Smith brothers, "The Smiths and the Dalys have always been kind, loyal, supportive, and very helpful. . . . But only to each other!"[5]

Mike attended Saint Thomas Aquinas Grade School from first through fourth grades. But when his mother insisted that the school advance her son from third to fifth grade, a practice common among competitive, high-society families, the nuns refused. In response, Mrs. Daly removed Michael from Saint Thomas and enrolled him in the sixth grade at Pequot Public School.

The school year did not begin well for Mike. He was young for his class, skinny, and not yet very tall. In addition, his father insisted that he wear knee pants, high shoes, and a beret to school, a mode of dress popular among the pre-World War I upper class and modeled on Reginald Birch's pen-and-ink drawings of Little Lord Fauntleroy, the hero of Frances Hodgson Burnet's eponymous novel. Mike's dress attracted negative attention. Students tagged him "Little Lord Fauntleroy" and "couldn't wait," in his words, "to give me a shot." Mike began coming home with a bloodied nose. When his father asked why he was getting into so many fights, Mike explained that bullies at school had zeroed in on him. At that, his father rolled back the rug and taught his son some boxing moves. He then put Mike in touch with a sixty-year-old boxing instructor who had been a lightweight fighter. There the youngster learned some additional moves. A short time later, when one of the bullies accosted Mike on his way to school, he responded by putting "a move on the guy." He didn't knock him down but did shake him up. The bully never bothered Mike again. Shortly thereafter Mike's dad relented and bought him some knickers like those that the other boys his age wore to school. His love of boxing, whether engaging in the sport, attending matches, or listening to fights on the radio, remained with him for the rest of his life. He would press his ear against the radio console when static or a weak signal made broadcasts hard to hear. And he enjoyed shadowboxing in his room. (In June 2005, when he was nearly eighty, Mike somewhat sheepishly "confessed" to the author that he had gotten so "worked up" after watching a televised boxing match, that he found himself shadowboxing.)

Mike's newly demonstrated pugilistic skills, along with his new long pants, his winning personality, and his enthusiasm for sports, made his school life much easier and more enjoyable. He loved the outdoors, was happy-go-lucky, and became the unofficial leader of a group of five friends who hung around and played sports together. But he did not enjoy his classes. In particular, he found math a real burden. Skipping the fifth grade had disadvantaged him mathematically because he had missed some basic building blocks. Those lacunae would bedevil him throughout high school and into college.

His parents also pushed Mike in the social sphere, insisting when he was twelve or thirteen that he take dancing lessons and attend cotillions. Still shy around girls, Mike hated the whole agonizing experience. Much later in his life he recalled ruefully: "Oh boy, the end of the world. I wasn't a very good dancer."

Mike's parents had Jesuit friends at Paul Daly's old school, Loyola, in Manhattan. Believing that their son would benefit from the kind of Jesuit high-school education Paul had received and wanting him to learn to speak French, they transferred Mike to Loyola for the eighth grade. Mike commuted into the city every day with his father and in the afternoons often visited his maternal grandmother, Mary Anne Gilroy, who lived near the school. Jesuits at Loyola, believing that Mike would profit from a boarding-school experience, suggested his parents enroll him in Georgetown Preparatory School, a Jesuit institution in the Maryland countryside outside Washington, DC. In September 1937, Mike arrived at Georgetown Prep as a freshman. The published tuition fee for resident students was $1,500, but the school often made adjustments based on a family's economic circumstances and size. The Dalys, like many other families who boarded their sons at the school, received a $500 discount.[6]

The Duke of Wellington supposedly declared that the battle of Waterloo was won on the playing fields of Eton. Though probably apocryphal and definitely hyperbolic, Wellington's statement paid tribute to what he regarded as the key role of English public schools in shaping the character of the British officer class. For Michael Daly, Georgetown Prep played a similar role, fostering physical skills, habits of mind and faith, and elements of character that later enabled him to play a heroic role on the battlefield. At Prep, Mike learned how to subordinate himself to the achievement of a common endeavor, a larger purpose. A budding leader, he also sometimes evidenced a reckless disregard for institutional restraints, a tendency that would lead to trouble over the next few years.

The oldest Catholic boys' high school in the United States, Georgetown Preparatory School was founded in 1789 by the Reverend John Carroll, later the first Catholic bishop of the new nation. Originally part of Georgetown University and located in the nation's capital, in 1919 the school relocated to Garrett Park, in the Maryland countryside northwest of the city. Then, in 1927, Georgetown University and Georgetown Preparatory School became separate corporate entities. During the worst years of the Great Depression, enrollment plunged by 50 percent and the school found itself in a precarious financial situation. By the time Mike Daly arrived, however, enrollment had stabilized and even begun to increase.[7]

The school occupied ninety-two rolling acres. At the highest point stood the main school building (now known as Boland Hall), its signature white cupola topped by a copper dome. The red-brick building, 300 feet long and featuring Georgian architecture, contained classrooms and dorm rooms and had two perpendicular wings, each 90 feet long. The north wing contained the infirmary and additional dorm rooms; the south housed the students' dining room and Jesuit faculty quarters. The building could comfortably accommodate one hundred boys. The extensive grounds provided facilities for ten tennis courts, two baseball fields, football and soccer fields, a rifle range, a quarter-mile track, and a nine-hole golf course. A small, wood-frame gymnasium housed a basketball court. When Daly arrived on campus, the campanile of the recently completed Italianate Chapel of Our Lady of Lourdes soared ninety feet above the campus. Topped by a simple copper Latin cross and visible from almost anywhere on campus, it testified to the religious mission of the school.

The Georgetown Prep catalog declared that the institution endeavored "to develop the intellectual faculties, to train the moral instincts, and to form character." Prep sought to prepare the boy not only to enter college and later a professional or business career, but also to "take his place in the world as an educated Catholic gentleman." For Paul Daly, those last three words resonated deeply. So also did Prep's reputation as "a select school" for those gentlemen. As the minutes of one meeting of the Jesuit community at Prep put it, "The school exists, at least in great part and was established, to care for Catholic boys whose parents would otherwise send them to a high-class non-Catholic school."[8]

Mike entered a school whose curriculum emphasized religious and academic instruction, elocution, and competition in classrooms and on the playing fields "in order to develop qualities of mind and character most needed for future Catholic leaders." The course of studies and pedagogy had its roots in the Jesuits' venerable *Ratio Studiorum* with its emphasis on languages, both classical and modern, and its goal of producing men who possessed *eloquentia* in both the written and the spoken word. Believing that competition—"healthy rivalry"—fostered enhanced performance among students and teachers, the Jesuits mandated that all students in their schools in the eastern United States take common final examinations prepared by a Central Board of Examiners. The board then published each school's results for comparison.[9]

Just turning thirteen as school began, Mike was younger than most of his classmates and was living away from home for the first time. Nevertheless he adapted well to the rigorous and regimented life at Prep, a task made easier by the presence of two friends from Loyola: the McDonnell brothers—Charles E. ("Bishy") and Thomas Murray.

On three of the five days of the week, Daly had to rise at 6:45 a.m. to attend the required 7:00 a.m. Mass. On other days he could sleep in until 7:15. Breakfast was served twenty minutes later, followed by an hour of study between 8:15 and 9:15. Classes met six days per week but not on Wednesday or Saturday afternoons. The academic day consisted of five forty-five-minute class periods with an additional ten-minute recess between second and third periods and a forty-five minute lunch period, during which the predominantly African American kitchen staff served the students at tables covered by linen and china. A three-hour sports block, which Daly eagerly anticipated throughout the day, followed the conclusion of classes. Students who had failed that day's recitation in any subject, however, had to attend an hour of supervised study between 4:00 and 5:00 or 5:00 and 6:00. In the winter months or during inclement weather, students could engage in hobbies— wood burning and painting—or attend classes in boxing, fencing, music, and the production of one-act plays. The students ate dinner between 6:00 and 7:00, after which they had a two-and-one-half-hour study period with a ten-minute recess from 8:15 to 8:25. "Lights out" followed at 10:00 p.m.

After Saturday-morning classes, students were permitted to go to Washington between 11:45 a.m. and 6:00 p.m. via taxi or the "Toonerville Trolley" line that ran just west of the campus. Jesuit scholastics—seminarians teaching at the school who also supervised resident students in the dorms and whom the boys addressed as "Mister"—accompanied the younger students to town. As for spending money, parents deposited a check with the school treasurer, and the headmaster dispensed it according to his judgment and the parents' wishes. Back on campus on Saturday nights, students often viewed movies in the school theater in the basement. The more adventurous among them, who entertained notions of sneaking off campus for greater weekend excitement, knew well the risk they took. The school catalog stated categorically: "Students are not to leave the grounds at any time without the prior permission of the Headmaster. Any student who leaves the grounds at night without permission thereby severs his connection with the school."

Sundays began with Mass at 8:00 a.m. After breakfast, the boys had to pass room inspection. (House men cared for rooms and cleaned them each weekday.) With the exception of lunch, from 1:00 to 2:00 p.m., the boys had the day free until Benediction, at 5:45 p.m., followed by supper and a study period.[10]

Daly's academic load at Prep included four years each of English, Latin, mathematics (through plane trigonometry), and religion. He also took two years each of Greek, French, and history (ancient and United States), as well as a year of physics. Intelligent but not academically driven, and lacking confidence and skills in math, Mike nevertheless occasionally earned second honors during his first two years. He particularly enjoyed studying history and Latin, and he especially liked and admired Father Kelvin "Scotty" Mac-Kavanagh, a legendary master teacher who taught Latin, English, and French; Father Bernard Kirby, who served as Prefect of Discipline and moderator of athletics; and coaches Tom Keating (football) and A. J. "Gus" Coupe (basketball). Still, he found it hard to sit still in class, tended to be disorganized in his studies, and did not particularly like to read (although as an adult he came to love the written word, especially poetry, and became a voracious reader of nonfiction).[11]

Tall and lanky—one classmate recalled him as "built like a pencil"—Mike played football, basketball, and baseball for four years, earning a varsity letter in basketball his junior year and in all three sports as a senior. He also served each year as an altar boy. He belonged to the rifle club during his freshman year, and to the Sodality of the Blessed Virgin Mary, an organization common in Jesuit schools that promoted devotion to Mary. Mike competed in horse shows during his freshman year. During his sophomore year he joined the debating society and, in the after-dinner hour, emerged as one of two "kingpins" of the early evening ping-pong games. As a junior, he wrote a piece for the *Little Hoya* entitled, "Prep Spirit" and served as a cheerleader during varsity football games. (He also played on the junior varsity football team.)

Energetic, personable, funny, friendly, happy-go-lucky, and "a bit ornery" and mischievous, Mike made friends easily, his closest being the McDonnell brothers and Thomas Coakley. Classmate Robert L. Barrett remembered Daly as "a real nice fella—always smiling and laughing, full of the devil but not looking for a fight. He danced to his own tune, but there was no malice, just a 'devil may care' attitude. He was fun to be with." Daly's room on the second floor in the north wing became a gathering place for evening "bull sessions" in his senior year. During one of them, according to the 1941 yearbook, "'Romeo' Daly tells us of Henrietta." The yearbook also admiringly noted Daly's "fancy stepping" in a "hot Conga chain" at the annual Tea Dance held at the school on December 7, 1940. Standing 6'2" and weighing 165 pounds, Daly, recently and overwhelmingly elected senior class president

Michael Daly, Senior Class President, Georgetown Preparatory School, 1940–41. *Courtesy Georgetown Preparatory School.* Mike's parents decided to send him to Jesuit-run Georgetown Preparatory School, the oldest Catholic boys high school in the country, located in the Maryland suburbs of Washington, DC. Popular, fun-loving, friendly, intelligent, and athletic, the 6'2" Daly attracted a wide circle of friends. But he also had a mischievous, antiauthoritarian streak that often landed him in trouble. A disciplinary infraction, for example, cost him his office as president of the senior class.

by his classmates, cut a dapper figure in his well-tailored suit as he posed with the other members of the recently elected student council for a photo on the steps of the main building. He exuded teenage cockiness as he stood slightly sideways on the steps, left hand in pocket, his hazel eyes (below slightly hooded lids) focused on the camera, his strong unsmiling mouth and aquiline nose, and his naturally raised eyebrows all contributing to an air of patrician haughtiness. Next to his name on the "Senior Quotes" page in the yearbook appeared the words, "Step aside, Freshman."[12]

Although the rangy Daly did not develop into a star athlete, coaches and teammates recognized him as an enthusiastic and determined competitor, a team player who hated to lose. "He wasn't a star," fellow football player Barrett recalled, but he was "pretty good." Barrett noted that Daly "had a good set of hands" to go with his height and "went all out when he had to and rested when he didn't." As the school newspaper noted in Daly's junior year, "Let's talk it up out there" became his signature exhortation from the bench or sideline to his teammates whenever he was out of the game. In his senior year, Daly played in most varsity football games as a regular substitute at both offensive and defensive end. The team finished with a record of 4–1–1, and in its final game of the season broke a ten-year winless streak against

Daly's Specialty

Football. *Courtesy Georgetown Preparatory School.* Daly earned a letter in varsity football, playing regularly as a substitute offensive and defensive end. He was not a star athlete, but his teammates remembered him as a "team player" and a "determined competitor" who hated to lose. He was deeply and positively influenced by Coach Thomas Keating and Assistant Coach Albert Charles "Al" Blozis, world record holder in the shot put, and future all-pro offensive tackle for the New York Giants. "Daly's Specialty." (Below) *Courtesy Georgetown Preparatory School.* Mike Daly loved team sports. In his senior year he lettered in varsity basketball and baseball as well as football. Drawn to the ideal of subordinating oneself for the good of the team, he had no disciplinary problems playing athletics.

archrival Iona Prep from New York. In that contest, Daly was knocked out tackling a runner. "An ignominious end to the season for me," he said later.

In basketball, Daly played forward on the varsity team as a senior coming off the bench—sixth man on a mediocre (11–13) team. Barrett remembered Daly as a player who "would feed you when you were open" and who "had a good shot." (Playing in Prep's wood-frame "gym," Daly and the other players sometimes had to loft their shots over a low-hanging rafter.) The team closed the year strong with an upset victory over Saint John's and thus earned an invitation to the *Washington Star* Basketball Classic. In the spring, Daly also roamed centerfield on the varsity baseball team—a team that had an uphill season until it won its last three games against strong opponents, including the top-ranked squad in the area, Washington and Lee.[13]

Daly also had become something of an impulsive risk taker and a mischievous rebel—traits that recent social science research identifies as characteristic of many Medal of Honor recipients. Back home he drove a Model T Ford that had belonged to his grandmother, and he drove it hard. Twice he had accidents as a result of driving too fast for road conditions. And like many teenage boys, he found himself increasingly at odds with his father. As in most father-son relationships, the two butted heads as Mike grew older and more independent. Mike came to see himself as a very different kind of person from his father: less cerebral, more antiauthoritarian, rebellious, and trouble-prone. His youngest sister, Alison, remembered Mike arguing with his dad. The arguments invariably followed a seemingly scripted pattern. As the words became more heated, Paul Daly would admonish his son to "Keep a civil tongue in your head!" and order him to "Go to your room!" Mike would stomp up the stairs and slam the door, which angered the father even more and led him to go get Mike, bring him back downstairs, and go through another argument. Clearly both father and son were strong willed and stubborn. Their sometimes-strained relationship during these years also proved painful and troubling to Mike, for Paul Daly still remained the lodestar of his life.[14]

Mike was never malicious or mean, but his impulsiveness, willfulness, and cockiness frequently landed him in trouble at Prep, where he became known as something of a "wise guy." His infractions involved tardiness, skipping classes, misbehavior, and violations of the school dress code requiring that students wear a jacket and tie to class and to the dining room. As a result, he sometimes lost the privilege of accompanying his classmates on school field trips. He often had to serve "JUG" (a tongue-in-cheek acronym for "justice under God"), which consisted of walking the outdoor track for forty-five minutes prior to athletic practices. Daly also occasionally showed flashes of an "Irish temper." One Jesuit scholastic accused him of throwing a Coke bottle at him during an argument, though Daly later insisted that he had purposely thrown the bottle out the window never intending to actually hit the scholastic standing next to it. But such outbursts occurred only rarely. For the most part, Daly kept his temper under control.[15]

No one could say the same about his room or his personal schedule. His dorm room was messy, and his lack of punctuality became a standing joke among his classmates. The student editors of the *Little Hoya* noted his chronic lateness in returning to school following holidays, quipping in their October 12, 1939, edition: "It surely is quiet around here. Say, has Mike Daily [sic] returned to school?" In September 1940, at the beginning of his senior year, Daly arrived four days after the beginning of classes, just in time, the yearbook later noted, for a school holiday! Daly later observed about his days in high school: "I was full of myself. I got by living for the next game." He was stripped of his senior-class presidency as a result of his many disciplinary infractions, including, his sister later recalled, something about his taking a school tractor for an unauthorized drive at night. On weekends, Daly and some friends occasionally made their way down to the burlesque shows in Washington, DC, although the time demands of academics and athletics as well as generally strict supervision by school officials did not allow much opportunity for such escapades. Most Saturday nights featured a film in the school theater, snacks from the school store, and bed check by 11:00 p.m.[16]

Despite finding himself often in trouble at the school, Mike had great respect and affection for many of the Jesuits and lay teachers there. He idolized Albert Charles "Al" Blozis, a 6'6," 245 lb. football tackle and three-time national shot-put champion at Georgetown University, who assisted Coach Keating with the Prep team and took a personal interest in the boys. (In 1941, UPI named Blozis, along with Joe Louis and Ben Hogan, the outstanding athletes of the year. Blozis went on to earn "All-Pro" recognition playing professional football for the New York Giants from 1942 to 1944.) Daly especially appreciated Father Kirby, the Prefect of Discipline, in whose office he spent so much time. Mike appreciated Kirby's blend of stern authority and personal kindness—his willingness to forgive even as he meted out punishment for Daly's many infractions of school rules. Kirby repeatedly urged Daly to develop "more self-control," and Mike continually resolved to do better. But invariably he would "fall" again, genuinely puzzled as to why he could not seem to avoid getting into trouble, especially since he seemed to have no disciplinary issues on athletic teams. Team sports appeared to give him both a physical outlet and an emotional focus that encouraged him to harness and direct his skill, energy, and daring in the service of a cause greater than himself: the good of the team. Others depended on him, and that called forth Mike Daly's best efforts.[17]

All this was part of the personal and spiritual development that lay at the heart of the school's larger curriculum and produced the "muscular Catholicism" expressed in Daly's article on "Prep Spirit." He began by praising the hard work and "high spirit" that the varsity football team had brought to its preparation for the game with highly touted Woodrow Wilson High School and that had resulted in a 6–0 Prep victory. He especially acknowledged Coach Keating as a crucial factor in the victory because he instilled in his team "this dogged *will to win.*" But Daly broadened the notion of "spirit" by pointing to another reason for victory that he believed no one should overlook. Before each game, he noted, it had long been a tradition at Prep for the team and the rest of the student body to attend Mass and receive Holy Communion. "It isn't enough to have the will to win," Daly wrote, "for in football as in later life we need the help of Our Lord at all times. We gain this help through the Sacraments, especially Holy Communion." More than sixty years later, Daly remembered "praying in that beautiful chapel" and the Jesuits' emphasis on the virtues of gratitude and generosity. He noted: "Georgetown Prep and the Jesuits nurtured in me a strong (if unconventional) Faith—*a fixed belief in the betterment of man*. For this I will forever be grateful." His conviction that God would ultimately redeem humanity no doubt contributed to his personal sense of well-being and confidence. Paradoxically, it may also have provided a pretext for the teenager to rationalize and minimize his frequent misbehavior. After all, God would understand, would ultimately forgive him. But Daly's faith also fostered in him a sense of obligation to recognize God in others and to help them when they needed it—a reinforcement of the values taught at home by Jesuit-educated Paul Daly. This faith would become the guiding principle of Daly's life. For now, seeds had been sown.[18]

Although he had not distinguished himself as an outstanding student during his time at Prep, Mike had done "well enough," maintaining averages of 84.6 and 84.8 in his junior and senior years, respectively. (The school required a minimum average of 80 to be recommended to college.) In 1941 he graduated twelfth in a class of twenty-eight seniors and, in an ironic twist, given his aversion to the subject, he finished fourth in the balloting for the Commencement award in mathematics. He graduated Prep having completed a rigorous academic course of studies, one that left him, in his own self-deprecating words, "scholastically competent."[19]

3   A Disappointment to His Family

New York City, Summer 1943.

Mike Daly had not had an easy or successful first year at West Point. He had survived a brush with the Honor Committee and the incessant hazing of the senior cadets (whom he seemed to infuriate continually), but he still faced his old academic nemesis, math, and its academic "relative," mechanical engineering. He had won a narrow reprieve the first semester but succumbed in the second by failing math. Unless he could pass a re-entrance test at the end of the summer, he faced possible dismissal. At the urging of his father, who had returned from the South Pacific in May 1943 and was stationed at Fort Lewis, in Washington State, Mike grudgingly enrolled for summer remedial classes with the brilliant tutor, Jacob Silverman, who had helped prepare him the previous year for his West Point entrance exam. Members of the remedial class included George Patton IV, son of America's most aggressive field commander. A tiny (5'3"), balding man, Silverman wore suspenders and sported an enormous black mustache. And he swore colorfully. Patton remembered him saying: "George, George, you son of a bitch! You pay attention, George. And don't write like fly shit!" Silverman also enjoyed a reputation for successfully tutoring cadets to pass the readmission exam. During the sweltering summer after the West Point term ended, Mike Daly found himself at Silverman's Bronx home "sweating," both figuratively and literally, under Silverman's tutelage.[1]

Following graduation from Georgetown Prep, the sixteen-year-old Daly stood at an important crossroads. His father, unaware of his son's private misgivings, wanted him to attend the United States Military Academy at West Point. Michael's last two years at Prep had corresponded to the beginning of World War II in Europe. In November 1939, two months after Hitler's invasion of Poland but about seven months before the German blitzkrieg swept through France, a poll of students at Prep found that 68 percent opposed US entrance into the war. The same percentage thought that the United States would not eventually be drawn into it, as opposed to 32 percent who held the opposite views on both questions. Seventy-two percent, however, indicated their willingness to fight if a foreign power invaded South America. In the next issue, 86 percent of the predominantly Republican student body expressed opposition to FDR's running for a third term, an opinion shared by Mike and his parents.[2]

Because Mike would not turn seventeen until September, too late to apply for admission to the Academy for the 1941–42 academic year, his father arranged for him to spend a postgrad year at Portsmouth Priory,[3] a Benedictine boarding school about six miles outside Newport, Rhode Island. This would give Mike a chance to strengthen his academic skills, particularly in math (precalculus), chemistry, and physics. At the Priory, Daly grew taller and more muscular and improved as an athlete. He played football on a team that included Robert F. Kennedy, did little work in the classroom, and sneaked into nearby Newport to drink with his friend, Kevin Hughes. Mike had been raised in a household in which alcohol flowed freely. According to a close family friend, the Dalys had a reputation for pouring drinks for friends and family at almost any social gathering in their home. One person described their style of drinking as "joke-filled fun punctuated with a lot of 'goddammits,' as in, 'Goddammit, Tim Smith, I remember when. . . .'"[4]

Toward the end of Mike's first semester, the Japanese attack on Pearl Harbor plunged the United States into war. Gen. George C. Marshall, the army chief of staff, designated Brig. Gen. Alexander "Sandy" Patch, Paul Daly's close friend, to go to the South Pacific to organize the reinforcement and defense of New Caledonia, a strategically located French-controlled archipelago that lay between Australia and Fiji.

According to his biographer, Patch was a tall, lean, ramrod-straight officer with piercing gray eyes and something of a scholar's air. His thinning red hair, by then gray, had earned him the nickname "Sandy" at West Point, where he and Paul Daly had become close friends. Their friendship deepened during the first months after the arrival of the 1st Division in France, where it was "broken in" near the French garrison town of Toul, just west of Nancy. During quiet periods the two men and Sandy's brother, Dorst, sometimes would slip away to a "watering place" in Nancy, where, in Paul's words, they would "have a hell of a time." Daly's daughter, Madge, recalled that her father and Patch "got on enormously well." Their contrasting dispositions—Patch tightly wound and high strung, Paul unruffled and calm—complemented each other. Though both were aggressive in combat and astringent in humor, each was modest and quiet and disliked off-color stories and jokes involving sex. Army historians characterized Patch as a "professional soldier's general who was more at home with his own staff and troops than with outsiders and less concerned with the prerogatives of command than with getting the job done." The self-effacing Patch did not seek the limelight, which he regarded as self-serving, and wanted no undue credit for performing his job as a professional soldier. Rather, he wanted the credit to go to his soldiers.[5]

Patch asked Paul Daly, then fifty years old, to return to active duty to serve under him in Task Force 6814, which was activated at the New York Port of Embarkation on January 14, 1942. Daly also received a call from Gen. George C. Marshall inviting him down to Washington, DC, for a briefing on the mission. Daly agreed to serve but first had to submit to an army physical examination—an exam that did not reassure his examiners. The doctors noted old wounds on both legs, an untreated double hernia, and hearing loss suffered as a result of shelling during World War I. One of Patch's staff officers explained, "The medico said Daly was a wreck, but Patch told the doctor to pass him and assumed responsibility for it." In early January the army approved Paul Daly for service with the rank of lieutenant colonel.[6]

As it turned out, Paul's decision to reenter the army had immediate and unforeseen consequences for his son Mike. On the evening he learned that the army would recall him, Paul telephoned Portsmouth Priory to tell Mike he would leave soon for the South Pacific. Because students did not have phones in their rooms, Paul's call went first to the headmaster, who then went to Mike's room to fetch him. Mike, however, was nowhere to be found. He had sneaked into Newport with his friend, Kevin Hughes, where he spent the better part of the night at a bar. The headmaster informed Paul of his son's absence and left a note on Mike's pillow instructing him to see him in the morning. On returning to his room around 4:00 a.m., Daly found the note and realized the gravity of his situation. Needless to say, he did not get much sleep in the few hours before dawn. That morning he reported to the headmaster's office, and by the end of the day he received word that he had been expelled.[7] Mike's late-night hijinks at Portsmouth Abbey suggest that, perhaps at a subconscious level, he sought to short-circuit his father's plan for him to attend the United States Military Academy.

Feeling disgraced, and at the same time caught up in the patriotic surge that followed Pearl Harbor, Mike tried to persuade his parents, particularly his mother, to give permission for him to enlist in the army at seventeen. They refused, still focused on securing him an appointment to West Point. Mike found the experience "deflating" because he wanted to serve as soon as possible.[8]

Meanwhile, father and son did not see each other before Paul Daly left for New Caledonia to serve as Patch's chief of intelligence for the Americal ("Americans in New Caledonia") Infantry Division. In the South Pacific, Paul would continue to distinguish himself, even as his son faltered back home. In October 1942 the Americal Division's 164th Infantry Regiment was sent to

Guadalcanal to relieve the 1st Marine Division. On October 13, 1942, it went into action against the Japanese, becoming the first US Army unit to conduct an offensive ground operation against the enemy in any theater. On November 19, Patch arrived on Guadalcanal, and the next day he assumed command of the western sector of the beachhead as the 1st Battalion of the 182nd Infantry attempted to take the offensive. Heavy resistance, however, stymied the battalion and threw it into confusion and disorganization. Visiting the regimental command post, Patch showed energetic leadership. His calm presence helped the battalion to regroup. The next day, the 1st, along with the 3rd battalion of the 164th Regiment, renewed the attack. When they faltered, Patch, accompanied by Daly, attempted to encourage the men by visiting front-line command posts 100 to 300 yards from enemy lines.[9]

After Patch assumed command of the entire offensive on Guadalcanal, on January 1, 1943, he appointed his trusted comrade Daly commander of the battered, disorganized 164th. Through skillful leadership and effective planning, Daly reorganized and rehabilitated the regiment, restoring it to a high standard of combat efficiency. One key to Daly's approach involved the importance he attached to developing the junior officers who served as platoon leaders. In a speech to a gathering of his platoon leaders on the eve of the regiment's commitment to Guadalcanal, Daly emphasized the central role they would play in the success of the regiment. "You have the most important job in the army," he declared. "You are the men who get the pushing done. A regiment with good platoon leaders is a good regiment. . . . Officers in higher ranks tell the men to go on. You are the ones who tell them to come on. You have the most dangerous job in the army." He waxed eloquent about the compensations of such a job, about the immense feeling of pride after a successful attack against a tough enemy, and about the exhilarating realization that thirty or forty men were willing to follow anywhere their platoon leader took them.

He warned them, however, to avoid a common temptation of junior officers: overt sympathy for their men. "Feel all of the sympathy you like toward your men," he told them, "but don't let them know how you feel." He then drew on his experience with horses for an analogy: "If you had a good race horse you would treat him like a million dollars, lavish every care upon him, but when the day came you would be ready to ride him to death. I don't mean to sound too hard-boiled, but race horses are for winning races and infantrymen are for winning battles." He preached a brutal reality that he believed essential for good leadership and ultimate success in battle. He assured the junior officers that he meant his speech not as a battle pep talk but confidently expected "that when the time comes you will do your best and that will be enough."

Yet, for all his cold realism, Paul Daly was also a high-minded idealist. Switching gears, he returned to a more inspiring and elevating note, exhorting them to keep in mind the larger meaning of the war. "Don't, in the welter of fatigue, confusion, and boredom, which is soldiering," he urged, "forget you fight for a great cause, a great tradition. We are not fighting for land or trade or to help England. We are fighting for everything that for us and men like us for centuries has made life worth living. The fight can be lost and would be lost, except for you and those like you." Ever the amateur military historian, he closed, "The same heat is on you that was on the Spartans at Thermopylae, on Don Juan at Lepanto. And God be with you."[10]

Paul Daly's concern about the crucial need for first-rate junior officers led him back to his ambitions for his son. Paul stood convinced that, the escapade at Portsmouth Priory notwithstanding, Mike would make a fine army infantry officer. He yearned to see him earn a commission by joining "the long gray line" of West Point graduates, something he himself had failed to do. Paul Daly's ultimate confidence in his son's potential and his own desire to see him at the United States Military Academy remained undiminished. But even though Mike did not share his father's enthusiasm for West Point, he said nothing, fearing he would further disappoint and burden his father, who had enough on his mind fighting the Japanese. But in this silence lay the seeds of yet another misadventure.

Despite his expulsion from Portsmouth Priory, Mike still secured an appointment to West Point because of his family's social and political connections. Richard Joyce Smith put in a good word for Mike with his good friend Senator Francis T. Maloney of Connecticut, who then selected Mike for appointment to the Academy. Feeling an obligation to his father, Mike nevertheless convinced himself that he would avoid going, that somehow, academically or physically, he would not qualify. His stint with Jacob Silverman, however, proved surprisingly effective, enabling him to pass the Academy's entrance exam. As for his physical exam, Mike passed despite some initial concern on the part of doctors about his malocclusion (misaligned bite). As Mike put it: "I was unhappy with it, but I was in disgrace after Portsmouth, people had done favors for me, and my Dad was strong for it, so I got carried down the stream. I felt trapped." In July 1942, Mike found himself at a big send-off party at his home. His father, serving in the army, could not be present but no doubt was pleased that his goal for his son had come to fruition.

On July 15, 1942, Mike reported to West Point to begin the "Beast Barracks" or plebe summer of the compressed three-year course. Standing 6' 3," he was assigned to Company H-2. (Assignment to companies was by height so that the cadets would present a uniform appearance when marching.) At

Plebe Daly. *Courtesy Special Collections and Archives Division, United States Military Academy Library.* Mike's father wanted him to attend West Point. Mike had no desire to do so, but he acceded to his father's wishes, with unhappy results.

seventeen he was younger than many of his fellow plebes, but his height and physicality led people to mistake him for one of "Blake's boys," football players whom legendary coach Earl "Red" Blake brought to the Academy to restore Army football to national prominence. Daly did play football, basketball, and baseball, but on company and battalion teams rather than varsity. He also enjoyed some success at boxing.

Daly had no problem with the rigors of physical training at the Academy, but he hated the regimentation and hazing that were an integral part of plebe life, and he bridled at what he perceived as the arbitrary wielding of power by upperclassmen. This included the requirement that plebes rise before reveille and pitch a tent in the dormitory hall "with all of your stuff in a particular way." Then, when reveille sounded, the upperclassmen kicked down the tents, and Daly, like the others, had to scramble to move all his things into his room and get down to formation on time or receive demerits. By January 1943 he had accumulated almost a year's worth of demerits—for lack of punctuality, talking without permission, improper uniform (such as failing to fold his socks with the smooth end at the front), creating a disturbance by forcibly taking a fellow plebe from the barracks and burying him in snow at 7:30 a.m. Each demerit had to be "walked off" with one hour of marching in full uniform in the square. The greatest single number of demerits that he received, however, involved something far more serious.[11]

The incident occurred in the early morning hours of October 22, 1942. As usual, Daly found himself running late reporting for guard duty. It was raining, and to save time, he did not put on his blouse but simply threw on his raincoat over his T-shirt. Those serving as relief for men on guard duty marched in a body to the various sentinel points around campus, where they replaced the men already there. During wartime, cadets walked guard duty carrying loaded weapons, though regulations stipulated that cadets keep their rifles on safety. When a relief column arrived, the guard on duty removed his ammunition clip from his weapon and gave it to the man taking his place, who then inserted it in his own rifle. As Daly arrived at his guard post and moved to relieve the man already there, he felt distracted and preoccupied, fearful that a cadet officer would discover his uniform violation and add to his mounting number of demerits.

The cadet captain of the guard stood close in front of Daly as the exchange of the ammunition clip took place under an arched vehicle shelter (called a "sally port") atop which stood a barracks housing upperclassmen. The other members of the detail stood close by at attention. The cadet captain bellowed, "Lock your piece!" Daly, with eyes straight ahead, reached down to check the safety, which in his haste that morning he had failed to do, and, mistaking the trigger for the safety-locking mechanism, discharged his weapon. The bullet struck the stone top of the sally port and fortunately ricocheted in such a way that it struck no one. Needless to say, the incident shook the captain of the guard. Improperly discharging a weapon counted as a serious offense at the Academy, indicative of dangerous carelessness. Daly recognized that there would be dire consequences, including even more undesired scrutiny from cadet officers.

But two hours later he compounded his difficulties. While still on guard duty he sat down on the running board of a cook's car parked in the alley leading from the sally port to the kitchen of the cadet mess (Washington Hall). Daly made sure to sit on the running board on the far side of the vehicle, using the car to hide him from prying eyes. An officer of the guard, however, came to check the position and discovered him. Daly lamely explained that he had been "investigating" a noise under the car. Publicly admonished from the "poop deck" in the dining hall in front of the entire corps of cadets for his two offenses, Daly was placed on special confinement to campus and required to march off the considerable number of demerits he received. He could not attend football games, and on Christmas Day he spent three hours in the morning and three in the afternoon walking his punishment tours.

For Daly the wintry gloom of West Point in which he "walked the area" reflected his mood. The key to surviving plebe year was to maintain a low profile, something Daly seemed incapable of doing. For this he had earned a reputation as a "slacker" and a "cut-up" and thus incurred the wrath of the upperclassmen. For example, shortly after the rifle incident, Daly stood in ranks before mess call enduring more verbal abuse from his "special tormentor," a hard-nosed cadet officer who seemed to delight in hazing plebes—Daly in particular—by insisting that they hit the deck and do push-ups, which the officer proceeded to do with one arm. The cadet officer berated Mike about discharging his weapon, complaining that the bullet came within "six inches" of his room. "Mr. Daly, did you know that you might have killed me?" he asked rhetorically in admonition. Of course, the better part of wisdom required that Mike take his medicine and remain silent, but he was too independent and rebellious, too mouthy and irreverently witty for that. As the cadet officer started to walk away, Daly muttered loud enough for him to hear, "Too bad I didn't!" The enraged officer came back at him "triple level" and kept at it for the rest of the year.[12]

Whenever Daly had the opportunity to tweak the cadet officers, he did so. Cadets marched to and from class in formations of twelve according to grades, with the best grades leading. When Daly's name mistakenly appeared at the top of the class instead of the bottom for Mechanical Drawing, he seized on the one opportunity he would ever have of leading his formation. He took delight in the surprised and sullen expressions of the upperclassmen as they saw him leading the formation, and to rub it in he brazenly led his formation on an extra tour around the square.

Daly expected that he would fail math and be dismissed from the Academy at the end of the first term in late January. Therefore, as the end of the semester approached, he invoked an Academy tradition called "recognizing" oneself as leaving, thereby gaining freedom from hazing and from regulations in the dining room requiring that plebes eat at "full brace"—sitting at the front of the chair at rigid attention, chin back, looking straight ahead. To his amazement, however, he squeaked by with a conditional pass in math after passing a special exam given to those in danger of being "turned out."

In his words, "All hell then broke loose." For appearing to have gamed the system, he became the target of even more intense hazing by outraged upperclassmen. Things got so bad that fellow plebes James Shilstone and Bill Thornton sought sanctuary for Daly by taking him "above the plain," to the Cadet Chapel. Dedicated in 1910 and combining the shapes and techniques of Gothic architecture with the massiveness of a medieval fortress, the chapel was constructed of native granite. It featured the largest pipe organ in the world, and among the beautiful stained-glass windows was the great Sanctuary Window inscribed with the Academy motto: "Duty, Honor, Country." There, services were conducted for Protestant cadets, faculty, and the public. (Daly normally attended Sunday Mass at the Catholic Chapel of the Most

Seeking Sanctuary. *Courtesy of James P. Shilstone.* Daly, on the left with fellow cadet James M. Shilstone, disliked life at West Point. He especially resented the traditional hazing of plebes by upperclassmen and made no attempt to hide his feelings from the cadet officers, who resented his antics and attitude. During his first semester, Daly accumulated almost a year's worth of demerits. On Sundays, in an attempt to give him some relief from the wrath of the cadet officers, Daly's friends took him up to the Protestant chapel grounds, where hazing was forbidden.

Holy Trinity, also a Gothic structure, whose stained-glass windows depicted Christian soldier-saints and memorialized West Point graduates killed in the service of their country.) Because the Academy forbade hazing "above the plain," Daly could enjoy a brief respite from the fury of the upperclassmen. A photograph snapped by Thornton on that day shows Daly bundled up in his greatcoat, with the collar of his cape upturned and buttoned around his neck, standing next to Shilstone. He may have felt besieged and bloodied, but his jaunty smile and slightly tilted cap indicate that his spirit remained unbowed.[13]

Daly's perceived willingness to play fast and loose with rules eventually led him into serious trouble involving the Academy's most hallowed set of regulations: the Honor Code. Formalized in 1922, the Honor Code specified that "a cadet will not lie, cheat, steal, or tolerate those who do." Throughout his time at West Point, Daly had qualms about aspects of the honor system, particularly the part requiring that a cadet report any breach of the code that he might witness. Daly drew a distinction between violating one's own honor and reporting a violation by another, thereby possibly destroying that cadet's career or ensuring that he would suffer "shunning" from the rest of the cadet corps. In short, Daly did not buy into the code and this, coupled with his characteristic inattention to detail, almost led to disgrace.

Daly's difficulties began after a student officer gave Daly some demerits for being late to reveille and then inadvertently wrote down the wrong date for the infraction. Seemingly drowning in demerits, Daly thought he saw an opportunity to avoid more and seized on the discrepancy in the date. He challenged the demerits on the grounds that he had not been on duty on the exact date of the infraction specified by the student officer's report. Daly did not realize (but should have) that by challenging the demerits as he did, he risked violating the Honor Code's prohibition against "quibbling." To his surprise and dismay, he found himself summoned to appear in the dead of night before the cadet-run Honor Committee on the top floor of Nininger Hall, a building made more ominous to Daly by its Gothic turret topped by battlements. In the dimly lit room, Daly sat in the center of a circle of cadets. For one of the few times in his life up to that point, he felt deeply afraid. If the committee ruled that he had violated the Honor Code, the entire Cadet Corps would shun him even if he weren't dismissed from the Academy. He would suffer disgrace, and a cloud would hang over his reputation. Fortunately for him the committee did not convict him, letting him off with a warning.[14] Math proved his undoing, however, and during the summer, Daly found himself with "Doc" Silverman in the Bronx, cramming for the readmission exam.

Because Madeleine Daly and the younger children had joined Paul at Fort Lewis, Mike took friends such as Bill Keeley and Billy Grimes to Fairfield on weekends, where they had the run of the house. One Saturday afternoon, emboldened no doubt by alcohol, Daly and Grimes went down to the public dock in Southport. There they found a small, unattended sailboat, which they navigated out into rough water in Long Island Sound, where it capsized and sank. Daly and Keeley were swimming toward the distant shore when, luckily for them, they were plucked out of the water by a passing boat rather than by the harbor-patrol craft they could see in the distance. The loss of the sailboat weighed on Daly's conscience. Later, during the war, he borrowed money from a soldier he knew from Fairfield and sent the cash in an envelope addressed to "Owner Lost Sailboat, The Dock, Southport, Connecticut." In an unsigned note, Daly explained that he had inadvertently sunk the craft that he had "borrowed" from the pier and asked that the money be given to its owner. (Daly repaid the soldier after the war.) Impetuous and reckless Mike sometimes might have been; malicious, mean-spirited, or dishonest he was not.[15]

Daly plunged into Long Island Sound, but he had difficulty immersing himself in his studies with "Doc" Silverman. He did not want to return to the Academy. According to Patton, one steamy afternoon with the mercury approaching 100 degrees, an exasperated Daly stood up, threw his books into the corner of the room and declared: "Dammit! That's it! I'm going to war." He ended up sitting for the readmission exam but, on the subway ride there, decided that he would purposely fail it. He did and was dismissed. Mike returned home, having yet again disappointed his parents but glad to be done with West Point and eager to get into the fight raging abroad. His only concern was that the war would end before he saw action.[16]

After leaving West Point, Daly felt conscience-bound to enlist rather than wait for the draft. He had internalized an ethic of service, duty, and noblesse oblige from his father: the belief that "it was only right for the privileged class that had received so much from the nation to be the first to serve in time of danger." Mike had not yet told his father of his immediate intentions, but he determined to enlist in the infantry. He had prepared for it at West Point, and it was part of his family heritage—such a part that it sparked a family spat. One evening at dinner during the period between the Priory debacle and his entrance into West Point, Mike, who had closely followed news of the great tank battles raging between the Germans and the Russians, ventured the opinion that tanks were changing the way war was fought, that they were becoming more important than the infantry. Sitting at the other end of the big dining-room table, his mother disagreed, saying she did not think tanks would make much of a difference. When Mike persisted in his opinion, the tone of the conversation became charged. Then, suddenly, Madeleine Daly flung her half-filled martini glass at her son. Loyalty to the infantry ran deep in the Daly household![17]

When Mike told the recruiting sergeant that he wanted to enlist in the infantry—at this point in the war enlistees still got their pick of service branch—the sergeant replied, "That's one request that you'll get, soldier." Most of those enlisting chose a different branch. Indeed, the army, through its use of the Army General Classification Test and its designation of inductees according to their civilian skills and educational level, tended to assign men with the lowest intelligence scores, education, and civilian skill sets to the infantry. Those with higher test scores, better education, and demonstrable civilian skills needed by the army went to the Army Air Corps and other branches—"a monumental misjudgment" in the words of military writer Max Hastings. Daly's educational level, a high-school diploma and one year of college, placed him in roughly the top 15 percent of recruits. Clearly he need not have ended up in the infantry. But for him the infantry truly was the "Queen of Battle." It offered him a chance to test, prove, and redeem himself in his own eyes and those of his parents. Finally, he also saw the war as a stark contest between good and evil—one that the United States simply must not lose—and it called forth in him ideals planted years before as father and son sat reading the *Song of Roland*.[18]

On hearing that his son had enlisted, Paul Daly reiterated those ideals in a letter written on September 4, 1943, from Fort Lewis. Whatever disappointment the father might have felt as a result of his son's performance heretofore, he seems never to have doubted Mike's courage or leadership potential as a warrior. "I am sorry that I shall not see you before you begin your all-out soldiering," he wrote in pencil on blue-lined paper. He reassured Mike that he would "get along all right" and reminded him that he was "a member of an old, honorable brotherhood" that included the men who stood at Thermopylae and Bunker Hill and who scaled the walls of Jerusalem and charged at Balaklava and Cold Harbor. "Never be surprised by the enemy or your superiors," he urged, and "never make excuses" or "be afraid to assert yourself whenever the situation requires it to your men or to General Marshall." Knowing his son, he added, "Be a good fellow, but not too much of one." He pleaded that Mike "try, try to get a commission" as soon as he could. "Your country has spent money educating you for this job," he lectured, "and if a gentleman is not a leader there isn't much excuse for him. . . . Get out front and stay there," he advised. "Take care of your men's health, feet, training, and of your own." Then he returned to an old theme, the getting of wisdom. "Use your head as well as your heart. Remember the first book I think that I ever heard you read. 'Roland was brave and Oliver was wise.' Heroes are all very well but it takes soldiers to win wars." He closed by telling Mike that his mother would return home at the end of the week, asking him to "Give my love to the children," telling him to take care of himself, and invoking God's protection for him. He signed the letter "Your affectionate father, Paul G. Daly." In a postscript he suggested that Mike enlist as "Michael J" or as "Michael" with no middle initial in order to please his mother.[19]

Several weeks later, just before Mike reported for basic training, his father penned another letter to his son, on a most appropriate day, September 29, Michaelmas in the Christian calendar, the feast day of Saint Michael the Archangel, patron of righteous warriors, and Mike's namesake. To highlight the significance of the day for his son, Paul dated the letter "Michaelmas, 1943." He began by noting that by the time he wrote again, Mike would be in the army. Acknowledging that his recent letters had mostly contained advice, he said, "I shall give you a little more." He assumed Mike would soon become an officer, and because the elder Daly had "seen a good deal off and on of this man's army," he thought his son "might as well have the benefit, if any," of his observations. He then gave a succinct tutorial, complete with two diagrams, on leadership and small-unit tactics.

  1. On life in the army: "Don't let the mud and dust, the personal discomfort and waiting around . . . incompetence and self seeking . . . get you down. Contrary perhaps to the laws of physics, the scum settles to the bottom after the shooting starts.

2. On responsibility: "Accept willingly any responsibility put on you and see that your subordinates accept theirs."

3. On fear: "I dare say you will sometimes be afraid in action. Everybody is at times as far as I know. The only important thing is not to let the men see it. Most men only advance because they see somebody else advancing, run because they see somebody else run."

4. On caring for troops: "Take care of your men's food and quarters, health, feet. . . . But the most important thing is to have your men convinced that you know your business, that you understand fighting. Like hounds, men will always love the man who feeds them or the man who shows them sport."

5. On cover: "Here, I see everyday platoon leaders letting their men advance by rushes and fall down at about 20 yards or so wherever they happen to be, on forward slopes and other exposed places [despite] often good cover within a few feet. Whether you are a corporal, sergeant or officer teach your men to use every available bit of cover and fold of ground, if they fall in a bad place, which they shouldn't, to crawl, roll, or run to a better one. This, plus discipline is . . . the school of the soldier."

6. On infantry tactics: "There is no mystery about warfare. The object of infantry tactics is to get in the enemy's flanks and rear . . . It is essential to hold and hit him. If you can get surprise, which you must always seek, by every means, you may be able to hit him without holding him. Hold with the weakest possible forces so that you can put all you can into the hit. Envelopment is the most effective way but sometimes small units will have no chance to envelop until they make one by penetration. Because of . . . numbers . . . Alexander had to do this at Arbela and Napoleon at Austerlitz, and platoon commanders will often have to. At Waterloo, Napoleon thought he could bull his way through Wellington's infantry and got defeated."

Mike may not have realized it then, but he would come to appreciate and employ much of his father's wise advice.[20]

Thus instructed, Mike was sworn into the army and reported for seventeen weeks of basic training to Fort McClellan in Anniston, Alabama. Located at the southernmost end of the Blue Ridge Mountains, Fort McClellan served as a US Army Infantry Replacement Training Center (IRTC), one of twelve throughout the nation. The centers went through two phases. Between 1941 and mid-1943, they were shaped to the needs of mobilization as the US Army transformed itself from a constabulary force of 170,000 enlisted men and 13,000 officers to an army of conscripts and volunteers numbering 8.3 million. In the second phase, from mid-1943 to 1945, the centers focused on supplying overseas replacements. By war's end, the replacement-training agencies of the combat arm—infantry, cavalry, field artillery, coast artillery,

Recruit. *Courtesy Daly Family Photos.* Having disappointed and embarrassed his parents by his dismissals from both Portsmouth Priory and West Point, Daly yearned for a chance to redeem himself. Shortly after leaving the Academy, he enlisted in the US Army and requested the infantry as his branch. Daly (top center) liked and enjoyed the guys in his training platoon at Fort McClellan, in Alabama. He did not find the physical training all that demanding. Indeed, he found it a relief from what he regarded as the mindless nitpicking and hazing at West Point.

antiaircraft, armored, and tank destroyer (TD)—had graduated 2.5 million replacements. Daly was a product of this massive undertaking.[21]

Having been introduced to army life at West Point, and having been toughened both physically and mentally there, Daly found basic training relatively easy. Certainly it was less onerous than the hazing by upperclassmen at West Point. Just as he had done when he played athletics at Prep, Daly became a team player at Fort McClellan. Once again he sensed that he was part of something bigger than himself: winning the war. He could put up with the hardships, inconveniences, annoyances, and indignities of basic training: numerous rules and regulations governing the minutiae of life, inspections and boring classroom instruction on such things as military courtesy and discipline, long hours of physical training and conditioning marches, fatigue details such as kitchen patrol, guard duty, and janitorial "policing" of barracks and grounds—and shouting drill sergeants. They were the means to the end he craved: getting into the fight. Apropos of preparing for that fight, he most enjoyed the hours of training devoted to qualifying with the M1 Garand rifle and to familiarizing himself with and firing the M1918A-2 Browning Automatic Rifle (BAR) (in effect a light machine gun, though it weighed between sixteen and nineteen pounds), the Browning M1919A-4 Medium Machine Gun, and the 60-mm M2 mortar. In addition he liked his fellow trainees and the camaraderie that developed among them. But all the time he carried the psychic burden of having failed at West Point and of having "messed up a lot" during the previous two years.

That burden eased somewhat for Mike as a result of a visit from his cousin, John S. Riley, a visit that had a profound impact on him. Riley, the oldest child of Daly's mother's sister, Estelle, was a few years older than Mike. A graduate of Georgetown University and a newly commissioned infantry captain in full-dress uniform, Riley represented something special to Daly: a contemporary model of manliness, combining physical strength and courage with compassion and consideration for others, especially those younger than himself. The eldest son in a large family, Riley seemed to Daly the "epitome of what I wanted to be." Riley's encouragement, support, and affirmation gave the new recruit a tremendous boost that he never forgot. Daly excelled during basic training and, in recognition of his outstanding performance, was offered a job as a member of the IRTC cadre, the core group of officers, noncommissioned officers (NCOs), and enlisted men who conducted training of new recruits. This would mean additional instruction for Daly and possibly an opportunity to attend Officer Candidate School (OCS). Daly, however, declined the offer. "My dad is overseas, sir," he explained, "and I might miss the war."[22]

While Mike honed his military skills in Alabama, the rest of the Daly clan gathered in Palm Springs, California, to celebrate Christmas 1943 with General Patch and his wife and daughter at a house Paul Daly had rented. Paul served as Patch's Deputy Chief of Staff for IV Corps, headquartered at Fort Lewis, Washington. Toward the end of the year, Patch and his headquarters moved from Fort Lewis to Camp Young, California, where Patch assumed command of the vast, 18,000-square-mile, California-Arizona Desert Training Maneuver Area. Patch awarded Daly the Legion of Merit for his outstanding performance of duty at Guadalcanal from November 15, 1942, to February 28, 1943, both as an intelligence officer for the division and, subsequently, as commander of the decimated and disorganized 164th Regiment, which he had restored to combat efficiency. Later, in a typically self-deprecating and offhanded remark about his medal, Daly wryly noted that "Guadalcanal was tough on squads and platoons but easy for a colonel except that the hills were too steep for jeeps and they wouldn't get us a horse." He dearly missed his horses, especially White's Hill, a two-year-old foaled on the Daly estate that gave promise of a notable career. Alluding to her husband's June 1943 visit home on leave, Mrs. Daly laughingly told a reporter that her husband "couldn't get home fast enough to see how the horse had come along. I swear," she observed, "he said 'hello' to the children and *kissed* the horse—or very nearly."[23]

By April 1944, Mike Daly had finished basic training and had reported to the overseas replacement depot at Fort Meade, Maryland, about ten miles southwest of Baltimore and near US Route 1, which linked Baltimore and Washington, DC. Thanks to Fort McClellan's calorie- and carbohydrate-intensive diet, he now weighed about 190 pounds. At Fort Meade, while awaiting shipment overseas, he again found trouble. Having gone down to Washington, DC, to see a girl he knew from back home in Connecticut, Daly stayed late. He took a taxi back to Fort Meade in an attempt to make morning formation, but he failed and had to paint the mess hall as punishment. Daly subsequently reported to Camp Shanks, New Jersey, outside New York City, to await transport to Britain as an infantry replacement. A few nights prior to departure, he and some friends left camp without permission and made their way into the city to hear singer Nat King Cole at the Zanzibar Club off Broadway. As Daly and his friends emerged from an enjoyable night of music and partying at the club, an MP asked to see their passes. When they could not produce them, he promptly arrested them. As a result, Daly spent the entire ten-day (April 15–24) trans-Atlantic voyage to Britain in the bowels of the transport ship cleaning pots and pans in the officers' mess.[24]

Once more he had "messed up" by flouting rules and regulations—a pattern that had persisted at least since his days at Prep. He had something of an entitlement mentality: rules applied to others but not to him. He could goof off and challenge authority because he had no worries about money, career, or family. His father had shown himself willing to step in and ameliorate major messes. But Daly's life and attitude were about to change dramatically as he entered the theater of battle—a stage on which his best self would soon emerge.

4 Initiation

Weymouth, England. June 4, 1944: D-Day minus 2.

On Sunday, June 4, when Mike Daly and other members of the 18th Regiment came off their ships, they sought the help of the Almighty. There, on the pier, they attended Mass. Behind them lay anchored the LCI(L)s (Landing Craft Infantry, Large) that would take them to Omaha Beach. Similar scenes were enacted at the various ports along the southern English coast that Sunday. At a Mass celebrated by Maj. Edward J. Water, a Catholic chaplain from Oswego, New York, a photograph snapped by an infantryman captured the poignant and dramatic scene. Father Water, dressed in his priestly vestments, stands with upraised right hand and delivers the final blessing in the sign of the cross. The young men kneel reverently, some with heads bowed, others with eyes upturned, gazing earnestly and intently at the priest, some beginning to cross themselves, all knowing that their lives hang in the balance. Mike Daly was one of the soldiers that Sunday who made the sign of the cross with that terrible realization in mind.[1]

During his summer prepping for West Point's math re-entrance test and later, during infantry basic training in the States, Daly had expressed fear that the war would end before he had a chance to fight. He need not have worried.

On April 14, 1944, Daly and his fellow infantry replacements—part of the 108,463 troops shipped to Britain that month—had landed in Scotland and been moved immediately to Minehead, in southwest England. Living in tent cities, isolated from contact with the locals, suffering from boredom, the thousands of GIs kept in shape for the eventual invasion by long marches that included many hills. The men lacked shower facilities and only occasionally could take a dip in a nearby river. A planned visit by heavyweight champion of the world, Joe Louis, promised some relief from the monotony. Louis's forthcoming visit excited Daly, who loved boxing and followed it closely. When Louis offered to spar with willing soldiers who signed up to face him, Daly eagerly placed his name on the list. "I thought that maybe I could slip one shot past him," he later recalled. But because Louis could not make it,

Final Blessing. *Courtesy, National Archives.* As the troops prepare to embark for Omaha Beach, Maj. Edward J. Water, Catholic chaplain from Oswego, New York, gives the final blessing at the end of a Mass he celebrated on a pier in Southampton, England. Daly attended such a service on that same Sunday in Weymouth. In the background can be seen the large landing craft that would transport the men to the beaches.

Figure 1: Organization Table: US Infantry Division

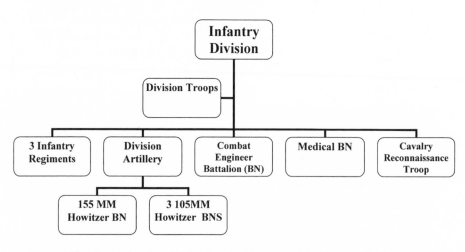

Source: Keith E. Bonn, *When the Odds Were Even: The Vosges Mountains Campaign, October 1944–January 1945* (Novato, CA: Presidio Press, 2006), 53.

sending his sparring partner in his place, Daly never got his chance. Willing to go it alone with "the Champ," the nineteen-year-old clearly spoiled for a fight with the Nazis.[2]

Preparing for that fight, Mike had a surprise visitor: his father. Colonel Daly had followed Patch to an assignment in North Africa. As a result of Patch's earlier success at Guadalcanal, General Marshall sent him to the Mediterranean Theater of Operations. Initially Patch and his headquarters staff of IV Corps, including Paul Daly as Coordinator of Strategic Services, were stationed in Algiers. Colonel Daly then took command of the 65th Infantry, an all-volunteer Puerto Rican regiment attached to Patch's headquarters. Very soon after his arrival in Algiers, Patch learned that Eisenhower had named him to replace the brilliant, mercurial Gen. George S. Patton Jr. as commander of the Seventh Army. Patton had set off an uproar back in the states when the public learned that, during the Sicilian campaign the previous May, he had slapped two soldiers suffering from battle fatigue in a hospital. Having furloughed Patton from his command for months and with the invasion of Normandy looming, Eisenhower, who in December 1943 had been named Supreme Commander of the Allied Expeditionary Force, ordered his most aggressive and controversial general to Britain to take command of the new US Third Army. In that capacity he not only would train the new division for combat but also would function as a decoy during the initial stages of the invasion. For his part, Patch would take charge of planning and executing the proposed Allied invasion of southern France—operation Anvil—later changed to Dragoon. Patch, in turn, placed Paul Daly in charge of combined Allied special operations for the invasion. Originally scheduled to occur simultaneously with operation Overlord, Dragoon was delayed and would not be launched until August. Indeed, until it actually occurred, the invasion remained up in the air, opposed by Churchill but pushed by Eisenhower.

In response to a request by Gen. Jacob L. Devers, commander of Sixth Army Group, to which Patch's Seventh Army belonged, Supreme Headquarters Allied Expeditionary Force (SHAEF) granted permission for Patch and two of his staff officers to accompany Devers to the United Kingdom for two weeks "for consultation and to acquire information concerning future operations." Patch requested that Colonel Daly accompany him, and the party set out from Algiers on May 12. Once in England, Patch and Daly took the opportunity to tour the countryside, visit General Patton's headquarters, and drop in on their sons. Capt. Alexander McCarrell ("Mac") Patch III, an infantry officer in the 315th Regiment of the 79th Division, was stationed at Wilmslow. Mike Daly was encamped just outside Taunton. Colonel Daly arrived at Mike's camp on May 18 in a jeep with a driver. Father and son took the jeep for a drive together. During their conversation, Paul Daly told

Mike that a colonel he knew at West Point had told him Mike flunked his re-examination in such a way as to show that he clearly did not want to be there. Paul Daly seems to have recognized and accepted Mike's aversion to the Academy. After the visit, the colonel noted in a letter to his wife (who was busy managing the family real-estate interests from his New York City office) that Mike seemed fine, despite smelling a little "gamey."[3] But Paul Daly did more than simply visit his son.

Once again the father used his connections and influence on his son's behalf. Paul Daly had remained close to a number of officers with whom he had served in the 1st Division during World War I. One of these, Maj. Gen. Clarence R. Huebner, now commanded the 1st Division. Paul told his old friend that Mike was eager to be assigned to a line outfit and to get into the fighting as quickly as possible. Paul also probably expressed a desire to see his son serve in his old regiment under his friend. Thus it was that Mike suddenly received orders assigning him to the 1st Division and ordering him to report immediately. It was unusual for a private to be moved individually, without his unit, and Mike was puzzled, although he probably sensed that his father had been at work behind the scenes. He boarded a train in full battle gear, conscious that his body odor probably made him an uninviting traveling companion. He headed first to London and there, at Victoria Station, transferred to another train heading south. Upon his arrival at division headquarters, he received a notice that the division commander wanted to see him. When Mike arrived at the general's headquarters, Huebner greeted him graciously and told him he had served with his father during World War I. Mike had no idea of the date of the invasion of France, but Huebner said: "It's coming up. It will be tough, but I hear that's what you want." Mike confirmed that, which seemed to please the general. He told Daly he would send him as a rifleman to Company I, 3rd Battalion, in his father's (and Huebner's) old infantry regiment, the 18th.[4]

Like all American infantry regiments, the 18th consisted of approximately 3,000 men divided into three battalions of approximately 850 men each. Within the battalions lay the heart of the infantry regiment: the rifle companies, designated by letters of the alphabet : A (Able), B (Baker), and so on. According to their table of organization, infantry rifle companies contained 187 enlisted men and no fewer than six officers, including a 35-man headquarters contingent with 28 communicators (radiomen) and cooks. Because planners anticipated heavy casualties during the invasion of Normandy, the rifle companies were overstaffed with officers and with enlisted men. As the war in Europe progressed, however, rifle companies seldom operated at full strength.

Figure 2: Organization Table: US Infantry Regiment

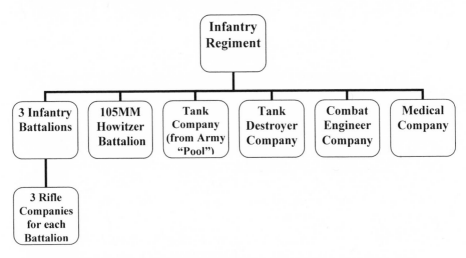

Source: Keith E. Bonn, *When the Odds Were Even: The Vosges Mountains Campaign, October 1944–January 1945* (Novato, CA: Presidio Press, 2006), 54.

In Company I, Daly was assigned to the first platoon, which was led by a second lieutenant and divided into three twelve-man squads under a sergeant. These squads composed the basic building blocks of the company. Each man in the squad had a particular responsibility. Two served as scouts, two manned the BAR, which provided additional fire support, and each of the remaining eight carried an M1—one configured as a sniper rifle and the others equipped to fire grenades. These roles periodically rotated from man to man. In the standard attack formation for a battalion, two rifle companies (the third was held in reserve at the rear) followed by the battalion headquarters walked or ran in an extended line of about four hundred yards toward the enemy position, each rifleman firing from the hip. In actual combat, however, confusion and chaos (the "fog of war") characterized many infantry engagements.[5]

Unknown to Daly at the time of his assignment, Gen. Dwight D. Eisenhower had designated the 1st Division "Force O," meaning that in just a few days it would spearhead the landing on Omaha Beach as part of the long-awaited assault on Hitler's "Fortress Europe." For several months the regiments of the 1st Division had trained intensively for the invasion, and in April 1943 the 18th had taken part in tactical exercises at the Assault Training Center at Woolacombe and had participated in a "dry run" amphibious

Figure 3: Organization Table: Rifle Company, 1944

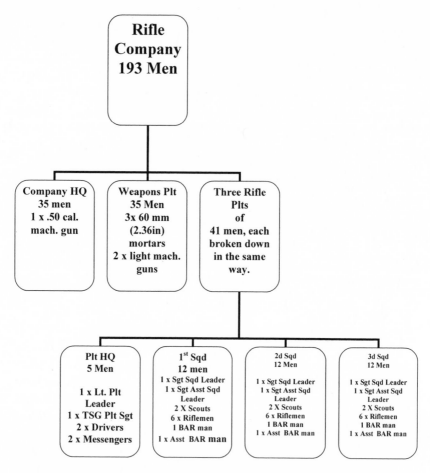

Source: Robert S. Rush, *GI: The US Infantryman in World War II* (Oxford, UK: Osprey Publishing, 2003), p. 27.

landing on the Torquay Peninsula on the English Channel in southwest England. Daly had missed much of that training, but he would get his wish to serve in a front-line infantry company. For his efforts he would receive the Combat Infantryman Badge, an award established in 1943 to recognize those who served satisfactorily in combat. The award included an additional ten dollars per month in pay—"princely" recognition of the fact that combat infantrymen bore the brunt of the fighting, bleeding, and dying. Eventually infantrymen would account for 80 percent of American casualties in Europe.[6]

On May 25, Daly found himself, with all other troops of the 1st Division, sealed within the marshaling area at Marabout Barracks, Dorchester, where briefings of troops and leaders began. These included the salient landmarks of Omaha Beach and a warning that German defenders at Omaha Beach now included not only elements of the mediocre 716th Infantry Regiment but also the more experienced and offensively capable 352nd. The 1st Division's orders were to seize the part of Omaha Beach labeled "Easy Red"—a mile of sand littered with barbed wire, minefields, and antitank obstacles. Fronting the beach was a hundred-foot-high plateau in which five gullies served as exits inland, the principal one, Saint Laurent Draw [E-1]), ascending from a small stream known as le Ruquet. After clearing these hurdles, the division was to drive southward from the beach through high ground to secure the area between the Aure and Drôme Rivers. For purposes of the invasion, each regiment was designated a Regimental Combat Team (CT), "a task force consisting of a regiment of infantry, a battalion of light artillery, and essential units of other arms such as tanks and TDs in suitable proportions," to enable it to be self-supporting in combat. The 16th and 116th CTs would constitute the first wave of the assault, the 18th and the 115th CTs the second.[7]

A note of lightheartedness crept into otherwise serious preparations when each company received a bulk order of condoms. The men were to use them to waterproof cigarettes, candy bars, flashlights, rifle muzzles, and so on. In fact, it was suggested that each man put a dozen loose in his pockets in case he had to cross a river or canal after the landing. Second Lt. Robert F. Stringer, of Company I, recalled that after he was wounded in the hip and taken back to the hospital, a nurse had to cut off his trousers and so emptied his pockets of their contents. When she came to the condoms, she smiled and deadpanned, "I don't think you will be needing these in the immediate future." Stringer "did not correct her in her thinking."[8]

On the drab afternoon of June 2, Daly's 3rd Battalion received the signal to load up and move out to the port of Weymouth. As the truck convoy carrying the men inched its way along the jammed English country road leading to the port seven miles away, men, women, and children gathered to wave at the troops and wish them "god speed." The heavily encumbered troops boarded their navy transports and then waited anxiously for three days amid swirling rumors of when the invasion would actually begin.

Because of terrible weather, Eisenhower postponed the invasion from June 5 to June 6, when, according to a young meteorologist, weather conditions barely adequate for an invasion would prevail. The morning of Monday, June 5, dawned stormy, but by noon the weather had calmed and a palpable sense of excitement mixed with dread and tension ran through the men as they watched the bustle on the waterfront. Then each ship received a bundle containing a letter for each soldier from General Eisenhower telling him that he was about to "embark upon the Great Crusade" that would

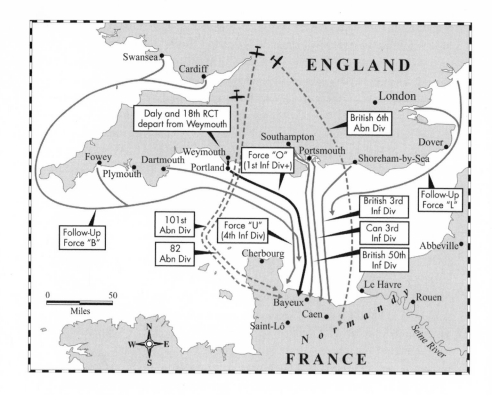

"bring about the destruction of the German war machine, the elimination of Nazi tyranny . . . and security for ourselves in a free world." Eisenhower wished his men "Good Luck!" and closed by urging all involved to "beseech the blessing of Almighty God upon this great and noble undertaking." That evening at 1800 the convoy of landing craft carrying the men of the 3rd Battalion embarked from Weymouth.[9]

Daly and most of Company I traveled in the relatively long (158 feet, 6 inches) and narrow (23 feet, 3 inches) LCI(L)-536. Its crew of three officers and twenty-one sailors transported six officers and 182 enlisted men of the overstrength infantry company. Because the deck was wider than the prow, troops would exit on each side of the ship by way of a gangway. Both gangways gave onto a ramp that was to be lowered onto the beach. Owing to the steepness and narrowness of the ramps and the time required for the men to disembark, however, the LCI(L) would not be used in the first waves of the assault. That task fell to the Landing Craft, Vehicle, Personnel (LCVP), or "Higgins Boat," a shorter (36-foot), faster vessel capable of carrying a platoon.[10]

As LCI(L)-536 made its way across the Channel, Daly, like most others, did not sleep. Some played cards—they had recently received their pay—and then turned to a big game of craps. Daly, the newcomer, tried to acclimate himself to the people in his squad. Having missed the pre-invasion training and landing drills because of his late arrival in England, Daly sought out and listened intently to men who had experienced the North Africa and Sicily campaigns. The presence of such veterans was critical to unit cohesion and combat efficiency and to the transformation of replacements into effective soldiers, especially once shells and bullets started flying. Daly had no feel for battle, and he had trouble envisioning it, but because many veterans seemed nervous, he expected a difficult time on the beach. Despite their own nerves, these veterans made an effort to calm and reassure the "rookies," a gesture Daly deeply appreciated.

Daly later said he had not been "a very strong formal religious person" but found himself "praying a lot in the Army." In the early morning hours he again turned to a higher power, invoking the intercession of both Saint Maurice, the patron saint of infantry, and Michael the Archangel. He particularly asked for strength, courage, and guidance so that he would not let down his comrades. Throughout the war, Daly would turn to his two "spiritual veterans," often repeating the traditional Catholic prayer to Saint Michael and a prayer he had learned as a child: "Lord, please give me the strength, courage, grace, and forgetfulness of self so that I might do what is right. Amen."[11]

The morning of Tuesday, June 6, dawned gray, cold, and windy, with choppy seas. According to Lieutenant Stringer, just prior to the start of the tremendous naval bombardment that would commence the operation, the men of Company I (those not suffering from seasickness) sat down to "a tremendous breakfast" of bacon, eggs, and coffee served on white linen and china with silverware. A few wags voiced gallows humor by comparing their breakfast to that of condemned men in a penitentiary on the morning of their execution.[12]

Packed into the landing craft, Daly once more experienced the army reality of "hurry up and wait." The timetable called for the 18th CT to start landing on the Easy Red sector of the beach in column of battalions beginning with 2nd Battalion at 0930, followed by 1st Battalion, and finally the 3rd Battalion commanded by Lt. Col. Joseph W. Sisson. The stiff resistance encountered by the 16th CT when it hit Omaha Beach at 0630, however, forced a revision of the invasion schedule for other units. After passing the line of departure, the first wave of landing craft carrying the 2nd Battalion of the 18th CT found it difficult to maintain formation and steer a straight course because of congested traffic toward the shore, where the 16th and 116th CTs remained pinned down on the beach. As a result, the 2nd Battalion did not start landing until about 1030.

To complicate matters, as the lead elements of the 18th landed in front

Figure 4: Order of Battle at Omaha Beach, including Michael Daly's Company I

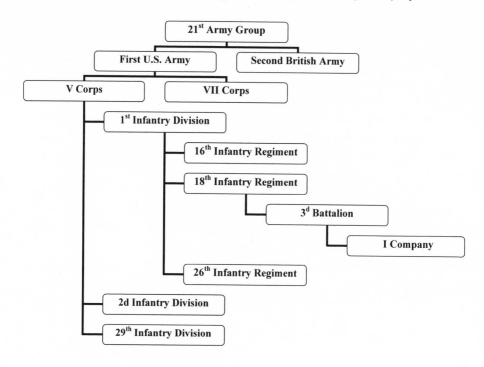

of the Saint Laurent Draw, so also did the 115th Regiment. This resulted in confusion and partially scrambled units.[13] Mines and underwater obstacles also posed a serious danger to the landing craft ferrying troops to the beach. They proved such a hindrance to the LCI(L)s that most of the 3rd Battalion, including Daly's platoon, had to be transferred to the smaller, more maneuverable Higgins Boats.[14] Daly recalled later that as he descended the "scramble net" (cargo-net rope ladder) from his ship onto the cramped landing craft, he could hear a recording of Winston Churchill's stirring words over the public-address system, words that resonated with the young soldier: "How our world was hanging in the balance and our glorious mission was to free another people from a terrible oppression."[15]

Descending the scramble net was no easy task. First, there was the sheer weight and bulk of his gear. He wore a canvas assault vest with four pockets in front and two in the back to carry toilet articles, extra underwear and socks, rations, a raincoat, hand grenades, a bayonet, matches, an entrenching tool, and two quarter-pound blocks of TNT to enable him to blow a foxhole instantly if needed. Other equipment included three or four grenades, M1, 150 rounds of ammo, and gas mask, not to mention his helmet and the pack on his back. Thus encumbered with more than sixty added pounds, he was expected to hit the beach. But for now he had to negotiate the shorter distance between his LCI(L) and the Higgins Boat. Swells in the rough sea caused the smaller landing craft to drop and rise considerably as the weighted men tried to step off the net to its deck. One might prepare to step off the rope when suddenly the craft dropped off many feet below. Daly made it without incident, but one man fell and broke his leg.[16]

Daly's landing craft had to circle in the choppy seas for several hours. Each man had been issued a "puke" bag for seasickness, and many used it repeatedly. Daly did not, for which he was grateful. As the landing craft circled and shells (dubbed "flying boxcars" by the men) screamed overhead on their way toward targets on shore, Daly felt both anxiety and excitement. He was eager to enter the fray on the distant beach.[17]

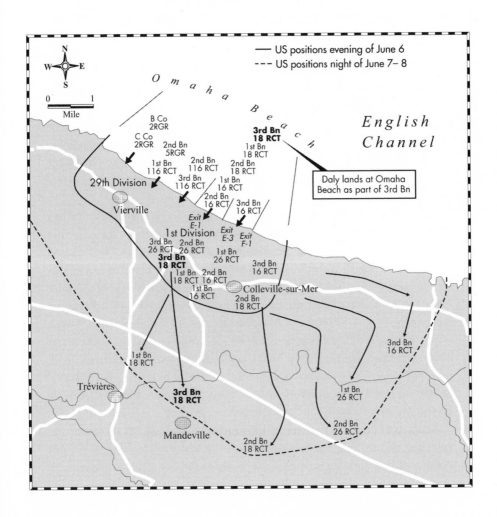

Unlike the other invasion beach sites (Sword, Juno, Gold, and Utah), five-mile-long Omaha Beach formed a shallow crescent, with German artillery protected in pillboxes on the bluffs at each end and at intervals in between. The artillery therefore had interlocking fields of fire into the flanks of the Americans on the beach, placing them in a deadly crossfire. As a result the first invasion waves of the 16th and 116th CTs had paid a terrible price, and they found themselves pinned down for hours before they managed to move off the beach. They succeeded not only because of inspired leadership on the beach and the soldiers' courage and tenacity, but also because the German coastal defenses at Omaha Beach were incomplete and relatively lightly manned. In addition, Allied naval fire helped neutralize German gun emplacements. And although the Germans could fire point-blank at the invaders, their machine gunners could manage only about four hundred rounds per minute—and those in short bursts—lest the barrels melt. They simply could not shoot all the Americans landing on the beach—although they came perilously close to hurling that first wave back into the Channel.

When the 2nd Battalion of the 18th landed, at 1030, it joined some elements of the 16th moving off the beach and up the cliffs, trailblazing for Daly and others who would follow. Daly's 3rd Battalion began landing at 1340. In the preceding three hours the 16th, 116th, and 115th Regiments and the 2nd Battalion of the 18th Regiment had neutralized many enemy positions on the bluffs. Enemy artillery located inland, however, kept up a steady fire on the beach and on landing craft in three- and six-round volleys, while some remaining snipers in the hills still posed a considerable danger to troops coming ashore.[18]

As Daly's landing craft neared the beach, it encountered both artillery and mortar fire. In his effort to get the men to the beach itself, the coxswain also had to maneuver around the ubiquitous mines and pilings. Nervous and off-course, he finally disembarked the men in three and one-half feet of water, through which they waded approximately fifteen yards to shore. A later Navy report indicated that the transport group ferrying the 18th Regiment lost twenty-two LCVPs, two LCI(L)s, and four LCTs (Landing Craft, Tank), nearly all as a result of being staved in by log ramps or hitting mines. After-action reports indicated that although personnel losses were relatively light, more than eighty of the ninety-six casualties suffered by the 3rd Battalion on D-Day occurred as men debarked from their landing craft and made their way to the water's edge.[19]

William Hale Jr., a member of I Company, observed: "In the water . . . you can't do anything but get through [it]. You can't be shooting. You can't dodge. All you could do is try to get up on that sand as quickly as possible."[20]

D-Day Landing at Omaha Beach. *Courtesy National Archives.* Because the large landing craft were experiencing problems from German fire as they approached the beach, a number of 3rd Battalion troops, including Daly, were transferred to smaller landing craft, popularly known as "Higgins Boats." One is seen here approaching the "Easy Red" sector of the beach.

As Pfc. Lewis C. Smith hit the beach, "The soldier on my right had his head blown off; the one on my left had a hole in his back about twelve inches wide." Jettisoning his heavy pack and gas mask, Daly struggled through the water and around mined obstacles, desperately trying to keep moving as the wounded and dead floated around him in the surf. Because he had grown up around the waters of Long Island Sound, he knew how to bob and work his way in, but later he said: "The kids from West Virginia and other landlocked states found the going even more difficult." He grabbed one badly injured man and dragged him onto the beach. There he found himself in the midst of utter chaos: the beach littered with wrecked vehicles, equipment, and broken bodies. Smoke, deafening noise, the cries of wounded men, exploding mortar shells, and small-caliber fire, the stench of cordite and death, all combined to create a surreal experience.[21]

Pumped with adrenaline and caught up in the confusion, the lanky Daly stood on the beach momentarily—violating Sgt. Smith's admonition to his men before landing: "Keep your eyes open and your ass low to the ground!" Unaware of the inviting target he presented, Daly tried to get his bearings and identify the peculiar sounds—similar to a light snapping of fingers—passing by his ears. He was, in his own words, "so green" that he didn't realize that the sounds came from bullets whizzing by! Suddenly he felt the full force of a boot kicking him in the butt and heard the voice of Sgt. Joseph L. Bognar, whom he knew from Fairfield, yelling, "For God's sake, Daly, get down and move off the beach." Daly hit the ground and started to crawl to the slim protection from direct fire afforded by a sand dune. He and others lay on the rocky shingle at the base of the dune created by the farthest advance of the high tide. The dune afforded some protection, but when exploding mortar shells shattered the surrounding shingle (slippery, polished stones deposited by the high tide), it became additional sharp-edged shrapnel.

Most mortar fire was random, and most enemy artillery fire was directed at landing vessels. German snipers firing from the bluffs, however, continued to pick off men below. Joseph Balkowski, the leading expert on Omaha Beach, writes: "Omaha Beach unquestionably remained a dangerous place through nightfall. Even worse, lethal enemy artillery fire fell on the beach all afternoon. . . . The randomness of it all was startling: one second a buddy would be by a GI's side, and the next he would be lying on the sand oozing blood—or maybe even blown to bits."[22]

Brig. Gen. Willard G. Wyman, the highest-ranking officer on the beach, realized that he needed to get the men off the beach and to the first ridge (designated the Beach Maintenance Line) as soon as possible, clearing out remaining German machine-gun nests and artillery positions in the process. As a result, as soon as the 3rd Battalion cleared the beach, it was ordered to make its way toward the Saint Laurent Draw through a narrow marked minefield cleared by combat engineers. Troops from the first assault wave and from the 2nd Battalion of the 18th had already managed to climb the draw and eliminate some enemy strong points. Enemy fire that continued to hit the beach area, however, impeded efforts to reorganize the 3rd Battalion, and enemy minefields made movement beyond the beach difficult and dangerous.[23]

Daly and other men of the battalion began to crawl through a marked minefield only to halt after a short distance when sniper fire inflicted a number of casualties. The fate of two Bangalore torpedo men attached to Daly's company illustrated the peril. They carried explosive charges on the end of long, extendable tubes, enabling them to clear obstacles indirectly. Their job was to blow a hole through the barbed wire and the minefields on the slopes. As Daly watched, one torpedo man went forward and was killed by sniper fire, and the second, who followed, shared the same fate. Daly recalled their action as the bravest he saw that day because, as he observed later, they had to know at the time that they had no chance of succeeding. Ironically the sniper poured so much fire into the bodies of the fallen soldiers that he unintentionally cut a hole in the wire. Flanking action by two or three riflemen from Company L led to the sniper's capture and enabled the battalion to proceed.[24]

At that point, Pvt. Willie W. Sutherland, the oldest man in I Company, a "gung-ho" thirty-year-old who carried a flamethrower, found himself in the lead. He noticed that a field of cattails to the right of Saint Laurent Draw showed no sign of having been disturbed—no broken cattails, footsteps, or such. Surmising that it was free of mines, he led the men of the company through the field and up the bluffs. Ascending the draw in single file within the narrow boundaries established by the white tape, cloth, and toilet paper laid down by the engineers to indicate a path through the mines, Daly passed grisly sights: GIs who had fallen during the initial ascent or had strayed into the minefields. The 3rd platoon lost one man to a mine, a teenager named Cox. A former boxer and "perfect specimen of an eighteen- or nineteen-year-old," according to Lewis Smith, Cox stepped on a mine that "blew him away." Some antipersonnel mines blew off legs. When the "Bouncing Betty" was tripped, it propelled itself upward about five feet and exploded at face level. The most psychologically unnerving, albeit far less common, mine was the "Castrating Pencil," a little tube with a bullet that had a soft percussion cap set on a pin. Stepping on it would cause spikes to explode, driving a sharp pencil into the groin.[25]

In addition to avoiding mines, Daly and his companions had to contend with German rifle and machine-gun fire zeroed in on gates and breaks in hedges. Daly gingerly followed the man in front of him, intermittently firing his weapon at snipers and hitting the ground when mortar shells exploded nearby, all the while struggling to stay on the designated path.[26] He felt a keen appreciation for the men who had risked and given their lives to clear the trail that he trod gingerly. As Thomas McCann, a member of the Intelligence and Reconnaissance Platoon of the 18th later recalled, "We saw . . . sights I had never seen before and hope to never see again." Despite the scenes of carnage, Daly tried to stay focused on his task by reminding himself that the guys in front of him and those behind relied on him. "I said my prayers," he recalled later, "and moved on."[27]

Once on the ridge, the battalion faced only sporadic sniper fire. By 1900 it had pushed about twelve hundred yards south of the beach and then paused to reorganize into assault and reserve companies. By 2400, Daly and Company I had crossed the Vierville-sur-Mer—Colleville-sur-Mer road. There, among thick hedgerows surrounding pastures and apple orchards, he and his comrades dug foxholes for the night. They found no enemy in front of them but discovered that a large number remained behind them, between their positions and the village of Colleville. "Constant small skirmishes with enemy positions . . . and small fire fights kept up all throughout the night as the enemy attempted to escape." Many D-Day veterans recalled shivering through the night in still-wet uniforms, some with only their cellophane gas capes to serve as windbreakers. Daly experienced it differently. He had gotten his wish to fight the Germans. He was too "wired" from his first combat to feel cold or sleepy. On that moonlit night sleep proved elusive for most of the men. It had been one long, seemingly never-ending day: "the longest day."[28]

5   Proving Ground

THE BATTLE OF NORMANDY

Normandy, June-July 1944.

As the battle for Normandy raged, Mike Daly consistently volunteered for the most dangerous assignments: night patrols and sniping. Serving as a sniper was risky business, made worse because soldiers on both sides generally loathed enemy snipers. On one memorable occasion, when Daly had been ordered to find a good vantage point in an area from which the Germans had withdrawn, he went forward and climbed a thickly leafed maple tree. Then the Germans moved back into the area and camped right under his tree! Daly could have shot a couple of them, but then he would "have been a dead duck." He remained quiet, barely moving in the tree as the Germans periodically came and went. The loud noise of their supply trucks served Daly well, covering any sound he might make. When his need to urinate became intense, Daly waited until the soldiers moved from under the tree and then relieved himself into his helmet. He gently and intermittently poured the contents down the tree trunk rather than risk exposing his position by dumping it in one place on the ground. When darkness finally descended and the Germans again pulled back, Daly climbed down from the tree and stealthily returned to his lines. Embarrassed to admit that he had not accomplished his mission, Daly reported to his platoon sergeant that he thought he might have "bagged a couple of Germans," although, wisely, he had never fired a shot. Both "Oliver" and Paul Daly would have approved.[1]

On the battlefield, many of the personal characteristics that had proven problematic for Daly before the war became assets. Combat also sharpened his focus and his sense of responsibility. "The guy next to you relied on you. You couldn't afford to let him down, or the larger cause for which you were fighting."[2] In the combat zones of France and Belgium, Daly rose to the occasion, proving himself an extraordinary warrior. At 1215 on June 7, the 3rd Battalion moved out along several hedgerow-bordered trails toward the village of Surrain about one mile away, but not before a sniper had wounded Daly's company commander, Capt. Herschel T. Coffman, who was replaced by Lt. Robert E. Hess. By 1530 they were in Surrain, receiving wine, flowers, and fruit from joyous citizens who earlier had watched the Germans withdraw without a fight. The battalion did not encounter opposition until it crossed the Bayeux-Isigny Road, about a half-mile from the village. There it ran into its first artillery fire since leaving the beach. Around midnight, having covered about two miles, the battalion moved into a defensive position just southeast of Mandeville-en-Bessin. At 0200, however, an enemy patrol in excess of thirty soldiers, ardent *Hitlerjugend* (Hitler Youth), whom the battalion journal described as "half insane or doped," penetrated the lines and entered the battalion rear-command post and motor pool, killing, capturing, or wounding several officers and men. Fortunately for the Americans, the GI captives overcame their captors and made seven of them prisoners. Meanwhile, American troops counterattacked and hunted down the invaders. Following point-blank firefights that raged throughout the night and into the dawn, ten Germans had been killed or wounded and sixteen captured.

Throughout the rest of the day and night, Daly's company came under small-arms and artillery fire from Trévières. It found itself operating against two large enemy patrols and observed large groups of enemy to its south. Fortunately members of I Company managed to take a dozen German prisoners from the 17th Engineer Battalion and 916th Grenadier Regiment, including a German NCO who had a complete map of the defensive positions of the 352nd Infantry Division. Relieved by the 3rd Battalion of the 9th Infantry on the morning of June 9, Daly and his fellow "grunts" received word to march back to an assembly area near Mosles, where they were given their next mission: cut the Bayeux–Saint-Lô highway and railway south of Blay and east of the expansive Cerisy Forest with the town of Vaubadon as the objective. The battalion ran into heavy opposition almost immediately and during the next five days would suffer eighty-eight casualties.[3] Using the secondary dirt road from Mosles to Blay as an axis of advance, the 3rd Battalion encountered enemy strong points consisting of automatic weapons and snipers in the *bocage*—eight- to ten-acre pastures and orchards enclosed by hedgerows consisting of raised banks of earth two meters high on top of which grew thickly matted bushes and beech, oak, and chestnut trees that created a leafy canopy. This was a landscape feature that American commanders planning the Normandy campaign had not taken into account sufficiently. Maneuvering tanks on the narrow roads between these embankments proved very difficult and dangerous. The *bocage* provided perfect defensive terrain for the Germans and proved deadly for American soldiers, who had to take the countryside hedgerow by bloody hedgerow. The casualties included Pvt. Cliff Hicklin, who had become Daly's closest companion.

The Germans, expecting to be cut off from one another, had trained to

Figure 5: Cross-section of typical Normandy hedgerow

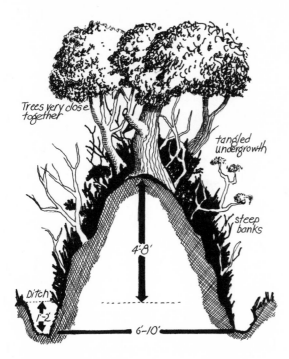

Source: "Fighting in Normandy." *Combat Lessons* 4 (1944): 5–19. http://www.lonesentry.com/normandy_lessons/index.html.

fight as individuals and in small groups in the hedgerows. They would wait until Americans were crossing a hedge and then attack, sometimes using mortars and artillery presighted on the single entrance into a field. They dug rifle pits behind the hedgerows, and in each corner they tunneled openings for machine-gun positions. German small-unit infantry doctrine stressed the primacy of the MG 42 machine gun in achieving fire superiority. An extraordinarily mobile and lethal weapon, the MG 42 could fire 1,200 rounds per minute. Each nine-man German infantry squad was issued one, giving them greater firepower per squad, platoon, and company than the Americans, who relied on the BAR—whose rate of fire was 600 rounds per minute—for fire suppression. Thus armed, German troops converted each enclosed field into a small fortress.[4]

Daly remembered: "We attacked hedgerow by hedgerow. A typical day in the hedgerows: sometimes nothing happened, sometimes a lot. The Germans didn't defend every hedgerow but defended a lot of them. Taking them involved all too often the necessity of going straight at them. Creep or crawl

Hedgerows. *Courtesy The Colonel Robert C. McCormick Research Center.* During the treacherous and bloody combat in the Normandy *bocage* (farmland crisscrossed by hedgerows), Daly's best buddy in the platoon was killed.

toward the hedgerow, get up and rush only at the last second—get behind something and keep crawling. You had mortars and artillery behind you."[5]

Daly and his buddies also welcomed the presence of tanks, which at first had foundered in the hedgerows. The narrow lanes afforded them little room in which to maneuver and very poor lines of sight. In addition, when they attempted to climb over the thick hedgerows, they often exposed their unarmored bottom to enemy fire. Then a GI named Curtis G. Culin came up with the idea of welding metal "teeth" to the front of tanks, which enabled them to rip and bulldoze openings in the hedgerows. Other GIs came up with an even more effective approach: attaching two sharp metal prongs to the front of the M4 Sherman tanks. The tanks could puncture a hedgerow embankment with the prongs and then back out, creating two three-foot-deep holes that could be filled with explosive charges and detonated, creating an opening wide enough for tanks and infantry. Some tankers settled on a quicker tactic that involved ramming the middle portion of the embankment at high speed demolishing the upper portion, including vegetation, and creating a passage for tanks and infantry. Using these tactics, tank/infantry teams proved effective in clearing out the hedgerows. Those that proved too resistant were bypassed and left for the 2nd Battalion to clear.

Success in war usually hinges on small-unit action, not massed armies clashing on broad fields. Small-unit action was part of a bigger picture that generals might grasp but that GIs, focused on their immediate mission in the field, definitely did not. "I was a private and had a very limited perspective,"

Daly remembered. "Usually there was someone beside me. When we saw someone firing at us, we fired back. I tried to be as aggressive as I could."[6]

During the early afternoon of June 10, as the battalion moved toward Vaubadon, Daly found himself pinned down along with the rest of Companies I and L in a woods near the town of Le Tronquay. More than a company of panzer grenadiers (mechanized infantry) and pioneers (combat engineers), well dug in, peppered the Americans with mortar, light- and heavy-machine-gun, and small-arms fire. Daly's company commander withdrew I Company to the east about five hundred yards and then attacked around the flanks. The Germans resisted stubbornly, but tanks from the 745th Tank Battalion attached to the 18th Regiment proved decisive in forcing the Germans to abandon their position.

By nightfall the battalion had reached Vaubadon. It had taken thirty prisoners and inflicted fifty casualties on the enemy while suffering twenty-two of its own. The 18th Regiment's rapid advance—essential to securing the beachhead at Omaha by pushing the Germans beyond the range at which their artillery could still hit the beach—had carried them more than twelve miles inland and had established the right flank of Maj. Gen. Leonard T. Gerow's V Corps on the confluence of the Vire-Elle River. A little further south, perched atop a cliff overlooking the Drôme River, the deserted village

On the beach. *Courtesy National Archives.* For days after the initial landings, German artillery continued to pound the beaches. Thus the Allies felt great pressure to push the Germans fifteen to twenty miles into the interior, beyond their artillery range. In the photo, a shell from one of the fearsome German 88-mm guns explodes on the beach.

Pushing inland. *Courtesy Roger Portier, Cobra Memorial, Marigny, France.* Daly's 18th Infantry Regiment, which had pushed southward into the Normandy countryside faster than any other regiment in the invasion, arrived first in the area of Caumont-l'Éventé, approximately eighteen miles from the beach. On June 15, 1944, in action near Lieu Béziers, Daly, acting as a forward observer, exposed himself to enemy fire in order to gain a better view of the enemy. He alerted his unit to a German flanking movement that subsequently was thwarted. For these actions, he received the Silver Cross.

of Vaubadon featured a chateau "surrounded by luxurious parks" that had served as German corps headquarters. There, thanks to army truckers, the Americans received needed supplies, including blankets, coats, and jackets of some kind for every man. In addition, Daly and his comrades in arms enjoyed a hot meal for the first time since landing.[7]

More pleasant experiences awaited Daly and his buddies in Balleroy. There the elated populace, including what seemed to some of the GIs a "dispropor-tionate number of good-looking young women," lined the road, tossed roses at the Americans, and waved homemade U.S. flags sporting only five or six stripes.[8] Even better, they introduced Mike and his buddies, such as Lewis Smith from Virginia, to calvados, the apple brandy of the region. It was so potent that GIs claimed it was "made of ground up grenades," and some allegedly even used it in their lighters. As the troops passed by, the grateful French stood, bottle and small "shot glass" in hand, and offered them drinks. Mike paused briefly, downed the fiery brew, and then resumed marching.[9]

NORMANDY: CAUMONT-L'ÉVENTÉ

Having secured the right flank of V Corps at the junction of the Vire and Elle Rivers, the 18th Regiment continued to push well ahead of 1st Division's other regiments. The next phase of its drive involved securing the left flank of V Corps by seizing the key town of Caumont-l'Éventé. It lay at the junction of seven roads and sat 750 feet above sea level, a site ideal for dominating the entire area with artillery. Further, the steeple of the parish church furnished a bird's-eye view for artillery spotters. General Gerow ordered the 26th Infantry to take the town and the 18th Infantry to secure the high ground to the west. Incredibly the Germans were slow in moving to Caumont, and the 18th Regiment encountered only light screening forces, which offered slight opposition. On June 13 the 26th Infantry captured Caumont with almost

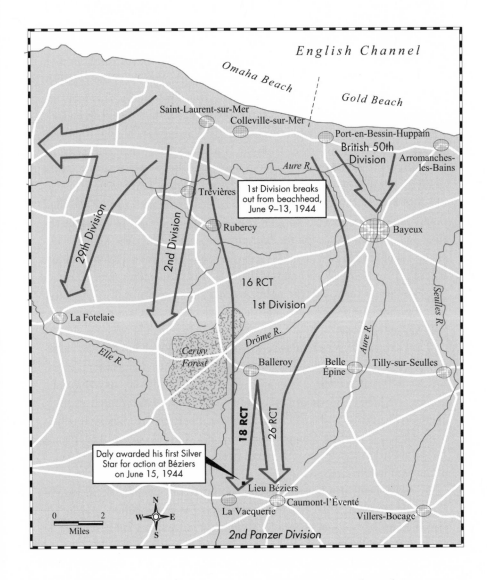

no opposition. One week after the D-Day landing, the 18th Regiment had advanced approximately twenty-two miles inland.

The British, on their right, and the 2nd Infantry Division, on their left, having encountered stiffer German resistance, had not penetrated as far southward. As a result, the 18th and 26th regiments found themselves occupying an exposed salient centered on Caumont. On the evening of June 12, Daly's 3rd battalion went into a defensive position near a tiny village known as Lieu Béziers, west of Caumont and a little north of the town of La Vacquerie. The Ferme Béziers, a large stone farmhouse on a rise in the gently undulating terrain, served as the battalion command post. Franklyn Johnson, a tanker in the 745th Tank Battalion attached to the 18th Regiment, noted, "A good network of gravel roads covered the area of orchards, pasture land, and cultivated fields dotted with stone peasant farm houses."

Daly and his comrades received orders to dig in until the units on their flanks could catch up. Fortunately the German 7th Army was too occupied trying to defend Caen from the British and Saint-Lô from the Americans to launch a full-scale counterattack against the 18th, but that did not mean Daly and his fellow "grunts" could take it easy. The Vacquerie-Caumont Road, approximately twenty-two miles from the Normandy beach, marked the front, and their right boundary was a small branch of the Drôme River on which stood the Moulin Béziers (a water mill). Young Bernard Marie, a twelve-year-old, and his ten year-old brother, Claude, lived in the area and helped their family raise wheat on what became a contested plot of land above the nearby river and mill and barely within the American sector. When the Marie brothers first caught sight of troops on the narrow road that passed by their family field, they immediately recognized them as American rather than German. They could not make out the uniforms, but they could not hear the harsh sound of hobnailed boots striking the road that they had come to associate with German troops.[10]

The Germans occupied the area across the Drôme River and the Vacquerie-Caumont Road, and each side continuously probed the other's lines. German forces numbered between 1,000 and 1,500 troops, and every day witnessed artillery exchanges (German guns made quick work of the church steeple), aggressive combat, and numerous skirmishes between reconnaissance patrols, especially near the Drôme River. At night, German self-propelled guns shelled the area often in short salvos of twelve, making it difficult for the men of the regiment to sleep.

At night, Daly also honed his combat and reconnaissance skills. He engaged the enemy in order to capture prisoners for interrogation, and he acquired knowledge about enemy locations and movements while striving to avoid detection. Officers picked a squad to conduct a patrol and then went over air-reconnaissance photos and maps with them to indicate their route and objectives. Members of the designated squad blackened their faces, necks, and hands with charcoal and, carrying no gear except rifles, slipped into the inky darkness of "no man's land," the contested area between the Americans and the Germans. Daly participated in many patrols and came to appreciate the canniness of his German opponents. During a planned ambush set up in the vicinity of Yvonniere, for example, the men spotted what they assumed to be an enemy patrol and prepared to spring the trap when the officer in command suddenly ordered them to hold fire. He recognized American helmets and fatigue jackets on the troops. Only too late, as the patrol passed out of range, did the officer realize that the Germans had tricked him by disguising themselves in American uniforms.

In such a setting, security remained a top priority. The men had to remain on alert during the night—as if, amid the artillery barrages, they could have slept. Often Daly and his buddies dozed during the much longer seventeen-plus hours of summer daylight. According to Dean Weissert, a sergeant in Company H attached to battalion headquarters, "Hygiene was a luxury." When he had the time, Daly, like Weissert, filled his helmet with water and then took a sponge bath and shaved. If any water was left, he washed his socks and hoped he would not have to put them back on before they dried. Medics stressed the importance of shaving because hair bristles made it more difficult for them to treat the wood-splinter wounds produced when shells hit and splintered trees.[11]

In this context, with each side jabbing insistently at the other, Daly proved a daring and adept combat infantryman, earning the plaudits of his company commander, Capt. Robert C. Hess Jr. Writing six months later, the captain praised Daly's superior performance and versatility as a rifleman, scout, BAR man, and assistant squad leader. He admired the consistent initiative Daly had shown, volunteering for dangerous missions such as sniping and night-reconnaissance patrols. On those patrols, he asserted, Daly had gained valuable information for both his company and the battalion. Hess noted that Daly "earned the respect and was admired by all with whom he associated." "On many occasions," Hess added, "he exposed himself to the enemy and took chances with no apparent regard for his life."[12]

On June 15, one such incident resulted in Daly's receiving his first medal for gallantry. A patrol from Company I moved towards Bienville but ran into very heavy resistance at the bottom of the shallow valley drained by a small branch of the Drôme River and had to retire. At 1900 the Germans heavily shelled the 1st and 3rd Battalions. When the artillery barrage hit his company positions, Daly was manning an observation post with his BAR. Mortar and artillery shells came crunching closer, and their rolling pattern indicated a counterattack. Disregarding his own safety, Daly moved his observation post farther out, to an exposed point, to gain a better view of the immediate terrain. "I was behind a tree," he recalled. "The mortars didn't get me. I could see green uniforms coming nearer. It looked like a company-strength deal. When they were two hundred yards away, I let them have it. Got ten or twelve. That broke them up. My own gang came on up and everything was OK." For his actions that day in exposing himself to enemy fire and thereby thwarting the attempted surprise enemy raid, he received the Silver Star. That medal is the third-highest military decoration (after the Medal of Honor and the Distinguished Service Cross) that the US Army can award for gallantry in action.

In combat the following month, Daly nearly duplicated his Silver Star performance by remaining at his observation post during intense enemy artillery fire while the unit on his right received a very strong counterattack. As he had done near the Moulin Béziers, Daly pushed forward with no cover to a point from which he could see an enemy formation to the front. He then called in American artillery fire that dispersed the Germans.

Sometime during late June or early July, Daly and Lewis Smith were "shooting the breeze" as they shared a foxhole, something they did occasionally. The two young men got along well. Smith admired how Daly carried and conducted himself. He thought Daly a fine soldier. He also found Daly friendly, pleasant, humorous, and easy to talk to—in short, "a nice guy." Earlier Daly had told Smith about his father's service in World War I and at Guadalcanal, and his own ill-fated sojourn at West Point. During this particular foxhole conversation, the talk drifted to combat medals. Daly observed matter-of-factly that the only medal worth winning—the only one that he would want—was the Medal of Honor. He did not expand on his reasons, and Smith certainly did not perceive him as a "glory hound." Perhaps, given his father's Distinguished Service Cross, anything other than the Medal of Honor seemed secondary, or perhaps he was simply trying to play down the Silver Star he had recently received.[13]

As a result of the 1st Division's defensive holding mission, it did not suffer the casualties sustained by other divisions of the First Army engaged in major attacks at the time. But the constant skirmishing, patrols, and artillery exchanges in the Caumont area cost the division 117 men killed, 1,994 wounded—most returned to action—and 86 missing in action. The weather during late June and most of July—cloudy, dreary, cold, and rainy—added to the discomfort and stress of the men who, in the words of one author, huddled "a bit closer to the ground" in their foxholes. Low clouds and limited visibility also shackled Allied air power, making it difficult to provide close air support for infantry and to interdict the movement of German reinforcements and supplies.[14]

NORMANDY: BREAKOUT AND BEYOND

On July 14, Bastille Day, after thirty-eight consecutive days on the line, Daly got a break from the dangers of combat when a battalion of the 10th Infantry relieved the 3rd battalion. Sent twenty miles to the rear to the town of Bricqueville, Daly enjoyed a shower, got some sleep, cleaned his clothing and equipment, watched movies, and participated in other recreational activities.[15] He stayed in the rest area until July 20, when he and the rest of the 3rd Battalion moved to a concealed assembly area in the vicinity of Verney-Haute. They were part of the consolidation of the 1st Division for an imminent attack, code-named Cobra, by the First Army—an operation that General Eisenhower and his commander of the First Army, Gen. Omar N. Bradley, hoped would produce an Allied breakout in Normandy.

Despite the frustrating, time-consuming, and bloody fighting in the Norman hedgerows and the supply problems caused by the lack of adequate ports—a gale on June 19 had demolished one of the artificial harbors constructed at Omaha Beach and damaged the other—the Allies had achieved an incredible build-up of forces. By the end of June, almost a million men had landed, along with some 586,000 tons of supplies, and 177,000 vehicles. Bradley's First Army included four corps with two armored and eleven infantry divisions, including the 1st Division. The British had approximately the same strength.

Near Caen, the British attempted to end the grinding combat in the hedgerows by breaking out into more open country. German armor, however, repelled them. But farther west the Americans enjoyed greater success. By July 18 the First Army had seized Cherbourg, captured the key road junction at Saint-Lô, and cleared the Normandy Peninsula generally to a line north of the Saint-Lô–Lessay road, thus enabling the First Army to mount Cobra.

The attempted breakout would come on the right near Saint-Lô in three phases: Phase I called for a massive, two-hour-and-twenty-five-minute air bombardment by approximately 2500 planes that included heavy and medium bombers, and fighter-bombers. They would rain down five thousand tons of high explosives, white phosphorous, and jellied gasoline on specific targets within an approximately six square-mile target area adjacent to and south of the Périers–Saint-Lô highway. Phase II required the first echelon, three infantry divisions, to open a gap in the German main defensive line, hold the gap open, and clear routes of advance for forces behind them. Phase III,

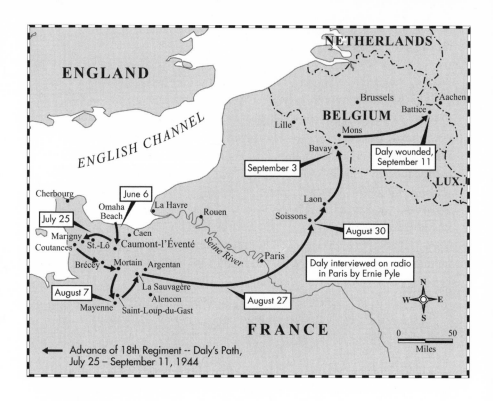

Map labels:

NETHERLANDS

ENGLAND

BELGIUM

• Brussels
Battice • • Aachen
Lille •
Mons

Bavay •

Daly wounded,
September 11

September 3

LUX.

Cherbourg •
June 6
La Havre
Rouen

Laon •

Soissons •

August 30

Daly interviewed on radio
in Paris by Ernie Pyle

July 25
Omaha
Beach
Caen

Marigny
Coutances • St.-Lô • Caumont-l'Éventé

Seine River

Paris

Brécey • Mortain Argentan

La Sauvagère

August 7
• Alencon
Mayenne Saint-Loup-du-Gast

August 27

N
W — E
S

FRANCE

0   50
Miles

← Advance of 18th Regiment -- Daly's Path,
July 25 – September 11, 1944

the exploitation echelon, called for the 1st Division to move through the gap and the 18th to strike at the town of Marigny. General Bradley later said, "To make certain that the blitz would get off to a fast start, I called on the Big Red One to pace it."[16]

The plan of attack called for the 18th to cross the Saint-Lô–Périers highway and proceed to the vicinity of Marigny. On July 25, behind an intensive aerial bombardment that utilized both tactical aircraft and bombers, the First Army attacked. Daly later recalled that, as he and his comrades waited in a somewhat swampy area, they could see and hear the roar of seemingly endless waves of bombers flying in from the north. Then, as more than 1500 B-17s and B-24s, 380 medium bombers, and more than 550 fighter-bombers dropped their tons of ordnance over enemy lines, the earth literally shook from the shock. Captain Sam Carter of the 3rd Battalion remembered, "When standing, your trouser legs jumped up and down. When you sat, your body shook. . . . We thought the Army Air Corps was never going to finish the bombing." Members of the 9th, 4th, and 30th Divisions had the same feeling, but it was because they found themselves on the receiving end of "friendly fire": bombs that fell short of enemy lines killed 111 American soldiers and wounded 490.[17]

By the second day, American troops had opened a big breach in German positions, whereupon armored divisions drove rapidly southward twenty-five miles to Avranches, at the base of the Cotentin Peninsula. The First Army turned southeastward, and the Third US Army, under General Patton, swung through Avranches into Brittany to secure ports.

Early in the morning of July 26, Daly's 3rd Battalion moved out in a column of companies with attached units. They advanced slowly because of the tanks accompanying them and because of the difficult terrain. They met little opposition until a point beyond the Saint-Lô–Périers highway not far from Marigny. The battalion commander prepared to have his force bypass the town because he thought the Germans had abandoned it. As a precaution, however, he ordered Company K to check it out. The men entered the town around midnight and ran into sharp enemy fire that inflicted a number of casualties. One platoon found itself almost trapped and barely succeeded in escaping. This forced a revision of plans to include capturing the town. The entire battalion withdrew to the north and took up positions for the remainder of the night with the intention of eliminating the enemy in the town in the morning.[18]

At 0630 on July 27, Daly and the men of Company I spearheaded the attack on Marigny, entering the town from the northeast. Daly's platoon moved southward through the city and, except for five or six snipers, who seemed to want to surrender, encountered no resistance before reaching the church, which stood on a high hill beside the main road to the south. By

Breakout. *Courtesy Roger Portier, Cobra Memorial, Marigny, France.* During Operation Cobra, the Allied breakout from the Normandy beachhead, Daly and the troops of the 18th Regiment encountered stiff German resistance at Marigny.

0745, the 3rd battalion had occupied the town. But as Daly and his platoon moved toward a little stream that flowed westward along the southern boundary of Marigny, things suddenly changed.

The stream marked the beginning of a sharp rise in elevation to the south. The terrain featured hedgerows and scattered trees with only a few buildings—an ideal defensive position that afforded excellent observation of the town, particularly the low ground on its southern edge. The stream presented no obstacles to infantry, but the tanks had to use the one small bridge over the stream. Daly's platoon approached the bridge in squad column led by a medium tank. The enemy let the tank approach to a distance of seventy-five yards before firing on it with a *panzerfaust* (a one-shot, shoulder-fired anti-tank weapon wielded by an infantryman). The tank withdrew to a curve in the road at the southern bank of the stream while Daly and the others sought cover in a small ditch. Thereafter they found themselves pinned down by fire from automatic weapons and rifles and by grenades. Over the course of three hours they worked their way back to a line near the stream. The 1st Platoon, rushing to the aid of the 3rd, also found itself pinned down. L Company joined the fray, and it too became pinned down. Soon thereafter, beginning at about 1300, enemy fire began to increase, first with light mortar shells and later with large 81-mm shells.

Throughout the afternoon of July 27 the two companies remained hunkered down in the face of the fire from the heights. Mortars were particularly worrisome because, in the words of Sgt. Troy D. Cox, who served with Daly later in the war, they were "silent killers. . . . You never heard them coming until they exploded. You could hear artillery a good ways off, and you did have a chance to take cover before it hit." The German fire that day was the heaviest Daly and his company had faced since Omaha Beach. They found it particularly galling because suppressing fire from American artillery was nowhere to be seen. The enemy observers on the high ground were "looking right down our throats." The fire was so well aimed that the troops had to crawl everywhere. And to make it worse, the men in Company I could not see their tormentors.

Between 1800 and 1830, moreover, the troops began to receive accurate and devastating fire from what Daly and his fellow soldiers regarded as the most effective and versatile artillery piece in the German arsenal: the 88-mm gun. The Germans employed it as their standard fieldpiece, as armament on the German Tiger tank, as an antiaircraft gun, and as artillery. About the "88," Bill Mauldin, cartoonist for *Stars and Stripes* (and a sergeant with K Company, 180th Regiment, 45th Division), wrote: "Their 88mm. is the terror of every dogface [his affectionate term for mud-caked GIs]. It can do everything but throw shells around corners, and sometimes we think it has even done that." Daly lay as flat as he could as the concussions from explosions shook the ground and his very insides, literally and emotionally. But having internalized his father's admonition about not showing fear, he struggled successfully to appear calm: "It seemed the right response." He also learned that artillery had its own unique sounds—a whistle when not going in his direction, a deafening roar when on top of him.[19]

The shelling continued unabated until shortly after midnight. Then it tapered off. Col. Elijah Peckham, the battalion commander, ordered patrols to investigate and by 0100 hours one of them reported that the Germans had begun to abandon their hilltop positions. Suddenly, about 0200, Daly and the others heard the uneven throb in the sky that came from the unsynchronized motors of Junker JU-88 dive-bombers. He dove for cover as the planes dropped flares and then their screaming bombs, which took a large toll among Company L. But just as the American saturation bombing of July 25 had gone awry, the JU-88s, mistakenly assuming that the Americans already occupied the crest of the hill, bombed their own troops, causing casualties and disorganization among them. At 0700 on July 28 a patrol of tanks moving southward on the road out of Marigny to the main road between Saint-Gilles and Coutances found that the enemy had withdrawn. In a classic understatement, an after-action report noted, "The Battalion was tired."

Daly could echo "Amen" to that. His company had suffered forty-one casualties that day, its heaviest combat encounter to date. Part of the explanation for the severe casualties came from Maj. Henry V. Middleworth in a later interview: "The 1st Battalion could not be ordered to fire long-range weapons on the hilltop resistance south of Marigny because of the uncertainty as to where they were. Radio communications [between units] were very bad." And the cannon company was unable to fire a single shot because nobody had been able to observe the enemy.[20]

On July 28 the 18th Regiment moved to Camprond by truck. Operation Cobra had reached a turning point. The German Seventh Army, suffering tremendous losses, had cracked and become disorganized between the Vire River and the west coast of Normandy. Despite putting up fierce pockets of resistance, it could no longer maintain a cohesive and coordinated front. Fleeing German columns clogged roads in the southwestern part of the area around Coutances and points farther south. The new mission of VIII Corps was to eliminate remaining pockets of resistance and push the Germans farther to the south. On July 30 and 31 the 18th Regiment moved by truck to an assembly point near Saint-Denis-le-Gast. It had moved out of Normandy's *bocage* into rolling, gentle countryside where armor could function as intended, in tandem with the air force. Morale soared as men anticipated kicking the Germans all the way back to Berlin. On July 31 the 1st Infantry Division moved out again, this time with the mission of seizing the high ground south of the Seine River near Brécey. The ultimate objective, however, was the commanding ground near Mortain and the security of the right (southern) flank of VII Corps.

The 18th crossed the Seine and moved toward Brécey, slowed only by skirmishes with armed reconnaissance units that it brushed aside. After marching twelve and one-half miles, Daly and the rest of his weary fellows mounted trucks and rode the rest of the way to the town, which they reached by nightfall, consolidating their defensive position on Hill 242, to the southeast, without contacting the enemy.

On August 2 the regiment pushed eastward. German troops manning isolated strong points offered considerable resistance, but the tanks quickly neutralized them. The march then continued to the high ground east of and overlooking Mortain, a small, ancient town astride the roads leading out of Avranches toward Brittany and southeastern France. The 3rd battalion moved eight kilometers to the northwest of Mortain to take the village of Juvigny-le-Tertre from elements of the 116th Panzer Division. After a brisk firefight, the battalion secured the village before dusk. On August 3, General Huebner designated the 18th Regiment to seize a commanding height, known as Hill 314, just east of Mortain. The 3rd Battalion began placing roadblocks along the network of highways and trails to the southwest of Mortain, the 1st Battalion took the town itself, and the 2nd Battalion moved onto a hill two kilometers to the northwest. That night the Germans shelled the town heavily. At about 1900 hours the following night, the Luftwaffe attacked, bombing the town for more than an hour and leaving it in flames. On August 4 the 18th repulsed an attack against the high ground east of Mortain.[21] The Germans hoped to stem the Allied advance and regain the offensive initiative at this place. Daly steeled himself for some very tough fighting.

But a change of plans removed Daly and his regiment from the imminent battle. At 1200 on August 6 the 30th Regiment relieved the 18th to enable it to move southward to Mayenne to protect the crossings over the Mayenne River as part of an unfolding plan to encircle and trap the German armies. Meanwhile, between July 7 and 12 at Mortain, the 30th Division, reinforced by the 3rd armored Division, turned back the last desperate German counterattack in Normandy spearheaded by the SS Panzer Lehr Division under Lt. Gen. Fritz Bayerlein. The Germans reeled back—broken. On August 9, 1944, eighty thousand German soldiers found themselves in a swiftly closing pocket. General Patton's newly activated Third Army barreled deep into France at Le Mans, and it seemed increasingly possible to trap the German Seventh and Fifth Panzer armies. The plan called for the Canadians to move southward to Falaise and Patton's forces to roll northward to Alençon and then to Argentan, leaving just a fifteen-mile-wide gap between Canadian and US forces. Closing this gap would seal the fate of twenty-one German divisions in what became known as the Falaise Pocket.

During that week of fierce fighting at Mortain, the 18th consolidated strong defensive positions on high ground surrounding the town of Ambrières-les-Vallées that lay approximately eighteen miles southeast of Mortain. Its mission: to protect Third Army's left flank. Battalion records described it as a time of "relative inactivity." What with patrolling and the inevitable firefights associated with it, Daly certainly did not experience "inactivity," relative or otherwise.[22]

Those "skirmishes" in the French countryside featured confusion, destruction, casualties—civilian as well as military—and sometimes even a bit of comedy. On one occasion when Daly was acting as company scout, he became separated from the rest of his unit when fighting broke out in a village and men fell and scattered. Daly turned the corner of a building only to find himself staring at a German soldier who had come around the other side. Both men reacted instinctively in the same way—by jumping back behind their respective sides of the building! Gathering his wits, Daly felt obliged to go around again and try to capture or kill the German. But he had disappeared.[23]

Even after his earlier close call as a sniper in a tree surrounded by German troops (or perhaps because he had failed to get off any shots), Daly continued to volunteer for sniping missions. According to Lewis Smith, he was finally "cured" of this penchant after another near disaster. With American and German forces separated by a river that ran through a ravine, Daly wedged himself into a tree overlooking the narrow valley and got off "some pretty good shots" at German troops patrolling the other side. But then the Germans responded with an artillery barrage from their 88s from which Daly narrowly escaped. Later, he emphatically declared to Smith that he would never again *volunteer* for a sniping assignment.[24] Whether that proved true, neither man could recall accurately many years later, but Daly certainly had not forgone his penchant for daring action.

SAINT-LOUP-DU-GAST

As the regiment shadowed and blocked German forces racing towards Falaise, headquarters assigned Company I the task of capturing the village of Saint-Loup-du-Gast. The village stood on the east bank of the Mayenne River about two and one-half miles southwest of Ambrières-les-Vallées and about eight and one-half miles north of the city of Mayenne. A bridge crossed the Mayenne River just below the village.

The people of Saint-Loup had endured German occupation for four years and bitterly resented their occupiers. The village being small, German troops were not stationed there. Rather, the command in Ambrières dispatched patrols. These stopped at farms and required the farmers to give them food, horses, and the like. When young French men reached the age of nineteen, they became eligible to be drafted as laborers for the Germans. The French underground resistance was active in Ambrières but not in Saint-Loup. One villager later said of German troops: "They looked rigid—like steel men [in their helmets and uniforms], not real men."[25] The villagers would pay a heavy price for liberation from those "steel men," and Daly would play a key role.

On June 6, with the wind blowing from the north, the villagers could hear the constant rumbling of the naval bombardment that preceded the D-Day landing. Beginning on June 7, Saint-Loup and other villages were bombed by B-17s. These raids especially targeted rail lines. Before a bombing began, American planes dropped leaflets warning civilians to stay two kilometers away from railroad tracks. Farmers often ignored the warnings, however, because railroad tracks crossed their fields, which had to be cultivated. Bombs also destroyed two houses in the neighborhood of Saint-Loup. On the night of June 9, the inhabitants of Saint-Loup could read newspapers in their fields by the light of flames from Mayenne. The Allied air raid there destroyed one-third of the city and killed 700 civilians, including the mother of one of the villagers of Saint-Loup. Those victims were part of the mounting toll of liberation in Normandy. Between D-Day and August 25, 19,890 French civilians were killed, not to mention the tens of thousands wounded, injured, and displaced.[26]

The carnage and destruction all around them left some embittered and many numb. But the villager from Saint-Loup who drove his horse cart to Mayenne to retrieve his mother's body for burial had another reaction. When a neighbor asked what he thought of the Americans in light of his mother's death, he replied: "They are freeing us. How can I be angry with them?" Several days later, thirteen Flying Fortresses hit Ambrières, leaving thirteen civilians dead. The population of Saint-Loup responded by digging trenches in the fields to serve as shelters in the event of further aerial or artillery bombardment, and they prayed for speedy deliverance by the Allies.[27]

In July a civil and military engineering group from the German construction company Organisation Todt occupied Saint-Loup. A small house next to the priest's rectory served as a guard post. Then, at about 1700 on August 5, the same day that the Americans liberated Mayenne, the Germans pulled out of Saint-Loup. The villagers mockingly observed that the fleeing German soldiers no longer looked so fierce. The Germans had intended to destroy the nearby bridge over the Mayenne River, but an accident with the detonator foiled their plans.

Initially the villagers thought the Germans had departed so precipitously because they feared more air attacks, but the next day they recognized that the real reason was the imminent arrival of the Americans, who signaled their presence by an artillery bombardment from guns placed in the train station at Ambrières. Despite the mayhem, however, both the 7:00 a.m. Mass and the later High Mass took place as usual. Word spread that the Americans were approaching, had liberated nearby towns, and would soon do the same for Saint-Loup. The total absence of German troops seemed to indicate that liberation was indeed at hand. One excited boy ran across the small bridge spanning the Mayenne River to give flowers to the American troops of Company I, who had stopped at the bridge. Neighboring farmers also gave the Americans calvados, and the soldiers in turn gave the local people chocolate, cigarettes, and tins of corned beef and pineapples.

The day passed in relative calm, although from time to time powerful detonations shook the houses. Then, because no Allied troops had yet entered Saint-Loup, the people began to worry that continued German resistance in the vicinity could spell the destruction of their village. American shelling of the area, beginning at 1800, confirmed their fears. Farmers took shelter in the hayfields, where they stayed all night.

The bombardment continued unabated until midnight, after which an hour's calm prevailed, "almost a silence of the dead," according to Abbé Louis Lévêque, the curé of Saint Loup-du-Gast. Suddenly the grinding sound of tanks and motor vehicles broke the stillness. The Curé thought, "Americans or Germans?" He ran to the door of his residence to investigate, wanting desperately to believe that the liberators had arrived. When three trucks stopped near the door, the priest incautiously asked in a raised voice, "American?" A sarcastic "Ya!" greeted him, and to his great consternation Lévêque realized that the troops were German. Happily for Lévêque, no one in the first vehicle understood French, and their attempts to communicate with him deflected attention from his imprudent first question. When a junior officer arrived who spoke French, he turned out to be a former student of theology, and he sympathetically warned Lévêque to get the people out of the village because there would be fighting. Later that day, August 7, with tank patrols increasing on the roads, the priest led the people of Saint-Loup to the American lines, where they stayed until August 13. During that time the Americans continued to shell Saint Loup in an attempt to dislodge the Germans.[28]

On Wednesday, August 9, elements of the 18th Regiment, including Company I, sent patrols toward Cigne and Saint-Loup. Daly reconnoitered Saint-Loup and then returned to his platoon to report the intelligence he had gathered. He armed himself with a BAR and then, as squad leader, led his thirty men into the village, pointing out targets to them and to the single tank and

Liberation! *Courtesy Roger Portier, Cobra Memorial, Marigny, France.* Despite the destruction associated with the Allied offensive, French villagers demonstrated their heartfelt thanks to their liberators, reaffirming in Daly the justice of the Allied cause.

M10 TD accompanying the squad. According to his commanding officer, Daly's cool leadership enabled the American troops to eliminate the enemy and capture the village, in the process taking some German prisoners. That night, however, the Germans, using a tactic Daly would see them employ with deadly effect throughout the rest of the war, counterattacked, wresting part of the village back from the Americans, who suffered eleven casualties— two killed, two seriously wounded, one lightly wounded, and six missing. The Americans controlled the hillock of Saint-Loup, and the Germans controlled the other side of the village. Having a front without definite lines made the American soldiers nervous, and they called in artillery that pummeled the enemy-controlled part of the village, including the church, the town hall, and a large château. On August 12 the Germans withdrew and Company I moved in along with Father Lévêque and the rest of the inhabitants. They returned to a shattered village—the chateau and the city hall were in ruins, and part of the church tower had been destroyed—but they were elated to be free of the "Boche" at last.[29]

NORTHERN FRANCE: PURSUIT

On the morning of August 13 the 18th Regiment shifted back to a full offensive mode. The 3rd Battalion entered Chantrigne unopposed, the Germans having fallen back during the night. As the battalion pursued them, the Germans moved northward to Sept-Forges and blew all the bridges over the Mayenne River behind them. Meanwhile, Company I drove out small enemy forces that had infiltrated the battalion's rear area, killing fifteen and capturing six.[30]

The 18th Regiment continued its push northward to La Coulonche, which overlooked a key valley that was in the rear of the German Seventh Army. A swift enveloping move forced the Germans to withdraw. On August 15 at 1730 the 3rd Battalion loaded into trucks with the mission of securing the high ground north of La Sauvagère. The regiment positioned itself along a dominant ridge in the vicinity of the town, placing it just ten miles south of Falaise, on the southern perimeter of the Argentan-Falaise Gap. The regiment had achieved its objective of funneling fleeing German forces into what resembled an elongated horseshoe that the Allies hoped would become a trap that bagged the German Army of the West. The Germans fought desperately for several days, until on August 16, Hitler gave the Seventh Army permission to withdraw across the Seine in hopes of salvaging as many troops and headquarters cadres as possible. Aided by rain and heavy mist that provided cover and negated Allied airpower for five days, eighty thousand troops fled eastward through the narrow Falaise Gap. They left behind 10,000 dead, 42,000 prisoners, and thousands of destroyed weapons, vehicles, and horses.[31]

As his unit passed through the picturesque French countryside with its rich dairy farms and orchards dotted with roadside crucifixes and statues of saints and of the Blessed Virgin, it seemed to Daly that the joy of the liberated inhabitants knew no bounds. Long lines of them dressed in holiday clothes thronged city streets, crying, clapping, shouting, and offering the ubiquitous bottles of wine to the soldiers. As the 1st Division pursued the fleeing Germans, it passed in an arc south of Paris, which the Germans had evacuated only recently and which Americans and Free French had occupied on August 25. So close, and yet so far, from the famous French capital. But fortune continued to smile on Daly. The war's most famous correspondent, Ernie Pyle, who frequently accompanied the 18th Regiment, scheduled a radio broadcast for the Armed Forces Network from Paris. When Pyle arranged to interview some men who had recently received medals for bravery in combat, Daly found himself in a jeep bound for the storied metropolis. As the soldiers entered Paris in the open vehicle, they received a tumultuous welcome. A sea of girls and women engulfed them, greeting them with flowers, lifting them out of their jeeps, and passing them around on a sea of hands. As Daly later observed, "This was pretty heady stuff for a teenager." But after the interview the teenager quickly returned to his regiment which finally enjoyed some "down time."[32]

When Daly came off the line, he could at last take a shower, wash his underwear, eat a hot meal, sleep, and read his mail. His former nanny, Mary

Martin, had sent him many letters. Keenly aware of his height and his daring disposition, and fearful that he would get shot in the head, she kept warning him to keep his head down. He also received some mail from his parents, although his father wrote infrequently because of the war's demands on his time. The letters he did write to his son continued in the instructional mode. His sister, Madge, wrote occasionally, as did several girlfriends, but not, according to Mike, "with any ardor." His younger brothers and sisters wrote occasionally. His male friends, all serving in the armed forces, did not know his whereabouts and, even if they had known, had little time for corresponding.[33]

During August and early September the "Big Red One" Division continued its rapid advance across northern France and into Belgium. On one of those days newly promoted Private 1st Class Daly rode a captured horse until the battalion commanding officer barked at him. A palpable euphoria swept the public in the United States and Great Britain and even Eisenhower's headquarters. Many predicted that the Germans would capitulate by Christmas. In the first week of September, 67 percent of Americans questioned in a Gallup poll answered that they expected the war in Europe to be over by Christmas, a sentiment shared by many GIs. The Allies' lightning advance, coming on the heels of the two-month slogging match in Normandy, and the sight of so much destroyed and abandoned German equipment across France led Daly to dare to hope that the end might indeed be in sight.

BELGIUM: STIFFENING RESISTANCE

But at the same time, tens of thousands of German troops, estimated at corps size, raced parallel with the Allied forces, seeking desperately to reach the fortifications of the West Wall (known to Americans as the Siegfried Line) on the German border, where they could reestablish defensive positions. (The Nazis had retained many troops within Germany itself for the defense of the Fatherland.) Those days featured, in the words of one author, "whirlwind, confusing encounters." On September 3 and 4, Daly's 3rd Battalion, along with the 1st Battalion and with the support of tank and TD units, killed hundreds of Germans and took 1,000 prisoners. The continuing clashes, however, strengthened Daly's perception of stiffening German resistance as Allied troops pressed ever closer to Germany itself, disabusing him of the hope that the Nazis would soon throw in the towel.[34]

On September 10, Daly's 3rd Battalion moved through Liège and across the Meuse river. A few German planes dropped bombs fairly close to the river crossing but were driven off by antiaircraft fire. The 3rd Battalion encountered no opposition until it reached the vicinity of the small town of Battice,

Belgium, about twenty miles southeast of the German city of Aachen and the Siegfried Line. On the outskirts of Battice lay a series of Belgian forts occupied since 1940 by the Germans. There a small force of about fifty infantry and one self-propelled artillery piece engaged the lead elements of the battalion briefly and then withdrew. Moving eastward, Company I approached Battice. For two hours during the late afternoon and early evening the Germans shelled Battice with heavy guns that were located to the northeast but that US aircraft could not find. The guns inflicted fourteen casualties that day, but the Americans took the town.

The following afternoon, at 1300, Daly's Company I spearheaded the 3rd Battalion advance northeastward from Battice toward Aubel. The highway connecting the towns across a beautiful, broad, saucer-shaped valley of farmland proved a perfect target for German guns perched on the high ground overlooking the valley from the northeast. During the entire operation, mortar and artillery fire poured down on the steadily advancing American troops. Up until that point, Daly had led a charmed life, especially in light of his demonstrated willingness to expose himself to enemy fire. Indeed, not long before, rifle grenades had killed two men directly in front of and behind him. As he moved across the open expanse of fields, however, Daly felt utterly exposed and vulnerable. Suddenly, mortar rounds exploded around him, sending jagged shrapnel ripping into his left calf. Experts estimate that "fragmentation devices" such as artillery shells and mortars accounted for more than half of all battlefield casualties during World War II. Daly found himself one of the 135,000 casualties suffered by the US Army and US Army Air Force between June 6 and September 14.[35]

Evacuated from the field, Daly spent six weeks recuperating in a hospital in England. During this period, Allied forces became bogged down in Arnhem, Holland, in the Hürtgen Forest, just inside Germany, and in Aachen, Germany. Hopes for a quick Allied victory before Christmas died that fall on the Western front. As Daly's leg healed, General Patch invited him to finish his recuperation at Seventh Army headquarters in Épinal, a town in the Lorraine region of eastern France. In early November, General Patch dispatched his personal plane, a converted B-25 flown by his personal pilot, Col. John Warner, to pick up Mike in England and fly him back to Épinal, just as he had done for his own son, Mac who had been wounded in October.[36]

In combat, Daly had demonstrated the courage and professionalism worthy of his upbringing and training. He had proven himself a valorous warrior. Patch would help him to the next level.

6   Becoming an Officer

December 1944, Seventh Army Headquarters, Épinal, France, General "Sandy" Patch commanding.

Mike was not the only Daly who would become a statistic on the lengthening list of US Army casualties during that fall and early winter. Even as General Patch offered Mike a commission as a second lieutenant and agreed to return him to combat as an officer in the 15th Infantry Regiment, 3rd Division, of Patch's 7th Army, Mike learned that near Fort Schiesseck, in Lorraine, his father had suffered a shrapnel wound that seriously damaged the sciatic nerve in his thigh. Before leaving to join the 15th Infantry Regiment at the front, Mike visited with his wounded father, who was awaiting transfer back to the United States. During their visit, Mike and his dad talked somewhat awkwardly, both avoiding the severity of the colonel's injury. Finally, Paul Daly remarked that because Mike's commission had just come through, he could use a few things. He then gave Mike his treasured pistol, a big Colt 45 he had won in a horse race. A nurse offered Mike her second lieutenant bars, which Paul pinned on Mike's uniform. Then they parted, the father's war finished, the son's about to enter a new, climactic phase.[1]

For General "Sandy" Patch, who would become a mentor for Mike Daly, the path to Épinal had begun on August 15, 1944, when the Allies finally launched Operation Anvil, the amphibious invasion of southern France. The Franco-American Riviera force consisting of Patch's Seventh Army and French Gen. Jean de Lattre de Tassigny's First Army quickly seized the important Mediterranean ports of Marseille and Toulon and then swiftly moved up the Rhone River to Lyon. US strategists hoped to bring more Allied force to bear against Germany's western border. At Lyon, Gen. Jacob Devers, commander of Sixth Army Group, subsumed the Seventh Army and the Free French First Army into his army group, which constituted the southernmost element of General Eisenhower's northern European command.

General Patch was one of the least well known of the high-ranking American military leaders of World War II. Tall, gray-haired, and bearing

Lieutenant Michael J. Daly. *Courtesy National Archives.* In late December, Daly joined Able Company of the 15th Regiment shortly after the regiment's bloody encounter at Sigolsheim, in Alsace. During the campaign to eliminate the Colmar Pocket, Daly would receive two Oak Clusters on his Silver Star ribbon (indicating a total of three Silver Stars) for his heroism.

a resemblance to movie star Gary Cooper, he appeared nattily dressed on the battlefield. He sported a silken Air Force map wrapped around his neck as an ascot and an elegant, black pistol holstered and worn from the waist of his army-issue riding breeches and regulation riding boots. He shared a love of horses with Paul and Mike Daly. Patch had a sharp temper that had led him into numerous fights when he was young but that he had learned to master as an adult. Self-possessed, modest, honorable, and physically brave—again, qualities he shared with his best friend—he also had a devilish sense of humor. As his biographer observed, "It was difficult to imagine him doing anything cheap or self-serving. He made firm friends, kept them, and liked having them around."

Soldiers, especially enlisted men, held him in high esteem because they saw in him "qualities that they admired in officers but did not always find. There was not a hint of vainglory, pomposity or pretentiousness" in his personality. He smoked Bull Durham tobacco and rolled his own cigarettes. He did not seek glory—indeed, he generally disliked the limelight and did not court the press, which often overlooked him. That changed, at least briefly, on August 28, 1944, when *Time* magazine featured his face on its cover following the amphibious landings in southern France and the push up the Rhone River. Patch, however, reportedly never even looked at it. He was known in military circles as a "finalist." "He was not flashy," said a member of his staff, "but the bottom line was that he always won." He was a warrior, like Patton, but abhorred pointless loss of life. Before an attack he would brood about casualties and was sensitive to what his soldiers might be going through—a sensitivity perhaps heightened by his own son Mac's service as

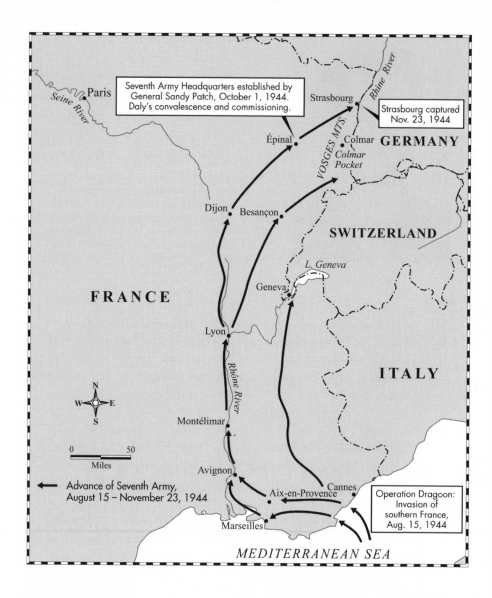

Seventh Army Headquarters established by General Sandy Patch, October 1, 1944. Daly's convalescence and commissioning.

Strasbourg captured Nov. 23, 1944

Seine River

Paris

Strasbourg

Rhine River

Épinal

Colmar
Colmar Pocket

GERMANY

VOSGES MTS.

Dijon

Besançon

SWITZERLAND

L. Geneva

Geneva

FRANCE

Lyon

ITALY

N
W · E
S

Rhône River

Montélimar

0   50
Miles

Avignon

Cannes

Aix-en-Provence

Advance of Seventh Army, August 15 – November 23, 1944

Operation Dragoon: Invasion of southern France, Aug. 15, 1944

Marseilles

MEDITERRANEAN SEA

the commander of a rifle company in the 315th Infantry. Once he had made a decision he considered sound, however, "he did not flinch." He fought boldly and aggressively, and once engaged, he accepted nothing less than victory.[2]

From September to November 1944, the Sixth Army Group, facing dogged resistance from the German Nineteenth Army in the midst of rugged terrain, chilling rain, a sea of mud, and then bitter cold and snow, struggled slowly and agonizingly eastward toward the Saverne and Belfort Gaps, in the Vosges Mountains of Alsace near the juncture of the borders of eastern France, Switzerland, and southern Germany. The area had been bitterly contested between France and Germany and had changed hands three times in the previous seventy-five years. One sergeant's observations captured the despair of the troops "The happy healthy people [of southern France gave way to] hungry and thin. . . . As for the scenery, that forest full of Christmas trees was lousy with snipers; those winding streams running through the valleys . . . only made their feet wetter and the full moon shone on the hills . . . making the GIs curse, thinking of the long fucking climb and the fucking mud and . . . more fucking mud on the other side."[3]

Beginning on November 13, however, while Mike Daly remained at Patch's headquarters, Patch's Seventh Army and General de Lattre's First Army began a well-planned offensive that poured through the German lines, captured Strasbourg, and moved quickly to the west bank of the Rhine River. In the process the two armies shattered the cohesiveness of the German forces—except those in a bulge, or pocket, that included the town of Colmar, near the Rhine, and extended thirty-five to forty miles westward, high into the Vosges Mountains. This salient, which had proven too tough for de Lattre's army to take at the time, became known as the "Colmar Pocket." The stubborn German salient did not concern Devers, who believed he could eliminate it soon enough. Instead, he wanted the Seventh Army to exploit its momentum and the wedge it had driven between German armies by crossing the Rhine above Strasbourg. Eisenhower, however, who did not have a very high estimation of Devers, did not concur. He had greater concern than Devers about the German "bulge" around Colmar. More important, he believed that Patton's more northerly route into Germany represented the soundest strategic approach. Eisenhower, therefore, ordered Patch's Seventh Army to strike northward in support of Patton's Third Army offensive in Lorraine. Patch, an effective leader and strategist who got along well and worked effectively with the much more flamboyant and better-known Patton, had no problem with this.[4]

But amidst the hard-won success on the battlefield, personal tragedy also stalked Patch. When the general first invited Mike Daly to finish his convalescence at Épinal, he had only recently suffered the shattering loss of his son, Capt. Mac Patch. The general's son was killed in combat on October 22, shortly after returning to his company from his father's headquarters, where he had been recuperating from a shoulder wound. Mike Daly had met Mac, a handsome, popular, friendly first classman (Class of '42) at West Point. Mac had made it a point to introduce himself to Mike, a gesture the beleaguered plebe had very much appreciated at the time. Mac had gone on to become, by all accounts, an intrepid infantry officer, rising to the rank of captain and earning the Distinguished Service Cross. The anguished yet stoic general drew some consolation from having the son of his best friend by his side—someone who had known and admired Mac and who displayed many of the same courageous qualities. Patch observed to his wife about Mike: "The boy is magnificent—six feet three inches tall and a lovely and attractive kid. He is still here tonight—although Paul has gone about his duties."

Mike often took his meals with Patch, including several dinners at which Patch entertained general officers. Mike sat at the table but spoke only when spoken to. One evening, he listened as General Patton turned the air blue with his profanity. At another dinner a high-ranking officer asked Patch how he got along "with that son-of-a-bitch, Patton." Patch, who admired Patton's brilliance as a warrior, did not begrudge him the publicity that surrounded him. Nor did he feel jealous of or threatened by Patton, who was five years his senior. He actually found Patton amusing and replied diplomatically, yet pointedly, "He's a good man to have on your side when you're in trouble."[5]

He felt the same way about his buddy Paul Daly, who remained an effective and dependable member of Patch's Seventh Army staff as well as a trusted friend with whom he could joke and unwind.[6] Of course, Patch valued Daly not only as a friend but also as an officer. The hard-charging Daly had impressed his superior with his energy, professionalism, aggressiveness, bravery, and ability to rejuvenate and improve the regiments he commanded. Patch knew he could count on Daly to get the job done. Consequently, when Patch became dissatisfied with the performance of the 398th Regiment of the 100th Division, he removed its commander, replacing him with Paul Daly on December 12, 1944. As was his wont, Daly gave particular attention to fostering initiative, leadership, and aggressiveness in the platoon leaders. He had great respect for and high expectations of these officers. "As important as is the assistance we get from the air and the artillery," he told a gathering of platoon leaders, "in the end, as always, the infantry goes in and pushes him [the enemy] out." He repeated almost verbatim the exhortation that he had given to platoon leaders on Guadalcanal with much the same positive effect on morale.[7]

His words had such a powerful impact because Paul Daly lived them. As part of the Allied drive against the Maginot Line, now strongly defended by Germans, Daly prepared, directed, and personally led the preliminary attacks against Forts Freudenberg and Schiesseck. In the words of the citation for the Silver Star that he later received, Colonel Daly demonstrated "unusual devotion to duty and complete disregard for his own personal safety during the period December 10–17, 1944." He had little tolerance for officers who did not lead from the front. When one of the three battalions in his regiment lagged in the attack, he went forward to see for himself what the problem was. He found the officer in charge giving orders from a deep foxhole. "It's pretty hot up here, Colonel," the officer allegedly said. "Too hot for you," Daly replied. "You're relieved!"

On December 14, even though the 3rd Battalion observation post found itself under hostile artillery, mortar, automatic-weapons, and small-arms fire, Colonel Daly insisted on visiting it to witness air and ground attacks. He joked that he had suffered from constipation but found this condition improved by shellfire! On each of the three following days he again visited forward positions. Officers such as Daly, who were veterans of World War I, clung to the belief that exposing themselves to fire without flinching or wavering instilled needed confidence in their men. This dangerous practice, however, often proved costly, both to the officers and to their units, whose efficiency and morale suffered when officers became casualties. And on Daly's third day of observation his luck ran out: a piece of shrapnel from an exploding mortar shell nearly severed the sciatic nerve in his thigh. His men went on to take Fort Schiesseck, but they would fight the rest of the war without him.

Patch wrote to his wife telling her that Paul Daly had been injured and would return to the States shortly. He added, "I have a deep friendship and respect for that man and I shall miss him greatly." (Shortly after the war, Patch, would tell W. B. Martin Jr., a friend of both Patch and Daly: "Colonel Paul Daly is the bravest man I ever knew in my life. He contributed immeasurably to my success.") Maj. Gen. W. A. Burress, commander of the 100th Division, wrote to Daly, "I can assure you from remarks I have heard from the younger officers here, that they had the greatest respect and admiration for your fine, cool leadership."[8]

While his father battled Germans, Mike remained in the relative safety of Seventh Army headquarters. Ironically, however, in that setting he found himself at great risk from the careless, reckless, self-defeating behavior that seemed to emerge when he was not actively engaged in what he regarded as important activity. He was great in the field but not so good in garrison. At Patch's headquarters he narrowly averted shooting himself in the foot, both literally and figuratively.

During his stay with Patch, Mike underwent oral surgery to remove impacted wisdom teeth. Because securing adequate supplies was difficult, the surgeon could give him only a small dose of Novocaine to deaden the pain. Woozy from the procedure and suffering from throbbing pain in his mouth, Daly returned to his room, still wearing his sidearm. As he sat in a foggy state on the edge of his bunk waiting for the ache to abate, he drew his pistol from its holster and pointed it at the floor. Suddenly—the sound of a shot—he had discharged the pistol. Shades of West Point—although this time he could cite more valid extenuating circumstances. Luckily the bullet only grazed the sole of his foot, leaving a burn mark on his boot. Had the wound been more serious, it might have seemed that he had "cracked" and given himself a "million-dollar wound" in order to avoid more combat—an offense punishable by court martial. Many years later, alluding to this incident and the earlier one at West Point, Daly wryly observed that discharging his weapon at the wrong time seemed to pose a challenge for him—at least off the battlefield.

On another occasion, Daly barely averted a serious accident while driving General Patch in a jeep to visit division headquarters. Daly had always had a "heavy foot," and this time was no different, even though snow covered the road. Driving too fast for road conditions, Daly suddenly came upon a slower-moving tank. Swerving around it to avoid a collision, he lost control of the jeep, and it ended up in a ditch. According to Daly, Patch "did not act very mad" about the near miss. Indeed the general commented to his wife in a letter, "Since John Warner brought Mike Daly here some time ago there has been no flying weather to get him back—He is still here and we enjoy Mike a very great deal."

Patch clearly saw in Mike many characteristics that he had loved and admired in his own son. He knew Mike to be a fine soldier, not only because of his Silver Star but also because of glowing performance reports he received when he asked Daly's former commanding officers whether he would make a good officer. He also knew, no doubt, of Paul Daly's strong desire that his son become an officer. As a result, Patch offered Mike a commission as a second lieutenant. In addition, perhaps as a way of trying to protect his best friend's son from the fate that had befallen his own, he offered to make Daly one of his personal aides-de-camp.

The offer of a commission struck Daly as unorthodox. He had never heard of a private being promoted to officer, and he figured his father was somehow involved. But the promotion was more than simple favoritism. The high casualty rate among company-grade infantry officers, such as Mac Patch, required that their number be replenished constantly. The War Department and commanders in the field agreed that "the one sure method of determining whether any individual has qualities which make him a successful leader in combat is to observe that man in combat." Indeed the War Department had issued directives authorizing and urging commanders to make battlefield appointments. Eisenhower had sent messages and letters to his subordinate commanders reminding them of the desirability of making as many battlefield appointments as possible. Patch agreed heartily that battlefield commissions represented the best way to procure the best officers, and he saw in Daly demonstrative proof of the qualities that made for an excellent officer.[9]

Daly's Commanders. *Courtesy National Archives.* Lt. Gen. Alexander M. "Sandy" Patch (on the left), Commander of the 7th Army, and John W. "Iron Mike" O'Daniel (on the right), commanding general of the 3rd Division, review troops. After being wounded by mortar fire near Battice, Belgium, on September 11, 1944, Daly was sent to a hospital in England. When he was released, General Patch, a close friend of Daly's father, invited him to Épinal, France, to finish convalescing at 7th Army headquarters. In December 1944, Patch commissioned Daly a second lieutenant and assigned him to the 15th Infantry Regiment of the 3rd Infantry Division.

As for serving as Patch's aide, Daly never entertained the proposal. He had known and admired the younger Patch, whose death had both angered and grieved him—as had that of his cousin, John Sherman Riley, whom he idolized and who had been so supportive of him after West Point. Both Mac Patch and Riley had served in the 79th Division (at that time part of General Patch's Seventh Army), and both had been killed at about the same time. Their deaths, and the fury Daly felt toward Germans, only strengthened his resolve to return to combat with the infantry. Daly accepted the offer of a commission—receiving the two gold bars of a second lieutenant on December 18, 1944—but declined to serve as Patch's aide, expressing his desire to get back to fighting. "I thought it was my job to be in the front lines," he later explained.

Patch obliged him and twice dispatched the newly minted lieutenant on a small plane back to the 1st Division just as it was becoming engaged in the Battle of the Bulge. On both occasions, however, bad weather forced the plane to return. Patch told Daly, "It's God's hand," and suggested he go to what Patch considered the best division in his Seventh Army: the 3rd Infantry Division ("The Rock of the Marne"), commanded by an officer known for his aggressiveness in battle, his old friend Maj. Gen. John W. "Iron Mike" O'Daniel. (O'Daniel had come by his nickname as a result of his heroism at the Battle of Saint Mihiel, during World War I. There he had fought for twelve hours despite being wounded in the face by a German machine-gun round.) Daly replied, "I'm all for it." Patch's staff took care of the paperwork, and on December 28, 1944, 2nd Lt. Michael Daly took over as leader of the 1st Platoon of A (Able) Company," 1st Battalion, 15th Infantry Regiment, 3rd Infantry Division. The 3rd Division, composed of the 7th and 30th infantry regiments as well as the 15th, was fighting in the Vosges Mountains. He would join a battle-hardened regiment that had weathered campaigns in North Africa, Sicily, Italy (where it had spearheaded the landing at Anzio), and southern France. Its proud performance during those operations had underscored the aptness of its regimental motto: "Can Do!"[10]

That "Can Do" spirit came at a terrible price throughout the autumn and winter. The Germans used mines, booby traps, machine guns, and skillfully sited mortars and artillery to inflict casualties and bog down the Allies, who also suffered logistical challenges, especially a shortage of gasoline and artillery shells. Even during lulls in the fighting, the tasks of digging, patrolling, and manning positions resulted in losses. Once the offensives had begun in Lorraine, the Hürtgen Forest, and the Vosges Mountains in the fall, casualties climbed rapidly. Mike Daly was one of 42,179 casualties (there were also 4,860 MIAs) suffered by the First Army between September 1 and December 16, 1944. During that same period, Patton's Third Army casualties totaled 53,182, and the newly formed Ninth Army suffered 10,056. In addition, the three armies sustained 113,742 nonbattle casualties, mostly trench foot—caused by prolonged exposure of the feet to damp, unsanitary, and cold conditions—and "combat fatigue," or combat-stress reaction. General Bradley later wrote that by early December, "We were mired in a ghastly war of attrition."[11] Shortly after a dreary, joyless Christmas, Mike left to join the 15th Regiment in eastern France at a village called Sigolsheim, near the Colmar Pocket.[12]

7   The Colmar Pocket

WINTER HEROISM

January 28, 1945, the Colmar Pocket, France.

Mike Daly and another man from Able Company trudged their way to Major General O'Daniel's headquarters for a regimental awards ceremony. On a snowy field O'Daniel presented the medals. Daly and many others admired the stocky, gruff, outspoken general. He carried a bayonet scar on his cheek from combat during World War I, and one of his favorite expressions in speaking to the men he commanded was, "Sharpen your bayonet!" He once declared, in his gravel voice, "I never felt better than when I saw a bunch of dead Krauts around on the ground." O'Daniel's troops admired him as a man of great personal courage who understood them and who himself had suffered the loss of a son in the war. Listening to some of O'Daniel's addresses during regimental reviews, Daly found himself stirred by what he regarded as the man's eloquence in explaining the critical importance of the Allied cause to the future of civilization and in assuring his men that free people around the world were watching them and praying for their victory. As O'Daniel pinned the oak-leaf cluster representing a second Silver Star on Daly's jacket, he made some encouraging comments and then asked the lieutenant if he was "ready to go back in there and get this thing over with." Mike's mumbled "I think so" was less "gung-ho" than O'Daniel had hoped for, and he said so. But this rolled off Daly's back. The laconic second lieutenant had nothing to prove; his actions said it all. Numbed by cold, fatigue, and combat, Daly and his companion turned around and made their way back through the snow to company quarters. The headline in the Bridgeport newspaper back home read, "Lieut. M. J. Daly of Fairfield Cited for 'Inspiring' Attack."[1]

The tough going that Allied operations experienced from September to December confirmed that the Germans had reorganized after their earlier defeats. General Eisenhower therefore determined to keep pressure on the enemy throughout the winter and deny them the freedom to reinforce their defenses. On December 7, 1944, in the Dutch city of Maastricht, Eisenhower met with Field Marshal Bernard Montgomery and Lieutenant General Bradley to plan an all-out offensive for the early weeks of 1945. Eisenhower decided that Montgomery's Twenty-First Army Group would carry the main effort, with secondary attacks in the south. Montgomery had argued that his army group should make a concentrated thrust across the Rhine north of the Ruhr River while the other Allied forces resorted to containing actions, but Eisenhower, who controlled the burgeoning American resources that Montgomery's plan would need, prevailed.

Before the Allies could fully implement the Maastricht plan, the Germans counterattacked in the Ardennes. Early in the mist-shrouded morning of December 16, Hitler launched the Seventh Army and the Fifth and Sixth Panzer Armies in an attempt to cross the Meuse, seize Antwerp, and split the Allied front. The "Battle of the Bulge" had begun.[2]

The Ardennes offensive forced Devers's Sixth Army Group to halt all offensive operations and extend its front northward. As a result, in January 1945 the German High Command launched Operation Nordwind, a major armor and infantry offensive against Patch's extended Seventh Army. A stubborn but flexible defense finally wore the German forces thin, but both sides suffered heavily in the bitterly cold weather during the worst winter of the century.[3]

On December 28, Mike joined Able Company, 1st Battalion, 15th Regiment, toward the end of a desperately fought, bloody, five-day battle for control of Sigolsheim, a town on the western Alsatian plain just east of the last line of the Vosges Mountains. On the day Daly joined Able Company, the Germans were resisting fiercely, their artillery and mortar fire reducing the town to rubble, but by the next day the 15th Regiment had taken Sigolsheim.[4]

Some high foothills just outside Sigolsheim also saw bitter fighting in the snowy, windswept weather. German troops still clung tenaciously to parts of Hills 216 and 351, both of which overlooked the town. Lt. Col. Keith L. Ware, commander of the 1st Battalion, which Daly had just joined, personally led a handful of men who, with a tank, succeeded in capturing enemy positions on the top of Hill 351—an action that earned him the Medal of Honor. Other units, meanwhile, completed the capture of Hill 216. Thus Daly found himself serving in a company that prided itself on leading the regiment in total number of medals awarded for bravery (thirteen Silver and twenty-two Bronze) and whose commander demonstrated the quality he most admired in an officer: leading from the front.[5]

The 15th Regiment's determined victory had opened the gates to the plain of Alsace to the east. But on New Year's Eve, Heinrich Himmler launched Operation Nordwind, the southern counterpart to the Ardennes-Alsace campaign (Battle of the Bulge) that raged to the north. The Germans attacked toward the vital Saverne Gap in the Vosges Mountains through which they hoped to link up with German forces engaged in the Ardennes. The Germans also forced a crossing of the Rhine River just north of Strasbourg that threatened the recapture of that city. During the first week of January, German morale soared on reports from their officers of great success in the Ardennes. They became convinced that they could change the course of the war and intended to present Strasbourg to the Führer as a late Christmas gift.

With an attack possible at any time, the 15th Regiment took up defensive positions with orders to hold the recently won ground "at all costs." All available men, including clerks, MPs, and cooks, were pressed into service organizing defenses. Initially Eisenhower ordered General Patch to pull his forces back from Strasbourg into the more easily defensible Vosges Mountains. The French, however, fearing a German massacre of those who had only recently welcomed and aided the Allies, bitterly objected to the proposal on nationalistic, political, and moral grounds and warned that they would fight for the city. In the face of this adamant opposition, Eisenhower rescinded the order. Fortunately for Daly, the 15th Regiment sector remained quiet. The German counteroffensive in the Ardennes ended in failure, as did the attempt to break out of the bridgehead over the Rhine River and take the Saverne Gap and Strasbourg.[6] The 15th Regiment sat perched on the plains of Alsace ready to help close the Colmar Pocket.

Daly found the men of his new platoon receptive and friendly, but they expressed astonishment among themselves at their new lieutenant's youth and boyish appearance. "The first time I saw him, he was a tall kid," remembered Sgt. Troy Cox. "He had wavy hair when he took off his helmet. I couldn't believe he could be an officer and a leader." Some of the men of the regiment were seasoned veterans who had served in Sicily, Italy, and southern and western France. But Daly also had demonstrated his own mettle as a warrior during his three months of combat from June to early September 1944. The members of his platoon knew he had served as an enlisted man, had seen combat, had received the Silver Star and the Purple Heart medals, and had attained an officer's commission—all of which increased his credibility with them.[7]

Daly had seen combat and knew what to expect, which steadied him as an officer. He had also seen company-grade officers good and bad in action, and he believed that he had learned from direct experience what worked and what did not. Now that he had become an officer, Daly felt a great sense of responsibility for the men under his command. He drew upon the lessons his father had imparted to him: the need for wisdom as well as courage because others' lives now depended directly on his decisions, and the need for an officer to lead his platoon from the front. Raised as a horseman by a horseman,

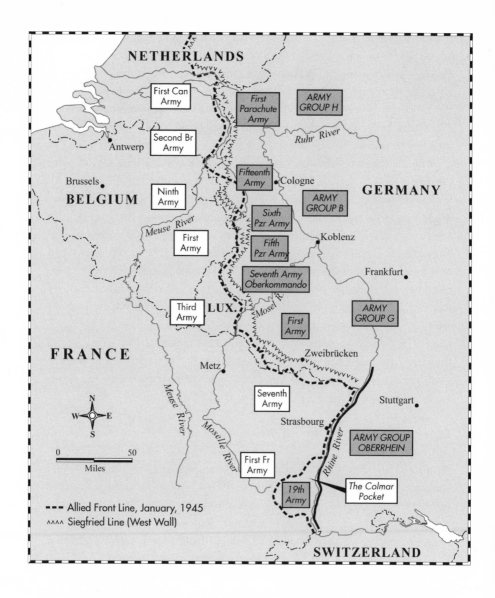

Daly internalized the advice often given to jockeys at tracks, and repeated to him by a World War I veteran friend of his father: "Get out in front and stay there." He knew he might well become a casualty again, but he did not dwell on that. He had a job to do, accomplishing his mission while leading and protecting his men to the best of his ability, and he intended to do just that.

He believed that he fought in a righteous cause—that Americans were duty bound to defeat the "terrible beast loose in the world." And he prayed that he would rise to the challenge and not fail his men. Now more than ever he took to heart his father's oft-repeated maxim that bravery consisted in being "more afraid of letting anyone know you are afraid than you are of what you are afraid of."[8] He had been preparing for this moment, at least subconsciously, since those bedtime stories of Roland and Oliver. Would he find himself capable of leading effectively as an officer? Would he show the right combination of bravery and wisdom? Did he have what it took? How far had he come? He would soon find out.

Many US history textbooks give the impression that after the Allied victory at the Battle of the Bulge, the war in Western Europe effectively ended—German resistance disintegrated, and the Allies sped effortlessly into the heart of the Reich to accept the inevitable surrender. The Battle of the Bulge and Nordwind did represent Hitler's last offensive campaigns in the West, but more than three months of bloody combat remained for Allied forces against a defeated yet resourceful foe that refused to surrender.

In January 1945, following the defeat of Hitler's counterattacks, General Eisenhower ordered Devers and his VI Corps in Alsace to launch a major offensive (Operation Cheerful) to eliminate the Colmar Pocket. This German salient west of the Rhine River, which took its name from the city of Colmar, measured 45 miles at its base on the Rhine and extended 25 miles into the Vosges Mountains. The perimeter around the pocket, which measured 130 miles, enclosed 850 square miles. Creating a 50-mile gap in the Rhine front of the First French Army, the German presence in the pocket threatened the rear of both the 3rd and the 7th Armies and thereby the entire Allied position in Alsace. It also drained Allied troops from what Eisenhower considered the more important front farther north, where he hoped for a deep breakthrough into Germany. The American and French forces in Operation Cheerful sought to strike the pocket simultaneously from the north and the south, push along the Rhine plain, and then pinch off the salient, thereby cutting off, trapping, and eliminating an array of German units that had concentrated west of the Rhine. Committed to holding the Colmar Pocket, Himmler brought in the elite 2nd Mountain Infantry Division from Norway and ordered his forces to hold the salient "at all costs."[9]

At the beginning of the Colmar offensive, Daly and the men of the 3rd Division found themselves attached to II Corps of the First Army under Gen. Jean de Lattre de Tassigny. In addition to German arms, Daly and his men faced a formidable foe in the weather. December and January had seen heavy snowfalls, but Allied meteorologists predicted that the weather would break in the latter half of January providing clear skies and roads for the offensive. Warmer temperatures in February, however, could melt the snow and turn the area into a muddy quagmire that would impede Allied operations. Thus General Devers pushed for the operation to begin as soon as possible. As it turned out, the meteorologists missed the mark badly. General de Lattre graphically described the terrible conditions faced by both the Allied and German forces during the Colmar campaign:

> As for the weather, it is impossible to imagine it more frightful. Though smiling on fine days, the Alsatian plain resembled an immense city of the dead, covered with a thick shroud of snow, from which emerged the skeletons of trees, haunted by croaking clouds of crows. And the sky, low and constantly grey, was only lit by the sinister gleams of fires or the blood-red flashes of gunfire. It was twenty degrees centigrade below zero, the wind howled, and there were over three feet of snow. Anyone with a roof over his head—and that was not the attacker—had a master card in the struggle. This truly Siberian winter was our enemy's best ally, and he knew it.

Prior to Operation Nordwind, Gen. Friedrich Wiese, the German commander of the Nineteenth Army, underscored the crucial importance of the weather to the German cause: "What will not return is the chance that the winter offers us. . . . Whoever wins the winter wins the war."[10]

Closing the Colmar Pocket required offensive operations in terrain ideally suited to defense. Small villages, towns, and extensive wood patches dotted the flat Alsatian plain that spread eastward from the base of the Vosges Mountains to the Rhine. In addition, numerous canals, irrigation ditches, and unfordable streams crisscrossed the area. German troops, increasingly armed with shoulder-fired *panzerfäuste,* posed a deadly threat to American armor. In an operations report dated January 5, 1945, Lieutenant Colonel Edson warned: "It has been learned that the Germans have more than a *panzerfaust* per man and that they are well trained and proficient in their use. The enemy holds his fire, and in many cases, is successful in knocking out a tank with the first round." He advised that tank and tank-destroyer fire cover all possible enemy positions in the approaches to a town prior to the attack. Tanks then could support and cover the infantry without moving up until foot elements definitely had cleared the sector of enemy infantry and "bazooka men."

The offensive plan called for coordinated attacks on both shoulders of the pocket by American and French forces. The main objective, however, was not the city of Colmar, but rather the town of Neuf-Brisach and the nearby bridge over the Rhine. Neuf-Brisach and the bridge lay seven miles east of Colmar. The Brisach bridge had proven invulnerable to earlier Allied air attack, and now Devers and General de Lattre hoped to secure it and to trap as many Germans within the pocket as possible. The four regiments of O'Daniel's 3rd Division (7th, 15th, 30th, and attached 254th) would thrust at Neuf-Brisach from the northwest shoulder of the pocket. In an operation it called Grand

Slam, the 3rd Division would cross the Fecht river at Guémar, the River Ill at Maison-Rouge, and the Colmar and Rhine-Rhone canals to cut off the city of Colmar from reinforcements from the East, thus assuring its fall. Troops would then move southward between the Rhone and Rhine canals to capture the town of Neuf-Brisach and the Brisach bridge over the Rhine.[11]

Opposing them were the men of the Nineteenth Army under the command of General Wiese's replacement, Gen. Siegfried Rasp. Rasp hoped to tie down Allied forces west of the Rhine to afford the German army time to redeploy units to the Eastern Front and to reorganize those units remaining east of the Rhine. The Nineteenth Army had been battered by the US Seventh Army and the Free French forces during the Vosges Mountains campaign. Its divisions were "under strength, underequipped, and undertrained." They possessed, for example, only about sixty-five operational tanks and assault guns. Still, Rasp had some advantages that would allow him to slow the Allies. He possessed some 22,500 highly motivated, albeit undertrained, troops, whereas the Allies thought he had only 15,000. His army, moreover, possessed plentiful supplies of mines, food, and small-arms ammunition, the advantage of short interior lines of communication, a secure rear area, and the ability to transform the numerous small Alsatian towns into formidable defensive strong points. And then, of course, there were the "great equalizers": weather and terrain. The Colmar Pocket would be no Allied cakewalk. Of that, Daly and the men of Able Company needed no convincing.

On January 20, 1st Corps of the French First Army began the operation, attacking northward from Mulhouse in a driving snowstorm with strong armor and infantry forces. This action drew armor of the German Nineteenth Army and the arriving 2nd Mountain Division to the southern part of the Pocket. Two days later on the night of January 22, the anniversary of the Anzio landings in Italy, Major General O'Daniel committed his 3rd Division in Operation Grand Slam. In the early-morning hours the 7th and 30th infantry regiments with the 15th Regiment in reserve staged a surprise crossing of the Fecht at Guémar before the Germans could react, and they positioned themselves for an attack to the south. By noon the 7th and 30th had captured Ostheim, cleared the Colmar forest, and arrived at the River Ill, which the infantry crossed using rubber boats.

Troops of the 30th then proceeded down the east bank of the Ill and, after a brief skirmish with a small detachment of German troops, captured a 100-foot-long timber bridge and a crossroads about a mile away. The location was known as Maison Rouge because of a nearby farm complex painted red. The Germans believed they had to deny the Allies access to the bridgehead across the Ill because, according to a later army study, it opened "like the neck of a funnel into the whole area of German resistance around

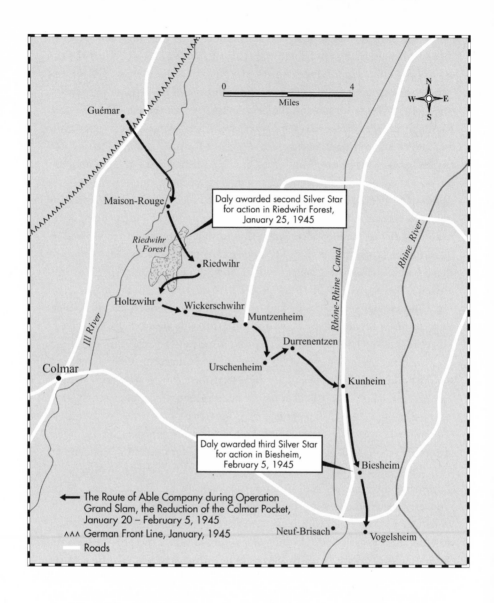

Daly awarded second Silver Star for action in Riedwihr Forest, January 25, 1945

Daly awarded third Silver Star for action in Biesheim, February 5, 1945

← The Route of Able Company during Operation Grand Slam, the Reduction of the Colmar Pocket, January 20 – February 5, 1945
ʌʌʌ German Front Line, January, 1945
— Roads

Guémar

Maison-Rouge

Riedwihr Forest

Riedwihr

Holtzwihr Wickerschwihr

Muntzenheim

Durrenentzen

Urschenheim

Colmar

Kunheim

Biesheim

Neuf-Brisach Vogelsheim

Ill River

Rhône-Rhine Canal

Rhine River

the Colmar Canal" and, once captured, "might well become [as it in fact did] the distributing point for American forces pushing to the Rhine."

At Maison Rouge, however, near-disaster ensued. Col. Lionel C. McGarr ordered infantry units southward toward Riedwihr and Holtzwihr. Meanwhile, with his engineers concurring, he judged that vehicles, including tanks, could use the bridge once engineers had reinforced it. Increasingly anxious about lack of armor and antitank support east of the Ill, he pressed his engineers to complete the reinforcement. They attempted an expedient, but the bridge collapsed under the weight of a Sherman tank attached to the regiment. The tank dropped "like an elevator" about fifteen feet into the swift current that was three to four feet deep. The Sherman lay tilted but upright in a riverbed of mud without natural rock formations or outcroppings. Until the engineers extracted the tank and repaired the bridge, the troops on the east side of the river had no armor support—a very dangerous situation, especially in light of the Germans' seemingly uncanny ability to extract a terrible price for Allied mistakes.

The 30th Regiment could not delay its offensive while the engineers worked frantically on the bridge. It had to coordinate its attack with simultaneous drives by the French on its left and the 7th Division on its right. Using a footbridge laid across the Ill north of the helpless tank, the 1st and 3rd Battalions of the 30th moved south and east across a thousand yards of snow-white flatland, entering a section of woods on the outskirts of the villages of Reidwihr and Holtzwihr. Unfortunately, fierce resistance elsewhere had held up both the French and the 7th Regiment, leaving the 1st and 3rd Battalions with dangerously exposed flanks and facing a powerful enemy.

At 1630 the hammer blow fell: the Germans counterattacked ferociously with infantry and four heavily armored and lethally armed *jagdpanzer IVs* and *jagdpanthers,* 75-mm and 88-mm assault guns mounted on Panzer IV and Panther tank chassis. (Infantrymen invariably identified German tanks as "Tiger" tanks, the largest and most fearsome in the German arsenal.) The heavy guns shredded and routed the 1st and 3rd Battalions, which had no supporting armor of their own. Only those soldiers toward the rear of their respective companies survived. The panic-stricken men ran headlong two miles back to the shelter of the Colmar woods at the Maison Rouge bridge site. Then, despite the 15-degree weather, they waded across the Ill River through waist-deep icy water, producing even more casualties.[12]

The combat at Maison Rouge illustrated what Audie Murphy, a lieutenant in 15th Regiment's Baker Company (and the most highly decorated American soldier in the war), later observed about German soldiers: they showed themselves masters of active defense by using the slow fighting retreat, giving ground stubbornly and bitterly, while battering American ranks with tanks, artillery, and mortars. The Germans built their defensive doctrine around the counterattack: persistent local counterattacks. The units staging these attacks, which varied in strength from a company to a battalion, often used tanks and tank destroyers closely integrated with infantry. With lengthening nights and sometimes limited air observation and photography during the day, the enemy could mass forces in an assembly area close to US lines and still avoid detection. Then, taking advantage of the morning fog or haze, they could attack and engage US forces quickly. These conditions and the proximity of wooded areas greatly increased the necessity for alert observation posts, listening posts, air-observation posts, aggressive patrolling, and defensive preparation for a variety of eventualities. Enemy artillery fire also increased appreciably, one of the most significant changes since the Normandy operations. The same weather conditions that limited aerial observation and photography made it more difficult for American artillery to locate and thus neutralize enemy guns.[13]

American troops found fighting in the woods in the Colmar Pocket especially challenging. The forests were dense, and although most trees were bare of leaves in the winter, there were evergreens. Maintaining formation in the woods proved difficult. In order to do so, a man had to keep the soldier next to him in sight. The Germans knew the forests and had built camouflaged strongpoints. Concealing tanks in the woods, they dominated the open fields across which Daly and his men had to advance. In his memoir of the war, Audie Murphy described German units in the forests as lying "like coiled snakes, striking suddenly and viciously." Sometimes their patrols surprised American forces, and sometimes the Americans stumbled onto a German strongpoint. Because the Americans were pressing the offensive, they were more vulnerable to ambushes. When those occurred, GIs would fire into bushes and at trees but often were unable to see the enemy, clad as they were in white parkas and pants—"spook suits"—that blended into the snowy terrain. Sometimes fighting involved individual duels between American and German soldiers separated by a few yards, each sniping at the other from behind trees. Sometimes, hand-to-hand combat ensued. Tree bursts from German artillery—shells exploding in the treetops—proved especially lethal, sending flaming branches and red-hot shrapnel to the forest floor. As Daly had already seen in Normandy and elsewhere, the Germans showed themselves resourceful, tenacious, and resilient foes, skillfully using combined infantry and armor, as at Maison Rouge, to bloody the Americans when they erred.[14] Now Daly and Able Company would get their baptism of fire together.

On receiving news of the disaster that had befallen the 30th, O'Daniel sent the 15th Regiment hurrying to the site of the footbridge over the Ill. He instructed the regiment to assume the mission of the 30th and to counterattack at once over the Ill at the site of the original footbridge and also at Maison Rouge. There, using planks from the shattered part of the bridge, and the turret of the sunken tank as a center pillar, engineers had jury-rigged a narrow span. O'Daniel knew that his infantry, absent armor, would be chewed up, but he had no choice. He had to try to keep the enemy at bay while his engineers repaired the bridge. He could not let the Germans seize the initiative and concentrate their power.

At 0300 on January 24, Companies I and K of the 15th Regiment's 3rd

Battalion moved across the Ill to press the attack, and until just before 0700 they made good progress. At that point, however, the Germans launched another counterattack, with the same results as on the previous day: the two companies were battered, and the survivors fled for their lives back to and across the Ill.

At about noon on January 24 the 1st Battalion entered the fray, crossing to the east bank of the Ill by means of both the footbridge and the "turret bridge." Still without armor, they set out into the woods north of Riedwihr even as engineers back at Maison Rouge worked furiously to construct a bridge that would bear the weight of tanks and other vehicles. By midafternoon the engineers at last succeeded, but too late for the 1st Battalion, whose noon attack the Germans crushed, albeit with far fewer casualties than the 30th and the 7th had suffered. The 1st Battalion had maintained an orderly retreat because it had been able to call in supporting artillery fire. By late afternoon, the battalion had regrouped and prepared to counterattack, this time accompanied by tanks and tank destroyers, and by a ferocious artillery barrage that sent shells into roads, junctions, and trail crossings in the Riedwihr woods.

In his first experience in battle as an officer, Daly led Able Company southward from the road junction at Maison Rouge, where they had been held in reserve, to join the rest of the battalion in the attack on the woods. Both Able and Charlie Companies ran into fierce opposition from enemy infantry and tanks at the edge of the woods. They became disorganized and suffered heavy casualties as the Germans employed a large number of tanks in an effort to eliminate infantry support for American tanks. Daly later recalled this as his most desperate moment of the war. He found himself momentarily confused about whether to fight or to flee. He hated to "let people down by retreating" but realized that he had to extricate his men from the woods so that they all could live to fight another day. He gave the order to pull out and made sure that his men, running downhill as fast as they could in knee-deep snow, got out. Then he followed them. Oliver and Paul Daly would have approved.

Daly described the withdrawal as "urgent," not "panic stricken." Although the Germans did not pursue the Americans out of the woods, they did keep firing at them, hitting several more of Daly's troops. When Daly and company reached the Ill River, they had to swim or ford the stream. Icicles dripped from the soaked uniforms of the shivering men. Daly felt relief at having extricated his platoon from an untenable situation and at having gotten them to safety, but he felt embarrassed at the pell-mell nature of the retreat under fire. His first major engagement as an officer had ended in near calamity. Daly thought that his commanding officers might criticize him for the withdrawal, but they did not, apparently recognizing the wisdom of "flight rather than fight" on this occasion. Armored battles raged throughout the night as Daly's platoon and the whole company, much reduced in size by casualties, regrouped. (Sgt. Julian Leon Lebowitz, Able Company clerk, listed almost thirty men as missing or killed in action that day, with eight later confirmed as having been killed.)[15]

All companies in the battalion had suffered numerous casualties and found themselves seriously weakened. When Able and Charlie Companies were combined, for example, they still numbered only a handful of men. In that precarious condition, the 1st Battalion dug in at the edge of the woods. Reorganizing the scattered companies took almost all day.

At midmorning on January 25, German infantry, accompanied by armor, counterattacked Able Company, which lacked both armor and antitank weapons. The Germans breached the line, driving some men back and isolating others while opening a gap through which their infantry tried to move. Daly's platoon sergeant, Kenneth W. Johns, however, remained in his foxhole and defended his position with his carbine against heavy small-arms and automatic-weapons fire from infantrymen seeking to exploit the opening. Six hours of grueling battle ensued, at the end of which the remaining men of Able Company forced the Germans to withdraw, even though one of their tanks continued to roam about in the woods shooting up whatever it found. Sgt. Troy Cox of Able Company later recalled: "The big German tanks would scare you to death. Their 88-mm guns were wicked. They were so fast and accurate; if you were close enough to hear one of them go off, then it was too late to take cover—it was there!"[16]

By 1500 on January 25 the battalions prepared to attack again. The 3rd Battalion would take Riedwihr while the 1st and 2nd eliminated resistance in the northeast and northwest woods respectively. The drained 1st Battalion had only sixty riflemen, with Able and Charlie Companies still merged. In the dark of night, Daly led twenty-four of his men three hundred yards against a strongpoint at the edge of the woods that consisted of dug-in troops around a machine gun. The Germans often located strongpoints in an opening in the woods or near a wide path where supporting troops dug in. Sometimes they were backed by mortars and/or one or two tanks. Advancing to within thirty yards of the German machine gun and "with bullets striking inches away from him," Daly killed the gunner, enabling his men to capture the weapon. He then led his platoon three hundred yards over "heavily shelled and bullet-swept terrain" to clear the objective in three-quarters of an hour. Twenty Germans died in the attack and "many more were captured or wounded through his [Daly's] inspiring and aggressive leadership." Daly "went after the other guy and it was every man for himself." The next day, he and his men helped repulse yet another German counterattack of infantry

The Colmar Pocket. *Courtesy National Archives.* The winter of 1945 was bitterly cold and snowy in the Colmar Pocket. On the outskirts of the village of Riedwihr, a German antitank gun with US communication wire strung over it lies overturned in the snow. The village itself shows the effects of recent fighting. Daly was awarded his second Silver Star for leading an assault against a German fortified position in the Riedwihr Forest, near where this photo was taken. Riedwihr fell to the 15th Regiment on January 25, 1945.

and armor. (At the same time, about a half-mile away, on the outskirts of Holzwihr, Lt. Audie Murphy of Baker Company engaged in action that led to his being awarded the Medal of Honor.)

As the historian of the 15th Regiment notes, "In two days of violent fighting, the 15th Regiment had saved the Ill River bridgehead, cracked through the tight armor-tipped German defense, pushed southward over the network of streams and wood patched terrain, against continuous counter attacks and stubborn resistance, and established an important line from which the offensive could be carried across the Colmar Canal to the immediate front." But the regiment paid dearly in casualties among officers, NCOs, and enlisted men. Some companies numbered only fifteen men. Many 3rd Division veterans of the Anzio beachhead pronounced the fighting in the Colmar Pocket, especially around Maison Rouge, as "just about as severe as anything they had yet gone through." The frozen bodies of GIs stacked up like cordwood and the terrible smell of burnt flesh that pervaded razed towns and lingered in the GIs' nostrils gave grim testimony to the truth of their observation.[17]

In the Colmar Pocket a dark mood prevailed. Daly grew increasingly aware that in addition to brutal combat and high casualties—January would prove the bloodiest month for casualties in northwest Europe—the cruel winter weather of the Colmar Pocket "Icebox" endangered not only his men's health, but also their morale by increasing the physical and psychological difficulties of military operations. Daly and his men envied the felt boots and fur-lined white winter uniforms of the German 2nd Mountain Division that opposed them. Having come from duty in Norway after service on the Eastern front, the German troops were much better prepared and equipped for winter fighting than the Americans. GIs wore field jackets and sometimes bulky wool overcoats that they almost universally hated and that many discarded because they restricted movement so much. For camouflage they wore mattress covers, sheets, pillowcases, any white cloth, over their clothing. "Some genius decided that we would wear white sheet covers for camouflage," Daly remembered, " but the damn things flopped around, got wet, and then froze at night," making movement difficult and sleep impossible. Daly, and many others, quickly discarded the "suits."[18]

There seemed no escape from the cold. Trigger mechanisms of rifles froze, as did oil in and on the weapons. When troops slept on the floors of abandoned schoolhouses or warehouses, they curled in the fetal position, hands clasped together and pressed between the knees. Essential clothing included long johns and gloves (or trigger-finger mittens), along with knit woolen caps and scarves, windbreaker trousers to be worn over the standard olive drab and M1944 Shoepac boots. With leather uppers, rubber lowers, and moisture-absorbing insoles, these boots provided far better protection against water, especially in static positions, than the standard combat boot. But the early versions, which had no heels and gave no support to the arch of the foot, proved terrible for walking and especially for marching.[19]

In many units, especially those suffering from low morale, cold-weather injuries (notably trench foot and frostbite) became epidemic. Cold and wet caused these injuries, but improper foot care, inadequate footgear and clothing, and inactivity all contributed to the high incidence. Few of those affected by cold-weather injuries returned to combat duty.[20]

Inadequate winter clothing contributed to the incidence of trench foot because healthy feet (and hands) depend on a warm body. The shortage of winter clothing sprang in part from the tactical and logistical realities in August and September. The unexpected rapidity of the Allied advance to the German frontier strained already overburdened Allied logistical support. That fact and the prevailing conviction that the war would end before the onset of winter led the European Theater command and the War Department to place a higher priority on transporting fuel, ammunition, and food than on winter uniforms. Inadequate planning and coordination between the Theater command and the War Department further delayed getting winter wear to Europe. When the weather became bitterly cold, in December, frantic efforts were made to supply adequate winter clothing, but not until January did the situation begin to improve. Many front-line troops fought through the bulk of winter inadequately clothed.[21]

Moreover, even though about 90 percent of the troops in the Seventh Army, including Daly's Able Company, had Shoepacs (far more than any other Allied army in Europe), and even though the Seventh Army's prior service in Italy afforded it greater experience and therefore subsequent success in dealing with trench foot, many of its soldiers ignored rules governing the wearing of Shoepacs. Some did so out of carelessness and exhaustion, some deliberately. The Shoepac had to be fitted so as to permit the wearing of two or three pairs of socks. The lower part of the Shoepac, made of material that interfered with ventilation, caused the feet to sweat profusely, saturating both insole and socks. This left GIs vulnerable to trench foot unless they could wring out the insoles and don dry socks at least once every twenty-four hours. The "paddle-foot shuffle" seen in the ranks of American infantrymen that winter signified not just bulky clothing, inadequate arch support, and numbed or frozen feet but also psychological demoralization.[22]

"What is combat really like?" Troy Cox asked rhetorically in his memoir.

> I would explain combat as firing our weapons, throwing hand grenades, hearing artillery and mortar fire; tanks firing and airplane strafing. You are homesick; you are wet, cold, and hungry; you are tired, sleepy, and completely worn out; you are sick of C and K rations; you are tired of sleeping in foxholes; you are tired of dangerous patrols; you are tired of firing and being fired upon; you wonder how much longer you will be able to stand up under all of the pressure; you want the war to be over; you wish that you could go home and everything would be all right. You are sick of seeing the dead and wounded soldiers. You are wearied by seeing your buddies get killed. You pray that the war will be over. That, is what combat is really like.[23]

In the face of a war that seemed interminable, many troops came to feel hopeless and depressed. Carelessness sometimes reflected a wish to end the suffering through disease, injury, or death. Some even induced trench foot by failing to massage their feet or to change into dry socks. By March 1945, more men were missing from the lines because of trench foot than for any other reason. The 46,000 cold-weather injuries constituted 9.25 percent of all casualties in the European theater, the equivalent of more than three divisions! The longer men stayed at the front without relief, the deeper their funk became, although seemingly little things, such as a hot meal, a shower, or a few days' rest, could make a world of difference in terms of attitude. Daly later recalled that "feet presented a constant challenge." He and his

The "paddle-foot shuffle." *Courtesy National Archives.* American troops display what came to be called the "paddle-foot shuffle" as they slog alongside a tank near Riedwihr. Snow and mud plagued the GIs, many thousands of whom became casualties as a result of frostbite and trench foot. Daly worked hard and effectively to maintain his men's morale and to minimize casualties caused by foot problems.

fellow platoon leaders, with the help of the NCOs, minimized the incidence of trench foot by insisting that the men change their socks regularly and by personally seeing to it that they did. That most of the men did so conscientiously and without much overt supervision spoke to their resilience, perseverance, and confidence in their officers and noncoms.[24]

Troy Cox admitted that maintaining spirit and resolve in the midst of the bone-chilling cold and the wounding and deaths of fellow GIs became a challenge. He recalled a handsome, twenty-two year-old Texan named Trig who "was big into machine guns and mortars." Trig, a friendly guy, was "crazy about his girlfriend," whom he intended to marry after the war. "All he wanted to talk about was his girl," said Cox, and the rest of the men listened good-naturedly. Then one day they noticed that Trig was uncharacteristically quiet. When asked about it, he replied that he had received a "Dear John" letter from his girlfriend telling him she was going to marry another man. Cox and the others urged him to forget her, insisting that she didn't deserve him, that he was better off without her. But he could not get her out of his mind. He also felt he could not face the people back home. When the platoon next went into combat, instead of hitting the ground with the other men, Trig remained standing and kept walking forward. His death, Cox remembered, "tore people up."[25]

When asked how he and his buddies coped psychologically amid the suffering and death, Cox paid tribute to Pfc. Sam Tapp of Greer, South Carolina. "In almost every platoon there was a boy who never worried, at least on the outside," and who possessed a comedic sense of timing that could lift spirits. Tapp was just such a person. He invariably had something funny to say at just the right moment to ease tension, induce laughter, and elevate spirits. Still, Cox noted, Tapp's outwardly breezy air evidently masked tensions he did not share with the others. His hair became totally gray in the course of several months of combat. Throughout their time in combat, men such as James Elling clung to memories of their wives and sweethearts. "Just the thought of my getting back to you . . . is all I am living for now," he wrote in a letter to his wife. "However, I think that I have lived thru hell on earth."[26]

General Patch also showed the strain of war in a note to his wife on February 24. "In my quiet moments alone," he wrote, "I too get a great sense of depression—Not so much because of our loss [their son]—but because I think I see too much serious incompetence—And I wonder how long it can continue. Am getting so very, very many letters from parents of boys who have been killed, wounded, or missing from this Army. Nothing is more devastating than that—There is so little I can say—Also, I am swamped with letters from wives, mothers, sisters, etc. asking why I shouldn't rotate their loved ones home."[27]

Daly looked back on the Colmar Pocket campaign as his most difficult combat: the snow and cold, the frostbite and trench foot, the dug-in veteran German units. "We had to fight the weather as well as the Germans. We had to try to keep the trigger mechanisms on our rifles functioning." People wounded in the cold went into shock faster. In the field, food consisted of C rations: canned eggs and meat or just meat by itself, beans, and pork and beans; and K rations: dried meat and vegetables, crackers, cheese, a small package of cigarettes, a piece of gum, a small block of sugar, and a package of powdered drink that could be mixed in a canteen of water. Thin, hard crackers made from flour and known as "dog biscuits," Spam, and Hershey's chocolate filled out the bill. "When we were able to stop, Daly later recalled, there were field kitchens, but we were often on the move for days at a time." Daly and his fellow officers recognized the toll that this took on the mood of the men and occasionally were able to send word to the kitchen crew to cook up some hot food and send it up as close as possible to the front lines. Small groups would then go back a short distance and eat a hot meal, which worked wonders for the mood of the men.

Finding cover from the cold proved a constant challenge. The ground itself often froze so hard that troops found it nearly impossible to dig foxholes with their entrenching tool. If they managed to do so, they usually tried to find felled trees or fallen branches to use as overhead cover, both for added warmth as they slept huddled three to a hole and for protection against deadly shrapnel from German artillery air bursts.[28]

Daly had a very close call with German artillery in the wintry French countryside. Major Ware, who later became the 1st Battalion Commander, joined Able Company to lead the battalion in a march through knee-deep snow. At one point, Ware mistakenly led the men to the right instead of to the left, and when he recognized his mistake, the men had to retrace their steps through the drifts for about a mile. Outside a small town occupied by the Germans, Able Company took up its position in a wood that opened onto a field. Daly's 1st platoon faced the town.

A patrol moved out to make contact with the enemy. At about 2,200 yards from the town, it received fire from the Germans. The members of the patrol included two new replacements and a seasoned sergeant. When the Germans began to advance on their position, the sergeant ordered the men to fall back with him to the woods, but they froze. Daly and the platoon leader from the right flank of the patrol approached from nearby as the two men, expecting the Germans to throw artillery as well as troops at them, struggled to dig in encumbered by their bazooka. The two soldiers had managed to "excavate" a hole about two feet square and two feet deep when, suddenly, shells from the 88s began to rain down. Daly and the other three all tried to jump into the hole one atop the other. The shell hit a small bush several feet from them. Fragments hit the men's rifles, cartridge belts, and canteens, but nobody suffered a scratch, illustrating what one infantry veteran told historian Stephen Ambrose: "During a shelling, I could get my whole body under my helmet."[29] Quite an accomplishment for someone as tall as Daly!

Patrols added to tension, exhaustion, and the pervasive sense of danger. The typical reconnaissance patrol took place at night. It could involve a platoon-size force, but more typically it consisted of a twelve-man rifle squad and often an eight-man machine-gun squad. Patrols sought to ascertain the deployment of the enemy and to gain usable intelligence by capturing prisoners for interrogation. If he led a patrol, Daly would brief his men on their objectives and on how they would communicate with one another. He also checked to make sure his men had enough ammunition. As the patrol crossed the line of departure, he placed himself inside the formation and waved people on. Because the inky blackness of night made this difficult to do, the members of the patrol had to stay close to one another and communicate using hand signals or touch or by "passing the word" quietly down the line. Two scouts preceded the rest of the platoon by a short distance, feeling their way along and passing messages back to the rest, serving as the "eyes" of the platoon and as an early-warning trip wire in case of ambush. Patrols usually returned before dawn and were kept in reserve for the rest of the day to let the men get some sleep if conditions allowed. If not, they operated on adrenalin.

Sleep deprivation was a reality of war. Men learned to function with little sleep and to grab what they could whenever the opportunity presented itself. Speaking of the cumulative impact of these small-unit operations, Max Hastings wrote, "Each such small operation was a nerve-wracking ordeal for those required to creep in darkness across water-logged countryside, poised every moment for the explosion of a mine or trip flare, the rattle of enemy fire." He pointed to the pervasiveness of fatigue even in the absence of a major battle, because even "the simplest everyday tasks—cooking, finding a tolerable place in which to sleep, wash, defecate" became major challenges on the battlefield and sapped energy.[30]

In his memoir, Troy Cox captured well the feeling of the soldier on the ground: "There never was just a 'little' battle or 'unimportant' battle, because one bullet is all it took to get killed. You would always be hoping and praying it wouldn't be you. You were completely exhausted most of the time, but you were forced to stay alert in order to survive. You walked like you were in a trance, and you kept talking to God to help you."[31]

Fearing an American breakthrough, the Germans mustered what reserves remained east and southeast of Jebsheim. The Americans, however, shifted southward to the Colmar Canal, a fifty-foot wide, six-foot deep waterway with twelve-foot embankments and slow-moving water that had not frozen. The canal passed just north of the city of Colmar, connecting it with the Rhine River, to the northeast. Well-dug emplacements protected the canal, and the fortified towns of Muntzenheim and Bischwihr lay nearby. These proved no match, however, for Allied air power and artillery. Allied planes bombed for two days, and on the cold, clear night of January 29–30, eight battalions of artillery pummeled the target area. On January 29, for example, 3rd Division artillery fired a barrage of 16,438 rounds.[32]

As a result, in Operation Kraut, Allied forces quickly crossed the Colmar Canal and made quick work of the dazed, disorganized force on the opposite shore. Daly's Able Company, held in reserve along with the rest of the 1st Battalion during the initial crossing, later led the 1st Battalion across the footbridges to join in the broadening offensive to clear the remainder of the Colmar Pocket and isolate the city of Colmar. The Americans would accomplish the latter task by occupying the area east and south of the city to the Rhine River. In the face of the combined American-French offensive, with the Americans driving to the center of the pocket and the French increasing pressure at both the northern and the southern shoulders, the Colmar Pocket began to disintegrate. As the German 2nd Mountain Division was ground down and then shattered, the 15th Regiment and the rest of the 3rd Division "encountered only scattered, piecemeal units and no cohesive battle order or defensive organization."[33] Those "piecemeal units," however, remained deadly.

In the first hour of February 1 the third phase of operations opened with an offensive to the Rhine designed to cut the pocket in two. This meant crossing yet another strategic water barrier: the Rhine-Rhone Canal, which ran in a north-south direction. Able Company's objective was to take the bridge leading into Kunheim. During the first phase of the attack through the Durrenentzen woods west of Kunheim, all company officers senior to Daly became casualties. He took command of Able Company and pressed ahead toward the town. The Germans, well armed with tanks, artillery, mortars, and rockets, committed themselves to defending the approaches to the bridge. They had created strongpoints at its foot by sending reinforcements to man thick-walled, large houses just west of the span. A twenty-four hour battle ensued. After several hours, word arrived that the French had taken Artzenheim and its bridge, a mile and one-half north, making seizure of the bridge at Kunheim unnecessary. At that the 15th Regiment objective changed from crossing the canal to clearing Germans from the area up to the canal and from the bridge itself.[34]

As Daly and Able Company attempted to traverse a clearing near the bridge at Kunheim, they encountered a withering hail of machine-gun and small-arms fire as well as heavy mortar concentrations. Daly extricated his men from their untenable position, reorganized them, and then led them on a new route through a woods infested by determined German opposition. Staying in the lead, Daly exhorted and encouraged his men and impelled them forward in the face of a hail of fire until he found it impossible to move further. He then directed his men to dig in and hold their ground. He personally supervised and checked the placement of their positions, enabling them to withstand intense fire from the fearsome 88-mm guns that night. Daly's company also suffered numerous casualties as a result of machine-gun fire, directed from tanks at a range of 150 yards, and barrages of 150-mm rockets, known to GIs as "Screaming Meemies," fired from a *Nebelwerfer*, a combination mortar and rocket launcher. Referring to the rockets, one veteran said, "If they came close, it seemed like they were going down your collar." The firing abated in the early morning hours, and at dawn Daly discovered that the Germans had withdrawn under cover of darkness having suffered many casualties.

Coming off the line, Daly moved his company into former German barracks in the woods. There he thoroughly reorganized the men after their engagement, painstakingly checking their equipment and seeing to it that they were able to rest and bathe. The next day he turned over a fresh, victorious, and tightly organized fighting unit to the returning company commander. Meanwhile the 7th Infantry had taken Kunheim after the battered German forces withdrew from the town.

Daly, however, had no sense of elation or victory when a town fell because there was always another, and then another, and another after that. Max Hastings captured the nature of combat when he described it, not as a clash of mighty armies after the fashion of Waterloo or Gettysburg, but rather as "an interminable series of local collisions involving a few hundred men and a score or two of armored vehicles, amid some village or hillside or patch of woodland between Switzerland and the North Sea." The observant Troy Cox remembered later that bridges were especially hard to take and that on entering a town, American tankers usually blew down the church steeple because it provided an ideal vantage point for snipers. "Any elevated ground was difficult to capture," Troy recalled. "Intersections at highways were always a dreaded spot, because the Germans would always have those places zeroed-in by mortars and/or artillery."

Gene Palumbo, a tanker in Baker Company of the 756th Tank Battalion, which was attached to the 3rd Division, noted that when Americans went down roads, "The Germans would have that 88 lined up so it would shoot like a rifle. They could make that thing do anything. Every so often, say maybe every five or ten minutes, they'd shoot it down the road in what we'd call the bowling alley. We'd start down the road and time it. When we figured it was five minutes, 'Let's get the hell off the road!' And we'd wait. And you'd hear *shuuuuuuuuu*. That 88 was going down the road and if there was anything on the road it would go right through it. That's what they used to do when they knew that we were moving up at night on 'em."[35]

Troy Cox experienced the terror of direct fire from an 88 in the morning. Thinking everything was clear, his platoon began walking down the highway on each side in single file, as usual. Suddenly, a German tank opened up on them with an 88. Cox's squad took cover on the bank of the road, but it turned out to be the side the tank was on, and it fired point-blank at them. American tanks fired back and drove off the tank, but a young, married man with three young children was killed, and Cox's buddy, James Carter, lost an eye.[36]

In early February, nights in the Colmar Pocket took on a surreal aura. On February 3, 4, and 5 the 3rd Division used antiaircraft searchlights in its sector, creating "artificial moonlight." Ed Adams of Able Company remembered it as "an eerie sight with enemy artillery and small-arms fire coming in and we were as light as day beneath the lights which were aimed at the enemy emplacements." But most found the illumination a great help in bringing out terrain features and maintaining control within and between units. The artificial light also facilitated rear-area activities such as moving to an assembly area or to a line of departure and bringing up rations and supplies. Soldiers interviewed by battalion officers believed that the artificial light proved most effective when units operated in hilly terrain, but that the light tended to "skyline" troops on flat ground, inviting enemy fire. A consensus emerged that in a defensive situation the "moonlight" gave a great advantage to guards and outposts, enabling them to pick up enemy movements and thereby reduce the possibility of enemy infiltration, which the Germans used with devastating effectiveness. The light also definitely aided night driving, vastly improved the visibility of landmarks and targets, and, by increasing visibility, encouraged greater confidence among the men. Because the advantages appeared to outweigh the disadvantages, Lieutenant Colonel Edson recommended this method of illumination whenever possible on moonless nights.[37]

On the morning of February 3, Daly and his men returned to action, moving southward the three or four miles between Kunheim and Biesheim along a slushy, muddy road flanked by fields and interspersed with enemy pillboxes. The trunks of leafless trees beyond the fields stood dark against the steel-gray sky; the snow-covered Vosges Mountains loomed to the west; and across the Rhine, to the east, the mountains of the Black Forest bristled with German artillery. The 1st Battalion was charged with eliminating enemy forces in the rear of the 7th Infantry, some of whose units were engaged in the town of Biesheim, where fighting grew more intense.[38]

The fate of Biesheim, a village of eleven hundred about ten miles east of Colmar, mirrored that of many other picturesque communities in Alsace. Before the war it had ranked as the most prosperous canton of the Neuf-Brisach region. Although the residents had evacuated the village in 1940 at the beginning of fighting between Germany and France, most had returned after the French defeat, except for three or four hundred Jewish citizens, whose synagogue, cemetery, and residential area, on the "Rue de Juif," stood as mute testimony to the horrible tragedy engulfing them and their fellow European Jews. The Germans had great stores of food and munitions in the town along with armor and infantry who stood determined to defend the last bridgeheads over the Rhine. They knew that if Biesheim fell, Neuf-Brisach, the communications center, could not hold out. Its capitulation in turn would sever key communications and supply lines, sealing the fate of the Colmar Pocket and providing the Allies a possible springboard into Germany. The combat that ensued—including street fighting, bombing and strafing by Allied planes, and artillery barrages from both sides—reduced much of Biesheim to rubble.[39]

Daly's company pushed southward to a point 500 yards north of Biesheim and from there, in tandem with Charlie Company, proceeded a few hundred yards eastward and then swung to the south. Approximately two hundred yards north of the town, fire from three or four machine guns, manned by what Lieutenant Colonel Edson characterized as "fanatical infantry," hit the flanks and the front, pinning down the forward elements. At daylight, Able and Charlie Companies fell back. They then called in armor, and three tanks helped wipe out the enemy positions. The small units of the experienced 3rd Division earned well-deserved praise for their skillful use of infantry-tank teams. In the words of one historian, they "almost unconsciously perfected their . . . teamwork to a fine art, enabling them to overcome the physical fatigue that most of the soldiers . . . felt." The next day American troops mopped up pockets of enemy resistance north of the town and around the Jewish cemetery.

On February 5 the final mission began: moving southward to secure the vital bridges across the Rhine at Neuf-Brisach and thus to cut the enemy's last remaining avenue of escape from the crumbling pocket. Daly and his company, their uniforms covered with so much mud that only the shape of their helmets distinguished them from the Germans, slogged down a slushy road southeast of the village as part of the 1st Battalion's drive to the south. After trudging across 800 yards of flat, muddy, open field, enduring fire from 88s and heavy mortars that inflicted numerous casualties, Daly's platoon spotted a German strongpoint about two hundred yards ahead. At a crossroads southeast of the town stood a fortified two-story stone house protected by barbed wire and surrounded by a low stone wall interspersed at intervals with stone columns. At least twenty-five German soldiers were entrenched about the structure.

Three enemy machine guns opened up and caught Daly and his men in a crossfire. By that time, only nine of Daly's twenty-two-man platoon remained unwounded. Reacting quickly, Daly directed his men to withdraw down a ditch. Meanwhile he stood up squarely in the middle of the road, firing his pistol in order to draw the concentrated fire of the enemy upon himself while his men retreated. For thirty minutes he moved about in plain view of enemy machine gunners and infantrymen armed with submachine guns. They fired a hail of bullets at him. As he danced around, they ricocheted at his feet. At the same time he noticed a fifteen-man German patrol approaching on his flank, and he started firing his pistol at them. Killing two, he alerted his men to fight off the rest. Finally, he broke contact and raced toward his platoon most of whom were crawling on their hands and knees toward the edge of town and the cover of two machine guns set up there. Troy Cox was carrying the machine gun, which was very heavy. Many began passing him as they made for a big gate in the wall at the end of town. The Germans, of course, targeted the gate. The gunners on the heavy machine guns called on Cox to run as they provided covering fire. Cox did so, and with bullets whistling by him, somehow made it unhurt to safety. Daly, meanwhile, worked his way among the more seriously wounded, who were lagging behind the others, helping and encouraging them. Not until he knew that every wounded man had made it back safely did Daly himself enter the company area.

He then gave a concise and calm report on the enemy situation to his company commander. For his action in the road that day, Daly received a second oak-leaf cluster for his Silver Star ribbon. He came to feel particularly proud of the Silver Star. Years later he called it the "infantryman's or workhorse medal"—indicating valor in a specific instance, not just meritorious service.[40]

Because Daly's company had not dislodged the Germans from the strongpoint, they once again received orders to seize it. The depleted sixty-man company attacked across five hundred yards of farm field that had been plowed in the fall and was now thawing. Troy Cox recalled, "We couldn't run at all in the mud, and would fall because it was so soft." When he fell, he also dropped his machine gun into the mire. The quarter-size openings in the barrel meant to cool the weapon became packed with mud, rendering the gun useless, but Cox still carried it as he continued to slip-slide across the field. The deadly crossfire from the German machine guns and numerous submachine guns mowed down forty-one of the men. Only nineteen reached the position. When an American tank moved up and blasted a hole in the wall, both the 2nd and the 3rd platoons charged forward in an attempt to storm the opening. But a German gunner on the other side, in combination with the continuing deadly crossfire, repelled two attempts. Finally, one rifleman, Pfc. Deland Payne, working his way to within fifty yards of the breach, stood up amidst a hail of fire and blazed at the gunner with his M1 rifle until he killed him.[41]

After an enemy grenade wounded the company commander, Daly leaped to the front amid the confusion and led the last violent assault. Grappling with the nearest German, he shot him dead with his pistol and then ran from man to man, directing them to the cleverly held German positions. Finally, he led his men inside the stone wall surrounding the house and into the house itself. Firing his weapon, he yelled for his men to "Shoot the bastards!" inciting them to their utmost in the bitter close-range fighting. The result: nine enemy dead, six wounded, and nine prisoners.

Troy Cox went around to the backside of the house and there saw something he never forgot. A young, mortally wounded German soldier lay on the ground bleeding profusely. One of the Americans insisted that they couldn't just let him die—they had to do something. Another soldier went inside the house and emerged with a captured German medic, who knelt down to examine the young man while the GIs gathered around. Standing up, the medic said, "Kaput! Kaput!" Some of the Americans picked up the wounded man and put him on the porch. He never moved. Standing there, Cox experienced one of the paradoxes of war. "You shoot your enemy," he reflected later, "yet sometimes, it hurts to see even your enemy die. . . . I believe that was the first time that I had ever felt sorry for a German. I looked at the young man and thought, such a waste of a young life." Daly experienced similar feelings. Yet, in both their minds, the scene also reinforced the justness of the Allied cause. Both attributed the tragedy of the young man, and the larger tragedy of the millions killed in the war, to "a few leaders of a few countries . . . intent on ruling the world, no matter the cost in human life."

A German counterattack, however, interrupted Cox's reflections. As fire from enemy self-propelled artillery began wrecking the house, Daly directed his men to dig in and hold the position. The Germans maintained fire on the house, the crossroads, and the roads to the rear in an attempt to deny the Americans use of them. Then, as Able Company fanned out to secure other houses in the area, German tank and artillery fire took them down one after another while continuing to zero in on the crossroads. The company clerk, Sgt. Lebowitz, recorded approximately twenty-five missing or killed in action that day.[42]

While Daly and his company hung on at the crossroads, other companies of the 1st Battalion, along with those of the 2nd and 3rd Battalions, captured Fort Mortier, which commanded the northern approaches to the Rhine River bridge sites. The Americans swept southward to the bridges themselves, only to find that the Germans had demolished them. By nightfall of February 5 the shelling of Daly's men had ceased: the 15th Regiment had secured all its objectives. The next night the 30th Regiment scaled the walls of the old fortress town of Neuf-Brisach. The Americans now firmly controlled the designated area east of Colmar, including the approaches to the damaged railroad and highway bridges across the Rhine. A staff officer of the 136th Mountain Regiment (part of the German 2nd Mountain Division) stated that by the first few days of February the German supply system had broken down completely, lack of gasoline being the major consequence. A captured officer said that large numbers of casualties were primarily the result of accurate and intense US artillery fire. In turn the 15th suffered 744 battle casualties and more than 1,000 additional casualties from disease, exhaustion, frostbite, and trench foot. The 3rd Division as a whole suffered more than 4,500 casualties. Unable to retreat across the bridges, only 3,000 to 4,000 combat infantry of the now virtually destroyed German Nineteenth Army managed to escape to the east bank of the Rhine. The remnants of the German army were mopped up, and resistance in the division sector came to an end after the seventeen-day campaign.[43]

Daly had distinguished himself as an officer while serving as a platoon leader during the Colmar campaign, adding two Oak Leaf clusters to his Silver Star. When squads became bogged down during operations or he sensed that the situation hung in the balance, he would lead from the front. He knew that this was risky both for himself and for the platoon should he be wounded or killed, but his job as an officer was to place himself where he "could most decisively influence the situation." As he observed later, "You have to take the chance to get things moving." While control and tactical employment of his platoon were key responsibilities for a platoon leader, the exigencies of the battlefield demanded that many times he fight as a rifleman. Time and again, Daly's calculated audacity, which at first glance could appear foolhardy, served him well as a tactical weapon to confuse the Germans and throw them off balance.[44]

His commanding officers sang his praises. Writing on February 7, less than two months after Daly had joined the company, Maj. Kenneth B. Potter, commander of the 1st Battalion, characterized the young lieutenant's service as "exemplary, evidencing a very high degree of leadership, aggressiveness, and organizational ability under the most difficult of conditions." In recommending Daly for promotion from second to first lieutenant shortly after the actions at Kunheim and Biesheim, Potter not only praised Daly's initiative in twice assuming command of the company during battle, but also identified essential elements of the young officer's leadership: "a very high degree of aggressiveness," "cool courage and calculated daring," "high organizational ability," and "the utmost devotion to his men both in the height of combat and in the lull ensuing."[45]

Conviction and anger played their part in fueling Daly's forceful leadership in battle. He believed that the war represented a struggle between good and evil, and he regarded the German troops as "wild beasts"—agents of those who would drag the human race into a new barbarism. He would do his utmost to stop them. In addition, a growing visceral hatred of the Germans figured into the mix—a hatred born of the god-awful, day-to-day experience of war, a wounded father, and lost comrades, such as young Captain Patch, his cousin John Riley, and his boyhood idol Al Blozis, who had been killed on January 31, 1945, in the Vosges Mountains. Daly, after all, had yelled, "Shoot the bastards!" when leading the assault on the fortified house at the crossroads south of Biesheim. In engagements such as those, he killed Germans at close range. But as was said of Audie Murphy, Daly could lose his temper and fight ruthlessly without losing his head.[46]

For years after the war Daly remained angry at all things German, refusing to purchase or ride in German automobiles, including his stepson's BMW, but even after the heat of battle, he felt no elation at the sight of enemy dead. Indeed, at Biesheim, after having led the furious assault on the safe house, Daly shared the same sadness at the waste of life that Troy Cox experienced—at the thought that the young German soldier lying dead on the ground might have made more of his life than Daly ever would his. He believed strongly, nevertheless, in the justice of his cause—"a cause that could not be allowed to fail." He said later, "It was kill or be killed." Self-preservation, the protection of his men, and the defense of civilization all required killing German soldiers. In each combat situation, he had a job to perform—a mission to accomplish—that he hoped would contribute, in its own small way, to hastening ultimate victory and thus an end to the killing and a way home.[47]

For all his fury at the Germans, Daly, like most American soldiers, had a grudging respect for their tactical genius and tenacity and for their arms, such as the MG 42 machine gun; the 88; the Panzer IV, Panther, and Tiger tanks; and the *panzerfaust*. Man-for-man and weapon-for-weapon, Daly (like many American troops) believed that the more professional Germans were better. In the "frozen crust" of the Colmar pocket, however, during what one historian termed, "America's Unknown Battle," Daly and his fellow citizen-soldiers prevailed over a battered yet skilled enemy. In the process they effectively destroyed large elements of the German Nineteenth Army, including the 2nd Mountain Division, the 198th Infantry Division, and the 16th *Volksgrenadier* Division.[48]

On February 7, Gen. Jean de Lattre de Tassigny, Commanding General of the First French Army, issued a special statement expressing his gratitude to the 3rd Division. At the celebrations marking the liberation of the city of Colmar, Gen. Charles de Gaulle, leader of the Free French, awarded the Division the Croix de Guerre with Fouraggère, the first such award given to an American unit during the war. The 3rd Division also received a Presidential Unit Citation for the Colmar Pocket offensive. Ernie Pyle singled out the foot soldiers who had demonstrated "real heroism—the uncomplaining acceptance of unendurable conditions." Amidst those "unendurable conditions," Daly had mastered one of the most difficult challenges for the platoon leader: to lead and fight at the same time. Now, he and his men had a chance to rest—and to train for the next phase: the Battle for Germany.[49]

8   The Dragon's Teeth

The West Wall (massive fortifications constructed by the Germans along the Franco-German border to protect the Reich), Hiedelbingerhoff, Germany, March 15–20, 1945.

First Lt. Mike Daly, executive officer at company headquarters, received a frantic call telling him that the attack by Company A on the West Wall had stalled amid tank traps (called "dragon's teeth"). Worse, the company commander and a lieutenant had broken under fire and fled the field, leaving the pinned-down men to their fate. Catastrophe loomed. Without hesitation, Mike sprang into action.

Looking back on the fighting at the West Wall, Troy Cox later observed: "We really gained a good leader in Lieutenant Daly. Through his leadership, I believe many lives were saved. I was probably one of them." As a result of his actions, on March 18 the twenty-year-old 1st lieutenant became company commander, was recommended for promotion to the rank of captain, and received another decoration: the Bronze Star with V for valor. In the span of ten months, Daly had risen from private to captain and from greenhorn to company commander.[1]

From mid-February to mid-March 1945, prior to the action at the West Wall, Daly and his regiment enjoyed a respite at a bivouac area northwest of Colmar near Pagny-sur-Moselle, a small town between Nancy and Metz. General Devers promised the 3rd Division that it would be so distant from the front line that the men could eat ice cream. In March the heavens seemed to applaud the liberation of Alsace from Nazi oppression: spring arrived early and, in the words of General de Lattre, "all at once brought back the smile to the land of Alsace." Looking at what lay ahead of them, the GIs debated among themselves about how the Germans would react to fighting on their own soil. Some hoped and argued that they would collapse as soon as Allied units crossed the Rhine in force, others that they would make a last-ditch stand, fighting with greater determination and ferocity. Now that the men had lost their feeling of isolation from larger developments and strategy, news became important. They followed reports of British, Russian, and French movements with keen interest and allowed themselves once more to hope that they would survive the war. Talk of home became more common even as fear lingered that one bullet or piece of shrapnel might cost them the race near the finish line.[2]

The men of the 3rd Division engaged in a training regimen to prepare for the looming invasion of Germany. Instructors focused on developing leadership skills, military discipline, weapons firing, street and woods fighting, pillbox reduction, and river crossing. Daly had so impressed his superior officers during the Colmar Pocket campaign that in early February they began the process of promoting him. Later, Maj. Burton Barr, assistant battalion commander, said: "We were having a terrible time [in the Colmar Pocket] but here was this gangly guy, always where you could see him, not hiding his height, an easy target, as though he believed wherever he stood would protect him. He never told you about himself, but you wanted to follow him. He was a truly brave man." On February 24, 1945, Daly received promotion to the rank of 1st lieutenant. In a letter to Major General O'Daniel, Lieutenant Colonel Edson observed of Daly: "He has been one of the outstanding junior officers of this regiment."

O'Daniel in turn notified General Patch, who recently had inquired about him, that Daly had been promoted to the rank of first lieutenant on February 24, 1945. Enclosing the citation for the third Oak Leaf cluster to the Silver Star along with a copy of the order for promotion, O'Daniel observed, "He is a young man that any father or commander can be proud of. I would like more of the same pattern." Patch then sent a message to Paul Daly, who during his recuperation was confined to the couch in his Connecticut home, where he berated himself for having been wounded. (Even after his wound healed, Daly's injury left him with little flexibility in his leg, but he moved around, albeit slowly, and even occasionally rode his horses.) Patch took obvious delight in congratulating his friend on his son's performance and proudly wrote of Mike, "Under heavy fire and with many of his men hurt, he grasped victory from almost certain defeat."[3]

Daly also impressed 1st Lt. (soon to be Captain) Audie Murphy, who attended the battalion training exercise as an observer. Army brass had transferred Murphy from command of his beloved Baker Company to a "liaison" position in an attempt to keep the national hero out of harm's way in the war's waning months. Daly and Murphy were both Irish-Americans, and both were just twenty years old. Both had been raised on tales of World War I. (Murphy's came from two uncles who had served.) Physically, though, Daly and Murphy cut quite different figures. Both were thin, but 6'3" Daly towered over 5'5" Murphy. The two also came from starkly different socioeconomic worlds. Murphy, the sixth of twelve children, had been raised on farms by his sharecropper parents in Texas. His father had abandoned the family in 1936, and Murphy had quit school early to help support his mother and siblings. He hunted game, which helped him develop the uncanny marksmanship that later became his trademark in combat. "If I don't hit what I shoot at," he had explained to a friend, "my family won't eat today." He also plowed and picked cotton fields for one dollar a day, and he worked in a general store/garage/filling station and at a radio-repair shop. After Pearl Harbor the sixteen-year-old convinced his sister to vouch to the army recruiter that he was in fact the legal age of eighteen. Once in the army he convinced skeptical superiors through sheer force of will that he could fight as an infantryman. He saw his first combat in Sicily in July 1943, about eleven months earlier than Daly. Murphy had gone on to win a battlefield commission and to become the most acclaimed warrior in the US Army, receiving every decoration for valor that his country had to offer, and an additional five decorations from France and Belgium.[4]

During the course of the exercise, Murphy watched as Daly led his men in a simulated attack straight up a hill without maneuvering. A major chastised him for his audacity, insisting that Daly would have gotten everyone in his platoon killed. Daly responded that his quick movement up the hill would have prevented the Germans from digging in, thus making them less, not more, lethal to his men. Murphy approved of Daly's approach and respected him for what he knew of his combat experience and ability. When he overheard the exchange, he interjected his view that the major should listen to Daly because "he's been at it a while and has been very effective."[5] Both men were strong leaders, aggressive warriors, and risk-takers, but both differentiated between calculated audacity, which they considered an invaluable tactical weapon, and mindless impetuosity that would result in needless casualties.

The time in bivouac afforded not only training but also some well-deserved amenities: showers; recreation, including movies; day rooms; enlisted-men's clubs; and liberty passes to the city of Nancy and a chance to mix with the local women. In addition, for a contribution of 250 francs, officers such as Daly could attend one of the two officers' parties—dubbed the "Can-Do Officers Brawl"—scheduled for March 9 and 12. A memo from regimental headquarters urged "officers who are in good enough physical shape to appreciate smooth liquor and rough women" to attend.[6]

Whether Daly went to the "Officers Brawl" or not, he did secure a three-day pass and visited Paris. He traveled there in a jeep and, once arrived, ran into his cousin Rosselle Daly. In addition to some sightseeing, they spent most of their time "carousing" in bars, probably in "Pig Alley" (Place Pigalle), where women and cheap booze were readily available. On his last morning in Paris, Daly was scheduled to meet another soldier at 0600 to go back to the front, but he felt so guilty about his behavior while in the city that he got up early and in the cold morning darkness made his way to the Church of the Madeleine (Saint Mary Magdalene), overlooking the Place de la Concorde.

Mike believed that Mary Magdalene had been a great sinner who repented, and that was how he now felt. The church building, with its large exterior columns on all four sides, looked more like an ancient Greek temple than a Catholic place of worship. Daly entered through bronze doors larger than those of Saint Peter's Basilica in Rome. Fittingly, the statue of a crusader-saint—King Louis IX—stood to the left of the entrance, while the tympanum of the triangular pediment above the portico depicted the Last Judgment. Once inside the dimly lit church, Daly could make out the statue of Saint Joan of Arc, another warrior-saint, about halfway up the main aisle on the left. Warriors, rescuers, sinners, judgment, peace—all mixed together. Daly took a seat in the back of the church and "talked to God for a long while." Then he drove back to the war.[7]

Although the Germans had suffered nearly a million casualties on all fronts during the Allies' summer offensives, the Third Reich still had millions of men in uniform. The German army hastily organized nearly 230,000 of these soldiers into "fortress battalions" to defend the West Wall, a defensive barrier referred to as the Siegfried Line by the Allies, which extended from the Netherlands to Switzerland.

Nazi propagandists touted the invincibility of these defenses to the German people, but their construction had languished following the fall of France in 1940. Only with the setbacks in the west in the summer of 1944 had the Germans again resumed work on the line. Still, even unfinished and undermanned, the Siegfried Line appeared formidable. It consisted of hundreds of pillboxes with interlocking fields of fire, supported by an extensive system of command posts, observation posts, and troop shelters. Furthermore, the Germans had carefully integrated their man-made obstacles with the terrain. Prominent among these obstacles were tank traps. Known as dragon's teeth, they consisted of pyramid-shaped concrete pillars four feet tall and several feet thick attached to a concrete foundation that extended four feet into the ground. The pillars were placed five to eight feet apart in a staggered pattern.

In early September 1944, Hitler had placed the respected Field Marshal Karl Rudolf Gerd von Rundstedt in command of the German armies in the West and charged him with the defense of the Siegfried Line. Hitler had hoped to stop the Allies at the West Wall long enough for the German army to regroup and mount a major counteroffensive. That counteroffensive, of course, had failed, and now Allied armies prepared to enter Germany.[8]

March 1945 marked the end of the winter stalemate on the western Front. Early in the month the American Ninth Army had reached the Rhine River near Duisberg. The First Army had taken Cologne and seized the Ludendorff Bridge over the Rhine at Remagen, and the Third Army had crashed through the Siegfried Line near Bitburg and raced to the Rhine above Koblenz. Eisenhower aimed his primary efforts at Germany's most important industrial region, the Ruhr. The Third and Seventh Armies now stood poised to take the second-richest industrial prize for the Allied armies: a triangular island of land, the Saar-Palatinate, bounded by the Rhine on the east, the Moselle on the northwest, and the Lauter and the Sarre on the south and the west.

On March 11, General Patch issued Field Order No. 10, authorizing Operation Undertone to begin on March 15. Patch intended to smash the Siegfried Line, penetrate the Saar-Palatinate, destroy the enemy in the zone, and seize the west bank of the Rhine. His forces then would cross the Rhine, an objective that he and Devers had planned for the previous autumn—until Eisenhower countermanded them. Patch's March 15 plan assigned the main effort to XV Corps under the command of Gen. Wade Hampton Haislip. The divisions under Haislip included two of the most experienced in Europe, the 3rd and the 45th. Haislip referred to them as "these two superb divisions." Haislip's Corps also included the battle-tried 44th and 100th Infantry Regiments along with the untried 71st Infantry, and the 6th Armored Division that was to push through any opening achieved in the Siegfried Line. The divisions of the corps would push along the Rimling-Zweibrücken axis. After breaking through the Siegfried Line, Haislip's force would continue the main effort beyond Zweibrücken to Kaiserlautern and then on to the Worms area, where the Rhine crossing would take place. Units would receive significant support from XII Tactical Air Command. Patch coordinated the moves of his army with those of Patton on his left flank.

Prior to the offensive against the Siegfried Line, the 15th Regiment moved to an assembly area near Voellerdingen, France. On the evening of March 14, the 15th Regiment relieved elements of the 44th Division at a jump-off position just short of the Franco-German border. The West Wall lay two thousand yards ahead. In his message to the division just before the assault, O'Daniel declared, "The attack will be pressed with the ruthless vigor that has routed every enemy formation opposing the 3rd Division." In a flight of bellicosity ending with his trademark exhortation, "Iron Mike" added: "All men will be brought to the highest offensive spirit prior to the jump-off. Bayonets will be sharpened." The reality was that American artillery and air power, combined with the aversion most American infantrymen had to using bayonets, made it as likely that men would be struck by lightning as that they would use the weapon in combat.[9]

For Daly and the 15th Infantry the Battle for Germany commenced at noon on March 15, 1945, as they moved out from an area near Bining, France. Eventually it would take the 15th Regiment, with the rest of the 3rd Division, through the Siegfried Line, across the Rhine and Main Rivers, and deep into the collapsing Reich. During the next twenty-four hours, as it swept to the northeast, moving across the Franco-German border, the 15th Regiment took four towns. As part of the 1st Battalion, Daly's Able Company spearheaded the offensive. Initially the men encountered very little small-arms resistance, but minefields, heavy artillery, and mortars inflicted some casualties.

Daly's company also encountered danger from an unexpected source: American aircraft. As part of the lead element of the attack, Able Company had advanced more rapidly than other units. As Daly and his men moved across open fields toward a hill whose crest was covered with trees, some American bombers and their fighter escorts returning from a mission appeared in the sky over them. The troops were unaware that the Germans had constructed a dummy tank out of wood and placed it at the top of the hill. Apparently convinced that Daly's men were accompanying the tank, two fighters suddenly peeled off from the formation, came around, and dove. An officer standing close to Cox hollered for the men to stand up and wave, assuring them that the pilot would recognize them as Americans. They all did so while the officer tried to detonate a yellow smoke grenade to signal that they were "friendlies." Cox and his comrades froze, however, when one plane fired a short burst from its .50 caliber machine gun that sent dirt flying everywhere and then disappeared behind the hill. "We thought that he had recognized his mistake," Cox recalled, "but he suddenly came back around the hill from the other direction. We thought, 'Uh oh!'"

The officer continued to insist that the men remain standing, and he continued to struggle with the smoke grenade. The pilot, however, let loose again, and Cox and the others hit the ground, Cox dropping his machine gun by his side as dirt flew up all around him. He thought he felt something hit him as the plane passed over, and he worried that he might not be able to stand up. Luckily his fretting proved groundless. Scared to death, he scrambled to his feet and made for a nearby ditch. One of the guys yelled out, "Hey, Cox, are you all right?" When he answered, "Yes!" the soldier urged him to look at his pack. What he saw shook him deeply: the top of the pack had been shot away. And when he went back to pick up his machine gun, he saw that it too had been hit. The stock had been destroyed. Within a few seconds the incident was over. The frustrated officer had finally got the smoke grenade to detonate by shooting it full of holes. The scene of the frantic officer struggling to detonate the smoke grenade by shooting it might have provided some comic relief except that the cry of "Medic" went up. One man had been killed and another wounded. The men knew that, given the difficulties of communication between ground and air forces, "friendly fire" casualties were an unfortunate part of the "fog of war." They nevertheless found such pointless casualties particularly painful and galling.

Cox, Daly, and the other men of Able Company had to swallow their feelings and press on. During the night of March 15–16, Able and Baker Companies compelled most German troops, except for a light covering force, to fall back to the fortifications of the West Wall. In Hornbach, one platoon of Able Company fought a two-hour battle before the town fell—the first in the Reich proper to fall to the regiment.[10]

General Patch's official diary, kept by one of his subordinates, described the small towns and villages in this part of Germany as places where "the people and their cows live together in the thick-walled buildings and pile the manure in neat piles in the street." It noted that in their scheme of defense the Germans made use of the towns and that, for the Seventh Army, destroying the buildings represented the best means of dislodging the enemy: "The ground forces have come to think of the destruction of towns and the softening up of strong points by bombing and strafing as a necessary part of the attack." And destroy the buildings the artillery and fighter bombers did. The diary included this observation: "So intense has been the attack that scarcely a man-made thing exists in our wake; it is even difficult to find buildings suitable for CPs [command posts]. This is the scorched earth."[11]

The 3rd Division now began moving toward the portion of the Siegfried Line that ran in an east-west direction south of the city of Zweibrücken. After two or three days, during which they took a few small towns and fought some sharp engagements, Daly and his men could see the massive fortifications that were the West Wall. These were part of a fortified zone eight to twenty miles deep and four hundred miles long.

The Germans had worked ingeniously with natural terrain to create a defensive line as impregnable as humanly possible. Thousands of forts and pillboxes of reinforced steel and concrete—smaller than the forts on the Maginot Line—studded the region. These were camouflaged as farmhouses, barns, and country residences, with some built deep underground. Five fortified lines constituted the West Wall. Daly and his men would attack an area in the Saar-Pfalz sector. Some emplacements had been equipped with long-range guns, howitzers, mortars, antitank guns, flamethrowers, and field artillery. Unlike the defensive positions on the Maginot Line, each fort and pillbox commanded a wide field of interlocking fire that covered the approaches to neighboring fortifications. Difficult terrain along the Franco-German border, as well as the Rhine River, provided excellent cover for permanent as well as field fortifications.[12]

Dragon's teeth south of Zweibrücken, Germany. *Courtesy National Archives.* During their assault on the Siegfried line (West Wall), elements of Daly's Able Company became pinned down among antitank obstacles known as dragon's teeth, whereupon their company commander panicked and fled. Daly moved forward, took command, directed fire, and then led the men to safety. For his actions, he was awarded the Bronze Star with "V" attachment for valor.

The Germans had made impressive efforts to strengthen the Siegfried line, but in February 1945 the German high command ordered its First Army to give up seven divisions for service elsewhere. As a result, at the time of Patch's offensive, the Germans had only nine divisions between the Rhine and Saarlautern—not more than twenty battalions of infantry and approximately one hundred fifty armored vehicles, most of them self-propelled guns.[13] Therefore they resorted to their familiar "floating defense": a squad or platoon responsible for a given defensive sector would occupy different positions within the sector on successive nights. This proved effective against small-unit and limited-objective attacks but could not compensate for the manpower needed to withstand a full-scale attack.

The men of Daly's Able Company faced elements of the 37th SS Panzer Grenadier Regiment of the 17th SS Panzer Grenadier Division, a depleted but still dangerous outfit. Army intelligence estimated that the regiment had between 400 and 500 men, was highly mobile, and was capable of hitting hard and fast. It remained a constant threat. At this stage the German soldiers were war weary and bereft of hope for final victory, but they fought hard as long as they had leaders who gave them orders and saw that they were obeyed. Enemy units operated at about 60 percent strength, and 60–65 percent of that number were ethnic Germans from Eastern Europe and the Soviet Union. Despite its designation as a panzer unit, the 17th SS had lost most of its armored vehicles. American intelligence reported that observers had never seen more than four or five tanks of the feared Tiger class at any one time in

The Dragon's Teeth   125

the immediate vicinity of the enemy front line. Occasionally, however, they had spotted larger numbers of tanks in the German rear areas.

The part of the West Wall that Daly and his company would assault consisted of five separate rows of dragon's teeth and behind them a belt of machine-gun and antitank-gun positions (reinforced concrete, both open and covered) and then an antitank ditch backed up by more concrete pillboxes with interlocking fields of fire. Most pillboxes had only one machine gun, but some had two. Atop some pillboxes were cupolas housing machine guns. The men of Able Company would have to assault the West Wall across barren rolling hills that, except for occasional copses of trees, afforded little cover.[14]

Following a strong artillery preparation, the 1st Battalion would make the initial breach, destroying the barbed wire and mines in front of the dragon's teeth. Division headquarters held the other two battalions in reserve, ready to pass through 1st Battalion to continue the attack on the fortifications. Once the 1st Battalion broke through the line, its orders called for it to push rapidly to the Schwarzbach River, secure the two bridges and high ground immediately to the north, and then mop up the area east of the breach on the flank and behind the Siegfried defenses. A carefully briefed patrol sent out to the dragon's teeth at night drew small-arms, artillery and self-propelled-gun fire. The Germans were waiting.

Needless to say, Daly and his men dreaded assaulting the seemingly impenetrable fortifications. As it turned out, the first sergeant, who had been with Company A for well over a year, from the campaign in Sicily through Anzio, the Vosges Mountains, the Colmar Pocket, and now up to the Siegfried Line, had accumulated enough points to go home. A few members of the company had known him all that time. Knowing the danger involved in leading the first assault, those veterans went to the company commander and asked him to let the first sergeant stay back because he was going home the next day. The captain denied their request, noting that he might need him. The men begged, but the captain would not budge. The men were upset. They had tried to protect one of their own. The events of March 18 confirmed their apprehensions.[15]

At 0545 the 1st and 2nd Battalions of the 15th Regiment jumped off from the woods toward the German fortifications. They were supported by the massed fire of nine battalions of artillery, engineers with tank dozers to destroy dragon's teeth and fill antitank trenches, and demolition teams. Each of the five pillboxes they attacked had a single aperture for a machine gun, and the largest pillbox, camouflaged by netting, boasted walls three to four feet thick. Minefields lay between the woods that marked the line of departure and a small group of trees about 350 yards to the north. Foxholes and wire lay between the dragon's teeth and the pillboxes.

Path of Able Company through Germany and Austria, March 17 – May 8, 1945

Siegfried Line (West Wall)

Cologne

Rhine River

Czecho-slovakia

Bad Neustadt an der Saale

Frankfurt

Main River

Schweinfurt

Bamberg

Rothenbuch

LUX.

Worms

Miltenberg

Heroldsberg

Grossheubach

Nuremberg

Zweibrücken

GERMANY

Daly awarded Medal of Honor for action on April 18, 1945 in Nuremberg; gravely wounded the following day

Saarbrücken

Hornbach

Daly assumes command of Able Company during assault on Siegfried Line (West Wall); awarded Bronze Star

Strasbourg

FRANCE

Rhine River

Danube River

Augsburg

Munich

Salzburg

"Camp Daly"

SWITZERLAND

Austria

0   100

Miles

Able Company led the 1st Battalion in the assault at a point near the tiny farming village of Heidelbingerhof, just southeast of Zweibrücken. Preceded by a short, intense bombardment rather than a long one, the attack caught the Germans by surprise. They had expected that the assault would come the next day. Moving abreast of the 7th Infantry and to its left, the 1st Battalion immediately met with intense small-arms fire as it picked its way slowly ahead, closing on the trees about 350 yards ahead. Then the enemy opened up with a heavy concentration of artillery fire. The assault platoons of Able Company also faced furious resistance from small-arms, machine-gun, and artillery fire as they moved through the woods and then through an open field toward the dragon's teeth and the casements. During this action, the first sergeant, whose friends had vainly tried to keep out of the battle, was killed, greatly upsetting and angering many.[16] They had intended to destroy the wire and mines in front of the dragon's teeth using Bangalore torpedoes but couldn't reach them. Pinned down and strung out at intervals in a small ditch with practically no cover, the men began to dig in when, suddenly, their shell-shocked company commander and a panic-stricken lieutenant ran for the rear—abandoning them.

At that moment, 1st Lieutenant Daly, the executive officer of the company, had his platoon in reserve acting as the headquarters group. Realizing the gravity of the situation, Daly stepped into the command vacuum. Advancing through heavy fire, he took command and spurred the men forward by leading a squad in an assault on one of the pillboxes. Working their way to the right, they managed to reach the vicinity of the dragon's teeth. Their losses had been heavy, however, and direct fire from the pillboxes prevented them from advancing very far past the concrete obstacles. Judging their position untenable, Daly ordered a withdrawal, but only part of the company could respond. In their positions on the other side of the antitank ditch, Daly and the 1st and 3rd platoons caused a diversion that enabled two other companies to press the attack. They found cover behind large, round bales of hay, which the Germans pummeled with bullets in an attempt to set them ablaze.[17]

Soon the Americans found themselves in an even more precarious situation: artillery and mortar fire hit their stationary position. Recognizing the perilous situation of his comrades unless they could withdraw to more protected terrain, Pfc. Gordon D. Olson exposed himself and began firing his BAR in bursts, drawing the bulk of enemy fire on himself as his comrades withdrew. Despite exploding mortars that knocked him off his feet and a bullet that ripped off a portion of his ear, Olson kept firing at the slits of the pillboxes and at the trenches in which enemy infantrymen had taken cover. He took down three German soldiers who moved out of their shelter in an attempt to set up a machine gun, but one of them managed to shoot him in the leg. Covered with blood, Olson continued to fire, carefully spacing his shots in order to conserve his ammunition. He collapsed and died shortly thereafter.[18]

Daly also provided covering fire for his retreating men and was the last to return from the dragon's teeth. He regrouped and reorganized his company in a defensive position in a wooded area without suffering a casualty, and then personally reconnoitered over exposed and fire-swept ground, positioning his company behind a little copse of trees about a thousand yards from the dragon's teeth. For further cover, the men used trenches the Germans had dug all through the woods. They held those positions for the rest of the day, harassing the Germans with small-arms fire.

At about dusk, Lieutenant Colonel Ware came by and wanted to know why they hadn't yet breached the line. Ed Adams explained that the small-arms and machine-gun fire had been too intense. They needed tanks, Adams said, but the tanks could not move up because of a German antitank gun down the hill toward the right. The driver of the TD from the 601st who was accompanying Ware volunteered to go after the gun if someone would accompany him. Ware jumped on, and the TD took a wide path to the rear and circled back toward the line. After that, Adams heard two shell bursts and shortly thereafter a "terrible thumping sound" that grew louder as it approached the knoll. Daly and his men hunkered down in the waning light. To their great relief, the TD came into view. The TD driver and Ware had seen the antitank-gun emplacement at the same time that the antitank crew had seen them. Both weapons fired at the same time. The TD knocked out the antitank gun, but the enemy round went through the TD's rear idler wheel near the axle. The thumping sound that had so alarmed Daly and his men was caused by the tread pulling the two wheels back and forth. During the night, Daly and his men endured German artillery barrages that uprooted trees around them but, thankfully, caused no further casualties.[19]

Earlier in the afternoon, Able and Charlie companies had pressed the attack and seized the two pillboxes that constituted the first line of emplacements. The men used the captured pillboxes as shelter when the Germans loosed artillery and mortar barrages on the emplacements and the system of trenches the Americans now occupied. By noon on March 19 the 2nd Battalion had captured two more pillboxes, breaching the second line of defense. Initially American armor could not cross the big antitank ditch in front of the dragon's teeth, nor could the tank guns, firing from a distance, penetrate the thick concrete walls of the pillboxes. Finally a tank fitted with a dozer blade came up and began pushing dirt into the ditch. The small-arms and machine-gun fire directed against it by the Germans proved ineffective. Soon other tanks advanced and started firing their big guns at the dragon's teeth, breaking them and loosening their foundations. This enabled the engineers to blow them up with explosives. After a number of hours a road that tanks and trucks could use had been built through the West Wall.

Daly moved his men forward and spent the morning directing them in mopping-up actions against pillboxes. Without covering fire from one another, they became easy targets. Because most Germans had withdrawn from the line during the night, the Americans met little resistance. When they found a pillbox still occupied, they demanded that the Germans surrender. If the crew inside refused, Daly and his men attacked the pillbox from the rear, where the doors and lack of armament made it vulnerable. They blew the doors and/or threw grenades down the air shafts.

The American positions, two thousand yards south of the town of Contwig, were under direct antitank-gun fire. In addition, hundreds of antitank and antipersonnel mines—among the greatest concentrations of mines the regiment had ever confronted—hampered their advance. Allied airpower and artillery, however, relentlessly pounded the Germans and broke their back. During the night of March 19–20, Daly and the rest of the regiment witnessed an hours-long "German fireworks show" as the Germans disposed of their ammunition before pulling out in the early morning hours of March 20.[20]

When headquarters initiated a court-martial investigation against the past company commander, Daly and others refused to cooperate by pleading "insufficient recollection." The captain, a man in his thirties whose wife had recently given birth to a child, had served honorably and bravely up to that point. Daly recognized a reality that subsequent research in the European Theater of Operations confirmed: as the war progressed, veteran officers and NCOs with prolonged time on the front lines (90–120 days of continuous action or 200–240 days of cumulative action) became increasingly vulnerable to combat stress. This held true even in the 7th Army, for whom periods of rest and retraining had interrupted periods of intense combat. Daly saw no need to stigmatize the man for the rest of his life. Eventually both the captain and the lieutenant who fled the scene with him were listed as "neuropsychiatric casualties." The European Theater of Operations reported 102,000 of these, the vast majority stemming from combat exhaustion. Although "combat exhaustion" was not a reportable condition, it, like trench foot, significantly drained manpower from already overstretched units.[21]

Still, those units had breached the vaunted Siegfried Line in thirty-six hours at a cost of 45 killed and 175 wounded for the regiment. The decision to stand and fight west of the Rhine had resulted in another disaster for the German army: thousands of its troops were killed or captured, and the remnants of its surviving divisions were disorganized and in flight, incapable of establishing a cohesive line to the west. Eisenhower had predicted that the war would be won west of the Rhine River.[22] In that he proved prescient. But both Ike and men down the line, like Daly, knew that they would have to finish the war inside Germany itself against a desperate but still-determined foe. Much fighting and dying lay ahead in the war's final two months.

9 *"Discipline of Kindness"*

Western Germany, March 1945.

Michael Daly's men showed a willingness to follow him because they recognized him as a superb warrior and also because they felt that he had their best interests at heart. He modeled courage and confidence—an almost insouciant disregard for personal danger—when he sensed that his men needed protection, inspiration, or reassurance. He also skillfully used group psychology. During one operation, for example, Daly and his men needed to cross a draw on which the Germans were firing, but from a distance. When the men balked at making the crossing, Daly urged them forward, assuring them that the German fire was too high to hit them if they stayed low. As the group moved quickly across the open space, Daly heard a pained yell from one of them: "Daly!" the man shouted—the battlefield was no respecter of rank—"They hit me . . . *in the foot!*" By then, though, he and all the others were across the draw.[1]

General Eisenhower once said, "The most terrible job in warfare is to be a second lieutenant leading a platoon when you are on the battlefield." Platoon leaders accounted for approximately 31 percent of all casualties in an infantry division. (Company commanders accounted for another 30 percent.) Daly, however, relished his job as a company line officer leading men in combat. He regarded it as the highest honor and responsibility the government could bestow on an individual. He had always loved action and felt happiest when making a difference. As an officer he made a difference, and it called forth his best self. He bore responsibility for achieving his mission and for taking care of his men, and as a company commander (which he called the "best job in the infantry") he enjoyed greater autonomy in choosing the means. The well-being of his men became his passion, so much so that, for their sake, he repeatedly placed his life on the line. He had moved smoothly from enlisted man to commissioned officer and in the process had shown himself a decisive leader comfortable with command.

S. L. A. Marshall, deputy theater historian for US forces in the European

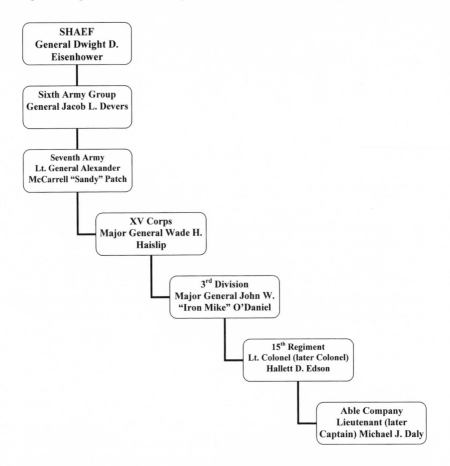

Theater, wrote: "The test of fitness to command is the ability to think clearly in the face of unexpected contingency or opportunity. Improvisation is . . . the essence of initiative in all combat just as initiative is the outward showing of the power of decision."[2] Initiative, clear thinking, daring improvisation— Daly had demonstrated each of these on the battlefield numerous times, and his men responded accordingly.

What happened to the irresponsible teenager of eighteen months earlier? Daly always contended that war did not change people so much as it removed masks and allowed "what's there inside to come out." It made people "more of what they are," so long as it did not push them beyond their breaking point. Clearly, in Daly's case, the experience of war had matured and sobered him and given him a sense of mission. He had always been inattentive to what he regarded as meaningless rules and regulations, and he continued so, but he had always been at his best when part of a team and able to focus on a larger goal. Now he had that goal, and others depended on him in life-and-death situations. Daly was a real romantic. Paul Daly's stories about Roland, Oliver, and the knights of the Round Table had taken root in him. In that, he was like his father, but he departed from his dad in being able to focus on individuals as well as causes. Mike Daly, for instance, could never view his men the way that his father did when he compared infantrymen winning battles to horses winning races.

The stark reality of war provided a setting that highlighted and channeled some of Mike's finest personal qualities: energy, athleticism, audacity, independence, aggressiveness, intrepidity, leadership, and courage—traits he had demonstrated before the war, but sometimes in ways that had led to trouble. Aristotle observed that courage makes all other virtues possible. Daly possessed courage in abundance, and other virtues flowed from that. For him war was the "refiner's fire"; it matured him and brought forth untapped reservoirs of wisdom, empathy, responsibility, patience, and selflessness in dealing with his men. War tends to brutalize men, but it ennobled Daly. Indeed, his strong sense of obligation to others and his desire to protect them became central to his understanding of his religious faith. He once said, "I always felt most at peace *doing* [his emphasis] something—doing something for people rather than just talking about it."[3]

Shortly after the war the great cartoonist Bill Mauldin observed that GIs "accept orders and restrictions, but because they are fundamentally democratic the insignia on the shoulders of their officers sometimes look a hell of a lot like chips." But historian Robert S. Rush and others note that many combat officers felt a sense of brotherhood not only with their fellow officers, but also with their enlisted men. This was particularly true among Officer Candidate School graduates and those who had earned battlefield commissions. Daly's previous service as an enlisted man gave him great empathy and respect for his men and great credibility with them. Pfc. James C. Elling, who had little use for officers, "idolized" Daly. He and the other men respected, trusted, and liked him implicitly, later describing him as "a natural leader," a "regular guy," and, in the words of Sergeant Lebowitz, "the bravest man I ever knew." Lebowitz recalled that Daly was by far the most popular and respected company commander the men had. He worked easily with the company headquarters staff, did not pull rank, berate, or condescend, and he demonstrated a passionate concern for the safety and well-being of his men.[4]

Daly's men admired his aggressive leadership, the skill and accuracy he demonstrated using his rifle, and his insistence on leading from the front. Time and again in battle he had shown them that he could quickly grasp and solve tactical problems—a trait on which their very lives depended. One of his men expressed his gratitude for Daly's efforts to keep him and the other men informed by telling them "what was going on and where we were going." Most especially, they appreciated his efforts to avoid the "wasteful casualties" that had proved so devastating to morale in other units. Decades later, Edwin K. Adams, who had served under Daly in Able Company from December 1944 until the end of March 1945, wrote to him, "Although we weren't close, I learned from you, which has helped me in my military career and also to make it through those last months of the war."[5]

Daly approached his men from the perspective of what he later called "a discipline of kindness," treating them with respect by focusing on what he considered the essentials, not "nitpicking." He led by example and by encouragement. As the company commander, even at the tender age of twenty, he became "the old man" in the eyes of his subordinates, most of whom were older than him. And Daly took to the role. He believed it imperative to bolster the confidence of his men and to be available when they needed him, on and off the battlefield. Enlisted men and officers found him approachable and accessible—"easy to talk to" as Lebowitz recalled. He participated in "bull sessions" with the men and provided a sympathetic ear when someone needed to unburden himself.

Daly recalled the night that a frightened lieutenant came to him to say he could not take it any more; he was cracking up. His wife had just had a baby he had never seen, and he was increasingly afraid of dying. Daly listened sympathetically and then told him he could do nothing about the painful separation from wife and baby, but he did know something about being frightened because he himself felt fearful at times. (He especially feared capture by the Germans, and vowed he would surrender only as a last resort.) The trick, he advised, was for the officer not to permit himself show his fear to his men. More than bombs and bullets, Daly cautioned, fear constituted the real enemy on the battlefield. He urged the lieutenant to say his prayers (Daly found himself praying a lot, especially while marching) and to remember that the men around him in the platoon were outstanding soldiers who would protect and sustain each other. Daly's willingness to engage the lieutenant on an honest, personal level and to encourage in him a sense of esprit and belonging eased the man's anxieties. He returned to his platoon and went on to fight well. (Later wounded, he was eventually reunited with his family.)[6]

As could be seen in his dealings with the lieutenant, Daly projected an air of calm and quiet confidence to the men in his company, many of whom were scared, homesick, and miserable in the tumult of battle. He understood the gnawing fear that ate at every man because he was something of a worrier himself, especially during quiet periods between fighting, when his imagination could run wild about what might happen to him. He controlled his

"Discipline of kindness." *Courtesy J. Leon Lebowitz.* Daly with NCOs and enlisted men of Able Company. From left: Pfc. Henry Birenbaum, Daly, 1st Sgt. Roy A. Kurtz, S.Sgt. Stanley A. Porucznik, Lt. Graham (squatting). Having served as an enlisted man himself, Daly empathized with and had great respect for his troops. He knew who needed encouragement and who would take the initiative in offensive operations. He made accomplishing the mission with minimal casualties his highest priority.

prebattle anxiety by getting outside himself: he prayed, and he focused on accomplishing the specific mission and the tasks that needed to be done. Daly reflected the kind of courage that historian Robert Rush describes as "the fixed resolve not to quit that must be made not once, but time after time." Managing his own fear and the fear felt by his men proved one of his greatest challenges and greatest achievements as an officer. In doing so, he drew upon his father's oft-repeated urging to fear only showing fear.

In a conversation with Gen. George Marshall shortly after he had returned from the Guadalcanal campaign, General Patch summed up his perception of front-line troops by observing, "The American soldier does not like to fight and does not like to die." In conversations with other army officials, he also deplored the tendency of the army to assign to the infantry the misfits and those who scored lowest on aptitude tests and to allow the best and brightest to escape into easier, less-demanding service or more glamorous units, such as the Army Air Corps. Maj. Gen. James Gavin of the 82nd Airborne shared Patch's views. Venting in his diary on January 18, 1945, Gavin bemoaned what he perceived as the lack of aggressiveness in American soldiers in regular units: "If our infantry would fight, this war would be over by now. . . . We all know it, admit it, and yet nothing is done about it. American infantry just simply will not fight. No one wants to get killed. . . . The regular infantry—terrible. Every body wants to live to a ripe old age. The sight of a few Germans drives them to their holes. Instead of being imbued with an overwhelming desire to get close to the German and get him by the throat, they want to avoid him if the artillery has not already knocked him flat." How to keep his men moving forward despite their fear and the ghastly scenes of carnage around them constituted a critical test of Daly's leadership skills.[7]

Daly's conduct on the battlefield both as a "grunt" and as a junior officer had shown him to be the antithesis of the infantryman described by Gavin. When fighting commenced, he moved into a "zone" of focused action, his senses acute, reacting both intelligently and instinctively. On the other hand, his battlefield experience taught him that, whereas most riflemen perform ably and fire their weapons in defense, many on offense, though they might start correctly against an enemy dug in and waiting, "go to ground" when the shooting begins in earnest. Relatively few NCOs and riflemen—about 20 percent—carried any attack. In Able Company, these included men such as Sergeants Ivan Ketron, Stanley A. "Proz" Porucznik, and Olaf Neswoog and Private 1st Class Elling. According to Daly, the strapping, blond-haired, blue-eyed, Elling "cut quite a figure." A locomotive fireman in civilian life, "warmhearted" to his buddies, and fierce in combat, the six-foot Elling had refused initial attempts by army authorities to assign him to a railroad battalion. "Hell no!" he exclaimed. "Give me a Browning, and let me go kill Nazis!" Daly described Elling as an outstanding soldier. "In a rifle company most people will behave well on defense. But when you have to go after the enemy . . . the same few soldiers lead every attack. Jim Elling was one of those soldiers. He was often there when things hung in the balance. You could never win a battle without such soldiers. He had and deserved the respect of everyone."

Daly regarded Ketron, Porucznik, Neswoog, Elling, and others like them as "salt of the earth guys"—the backbone of the company. Looking back on his experience, Daly once wrote, "They asked Wellington after Waterloo how he was able to defeat Napoleon and he replied that he had the better lieutenants. Able Company had the better sergeants."

Daly recognized that one of his critical responsibilities as an officer was to identify men who were natural leaders and to make sure they were promoted to the rank of sergeant. He wholeheartedly agreed with *Army Talk*'s assertion that "this is a sergeant's war." After all, of the ten leaders authorized in an infantry rifle platoon, nine were NCOs. These men led their squads of no more than a dozen men—the primary groups of an infantry division—and made it their business to identify and encourage the best fighters under them so as to animate the rest of the platoon.

Daly found that the best guys in combat were not necessarily those who were former athletes, or who were brash, loud, and overtly belligerent off the battlefield. Sergeant Neswoog, for example, was a dentist who had not played high-school sports. The self-starters on the battlefield, the truly aggressive, suffered the highest casualties, however, and their numbers had to be replenished—a responsibility Daly took seriously because he knew that his platoon's ultimate success and very survival depended on them. He attempted to model aggressiveness and initiative for his men by leading from the front. He wanted his men to know that he would not ask them to do anything he would not do himself. His example and encouragement helped keep them moving toward the enemy—the most difficult challenge faced by an officer, especially when his men ran into machine-gun, mortar, and artillery fire from dug-in positions. Daly sought to convince his men by word and example that, although it seemed counterintuitive, aggressive forward movement was the key both to achieving the objective and to bringing back as many men as possible. To stop on open ground, a natural urge to which many succumbed in the late autumn and winter of 1944–45, rendered them more vulnerable. The closer and more quickly they came to enemy lines, the safer they were from the artillery shells and mortar rounds that took such a heavy toll on GIs.

But unlike Gavin, Daly did not judge harshly those who hung back. He believed that most of his men did the best they could with what they had. Daly later said: "Everyone has a breaking point. You have a reservoir, but it can dry up if you are in combat too long. If a person had been in combat too long, he deserved some special consideration."

He came to understand his men's strengths and limitations. He reassured and encouraged the wavering, who at least played the important role of targets, forcing the Germans to disperse their fire rather than concentrate on those warriors who led the attack during offensive operations. The sense of shared danger formed a bond among the men who survived and remained with the company. Daly consciously attempted to promote high morale and unit cohesion among his men, recognizing what S. L. A. Marshall later noted: "On the field of fire it is the touch of human nature that gives men courage and enables them to make proper use of their weapons. . . . The thing which enables an infantry soldier to keep going with his weapons is the near presence or the presumed presence of a comrade." One member of Able Company remembered: "People got along and did their jobs. We would rather have been home but we were there. You did your job. We felt we were fighting for freedom—to wipe out Hitler. If we failed we'd be speaking German. I was also fighting for my buddies, and to go home."[8]

As a company commander, Daly played a different role from that of platoon leader. When the platoons were attacking in columns, for example, he usually placed himself near the front, but did not assume the lead position nearly as often as he had done before he became the commanding officer. He realized that his job required him to oversee and coordinate the attack but that he had to let the platoon leaders handle their platoons. Placing himself near the front, especially in crucial situations, gave him an accurate view of circumstances so that he could coordinate the actions of the various platoons by means of radio or runner. In short, he did more commanding and less fighting.[9]

One particular command challenge was leading the "green" soldiers who had been rushed to the European Theater as individual replacements in response to the manpower crisis arising from the intense combat of late fall and winter 1944–45. The manpower shortage had even deeper roots, going back to what some refer to as the "ninety-division gamble." Believing that technology and firepower would limit American casualties and thus allow for the use of fewer infantrymen, and keenly aware of the manpower needs of the economy, General Marshall, the army chief of staff, decided to limit the army to ninety infantry divisions (eighty-nine were eventually deployed) so that men could be channeled to war production and to naval and air power.

Of five million men drafted into the army, only two million served in combat roles, and in northwest Europe, even in 1945, barely 300,000 stood available as members of rifle companies or armored units for combat against Germany. As a result, many divisions stayed in line almost constantly, with corresponding stress and huge casualties. In the course of a year, infantry regiments of approximately three thousand men would lose twice that number killed, wounded, and missing in action. Daly's 3rd Division suffered 25,997 casualties during the war, the largest number of any division in the European and Mediterranean Theaters. The odds that a rifleman would survive the entire campaign unwounded did not much exceed Paul Daly's during World War I.

It was into this nightmarish scene that the young replacements entered. Congress had insisted that the army assign eighteen-year-olds to the front only in units, not as individuals, but the exigencies of war made that a dead letter. Anxious, uncomfortable, and confused, replacements sometimes became casualties even before reaching their new units. Often they arrived at night and took up positions without seeing the faces of those alongside whom they would fight or, sometimes, without knowing the names of their squad or platoon leaders. When morning dawned, their isolation sometimes continued. Historian Paul Fussell, who served in the European Theater, later claimed that veteran troops often would have nothing to do with inexperienced replacements, fearing they would do something stupid that would get themselves and others around them killed. He also implied that experienced troops put the "greenhorns" at points of attack as cannon fodder—a highly questionable assertion. Yet, even the term "replacement'—theater headquarters changed it to "reinforcement" in late December—connoted expendability.[10]

Daly later insisted that his company offered replacements moral support when they needed it most—at the time of their arrival. He and the NCOs had little time to orient a new man properly before he went into the line, but they tried to protect and help him. Often Daly greeted new arrivals at the edge of combat. He tried, not always successfully, to keep them out of harm's way as they learned the ways of combat. He reassured them that they had joined a great company and emphasized that they were all in the fight together. "Follow the experienced guys," he advised them. "The platoon sergeants will take care of you if you do what you're supposed to."

Despite Daly's best intentions and efforts, however, new replacements often suffered isolation and stolid indifference from veteran GIs. One night, Troy Cox and a new replacement were pulling guard duty together. Just before dark an officer came by and told the replacement to go out and take a bazooka off a dead soldier. He ordered Cox and the replacement to set it up by their foxhole, just in case they might need it. As the officer walked away, Cox realized that retrieving the bazooka would be hard and dangerous because Germans were out there. The scared replacement looked at Cox and asked, "Would you go get it for me?" Cox replied, "No way. He told you to get it and if you don't, it will stay out there." The frightened soldier then crawled out to the dead soldier, got the bazooka and its rounds, and crawled back to the foxhole. The two men set it up, ready to fire. At that point, neither man knew the other's name. The next morning the officers and some men walked by, and one of them said, "Look there, boys, see how that bazooka is set up. That's the way to do it." At that point, the replacement, Ed Adams, from Clarksville, Indiana, experienced his first feelings of acceptance.

Attaching themselves to and learning from "veteran" junior leaders (one became a veteran after four months) regardless of rank was the key both to the survival of replacements and to the ability of the platoon to keep functioning even with heavy losses and turnover. As long as replacements continued to arrive, and as long as there remained veteran junior leaders from whom replacements could learn and around whom they could rally, squads, platoons, companies, and regiments could continue the fight.[11]

Obviously Daly's best efforts and those of his NCOs could not keep all his men safe. His most trying and painful times in combat came when he found himself unable to relieve the suffering of his wounded and dying soldiers. One incident that occurred before he had become company commander particularly haunted Daly. It involved a young man who bore the same last name, but was no relation. Joseph Daly, a replacement, seemed nervous and lacking in self-confidence. When Mike noticed him hanging around headquarters, even though he should have been with his platoon, Mike sympathized with his plight and tried to offer words of encouragement. One bitterly cold night, Mike and about thirty-five of his men received orders to occupy an early-warning position in front of the line. They spread out on a wooded snowy knoll in a defensive posture. The Germans attacked their position using mortars, cutting them off from the main body. Mike knew that if they could hold out until morning they would get relief, and so he had his men lay down a great volume of fire to disguise their relatively few number.

During the action, Pvt. Daly was gravely wounded in the back and was both frightened and in agonizing pain. A medic attended him, and Mike tried to comfort him, but he had no way of getting the man back to the field hospital to receive the medical attention he desperately required. Instead, Daly watched as the medic, performing the roles of doctor, nurse, and chaplain, dressed the wound, administered pain-killing morphine, and comforted the boy, talking to him softly and gently until he lost consciousness and died. The experience of standing helpless, unable to remove young Daly, unable to rescue him, seared its way into Mike's consciousness, strengthening his resolve to get as many of his charges back safely from the war as possible. He never forgot Pvt. Daly.[12]

Nor did he ever forget the critical role played by the medics in his company, who performed so heroically and selflessly in combat. Unarmed and wearing the large emblematic Red Cross on a field of white on their helmets and on armbands, and seemingly heedless of danger as fighting raged, they sprinted or crawled to the wounded, bringing them aid and helping them back to American lines. Despite the provisions of the Geneva Convention that supposedly protected them as noncombatants, they often were exposed to hostile fire. As a result, Daly lost a number of his medics. Even though he did not have much personal contact with them, he knew the name of every medic who served in Able Company and stood in awe of them.[13]

Daly's men displayed exceptional endurance as they fought from one village to the next amid terrible scenes of carnage and destruction. Looking back, Daly recalled that as German forces retreated and the war dragged on, each day of combat filled him with a ceaseless tension: was the continuing war using up his luck and that of his men? As Mauldin's cartoon character Joe says to Willie while both GIs hunker down at night amid ruins and with bullets whizzing overhead, "I feel like a fugitive from th' law of averages." In his book *Up Front*, which featured the cartoon, Mauldin went on to write, "All of the old divisions are tired—the outfits which fought in Africa and Sicily, and Italy," which included the 3rd Division. "It doesn't take long to tire an outfit," he continued. "Those men have seen actual war at first hand, seeing their buddies killed day after day, trying to tell themselves that they are different—*that they won't get it; but knowing deep inside them that they can get it — those guys too know what real weariness of body, brain, and soul can be.*"(Mauldin's italics)

Like others, Daly felt that his luck was running out, but he was even more anxious for the members of his company. He thought a lot about his small hometown of Fairfield and of the people he knew there, but unlike many of his soldiers, he did not experience homesickness. Before joining the army and shipping overseas he had been away from home for long periods, first when he attended Georgetown Prep and Portsmouth Priory and then when he went off to West Point and later to basic training. Unlike some of his long-serving men—a number decreasing steadily as the war ground on—he was in action for four months before being wounded and then had six weeks of convalescence, followed by a return to the battlefield. His time in combat, therefore, numbered in the months, not years, and he had not left a wife or a girlfriend behind in the States. Most important, he felt responsible for others' lives, for their welfare, morale, and performance. "Having that responsibility . . . led me to do anything to cheer them up or encourage them and let them feel that they had as much support as possible." He saw himself as a "bulwark" for his men, keeping them focused on their mission and confident in their ability to survive and prevail.

Soldiers love to complain, and rightfully so, but Daly could not indulge in that luxury. "The situation helped me to forget myself and focus on the men." He once observed, "It's more conscience than courage when others rely on you." In practically every engagement he lost someone from his unit, but he could not allow himself to dwell on it. Saddened, he would whisper a short prayer and then slog on.[14]

Amid the passions of war, which Daly felt intensely, his conscience helped him to maintain his moral compass, to avoid descending into barbarity. During combat, some American soldiers did kill prisoners, but no court-martial was ever convened for these men. Historian Stephen Ambrose revealed that about one-third of the one thousand combat veterans he had interviewed said they had seen other GIs kill prisoners. Troy Cox also saw some men of Able Company—the same who showed compassion for the young, mortally wounded German at Biesheim—shoot a prisoner after being provoked by the death of one of their own at the hands of a sniper.

Daly, however, insisted on treating prisoners according to the rules of war. On one occasion, after Daly had assumed command of the company, but before he was promoted from first lieutenant to captain, his company found itself with thirty or forty German captives. Guarding them required diverting troops from combat roles. Because the company found itself under attack, their prisoners proved an even greater problem. One of Daly's fellow lieutenants suggested they shoot the prisoners so that they could better respond to the attack. Daly, however, exploded at the idea. "Goddamn it!" he shouted. "That's not what we're fighting this war for!!" The lieutenant then backed down, aware that Daly was prepared to shoot him rather than allow a blatant war crime.[15]

As a warrior and a leader, Daly had employed well the lessons his father had drawn from Roland and Oliver. He showed himself fearless in combat, continually exposing himself to fire, but also levelheaded and clear thinking—that combination of calculated daring and cool courage that his superiors had noted. Actual combat, he later recalled, induced in him "forgetfulness of self." Focused on the objective and his men, he thought better on his feet amidst the flux and chaos of battle than he did when planning things out. One man who served under him marveled at his skill with a carbine, referring to him as "a dead shot." The M1 was the standard-issue rifle, but Daly preferred the carbine. In close action it was lighter and shorter and had a bigger magazine, and at greater distances it was more accurate and powerful. Similarly, even though the Colt 45 pistol was standard issue for officers, he seldom used it because he regarded it as terribly inaccurate.[16]

Another member of Able Company observed that Daly "had God-given instincts." Those instincts told him that moving aggressively would keep the enemy off balance and result in fewer American casualties. "We didn't spend a lot of time maneuvering," he said. "We would put out scouts. A squad would go down the main street of a town while other squads moved forward on parallel streets." When he and his men did take fire, Daly proved adept at recognizing its source, quickly analyzing the situation, utilizing topography for cover, and maintaining steady fire on the enemy. His most frequent order to his men in combat was "Follow me" (the infantry motto) or "Cover me." One of his men later observed that Daly "was calm, laid back, but dangerous as far as the enemy was concerned. He wasn't a damn fool even though he was [often] way out front. He didn't charge machine guns with a bayonet. He was looking for the best route of attack that would provide the best cover for his men." And he did not hesitate to retreat when necessary in order to fight another day. As Daly himself noted, "Ya gotta survive."[17]

10 Götterdämmerung

THE FINAL BATTLE FOR GERMANY

Southwestern and southern Germany, March-April 1945.

During the last months of the war, as the Allies drove into the collapsing Reich, survival was constantly on Daly's mind, and on the minds of American troops in general. They faced shattered but often still fanatical elements of the Nazi Party, the *Waffen SS* (whose numbers actually increased to 830,000 by the beginning of 1945) and the *Hitlerjugend*. These in turn attempted to strengthen the resolve of the *Heer* (army [land forces]) and the *Volkssturm* (home guard) to fight to the death. In looking back on those final months, Daly noted that although many German units consisted of *Volkssturm,* "There were good specimens among them." The *SS,* he said, "remained formidable often even at the end." That the German army faced inevitable defeat made their bullets and their 88s no less deadly. The last months of the war saw emotionally and physically exhausted American troops in pursuit of despairing, yet still dangerous remnants of German units, all amid a shocked, terrified, and suffering civilian population—each group seemingly locked in a nightmarish spiral of death and destruction even as the war moved inexorably to a conclusion.[1]

In that context, every casualty took on added poignancy for Daly, but especially those involving men who had served in combat for a long time. Yet he realized that to end the war as swiftly as possible and thereby get himself and his men back home required keeping the pressure on the Germans, which paradoxically meant American casualties. With Germany obviously defeated yet still unwilling to surrender, Daly faced a daunting leadership challenge: motivating his men, none of whom wanted to die fighting a crumbling foe, especially in the last weeks of the war. That foe was still extracting a painful toll on the Americans. For example, Patch's Seventh Army Diary noted that between March 15 and March 23, battle casualties had been "very light, amounting to *only* 7,000." [Emphasis added] Patch clearly believed that the casualties represented a relatively small price to pay for, in the words of one author, "rolling up a major part of the surviving defenses of central Germany."[2]

The grim reality of that task filled Daly and his men with a sense of foreboding every morning as they awoke. Troy Cox recalled: "Every day was a dread . . . because we knew there was another town to take. I dreaded every day. Would I get it today? There seemed no end to it. . . . In town, there would be an intersection that you dreaded because the Germans had zeroed in on it. Even if we were designated as the reserve platoon and got a brief break, we dreaded being called back up." Dread operated like a black hole in the pit of the stomach—sucking the light from each soldier's day.

And death came capriciously. On Cox's first day of combat, for example, the company encountered a house at a crossroads that the Germans had converted into a strong point. As his buddy and fellow Mississippian, Leonard Dillard, moved past him, Cox said: "I hear we're going to take that house. Be careful." Leonard replied, "You do the same." Five minutes later, Leonard lay dead. Little wonder that each morning's sunrise inspired apprehension.

On March 22, after mop-up operations on the Siegfried line during which elements of the 15th Regiment eliminated pockets of resistance, destroyed pillboxes, and bulldozed dragon's teeth, most of the regiment gathered at Contwig. It then moved over a highway strewn with the detritus of war to an area south of Worms for another river crossing—this time the Rhine. SHAEF doubted that the Germans possessed the ability to maintain a discernable defensive line in the West, estimating that the *Heer* possessed only sixty-five reduced-strength divisions in the West, the equivalent of no more than twenty-six full divisions.[3]

Audie Murphy graphically captured the military situation that developed after the capture of the Siegfried line: "Beyond the Siegfried Line our forces consolidate; and the drive becomes like a great river pushing against a series of rotting dams. A dam breaks; and the torrent lashes onward until it hits another obstruction. Between the major points of resistance lie gaps protected by lines so thinly held that locating the actual front is often difficult. After we cross the Rhine, the dike crumbles; and a flood of men and arms pours over Germany."[4]

While no effective coordinated German defense line remained, German tactical genius asserted itself as German commanders improvised a defense centered on the *Kampfgruppe* (battle group). These consisted of personnel—infantry, armor, *Luftwaffe*, antiaircraft and service—pulled together from shattered units and stragglers. They numbered between 100 and 3,000 under the command of the most senior officer available.

The *Kampfgruppe* packed weapons that gave it significant firepower and enabled it to "punch above its weight," in the words of Max Hastings. One of these was the *panzerfaust*. A person could fire the weapon from a standing, kneeling, or prone position. The oversized warhead was mounted on the front of a steel tube 41 inches long and 1 3/4 inches in diameter. The projectile, kept stable in flight by steel fins, had a range of only thirty yards—its biggest drawback—but could penetrate up to 170 mm of armor or be used against troops. "When fired," Daly recalled, "you could almost see the thing going through the air. It looked like a football!" Armed with one of these weapons, a thirteen- or fourteen-year-old boy could destroy a tank, and many did. Firing at a tank at such close range, however, often proved suicidal, because smoke engulfed the person who fired the weapon, giving away his position. A *panzerfaust* round had a tremendous effect when fired into a cellar, where American soldiers might have sought cover during a counterattack. The sound alone of the explosion could damage a man's hearing and even give him a concussion.

Daly noted that surviving German units received great numbers of these weapons, thereby increasing the already impressive firepower they possessed in the MP 40 ("Schmeisser" or "Burp Gun"), the dreaded MG 42, and mortars (the "poor man's artillery").[5] They employed *panzerfäuste* to great effect when, in what they called "active defense," they counterattacked American forces.

The Rhine crossings began just south of Worms on the cloudy morning of March 26. The 2nd and 3rd battalions traversed the river in rubber assault craft and clambered onto the east-bank landing spots at 0900 and 1000 respectively. Daly's company and the rest of the 1st Battalion assembled in a wooded area and crossed by the same means at 1200, encountering little resistance except some sniper fire and occasional mortar rounds, which did little damage. At 2200, the 1st and 2nd battalions jumped off from assembly areas east of Lampertheim to face night combat in low, flat, heavily forested terrain. The enemy proved adept at using bicycles for mobility, but by midnight Daly had his company sitting on the objective, the autobahn, thus severing communications between Frankfurt and Mannheim.

Scouts captured an old man and four young boys who were manning a machine gun to protect the autobahn. The old man started to cry, saying he had not wanted to fight but that German troops had ordered him and the boys to maintain the position. He begged the Americans not to shoot the boys. The scouts released all of them to return to their homes. Daly's company also captured five 88-mm guns that the Germans had set up to destroy Allied armor using the highway, and they demolished several German vehicles that tried to break through the roadblock.[6]

Daly sought to maintain the momentum of the rout and keep the pressure on the Germans so that they could not reorganize. Able Company passed through Huttenfeld, a village secured earlier by Charlie Company, and made for the small bridges over two narrow irrigation canals to the east. Knocking out a German machine gun that guarded the first, the company swept over the bridges and continued to Laudenbach.

Before Able Company arrived, American Piper Cub scouting planes appeared in the sky over the town. On seeing the planes, most German troops left, but a few, led by two young regular army officers, remained. They constructed a slapdash barricade, but when the townspeople urged them to remove it and offer no resistance lest the Americans destroy the town, the troops, accompanied by a tank, withdrew to the terraced, partially wooded hills above the town. Daly ordered one of the tanks attached to his company to destroy the barricade by driving through it. Almost immediately thereafter, Able Company took heavy fire from rifles, machine guns, and 20-mm guns in the hills. This reflected the standard German tactic of constructing blocking positions or strongpoints on a road with a mix of one or two well-concealed tanks or assault guns protected by a ring of heavily armed infantry.

Daly responded using the method increasingly employed by American troops in dealing with towns that did not signify their willingness to capitulate by flying white "flags"—often sheets hung from windows and prominent buildings. He called for occasional shelling of the town and its surroundings from 0600 to 1200. The townspeople huddled in their cellars, but some hung a white sheet from the top window of the Catholic church. When the barrage ended and Daly's company entered, civilians—some nearly hysterical, others curious—milled about in the streets. Most felt relief that the Americans, not the Russians, had taken the town and that damage had been limited for the most part to collapsed roofs. Using loudspeakers, Daly ordered the townspeople to return to their homes and fly something white from their windows. He warned that he would destroy those houses not displaying the sign of surrender. Meanwhile, Daly's men subdued remnants of opposition in the town.

The relentless drive resumed through the rolling hills and thick forests east of the Rhine. By March 29 the 1st Battalion had reached Grasellenbach, almost thirty miles from where it had crossed the Rhine near Worms. As Able Company swept through Germany, a pattern emerged: brief firefights and skirmishes on the outskirts of villages and towns, often at hastily erected roadblocks, followed by the collapse of the resistance. Sometimes German civilians responded in a friendly manner to the arrival of American troops. When a baker in one village offered them cookies, the GIs insisted he eat one first, as a precaution against poisoning. Most of the time, however, the people would line the streets and just gaze at the troops.[7]

On March 29 the 1st Battalion moved fourteen miles to division reserve at Kirch-Brombach. There it received orders to proceed eleven miles northeastward, to the vicinity of Worth am Main, on the banks of the Main River southeast of the industrial city of Frankfurt. The Seventh Army had received orders to drive to the northeast to protect the right flank of Patton's Third Army, which had its sights set on the strategic Ruhr pocket. From there, on March 31, Daly's Able Company and the rest of the 1st Battalion crossed the Main River on foot using a partially demolished railroad bridge. Moving to the south-southeast, they encountered little opposition as they and other companies leapfrogged through picturesque villages in the Main River Valley nestled below the Spessart, a low range of hills to the east of the river. Arriving on the crest of Busig Hill above the farming town of Grossheubach, Daly ordered Able Company to pause while he sent out patrols to investigate the lay of the land and the location of German forces.[8]

Approximately six months earlier, on October 18, 1944, all German men between the ages of fifteen and sixty not serving in the military were conscripted for service in the *Volkssturm* (a national militia). By that time more than one hundred men from Grossheubach had perished fighting in the German army. Nevertheless, on October 24 all eligible sixteen-year-olds were ordered to report to the *rathaus* (town hall) and from there were sent to the *Heer* recruiting headquarters in Frankfurt. As they traveled to the office, the seventy-five youths learned that its staff had fled. Consequently the boys returned to Grossheubach. Before going to their homes, however, they celebrated their good fortune at the "Adler" *gasthaus* (inn).

About nine hundred refugees from other parts of Germany had crowded into Grossheubach. Many were relatives of village residents who took some of them into their homes; many others lived in modular barracks constructed near the cemetery. By the end of the year, about seventeen hundred people had found refuge in the village. But apprehension and anxiety grew as retreating German units of company size passed through, and as the ominous roll of artillery in the West grew louder, indicating the approach of the front.

Beginning in November, American fighter-bombers began to hit the area, and in February 1945, American planes dropped twenty-five bombs on the nearby resort town of Miltenberg and on the outskirts of Grossheubach. German government propaganda depicted the Americans as criminals and warned that Germans should fear the worst if they proved victorious.

In late March 1945 a company of German troops led by an SS lieutenant in his early twenties and composed primarily of sixteen- to eighteen-year-old German and ethnic German eastern Europeans arrived to defend the town. When the lieutenant established a command post in the bakery, he did not realize that two young women in a room behind the shop could overhear his telephone conversations, including the conflicting orders he received regarding the defense of Grossheubach. The lieutenant ordered his troops to construct defenses using Russian prisoners of war who worked on the local farms. Soon interlocking trenches covered the area, including along the Main River and the major road into town and at the foot of the terraced vineyards above the town on Bustig Hill.

On March 29 a few villagers were walking toward Kleinheubach, a nearby town, when Americans started shooting from Bustig Hill. The people fled home uninjured. One woman in the group, Louisa Dabor, who saw a young German sniper in a nest near the ferry site, told him he should stop—that there was no sense to this any longer. Later, at the same location, she found his helmet with a bullet hole in it.

The next day American tanks and mortars in Kleinheubach fired rounds into Grossheubach that landed in streets and fields. People sought shelter in cellars. The thirty to thirty-five in the wine cellar of the tavern agreed among themselves that someone had to do something. The daughter of the landlord and her sister-in-law went into the courtyard of the tavern, where they quickly fashioned a white flag from a sheet and a large pole used for picking vegetables in the fields. Then they carried the white flag to the church. One intrepid fifteen-year-old altar boy, Walter Repp, who lived near the church, went to the pastor, Father Kempf, and asked his permission for them to place the flag on the belfry. With the priest's consent, Repp climbed into the tower and placed the flag in a highly visible position. The bombardment stopped almost immediately.

Thinking the town had decided to surrender, Daly ordered his men to enter it cautiously. Unknown to Daly, however, the SS Lieutenant in command of German troops had no intention of capitulating. Appearing at the rectory with the deputy mayor, Felix Straubb, he summoned the priest, whom he suspected of having hoisted the flag. The confrontation drew a small crowd that included the women and Repp. The lieutenant demanded the name of the person responsible, but all present pleaded ignorance, knowing that the lieutenant probably would shoot whoever was named. He then drove to the home of the bell ringer and demanded to know who had raised the flag. When that person also pleaded ignorance, the lieutenant brought him back to the church. Some village men whom they passed on their way back to the church urged Repp to leave the flag in place. Threatening them with his pistol, the lieutenant forced Repp to remove the sheet. But during the course of the afternoon, many families emerged from their cellars and hung white bedsheets from the windows of their houses or placed them on their roofs. But when they heard exploding grenades and rifle fire, they fled once more to their cellars. Before entering his cellar, one resident hurriedly hung a sheet out his window, but the fanatical lieutenant happened by and threatened to shoot him unless he removed it.[9]

The noise that sent the townspeople scurrying for cover started when lead elements of Able Company made their way down the terraced slopes of the vineyards toward the road that abutted the Main River and ran into the town from the east. There they unexpectedly encountered enemy machine-gun nests that inflicted many casualties. Private 1st Class Elling, one of the hardy, proactive warriors on whom Daly relied, was serving as a scout for his advance patrol, and he seized the initiative—as usual. Using a hedgerow as cover, he made his way to an open field and then stealthily crawled across it to the vineyard where the Germans had established their strongpoints. Then he charged a German position all the while firing his BAR to deadly effect. At one point, a bullet hit his entrenching shovel spinning him around and knocking him to his knees. Nevertheless, he killed three and wounded one as they desperately fired at him. Walking from hole to hole firing his BAR, he so unnerved the enemy that they could not shoot accurately. Single-handedly he killed eleven Germans. He capped off his heroism when he spotted a thirteen-man special sniping patrol sent out for him. Crawling forward, he continued to fire, killing five more Germans and wounding two, whereupon the remaining six surrendered. After another short firefight involving other elements of Able Company, the remaining Germans surrendered. Private Elling subsequently received the Distinguished Service Cross for his actions that day.[10]

After knocking the stocks off captured German rifles to make them unusable, the American troops created a six-foot-high pile of weaponry. Then they conducted a house-by-house, basement-to-attic search for German soldiers. Meanwhile, some young German deserters who had taken refuge in the village captured the SS lieutenant and took him to a trench near the Main River to execute him. Before they could do so, however, American troops discovered them and rescued the lieutenant from sure death. Following their search of the town, the Americans bedded down in the barns that abutted many houses in the agricultural community.[11]

During the last two months of the war, American forces repeatedly encountered the situation that played out in Grossheubach. As the situation of the German army became more desperate, fanaticism increased among Nazi Party members, SS, *Hitlerjugende,* and military cadets. Joseph Goebbels, Hitler's chief propagandist, had done his job well over the years, and a whole generation of brainwashed youngsters had grown up under his and Hitler's sway. A significant number of them had experienced an awful "rite of passage" that involved an oath to sacrifice their lives for the Führer. "Goebbels' legman," Helmut Sündermann, cried: "The German nation is to be wiped off the map. German men are to be enslaved and deported to all corners of the earth. . . . When enemy divisions reach German soil, they must be attacked from every house, every village, every field, every hill. We must not leave a single blade of German grass which might feed the invaders."[12]

Ironically the failure of the July 1944 "bomb plot" against Hitler had strengthened the hand of the Nazis. Many young people believed that destiny had chosen Hitler to survive and eventually to prevail. *Time* magazine quoted *Gauleiter* (regional leader in the Nazi Party) Franz Hofer of Tyrol as telling "Hitler Maidens" to "stand faithfully and unflinchingly before, behind and beside the Führer. Victory is nearer than you think."[13]

By March 1945, however, that promise rang hollow to many. German civilians in the West increasingly recognized the futility of continuing warfare and wanted to surrender, to end what they now considered needless destruction and death, to save their homes, property, and lives. Desertions from the German army also continued to grow.

Nevertheless the SS, and other "true believers" several hundred thousand strong, clung to the desperate hope propounded by Hitler and high Nazi officials that new "V" weapons and a fight to the death would buy time during which the Allies would grow sick of the price in blood that complete conquest entailed. The supposedly fragile Allied coalition would break apart, and Germany would secure a negotiated peace with the western Allies. Failing that, *Götterdämerung* ("twilight of the gods," a collapse marked by catastrophic violence) would preserve the honor of the German nation and inspire future generations to preserve, and eventually restore to dominance, the ideology of National Socialism. In Grossheubach, and throughout the unconquered portions of the Reich, they used terror and intimidation to enforce their will on soldiers as well as civilians, instituting "flying courts martial" and hanging or shooting those who urged or attempted surrender.[14]

Many families in Grossheubach had relatives who had immigrated to the United States in the mid-nineteenth and early twentieth centuries, and a number of the villagers had lived in the United States for a while and spoke English very well. One such person was Rosa Zoeller, in whose three-story home on the east side of the village Daly established his command post. Mrs. Zoeller, whose husband was serving in the German army, had lived in New York City for twenty years and now resided in Grossheubach with her mother and her three boys, ages three, ten, and fifteen. Having been born in New York City, the older boys were US citizens, a fact that their mother made known to Daly and the other soldiers. The Zoeller family remained in the house while it served as the company command post. (Daly did not remember ordering any German families out of their houses. His men stayed in deserted houses, ruins of houses, and barns.)

American troops set up a mortar in the family garden to harass German troops defending nearby Miltenberg. Because some branches of a cherry tree obstructed the mortar, the men prepared to cut down the branches, but Rosa Zoeller spotted them from upstairs in the house and yelled down to them to stop because the cherries might be the family's only source of fresh food when they ripened in May. Daly heard her complaint and ordered his men to reposition the mortar. They did so by moving it to a nearby house that sat on ground even higher than the Zoellers.' When the troops told the owner, who had lost a leg in the First World War, that he would have to relocate, Rosa again went to Daly, who once again ordered the mortar crew to relocate, enabling the man to stay on his property. All this transpired as US Army surgeons, using the large table in the Zoeller's dining room, treated and operated on wounded GIs. When Able Company departed, the doctors left the helmets, fatigues, and jackets of two deceased GIs, and the older Zoeller brothers began wearing the uniforms. (Years later, the eldest Zoeller son, Gerald, joined the US Army and served in the 3rd Division.)[15]

As darkness fell, Daly sent a platoon to enter Miltenberg from the rear. There they found a strong force that put up a spirited resistance, preventing further penetration and even surrounding the platoon. The rest of Able Company swept around the flank to join the stranded platoon and hold the east end of the town while Baker Company prepared for a full-scale attack, supported by tanks, at dawn. In the face of such overwhelming firepower, the Germans quickly surrendered. Able Company had completed its mission in this portion of the Main River valley.

The 1st Battalion now moved sixteen miles north from Miltenberg to an assembly point at Heimbuchenthal. From there, Able Company rode atop tanks and tank destroyers across the meandering Main River and through woods for ten miles to Rothenbuch, a small, picturesque town nestled in a valley of the Spessart mountains.[16] The village sheltered hundreds of refugees from the Rhineland and the Saar. In March the flight-reporting service of the Luftwaffe had established a radio station on "Zoo Mountain," near the village, whose long-distance line led into the Rothenbuch village school. American fliers soon discovered it, and in the afternoon of March 25, fighter-bombers attacked and destroyed it in a raid that lasted about forty-five minutes. Earlier, at about noon, fighter bombers had strafed the village during the Palm Sunday procession, hitting the priest's house, a barn, and several other houses but otherwise causing only minor damage.

The raid terrified the residents and deeply impressed Mayor Anton Gessler, who previously had spoken of "final victory" and exhorted the village to hold out against the expected American onslaught. But now he changed his mind. On March 27 he burned important documents and, hoping to preserve his village from destruction, issued a call to its residents not to oppose the American soldiers. Rather, he urged them to behave calmly, stay at home with the windows closed, and attach a white sheet to their house. As a signal to American planes that his village intended to surrender without a fight, Gessler ran a white flag up the town flagpole. On hearing about the flag, however, the SS, in a replay of the scene at Grossheubach, sent troops to remove it and to arrest the mayor. The villagers hid Gessler, but a detachment of SS troops and *Volkssturm* remained to oppose the Americans. By March 26, American tanks had taken the nearby town of Lohr am Main, and American artillery had begun to fire on Rothenbuch, although most of the shells exploded harmlessly in the meadow behind the church.[17]

The German troops built defensive walls along either side of a road that ran along the base of the hill overlooking the southeastern entrance to Rothenbuch. The SS placed an 88-mm gun near the sports field, and near the gun the *Volkssturm* built an antitank barrier of ten or twelve felled spruce trees across the road. Daly could see that the men were older and, judging them unwilling combatants, chose not to fire on them from the heights above the town.

As a TD accompanying Able Company nosed over the hill overlooking the town, a shell fired by the 88 slammed into it, setting it afire. The rest of the armor pulled back and then edged back up to the crest of the hill, where they spotted and destroyed the 88 and its crew. Daly ordered a frontal assault by his company with support from tanks and TDs. At the same time, Charlie Company circled around the town and attacked from the rear without armor. A brief but intense fight ensued during which German troops fired small arms and machine guns from behind the stone wall at the base of the hill and disabled another TD with a *panzerfaust*. At the conclusion of the skirmish, thirty German troops lay fallen and seventy-two had surrendered. American fire had knocked out two enemy antitank guns.[18]

According to the chronicle of the children's home in Rothenbuch, which housed eighty preschool children, the nuns who ran the institution could not find a way to leave the town safely once the shelling started. Consequently the sisters and the children, with the parish priest and about forty others took shelter in the basement of the home. With communication between Rothenbuch and other towns cut off, the sisters had no idea how or where they would find food to feed one hundred twenty people. Then, out of the blue, Daly drove a jeep onto the grounds of the home and inquired about the children. Troops searching the houses in the village had alerted him to the sisters' predicament. Daly arranged for them to take the "remainders" from the American officers' kitchen three times a day. According to the school chronicle, these "remainders" proved so nutritious and filling that they largely satisfied the children. The sisters saw this as providential and noted, "Where the emergency is largest, God's assistance is next."[19]

Able Company and the rest of the 15th Regiment pressed their advance to the northeast in order to exploit the disorganization of the enemy. Daly saw village after village that had been reduced to rubble by bombing, artillery, and infantry combat with inhabitants living in the ruins of once-charming settings. On April 8 at 1715, Able Company pushed into Bad Neustadt an der Saale, one of Germany's spa cities, at the junction of the Franconian Saale and Brend Rivers in a wide valley of the Rhön Mountains. There, at the Brend, they came upon an enemy-held, explosive-wired bridge. That afternoon, twenty-one-year-old Sgt. "Proz" Porucznik, the 5'11," square-shouldered Polish-American whom Daly regarded as "an outstanding soldier," fought taller than he stood. As he led his platoon through heavy machine-gun and small-arms fire to secure and hold the bridgehead, five of his men were pinned down. To guide them to cover, he crawled fifty yards through grazing fire. When a company-strength force counterattacked, "Porucznick skillfully regrouped his squads, engaged the enemy for thirty minutes, and repulsed the attack." At approximately 2000 hours, Able Company arrived northwest of Bad Neustadt.[20]

On the night of March 16 the people of Bad Neustadt had seen fire on the south horizon coming from Würzberg, an important rail connection and the location of a number of hospitals. Fire bombing destroyed 85 percent of the city and killed two thousand, a fate that most in Bad Neustadt fervently hoped to avoid. Many, such as fifteen-year-old Ludwig Benkert, had heard wounded veterans home on leave from the Russian front declare that Germany was losing the war. The increased bombing in 1945 made that point crystal clear to the populace of the city.

Several days before American forces arrived, Walter Jacob Preh, a prominent industrialist who owned the Preh machine-tool factory, went to meet Dr. Otto Helmuth, the *gauleiter*, who had relocated with his staff from Würzberg to Bad Neustadt. Over dinner, Preh asked him not to resist the Americans. Helmuth supposedly agreed, issued an order to the effect that the city would not be defended, and had it posted all over the city on Saturday, April 7. Then, however, the three platoons of young SS troops stationed in Bad Neustadt received orders from Berlin to fight to the death.

On April 8, in Wollbach, a rural village north of Bad Neustadt, the school canceled classes, and the boys, who ranged in age from fourteen to sixteen, including Jacob Benkert, listened as officers from both the regular army and the SS urged them to enlist as "volunteers for victory." The SS officers promised the boys a "good time," but the SS troops were armed only with rifles, grenades, a few machine guns, and *panzerfäuste*. In response, *Kreisleiter* Andreas Ingebrand (the local Nazi Party leader) ordered the posting of signs announcing the defense of Bad Neustadt. The *obersturmführer* (a Nazi party paramilitary senior assault leader in the SS) stationed one platoon of troops in the western suburb of the city known as *Gartenstadt* (Garden City), another along the main street, and a third on the medieval wall near the north entrance to the "old city." Then he withdrew to the hills outside the city to "keep watch" from a distance.

As Able Company and its attachment of tanks approached Wollbach from the direction of Bischofsheim, they ran into another skirmish on the order of those earlier in Grossheubach and Rothenbuch. The platoon of German soldiers waiting in the Gardenstadt opened fire with heavy small arms, *Nebelwerfer,* and panzerfäuste. American tankers responded with machine guns, which they sprayed from side to side. Able Company scattered the SS platoon, inflicting casualties and capturing some. Then, proceeding down the Haupstrasse, the American column took fire from the platoon hidden along the side of the road. Again American firepower scattered the attackers, leaving some dead at the side of the road.

At the same time, American observation planes and fighter-bombers flew above the city. Reaching the tower that marked the north entrance to the "old city," Daly halted the bulk of Able Company and, in order to find the mayor to surrender the city, ordered three tanks to drive to the tower marking the south entrance. On the way, when one tanker opened his hatch and peered out, a sniper shot him, but his wound was only superficial. The medics found that the bullet had penetrated his helmet at such an angle that it spun around the inside almost harmlessly! Meanwhile, finding no mayor at the city hall, the tanks continued along a road that ended at Preh's factory.

A situation similar to that in Rothenbuch but with more tragic consequences now played out. On April 7, Preh had met at his factory with the deputy mayor, Carl Bonfig. (Ingebrand, who was mayor as well as kreisleiter, had fled the city.) Bonfig agreed to surrender the city to the Americans and set out for the *rathaus* to do so. But an air raid by American fighter-bombers led him to take a detour to his home, where he sought shelter in his cellar. When the American tanks found Preh at his factory, he told them that Bonfig would surrender at the rathaus (city hall) and agreed to ride there with the Americans. But of course Bonfig was not there. At that, Daly, who had joined the tanks, gave Preh thirty minutes to have Bonfig surrender the town and post white flags or suffer tank and artillery fire. Taking a white flag, Preh left to fetch Bonfig.

Unluckily for Preh, as he was walking to Bonfig's home, an SS officer, seeing the white flag, shot and killed him. Shortly thereafter, Bonfig arrived at the *rathaus* and surrendered the city. Resistance had collapsed after less than an hour's fighting. The Operations Report of the 3rd Division recounted that the action at Bad Neustadt represented typical enemy tactics during the month, consisting largely of sniper, *panzerfäust,* and modified antiaircraft 88 fire directed at American troops.

American casualties in Western Europe during April would total only slightly less than during February. Patch's Seventh Army would suffer its greatest single monthly losses since entering combat in August 1944.[21] For Daly and the rest, victory seemed so near, and yet so bloody far, especially with the city of Nuremberg looming as the next objective.

11 Nuremberg—Medal of Honor

Nuremberg, Germany, April 18, 1945.

Daly and his men were so close to surviving the war, so close to the end of the nightmare. One last hurdle remained: dangerous urban warfare in Nuremberg. The city had been flattened by air raids, but the shattered landscape afforded many sites for snipers and Nazi bitter-enders to extract a last measure of American blood. Sleep-deprived and running on adrenaline, Daly was haunted by the thought of losing more men so near the finish line. Getting them home focused him and put him into his "zone." He would do his damnedest to protect them. Almost as if he could will their survival, he appointed himself company scout and advanced thirty yards in front of the rest in search of the enemy. What happened next would make Daly a national hero.

On April 9 the 15th regiment moved to an area south of Schweinfurt, an industrial city and ball-bearing-manufacturing center whose air defenses earlier had proved so deadly to Allied airmen trying to bomb it. There, on April 11, Daly's life, would take a dramatic turn. American intelligence feared that Hitler and his highest officials intended to make a last stand in a mountain redoubt surrounding Berchtesgaden in the Alps of southern Bavaria, Austria, and northern Italy. Although reports about an "Alpine redoubt" ultimately proved unfounded, Eisenhower took no chances. To prevent remaining German forces from retreating to the rumored redoubt, Eisenhower authorized the Seventh Army to execute an arching sweep to the east and then proceed southward from Schweinfurt to Nuremberg, the shrine of National Socialism and the scene of massive prewar Nazi rallies. The 3rd Division then would continue to Munich and, finally, Salzburg, Austria.[1]

On February 21, 1945, as part of the devastating Allied air offensive directed against German cities, two thousand Allied planes had smashed the center of Nuremberg knocking out electricity and water. Despite this punishment, Reich Defense Commissioner Karl Holz, the *gauleiter* of Nuremberg (a protégé of Julius Streicher, the phobic anti-Semitic Nazi boss of Franconia),

pledged to defend the city against the American troops headed his way, signaling that urban warfare lay ahead. In the small village of Heroldsberg, just
north of Nuremberg, fourteen-year-old Friedrich Braun (who had lost his
father on the Russian front in 1943) and other members of the *Hitlerjugend*
received an order to report to Erlangen—eleven miles away—for service in
a "tank-hunting battalion." Gathered in an exercise area, each boy was to
receive a rifle and a bicycle with two *panzerfäuste* (mounted by leather straps
under the handlebar). An *SS* 1st sergeant lined up the boys according to
height. Those too short to straddle the bike he ordered to go home to their
mothers. The diminutive Braun did so, trudging through the night until he
reached his home. For other Germans, young and old, however, the war
would continue—for some to the death.[2]

Beginning on the evening of April 11–12, units of the 15th Regiment took
Schweinfurt and numerous villages along the Main River with little opposition. At this point, ever-present fatigue weighed heavily on Daly and his men.
A photograph snapped by Sergeant Lebowitz, the company clerk, graphically
captured Daly's weariness that spring. Returning to the company area at
dawn from leading a reconnaissance patrol, Daly appears gaunt, a study in
exhaustion, with his eyes nearly closed as if sleep-walking, nose clearly red-
dened and swollen, rifle slung over his right shoulder with his long right arm
and fingers keeping it straight.[3] The exigencies of ending the war left precious
little time for sleep.

To the limit. *Courtesy J. Leon Lebowitz.* Die-hard
resistance from *SS* troops and *Hitlerjugend* (Hitler Youth)
meant that combat and casualties continued in March
and April of 1945, even as it became clear that Germany
had lost the war. The constant tension of combat can
be seen in Daly's exhausted body and face as he returns
to camp from a reconnaissance patrol near Schweinfurt,
Germany, in April. The company clerk who snapped this
photo later wrote under it in his scrapbook: "Captain
Michael J. Daly . . . the best officer and bravest man I
have ever known."

The regiment crossed the Main River yet again, the infantry crowding atop tanks and TDs that sped southward through towns and villages. After encircling Bamberg, thirty miles north of Nuremberg, elements of the regiment encountered stiff resistance southwest of the town. Ten "Goliath" miniature tanks loaded with explosives were captured, but two others detonated, killing two GIs and wounding two. German planes, long absent from the skies, reappeared at night and dropped antipersonnel bombs. Mines, trip wires, and heavy sniper fire—some from civilians—slowed the advance but failed to stop it. Indeed, by April 13, two days after the regiment began the offensive, Bamberg, along with forty-three other towns and several villages, had fallen.[4]

The "whirlwind drive on Nuremberg" resumed without interruption until it reached Heroldsberg, one of a number of towns constituting a "flak ring" around the city. Most antiaircraft emplacements in Heroldsberg were self-propelled 88s. In addition to firing them at planes, the operators could level them against infantry, though not very accurately: the guns lacked sighting scopes. Still, at a range of five to ten miles, a German ground crew using its "quick fire" drill could loose fifteen to twenty rounds per minute. The four 88s and three of the 20-mm guns were located on the north end of the town, with three 88s and one 20-mm at the edge of the cemetery. Four machine-gun posts provided cover for the antiaircraft guns and for the two main entrances into the town from the north. On the main street, which ran through the heart of the town, the Germans had erected a tank barrier, but their commander had ordered them to keep it partially open to enable German troops and equipment to withdraw if necessary.

The German force in the town consisted of *Volkssturm*, regular troops, air-force personnel pressed into the role of infantrymen, *Hitlerjugende*, and some SS. In the latter stages of the war, the SS drafted men and boys into the SS; the *Waffen SS* remained voluntary. Continuing to the southwest, Able Company approached Heroldsberg from high ground around Kalchreuth. Tank destroyers spotted a German convoy in the distance including three ammunition trucks, five howitzers, and two prime movers towing an 88-mm and a 20-mm gun. The convoy sped ahead when the American TDs began firing. It had just about reached the shelter of the town, about a mile away, when one of the TDs scored a direct hit on the prime movers, completely destroying them and the guns being towed.[5]

When the units of the 1st Battalion, including Able Company, approached the outskirts of the town, at about 1800 hours, they moved cautiously. Receiving sniper fire from a considerable force of German troops in the nearby forest, Major Potter returned fire, followed by the rest of the 1st Battalion. During the thirty-minute artillery bombardment that followed, the Germans withdrew into the town.

Able Company moved down the main street in two columns flanking two pairs of tanks. When they spotted a teenager wearing an armband, they took him prisoner, thinking him one of the fanatic *Hitlerjugend* whom they feared. He belonged, however, to the *Hitlerjugend* Fire Brigade, whose members also wore armbands. The Americans forced the boy, four other civilians, and one captured Luftwaffe soldier to march closely in front of the first two tanks, in effect using them as human shields, a violation of the Geneva Convention. Daly evidently approved the tactic in hopes of providing greater protection for his men. The tanks stopped in front of the post office and each fired an air burst above the woods, which left the civilian hostages under the guns deaf for a week. Suddenly ten inexperienced German soldiers positioned down the street—eight on the left and two on the right—opened up with an inaccurate crossfire, using hard-to-aim submachine guns that tended to rise as they fired them. The Americans returned the fire. One German was so inexperienced that he did not know how to change the magazine. As he attempted to do so, American fire brought him down. In addition, about one hundred Germans, together with a 20-mm gun, were captured in a weedy area north of the town.

Sharp skirmishes continued at the antiaircraft emplacements, but by late evening one hundred fifty German troops, *SS* and *Volkssturm* (a few of them drunk) had surrendered. Even after having supposedly cleared the town, though, the battalion had to contend with lone snipers. In interrogating prisoners, American intelligence asked one question: "Where are the AA guns on the outskirts of Nuremberg?"

Moving out of Heroldsberg in the dark, Able Company lost two GIs when a mine explosion destroyed their jeep. Engineers had to be called in to clear mines and to help the men deal with three antitank barricades and massive numbers of trees felled across the road to Nuremberg. As the troops crept ever closer to the city itself, antiaircraft and artillery fire became heavy, and the Luftwaffe, employing its new jet fighter, the Me 262, began bombing and strafing the Americans.[6]

The US Seventh Army now approached Nuremberg from three different directions with two armored divisions, an armored cavalry group, four infantry divisions—the 3rd, 30th, 42nd, and 45th—and the support of massive airpower. The nine-hundred-year-old city occupied an important place in German history, having served as the unofficial capital of the "First Reich," the Holy Roman Empire, particularly from the 14th to the 16th centuries, when decrees required that the *Reichstag* (legislative body) meet there and that the imperial regalia and jewels be kept there permanently. The city was home to Albrecht Dürer, the greatest painter of the Northern Renaissance. Because it figured prominently in the Holy Roman Empire and because it was in south-central Germany, the Nazis chose it for their annual party conventions—the Nuremberg rallies—from 1927 to 1938. There Albert Speer constructed the massive structures that constituted Hitler's Nazi Party Rally Grounds. There also, in 1935, the Nazi government announced its infamous Nuremberg Laws (the cornerstones of German racist policies), and Julius Streicher, the *gauleiter* of Franconia, spewed his anti-Semitic venom. Daly and his men knew that Americans viewed Nuremberg as the "Nazi shrine" and that the capture of the city would be a sign of military and moral victory over National Socialism.

On April 12 the German High Command had ordered the unconditional defense of all cities. And because Hitler, Goebbels, and Himmler regarded Nuremberg as unique and feared that its fall would demoralize both the army and the rest of the German population, Hitler stressed that the forces in Nuremberg should fight to the last man. He found a willing accomplice in Karl Holz, the city *gauleiter.* The German force defending Nuremberg consisted of six to seven thousand troops, including a shrunken *SS* regiment of approximately five hundred soldiers from the 17th *SS* Panzer Division, two thousand Luftwaffe fighter pilots and ground personnel turned infantry, elderly antiaircraft soldiers, Russian volunteers of German ethnicity, young men in the Reich Labor Service, remainders of spare troops stationed in the city with wounded and recuperating soldiers, and a number of *Volkssturm* companies and *Hitlerjugend.* They faced a juggernaut in the Seventh Army with its 45,000 troops divided among infantry regiments and supporting elements. The fight would not be an equal one, but it would still be a dangerous one for the American troops.[7]

Systematic and relentless Allied bombing had reduced the city itself to rubble. Eight thousand of its citizens had perished in the air raids. But antiaircraft guns—most of them 88s that German troops could also train against American troops—still ringed the city, and Nuremberg's bombed-out buildings provided shelter for snipers equipped with machine guns, submachine guns, small arms, and *panzerfäuste.* On April 15, *Gauleiter* Holz vowed in a message to Hitler that no matter how desperate the situation, he "would rather stay in the most German of all cities under all circumstances and die fighting than abandon it." "Even if we have no weapons," he declared, "we will spring at the Americans and tear their throats open." Hitler responded from his bunker: "Now begins a battle of fanaticism that is reminiscent of our own struggle for power. No matter how superior our enemies' strength may be at present, eventually it will break—as in the past." To stiffen the backbone of the city's residents, the Nazis disseminated propaganda that the American troops intended to slaughter them.[8]

As in Heroldsberg, the defenders of Nuremberg established antitank barriers of various kinds in the suburbs and, in the city itself, on approaches to the walled old city. On April 16, General Patch surprised the Germans by ordering an attack, not from the west but from northeast and east of the city. The population sought cover, while Arthur Schoeddert, constable of the antiaircraft artillery, who read air-raid reports on the radio and was nicknamed "Uncle Valerian," failed to forward Holz's order to comply with the Führer's instructions to blow up gas, water, and electricity plants.[9]

For Daly and Able Company, the battle for Nuremberg commenced at dawn on April 17. The 1st Battalion of the 15th Regiment occupied the center with the 2nd on its left and the 3rd on its right. In the small villages north of the city, Daly's company encountered mines, heavy mortar fire, and an infantry counterattack that it repulsed thanks in part to a timely warning from Lt. Frank Burke, motor officer of the 1st Battalion. He had spotted German troops earlier and had singlehandedly killed many before their attack on Daly's company. Daly also encountered an incongruous situation in a wooded park on the outskirts of Nuremberg. As his men crouched in the woods with the city in the distance, young German soldiers and girls on their bicycles pedaled along a path into view. Because he did not want to risk hurting the girls, Daly radioed back to headquarters to report the situation and to ask what action he should take. He obtained permission to shoot over their heads in order to scare them away, which he did.[10]

The next morning, April 18, Daly led his company (which had not slept for twenty-four hours) into the city to confront the Nazi last stand. In a message to Hitler, Holz acknowledged that the military situation had become desperate even as "the final struggle for the town of the Party rallies has begun." He affirmed, however, that "the soldiers are fighting bravely, and the population is proud and strong," and he vowed to "remain in this most German of all towns to fight and to die." He ended by assuring Hitler: "In these hours, my heart beats more than ever in Love and Faith for the wonderful German *Reich* and its people. The National Socialist idea shall win and conquer all diabolic schemes." Hitler thanked Holz, who personally led raids against American tanks, for his "exemplary conduct" and awarded him the Golden Cross of the German Order.[11]

Once American forces broke the ring of flak guns, the fight became an exercise in urban warfare—costly, painstaking, street-by-street, block-by-block, house-by-house, combat, "defeating one more futile though dangerous counterattack launched by a few men, a squad, a platoon." All the while, American fighter-bombers and artillery kept pounding an already ruined metropolis. Fierce fighting raged along the ring around the old town and in the residential areas near Bayreuther Strasse (the main road into the city from the northeast). Those houses that had survived the air raids were destroyed. The Germans fought more bitterly and more fiercely as they retreated behind the high sandstone wall, complete with towers and a castle, that partially enclosed the old city.

To counter propaganda that they would kill civilians, the Americans used loudspeakers to tell the people that they should stay in their houses and cellars during the fighting. They further instructed them to put white sheets on their homes. The Americans compelled some German police to accompany them in order to give people instructions. Civilian residents of the city and its outskirts sought shelter in public bunkers and cellars. The grandfather of fifteen-year-old Max Goebel observed bitingly: "[The Americans are] getting ever closer with their cannons. I hope those last 'heroes' out there get lost soon, otherwise we too will be in trouble. I'm afraid there are some SS men who still want to win the war."[12]

As Able Company entered the city, it began to take sniper fire from civilians, firemen, policemen, and soldiers. A sniper killed two platoon scouts and then came out of hiding and surrendered. Enraged by the deaths of the two scouts, the lieutenant who led the platoon seized the sniper by the arm and pulled him down into the basement of a building. He stood the man against a wall, backed off, and then peppered him from head to foot with fire from his carbine. According to Troy Cox who witnessed the incident, "It was not a pretty sight." Knowing Daly's stand on the treatment of prisoners, none of

Nuremberg. *Courtesy National Archives.* Troops of the 15th regiment move through the ruins of Nuremberg toward the medieval walls surrounding the old city. The Nazi *gauleiter* of the city ordered a fight to the death. The rubble produced by relentless Allied bombing in the previous months inadvertently proved advantageous to German snipers. Daly's efforts to deal with such a threat to his men on April 18, 1945, led to his receiving the Medal of Honor.

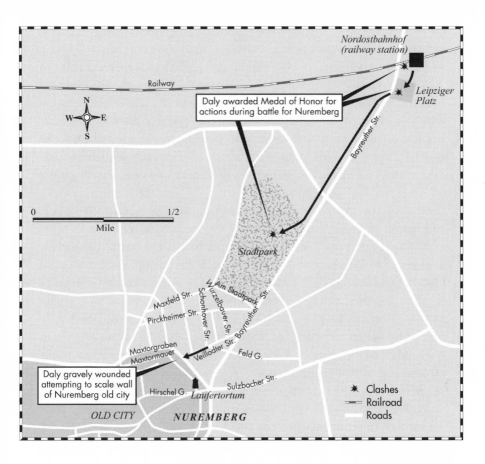

Nordostbahnhof
(railway station)

Leipziger
Platz

Railway

N
W—E
S

Daly awarded Medal of Honor for
actions during battle for Nuremberg

Bayreuther Str.

0   1/2
Mile

Stadtpark

Maxfeld Str.
Pirckheimer Str.
Schonhover Str.
Wurzelbauer Str.
Am Stadtpark
Bayreuther Str.

Maxtorgraben
Maxtormauer
Veilloder Str.
Feld G.

Daly gravely wounded
attempting to scale wall
of Nuremberg old city

Hirschel G.
Laufertortum

Sulzbacher Str.

✳ Clashes
═══ Railroad
___ Roads

OLD CITY

NUREMBERG

the men said anything to the captain, who remained unaware of what they
had done to the captured sniper.[13]

Recognizing the danger that snipers posed to his men, and intensely determined to bring back home as many of them as possible, Daly took the point
as they made their way down *Bayreuther Strasse.* What took place immediately thereafter would result in Daly's being awarded the nation's highest
military honor.

Initially, a machine-gun nest in a water tower pinned down the unit, but
Daly maneuvered into a position from which he was able to silence it with a
few well-placed carbine shots, allowing the company to move forward. Still
on the outskirts of Nuremberg, Daly found Bayreuther Strasse blocked by the
wreckage of a railroad bridge—part of the light railway line that ran around
the northern part of the city. As he swung to the right of the twisted wreckage
and led his men onto a low rail embankment with the ruins of the small sta-

tion—Nordostbahnhof—and some rolling stock to his left, machine-gun fire erupted from across the Leipziger Platz, raking the exposed party and killing and wounding a number of his troops. Daly emphatically ordered his men to take cover. Then Sergeant Cox saw "that long-tall boy running stooped over with his carbine." Daly sprinted across the tracks through a hail of bullets kicking up all around him toward the machine-gun nest. He reached shelter in some rubble about fifty yards from it. Jumping to a standing position, he fired his carbine and struck one of the enemy. He then sprinted to a new position, as machine-gun bullets riddled the earth around his feet, and he picked off the remaining two gunners.

Moving Able Company aggressively and quickly, Daly encountered a German patrol equipped with *panzerfäuste* and ready to strike at the tank attached to his company. Signaling for his men to halt and, in the words of his staff sergeant, Ivan Ketron, "taking his life in his hands," Daly moved out alone toward the ruins of a house. From there he observed three Germans to his front and then, before opening fire with his carbine, waited for another three to come into his gunsight. The German soldiers peppered Daly's position with a hail of automatic fire "that sent up eddies of fine white dust from the building he was shooting from." *Panzerfaust* charges slammed against the farthest wall of the building, but the captain coolly continued firing, killing all six members of the enemy patrol.

With artillery, machine-gun, and sniper fire resounding around them, Daly led his men to the debris-filled city park that served as the nerve center for enemy resistance. A well-concealed machine gun opened up on his men, and Daly started back across the street to locate it. He found it when it fired on him from a range of about fifty yards sending bullets between his legs. Daly killed the gunner with a rifle shot and then calmly directed his men to set up their own machine gun in a nearby crater. Standing beside it, he directed fire that killed the remaining three German gunners.

Still in the lead, Daly turned back into the park. As he paused to position his platoons, two Germans rushed from concealment and set up a machine gun only ten yards from where Daly stood. The machine gunner opened fire, killing a sergeant next to him. Seizing the fallen man's M-1 rifle from the ground, an enraged Daly engaged his assailants at point-blank range. The machine gunner died instantly, but the assistant gunner was only wounded. When he struggled to his feet firing a submachine gun, Daly brought him down with one more shot. Daly had killed fifteen Germans, wiped out three machine-gun nests, and destroyed an enemy patrol.

Col. Hallett Edson, commanding officer of the 15th Regiment, said of Daly: "He infected his men with some measure of heroism and demoralized the enemy by the uniform deadliness of his fire. . . . His heroism towered above the courage of those around him." Sergeant Kurtz claimed that "Captain Daly smashed a path into the heart of [words missing] by performing the combat duties normally done by a full company." And Sergeant Ketron declared: "If it hadn't been for what Captain Daly did at Nuremberg, I don't know how many of us would have pulled through. . . . There was no fear in him as he rushed strong enemy positions to save us from being cut to pieces."

When asked many years later, why, as company commander, he had assumed the scout position, he answered that he had not planned to do so—he just instinctively reacted to the dangerous situation that the company faced. "It seemed the thing to do," he said. Decades later, James Elling, himself a winner of the Distinguished Service Cross for his action at Grossheubach, hung a calendar that Daly had sent him and underneath Daly's name wrote, "My hero." For his actions that day in Nuremberg—actions that a War Department press release described as a story that "reads like a Hollywood script"—Daly would receive the Medal of Honor, one of the last for action in the European Theater.[14]

But to Daly those actions were just part of the bitter, chaotic, numbing struggle to subdue Germany and end the war. Able Company proceeded farther into the city—all the while receiving sniper fire. On April 19, after spending the night in the city park, Daly and his men made their way to their objective: the still-imposing wall that surrounded medieval Nuremberg, where not a single building remained intact. Daly and Major Barr, the battalion commander, who was accompanying Able Company at the time, encountered two parallel walls: the first about six feet high, and the second, twenty yards beyond, about twelve feet high, with towers ideal for snipers. Rubble lay everywhere. After climbing over debris to reach the wall (which in other sectors had proven impervious to direct fire from antitank guns), the company received orders to scale it.

Daly's Company had received numerous orders over the previous months designating them to spearhead missions. Daly liked and admired Barr, finding him an excellent leader who combined courage with empathy for the GIs he commanded. Daly enjoyed an excellent relationship with his superior officer and joked that Barr needed to learn the alphabet because it seemed the only letter he knew in tough situations was "A" (for Able Company). But standing at the wall, both Daly and Barr thought the order made no sense. Snipers lurked all about, and obeying the order would be well-nigh suicidal.

Barr and Daly decided to call back to headquarters to explain the situation and try to convince them to let the company search for an opening in the wall at another point. Those back at headquarters, however, believing

The wall. *Courtesy Stadt Archiv Nürnberg.* Looking north from the *Laufer Tortum* (a tower in the southeast corner of the wall surrounding the old city) in 1941. By 1945, bombing and artillery fire had destroyed or severely damaged all the structures in this photo, including portions of the wall, and had produced great piles of rubble on both sides of it. The arrow indicates the area of the wall near the intersection of Maxtograben and Veilloderstrasse that Daly scaled rather than send one of his men. The wound he incurred was nearly fatal.

it necessary to keep maximum pressure on the Germans, insisted that Able Company scale the wall at that location. Daly felt that their obliviousness to the situation jeopardized lives unnecessarily.

The orders stood, however, and Daly, who was operating on pure adrenalin, told Barr, "If anybody goes up, I go first." His sense of responsibility for his men took over instinctively. He couldn't send anyone but himself over that wall. If they wanted to follow him, fine. But he would not order them to do something he had not done first—and certainly not at this stage of the war. He had a "bad feeling" about trying to scale the wall because of his certainty that snipers lurked on the other side. But reflecting the optimism and sense of invulnerability of youth, even in one who had previously suffered a bad wound and had seen many men die, he figured he would probably take a bullet but would survive.[15]

It was about noon. With Barr hoisting him with his hands, Daly jumped up to grab the top of the battered wall, part of which had fallen as rubble, on which Barr stood. As Daly started to pull himself up and over, a sniper's bullet fired from below him tore through the right side of his face and exited the left, clipping his right ear lobe, passing through his palate, and fracturing both his upper and lower jaws.

Daly fell back. Still conscious, he began to choke on the blood that filled his throat. Sgt. Jesse Fisher, carrying ammunition forward, heard what sounded like someone snoring. The noise came from Daly as he struggled to breathe with blood in his mouth and throat. The quick-thinking sergeant, now under fire himself, reached into Daly's throat with his hand and literally scooped the coagulating blood and mucus from his air passage. He repeated the procedure as medics carried Daly back on a stretcher. Then, so that blood would not run back down Daly's throat, Fisher threw him face down onto the hood of a passing jeep filled with the wounded.

As the jeep bumped back to the aid station, Daly pulled his tongue out as far as he could in a desperate attempt to breathe. "I thought I was finished," he recalled in a later interview. "I'd seen enough face wounds. I remembered to be still. But it was like there was a pillow over my face. I knew I was suffocating." The men of Able Company gave him up for dead.[16]

The medical personnel at the first-aid station felt the same way and immediately summoned a Catholic chaplain, Rev. Francis B. Thornton, to administer the last rites of the church. Daly later said that when the priest walked in, he felt "a bit disconcerted," realizing how close to death he was. But he also felt an immense sense of relief because he still felt guilty about his wild time in Paris and needed to receive absolution. Thornton later wrote Daly a letter in which he said that he had rarely seen anyone more happy and grateful to see a priest than when Mike saw him enter the room![17]

The doctors at the 3rd Unit, 10th Field Hospital, performed an emergency tracheotomy and decided to operate on Daly the next day. Before he went to surgery, he had another visitor, General Patch, who described his visit in a letter to his wife: "It was a dreadful sight. He had a tube in his throat, could not speak, and was receiving a blood transfusion. I walked over to his bed and looked at him, and through one partly opened eye I felt that he recognized me and so I held out my hand and he took it. . . . When I left that evening, the doctor could not tell me whether he would pull through." Later, Patch told a newspaper reporter that he had doubted Mike would make it.

Meanwhile, Madeleine Daly received the third telegram from the War Department in eighteen months informing her that one of her loved ones had been wounded. In that same April approximately 41,000 other families received the same or worse news as a result of fighting in the European Theater. Thankfully, Patch turned out to be a better general than prognosticator. After the doctors operated on Daly, he was returned to his ward in good condition with a temporary bandage holding the lower jaw in place. A relieved Patch paid him another visit.[18]

Back at the walls of the old city, Barr refused to risk any more men in trying to scale the wall. He ordered them to move along it in search of an entrance. Late in the afternoon they, with other companies of the 18th and 30th Regiments, moved into the old city through Sulzbacher Strasse, at its junction with Maxtorgraben and Bayreuther Strasse. German units, however, continued to resist both the 3rd and the 45th Infantry Divisions, forcing the US forces to employ heavy artillery and bomber aircraft. At 1030, the German combat commander, Colonel Richard Wolf, ordered by the Army High Command to defend Nuremberg "to the last bullet," realized the hopelessness of the situation and sent an order via couriers to all combat units to cease fire at 1100.

Prominent Nazis, however, refused to do so. Many had taken shelter in the Palmenhof Bunker in the city police station, where they were surrounded by American troops. There, Nuremberg's Lord Mayor, Willi Liebel, committed suicide. Holz and his men fought on from the ruins of the station even though they no longer had numbers large enough to secure the big building from all sides. Most of those remaining planned an escape attempt that night. Calm and composed, Holz declined three or four offers from an American negotiator to surrender. He also refused to participate in the planned escape and indicated to one of his men (who survived) that he would commit suicide as the police headquarters fell. That evening though, he was seriously injured by one of the tank shells continually battering the station. He lived only five minutes.[19]

Nuremberg fell on April 20, the same day that Daly underwent his operation, and also, fittingly enough, Hitler's fifty-sixth birthday. That afternoon, General Patch reviewed a victory parade at the hastily cleared Hauptmarkt— also known as Adolf Hitler Platz—during which American troops raised the US flag over the city. The following day, Seventh Army Commander Patch, XV Corps Commander, Gen. Wade H. Haislip, and commanders of the 3rd and 45th Divisions, reviewed American combat units as they paraded through the heart of the city with army planes flying overhead. On April 22, following another victory parade by the 3rd Division through the Zeppelinfeld, the site of massive Nazi Party rallies, American engineers blew up the *hakenkreuz* (laurel wreath and swastika) perched above the tribune (speaker's stand) at the Nazi Party congress grounds, a powerfully symbolic event recorded by cameras and shown throughout the world.

The five-day battle for Nuremberg cost the lives of more than a thousand German soldiers and 371 civilians, with fewer than 150 GIs killed. Seventeen thousand defenders became prisoners. Some German sources insist that more than five hundred SS troops in the vicinity of Dachau and Nuremberg died at the hands of the American soldiers in the final days of the war.[20]

By V-E Day, May 8, Able Company had entered Austria. Near the city of Salzburg the company set up a tent camp that the men named "Camp Daly" in honor of their fallen captain. Sergeant Lebowitz, the amateur photographer who had taken a number of photos during the war, put together a scrapbook while at Camp Daly. Under the photograph showing an exhausted Daly returning from a patrol, Lebowitz wrote, "Captain Michael Daly—the best officer and bravest man I ever knew." Able Company of the 15th Regiment subsequently became known as "Daly Company."[21]

12 Escaping The Hero's Cage

Fairfield, Connecticut, August 24, 1945.

Shortly after 6:30 p.m., Capt. Michael Daly returned to a hero's welcome in his hometown of Fairfield. Banners reading "Welcome Home, Captain Michael Daly, CMH" hung all over town, especially along Boston Post Road (US Highway 1) in the business district. A crowd of more than two thousand, including a marching band, braved a downpour to line the platform of the Fairfield train station. As the young hero stepped off the special train that had borne him and his family home from Washington, DC, the band played "We Won't Go Home Till Morning," and the gathering greeted Daly with unrestrained cheering. Mike Daly was the toast of the town! The pride of Fairfield! When the cheering stopped, however, the twenty-year-old would face a dilemma: what to do as an encore with the rest of his life?

On April 23, 1945, a military plane evacuated Daly by air to Paris and then to the 105th General Hospital, in England, where his jaw was wired shut. He stayed in a ward that held only men suffering from facial wounds. He couldn't feel sorry for himself after seeing others so "horribly wounded." His own wound left him with a partially paralyzed palate that caused difficulty in enunciating clearly and also a noticeable hoarseness in his voice, but by the time he departed for the United States on board a hospital ship, he was ambulatory. During the voyage he used a problem he was having with his ear to entertain the other guys. As a result of the wound and his surgery, a small air passage had been created from his ear to his palate. When saliva formed in his mouth, Daly would pull on his cheek and spit it out his ear! Arriving in the States, he was flown to Cushing Hospital in Framingham, Massachusetts, outside Boston.[1]

His parents did not know the exact time and date of their son's arrival. Once he had checked into Cushing Hospital, Daly—who did not yet know that he had been recommended for the Medal of Honor—secured a pass and traveled home. He was anxious to see how his father's recovery was proceeding and to reassure his parents that he was physically whole and all right.

A hero's welcome. *Courtesy Connecticut Post.* A crowd of 2,500 welcomed Daly home to Fairfield, Connecticut. "This is the 'swellest' thing that ever happened to me," he told the cheering throng.

Glad to be back home to see his family and its menagerie of pets, including his horse, Woodsmoke, Daly nevertheless described feeling "strange" in the setting. About his war experiences he said little to either of his parents because he felt "awkward" doing so. His father was convalescing, and his mother, who struggled with bouts of depression, had a large family to manage. Mike did not want to burden them. Father and son, both veterans, had shared a common experience, and each surmised what the other had gone through. Actually, Mike rarely discussed his experiences with anyone in the family except perhaps to recount a humorous incident. When his sister Madge visited him at Cushing Hospital, however, where he was undergoing speech therapy, he did whisper to her that when he was in a tight spot, he thought of Roland and Oliver—an implied tribute to his father's influence.[2]

The parallels between Mike and Paul Daly's experiences at West Point and their gallantry on the battlefield raise two interrelated questions. How much did Mike consciously or unconsciously seek to emulate his father? And how much of his combat performance stemmed from an attempt to prove himself to his father or even to surpass his father's achievements? Reflecting about it decades later, Mike observed that his father's record influenced him in that it mirrored what his father stood for. "Brought up like that with a father like that—it became a part of me. I never gave it a particular thought. I never consciously thought, 'What would he do?' or, 'Would I do better than he?' At that juncture, what he stood for and the way he had raised me influenced me, but it was not as evident to me then as it became later." Mike claimed that during the war he did not feel that he was competing with his father for military glory. Indeed, he said, "I was always surprised by the medals." Still, Mike had talked about feeling the need to redeem himself in the army after his misadventures at Portsmouth Priory and West Point, and in this he now felt he had succeeded. But he considered his father the genuine hero of the family: the epitome of the gentleman officer who had been unfairly denied the Medal of Honor that Mike now wore.[3]

Convalescing at Cushing Hospital in July 1945, Daly received word that he would receive the Medal of Honor personally from President Harry Truman, one of the last two Medals of Honor awarded for action in the European Theater. On August 23 he traveled to Washington, DC. The drizzling rain forced the ceremony from the White House lawn to the gilded, chandeliered East Room. At twenty years of age, Daly was the youngest among the twenty-eight officers and enlisted men to be similarly honored. During the four years of war, 144 of the 440 Medals of Honor awarded during the conflict were given for deeds of valor in the European theater of operations during the eleven months between D-Day (June 6, 1944) and V-E Day (May 7–8, 1945). Daly's 3rd Infantry Division boasted 36 recipients, the most for any division in World War II.[4]

A correspondent from the *Bridgeport Sunday Herald* who reported on the ceremony disapprovingly described the ninety-minute occasion as "pompous, stilted, cut-and-dry, coldly impersonal, routine, lacking any emotional uplift." It "was grossly inadequate, if not grotesquely so," he complained. Those scheduled to receive their awards and about one hundred fifty proud family members and friends gathered in their assigned places. Daly's parents and his six brothers and sisters attended. Promptly at 10:00 a.m., music broke the silence that had settled over the audience, and all present rose as President Truman entered.

The awards ceremony began with each honoree receiving his medal alphabetically, one by one. An army officer announced Mike Daly's name when his turn came. Daly walked to the center of the platform and stood there while the army officer in a barely audible, sing-song voice read Daly's citation with the audience catching every third word. President Truman then placed the medal around Daly's neck. According to the *Bridgeport Sunday Herald*, Truman closed the ceremony "with a few prosaic sentences." The president then walked out, and army and navy officials, including the acting secretary of war, the secretary of the navy, and General George C. Marshall, army chief of staff, formed a receiving line and shook hands with the medal recipients. Daly offhandedly remarked to reporters, "Sometimes, things like this are harder to go through than battles." More seriously, he told newsmen

Medal of Honor recipients in East Room of the White House. *Courtesy Daly Family Photos.* Some of the twenty-eight officers and enlisted men who, on August 23, 1945, received the Medal of Honor from President Truman in the East Room of the White House. At twenty years of age, Daly (second row, two seats to Truman's left) was the youngest of those honored.

that he was "just lucky"—that "It is the 'guys' who didn't come home who deserve the medals."

The *Bridgeport Sunday Herald* included an insert in the middle of its story that read "Flunking Doesn't Matter to Dalys." It pointed out that in "flunking out" of West Point, Mike had followed in his father's footsteps and that both had become war heroes. Paul Daly expressed regret that Senator Francis Maloney, the man who had selected Mike as his appointee to West Point in 1942, had not lived long enough to know that his appointment had turned out "all right" after all. The senator's former secretary triumphantly claimed, "Senator Maloney was always a good picker of men. Daly was officer material, definitely, and Senator Maloney knew it. All those West Point people were all wrong, and Senator Maloney was right."[5]

Ned Morrill, who had served with Paul Daly in the 1st Division, paid tribute to both the son's valor and to the father's role in fostering it. He wrote: "I am reminded, Paul, of long dissertations by you, as we rode together many years ago, of the merits of thoroughbred horses: their stamina, heart, courage, and superlative performance which results in victories in the field for which they are trained. What I did not know, nor did you tell me that to these qualities can be added in men, those of intelligence, faith, religion, and family pride, which go to make the thoroughbred soldier which your son is." He went on to tell the colonel that he always considered him "tops in the 1st Division in 1918" and to assure him that he did not invent this opinion. "When it comes to gallantry in two wars," he continued, "I am sure that Michael would be the first to acknowledge the source of his inspiration." The son had received an inheritance, Morrill concluded "and with it has, by his own virtue, built a fortune of glory which he will transmit to your family, and our country, for years to come."[6]

After the Medal of Honor ceremony, Mike and his family entrained for Fairfield. There, greeted by a large crowd and escorted through a guard of honor, Mike climbed onto the closed-back top of an open roadster. Flanked by marching veterans and accompanied by the band, his officer's hat pushed back onto the crown of his head (making him look even younger than he was), Mike sat perched on the car as it made its way slowly past lines of smiling, shouting, sometimes tearful people. A police car led the procession, which included cars carrying Daly's family. General Patch had planned to accompany the family back to Fairfield, but pressing business in Washington, DC, forced him to cancel. Ignoring a raincoat that someone had handed to him, Daly smiled, bowed, and now and then leaned down to shake the hands of proud "Fairfielders" who ran out to greet him.

As Daly and family arrived at Fairfield's Roger Ludlowe High School, the town guard of honor escorted them to the auditorium platform. There Daly stood at attention as the cheering crowd of one thousand "took him to their hearts," in the words of one observer, giving him an ovation that lasted more than three minutes. During the ceremonies, various speakers paid tribute to Daly and his heroism. Herbert L. Emmanuelson, the state American Legion commander declared, "Captain Daly typifies the top in American manhood." First Selectman John Ferguson joined in the encomiums and added that Mike had received his type of courage from his illustrious father, "whose war record is comparable to that of his son." Monsignor William J. Blake, pastor of Saint Thomas Aquinas Church, praised the young hero, asked God to bless him, and echoing Emmanuelson, declared, "You are a chip off the old block." (Within a short time, Mike's mother took to saying, "He's a block off the old chip.") After receiving a scroll from the city, a blushing but ever-smiling Daly summed up his feelings as he spoke briefly to the audience. Alluding to his impaired speech—an unintentional reminder to the crowd of the wound that he had suffered—Daly said, "I can't talk very well but I want to say that this is the 'swellest' thing that ever happened to me. A heck of a lot sweller than getting the medal from the President."

Among the admiring crowd stood twenty-three year-old Ann Kirk Shaw, a Fairfield resident who worked as a riveter on F4U Corsair airplanes at a Bridgeport, Connecticut, assembly plant. An unconventional and daring young woman, she had, much to the chagrin of her parents, spent part of her salary on flying lessons at the Women Air Service Pilots program and had become a pilot. As she watched Daly, she was struck by his tall good looks, his amazing war feats, and his almost painful shyness.[7]

Fairfield could not seem to get enough of its young hero. Attention focused on him again when Fairfield marked V-J Day on the night before the officially designated day. Seven to ten thousand people turned out to watch the torchlight parade through town that began shortly after 8:00 p.m. and was followed by a block party at Legion Field. There, as Mike led a group of servicemen in the line of march from the back seat of a jeep, he received an ovation. On the town-hall green he reviewed the marchers in front of the town honor roll. Later, at Legion Field, he addressed a large throng that had gathered at the tennis courts for a program of entertainment and dancing. Again he apologized for his voice, but according to the local paper, he "received a Frank Sinatra reaction" from the young ladies when, in prefacing one of his remarks, he said, "Now take me . . ." All the girls yelled, "We will!"

After the laughter had subsided, a clearly embarrassed Daly made the serious point that he had intended—a point he had kept reiterating since receiving the Medal of Honor: "I was darn lucky, and that's an understatement, but we should never forget, on this V-J Day, the boys who never came back and should receive the medals."[8]

Father Kirby, Daly's old Prefect of Discipline back at Georgetown Prep, the Jesuit who had disciplined Mike and repeatedly urged him to develop more self-control and a greater sense of responsibility, no doubt swelled with pride and flashed his signature grin when Mike returned for a low-key visit with the faculty on September 23. Word got out among the students about Daly's presence on campus, and a number of them eagerly sought him out. One of the boys later remembered that Daly, dressed in civilian clothes, had spoken with them in an informal setting, and that he replied cryptically and with apparent embarrassment when they asked about his combat prowess and medals. The following month, the first-ever issue of the school's alumni newsletter, *Gprep Alumnews,* published a photograph of President Truman awarding Daly the Medal of Honor. Alongside the photograph ran a description of Daly's heroism at Nuremburg. At the end of the academic year, the student yearbook, the *Cupola,* featured the same shot. One gushing writer in the *Washington Times Herald* even attributed Mike's heroism to lessons he had learned playing athletics at Prep. Father Kirby surely hoped that he and the school had played at least a part in forming the hero Mike had become.

Father and son. *Courtesy Daly Family Photos.* Both father and son had been seriously wounded in Europe. Shrapnel from mortar fire severed the sciatic nerve in Colonel Daly's left leg, and Mike spent a year in and out of hospitals after being wounded in the palate and jaw by German gunfire.

In December 1945, *American Legion Magazine* ran an article, entitled "Daly Double," that featured both war heroes, father and son.[9]

Three months earlier, on September 15, Mike had celebrated his twenty-first birthday. To mark the occasion, Paul Daly enlisted his twelve-year-old son, Gilroy ("Roy"), to drive him to every bar in town, where he laid down a wad of cash and declared that the drinks "were on Michael." Privately, Paul Daly told his son he had never known a "gentleman" who had won the Medal of Honor," that they were "rough necks." Paul Daly probably meant his comment as a warning to his son about the pitfalls and temptations, especially to hubris and its partner, boorish behavior, that he might fall prey to. No doubt Paul hoped his words would spur Mike to conduct himself with the decorum Paul associated with gentlemanly behavior. Whatever his motivation, the comment stung Mike, but he never discussed it with his father. And as things turned out, Paul Daly would have reason for concern.[10]

Meanwhile, about a month after Mike's birthday celebration, the Dalys hosted another party. When General Patch, who had been stationed in Washington, DC, as chairman of a high-level board tasked with reorganizing the army, completed his final report, he called Mike's sister Madge, who worked in the Pentagon, and invited her to fly with him aboard his assigned B-25 to visit her parents in Connecticut. "I'm sick of all this, and I want see your father," he told her. Patch enjoyed the visit and left feeling refreshed, but he and the Daly family would never see each other again. Vulnerable to pneumonia, which he had contracted several times both before and during World War II, and having suffered a bout of malaria in the Pacific, Patch fell ill in November

1945. Initially doctors gave a positive prognosis, but his A-type pneumonia worsened, and he died on November 21, two days short of his fifty-sixth birthday. In the space of a year, Mrs. Patch had lost a son and a husband, and Paul Daly had lost his best friend. And the death of the old family friend who, as commander of the Seventh Army, had taken such a personal interest in Mike and been so instrumental in his gaining a commission, deeply saddened Mike, who had experienced so much death and loss.[11]

In addition to these trials, Mike also spent the next year in and out of hospitals as doctors dealt with complications arising from his injuries.[12] He had lost thirty pounds since being wounded. But his hospital stays did not seem to depress him. Freed from the burden of wartime—and perhaps also seeking to escape some bitter memories of combat—he acted the kid again. His irrepressible sense of fun and mischief turned his hospital sojourns into something of a party.

At Cushing Hospital he had to undergo some corrective surgery, including removal of the wires that bound his jaw. After the operation, as attendants wheeled him down the corridor with all of his face but his prominent nose bandaged, he heard a voice cry out, "I'd know that nose anywhere!" The voice belonged to Kevin Hughes his friend from Portsmouth Priory who in early 1942 had accompanied Mike on his ill-fated night trip into Portsmouth and with him had been expelled. Hughes had subsequently joined the army, served in North Africa, and then left his unit without permission to join the Rangers. He had been seriously wounded by machine gun fire at Anzio.

Kevin and Mike reconnected, having some great times in Cushing and at what Daly called the "surrounding gin mills," including Ken's Steak House, in nearby Framingham. "In those days it was a small place with a bar—steaks, mashed potatoes, salad, and all you could drink!" They spent hours there enjoying themselves, and they became friends with the owner. On one of Daly's visits to a bar shortly after having had the wires removed from his jaw, he got into a fight with a "braggart sailor." Looking back many years later, a close friend remarked, "When you were drinking with Michael in the early days, he would often start throwing punches whether in play or earnest by the end of the evening." As a result of his brawl with the navy man, he had to have wires reinserted into his jaw, and the doctor strongly admonished him to avoid any more fights![13]

When back in Fairfield, Daly began to date Ann Shaw. She was three years older and a Protestant, but the Medal of Honor recipient and the daring female pilot (who would become the first woman commercial-helicopter pilot in the United States) hit it off. He was a local hero, she recalled later, "with a fantastic, big, important family" and a "gruff" father, who scared her to death. They enjoyed one another's company and had, in her words, "an awfully good time" going "out on the town" with friends. Many years later she recalled that "he was fun to be with and to talk to" (although he did not talk about his wartime experiences). And he was very kind.

Because of his injuries Mike had to leave Fairfield for a while for treatment, during which time he and Ann lost touch.[14] In addition to his fragile jaw, partially paralyzed palate, and weight loss, Mike also had developed pleurisy, which subsequently became pneumonia and left him somewhat debilitated. He recovered quickly, but his doctors, fearful that the pneumonia might presage tuberculosis, sent him to Fitzsimmons General Hospital in Denver, Colorado. When he walked into his hospital room, Daly found that he had a roommate. A skinny, blond guy named Parnell "Paul" E. Bach was already bunked in. Daly took the open cot by the window.

Like Daly, Bach was a twenty-one-year-old. He held the rank of first lieutenant in the Army Air Corps. Bach remembered Daly as "tall, erect, impressive" with dark hair and a big, friendly smile. "He was an infantry captain. . . . He was wearing so many decorations I had to do a double-take to believe what I saw. He had *the Congressinoal Medal of Honor!* When Michael undressed to get into his bed, I saw wound marks everywhere. The guy had obviously been through a lot." Bach recalled that over time he managed to coax some stories out of Daly, but he found him extremely modest and reluctant to talk about his war exploits. Bach later wrote: "I have never met anyone more unassuming, polite, and kind. He was reluctant to speak of it at all." But he showed no reluctance about engaging in mischief.

Confined to the hospital for testing and further care, the patients could not obtain passes to go into Denver. The location of Daly's cot under a window, however, provided a handy solution to that problem. According to Bach: "He found ways to go through windows and under fences that would be good copy for cat burglars! He was a constant source of awe."[15]

When Daly did return to Fairfield between periods of hospitalization, and after he was discharged from the army in September 1946, with a disability that paid him $175 per month, he found himself feted as a hero and caught up in a heady whirl of partying. During late-night outings at local bars, especially Sullivan's Bar and Grill, a hangout for veterans, someone always seemed to want to buy him a scotch. He wasn't sleeping much, and he closed a lot of bars with his friends. "I spent a lot of time with people who had been in combat," he said later. "I met them in bars. We shared a natural understanding. We didn't talk about specific incidents, but we had a natural affinity with one another." Indeed, Daly almost never spoke about the war except to relate a humorous anecdote. A home movie taken of a uniformed Daly bestride his horse during the Memorial Day parade of 1946 reveals a

The hero's cage. *Courtesy Jack Ringel.* When Daly returned to Fairfield, he and his friends closed a lot of bars and even became involved in brawls. "I wasted a lot of time," Daly later said. "It took me a long time to grow up." In fact, it took him a long time to work through the emotional impact of the war. One night a close family friend said, "I think you should get a job." Daly took these words to heart. "I didn't want to become trapped in a hero's cage," he would later explain. "I had to get on with my life." The next day he landed a job with Atlas Supply Company, a subsidiary of Esso Oil. Uneasy in a large corporation, he ultimately started his own business— Daly and Associates—selling automotive accessories to oil companies.

pensive, somewhat burdened and detached figure—handsome, popular, and dashing, but lonely—caught in a hero's cage.

Mike's parents did not say much to him about his late-night hours, excessive drinking, and unruly behavior, but it was hard on them, and he sensed their unhappiness. Perhaps this was when Paul Daly made his disparaging remark about Medal of Honor winners. "The attention of being a hero throws you off track," Mike commented later. Some advised him to return to West Point. Old Gen. Frank Parker told Paul that he hoped Mike would return to finish his course. "I imagine," Parker wrote, "there will be no one to oppose his application." He added, "Were he my son, I should so advise him. Time lost now will be more than compensated in the long pull."[16]

Mike, however, had no desire to reprise his experience at West Point and could not see a future for himself in the peacetime army with all its "spit and shine." Others urged college and law school, but at twenty-one or twenty-two, Daly felt older than his years. With all the experiences he had during the war, returning to school with younger students didn't appeal to him. (As a result of the GI Bill, however, colleges were flooded with veterans, many older than Daly.) In truth, Mike did not want to return to school because he had never liked it. That would eventually constitute his greatest regret in life. "I wasted too much time. I should have gone back to school," he remarked more than once. This, even though he showed remarkable intelligence, cultivated an insatiable curiosity about a wide range of subjects, wrote elegantly, quoted epigrams and lines of poetry frequently, and generally became well read.[17]

Instead, like other Medal of Honor winners and many returning veterans in general, Daly felt himself adrift, disengaged—unable to determine what a "twenty-something" hero should/would do with the rest of his life. One night in 1946, Harry Holt, an elderly and distinguished neighbor and friend of the family whom Mike respected deeply, took him aside and said simply, "Mike, I think you should go to work." Mike experienced the man's words like a splash of cold water in his face. They woke him from his depression-induced lethargy. Discontented and uneasy with the course of his life, Mike took the man's words to heart. "I didn't want to become trapped in a hero's cage," he would later observe. "I had to get on with my life." The next day he landed a job as a salesman with Atlas Supply Company, a subsidiary of Esso Oil, headquartered in New Jersey. He moved to New York City and took a room in the house of a cousin of his father, a widow named Kathleen Madigan, who lived in Hamilton Park near Harlem.

But his wild streak, often fueled by alcohol, persisted. One friend recalled that the Dalys (including Madge, Roy, Bevin, and Dermot) "were offended if you didn't have a drink with them and would protest vehemently if someone tried to leave "early." He needed to steel himself for his get-togethers with the Dalys because drinking with them "in the early days was a contact sport," often ending "with fists flying," either in sport or in anger. Mike had fancied himself a good boxer since his father had arranged for him to have boxing lessons in the fifth grade. (Hence Mike's desire to spar with Joe Louis in England.) He loved the sport of boxing. Quick fists and a competitive nature, coupled with alcohol and pent-up emotions, proved a volatile mix. Daly later admitted, "It took me a long time to grow up."

During that interval, he continued to get into scrapes, one of them leading to a newspaper story quite different from the admiring pieces he had grown accustomed to. Shortly after Mike had started to work for Atlas, he, his friend "Bish" McDonnell, and McDonnell's sister were in a bar in New York City. They drank too much and got into an argument with the proprietor that escalated into a fight. When police arrived to break it up, McDonnell, pointing to Daly, indignantly and insistently proclaimed that they didn't realize *who* they were arresting. That led to a piece in the *New York Journal American* describing Daly as a "self-styled war hero" who had started a brawl on 42nd Street. Daly and McDonnell spent the night in jail, where Mike worried about the possible effect of the incident on his newly acquired job. The next day, Daly and McDonnell, represented by a lawyer, appeared before a magistrate along with the proprietor, who had bandages on his face. Thanks to the lawyer's efforts, the proprietor decided not to press charges, everyone shook hands, and the judge dismissed the case.

But incidents associated with alcohol continued to occur. Mike's office building stood next to the Biltmore Hotel, whose "Men's Bar" became a favorite "watering hole" for Daly and company. Because the hotel lay just across the street from Grand Central Station, Daly and friends would hit the bar before traveling back to Fairfield and then would continue drinking in the bar on the train. Not infrequently they would fall asleep, miss their stop at Fairfield, and be awakened by the conductor at the end of the line, in New Haven. Sometimes, however, Daly and his comrades would become cantankerous. One altercation involved Daly and his old buddy, Bill Keeley, who had "helped" Mike sink the sailboat in Long Island Sound and later had served as a Marine in the Pacific. Traveling in the bar car, they began arguing about "the Army vs. the Marines." A lot of pushing and shoving ensued. Before any blows were thrown, the conductor summoned the railroad police, who arrested both men. Daly spent another night in jail. Again a lawyer took care of the legal situation and arranged to have the charges dropped. Daly's parents were mortified by Mike's run-ins with the law, but they could do little except signal their disapproval of behavior that echoed the "bad boy" of prewar years.[18]

In truth, Daly's drinking and brawling behavior was not uncommon among returning GIs. Many who carried unresolved anger, guilt, and assorted demons of war with them turned to alcohol in an attempt to ease their transition back into civilian life. Daly had developed such a sense of responsibility for his men that the guilt of having survived while so many of them had not, and the grief he felt at their loss surely ate at him. Late-night drinking bouts would have helped anesthetize those feelings. Today we recognize Daly's restlessness, drinking, fighting, and sleeplessness as symptoms often associated with posttraumatic stress disorder.

Like many others of his generation suffering the same symptoms, however, Daly soldiered on. He traveled extensively selling Atlas automobile accessories to Esso gas stations. The company then assigned him to Canada for a year, where he lived in Toronto. One night, returning from a bar where he again had drunk too much, he missed a turn in a square in front of Upper Canada College and wrecked his car by hitting the school's wrought-iron gate. In truth he was still floundering, still unable to rekindle the self-control and sense of responsibility that he had shown on the battlefield, still unable to find his purpose, his niche in life.

Mike did not like working for a large corporation. He craved the independence of working for himself. After seven years, when Esso spun off Atlas, he decided to leave. In 1953 he started his own company, "Daly and Associates," and sold automotive accessories to Atlas-licensee filling stations. By then he knew his way around the business, but when he found that winning clients was slow going, he had doubts about whether he could succeed as a salesman. Nor did he think highly of his occupation. Later he would refer to himself as a "peddler" who had lived "a life of compromise." But because he now ran his own business, he took some accounting courses at Pace University and some business courses at Columbia University.

His father regarded his efforts to become an independent entrepreneur as less than a "high endeavor." He expressed the hope that Mike would stay with a large corporation, which he regarded as a more respectable and gentlemanly occupation than that of an independent salesman. He did not say anything else, but Mike perceived an attitude of disappointment if not disapproval. During those years, Mike and his father drifted somewhat apart.

By now in his early thirties and with his business struggling, Daly followed the suggestion of a family friend who was a judge. He explored the idea of attending law school. In May 1956, by passing a qualifying exam administered by the University of the State of New York (today the State University of New York), he earned a Law Student's Qualifying Certificate. This allowed him to apply for admission to any registered law school. He considered running for a seat in Congress, but when his brother Roy decided to do so, Mike deferred. More outgoing than his reserved, buttoned-down brother (who wore a sport coat and tie while campaigning on the beach), Mike took his brother around to introduce him to the local Democratic politicos who would select the nominee. Paul Daly, long active in Democratic Party politics in Fairfield, carried considerable weight in the party but privately thought that his scholarly, reserved younger son was better suited to be a federal judge than a congressman. And some party leaders agreed. They encouraged Mike to run instead of his brother, whom one of them referred to as "Little Lord Fauntleroy." Mike, however, saw that his brother really wanted the opportunity. And he believed that he himself just had "too many skeletons in the closet" from his immediate postwar years. And he was feeling pressure to start making money. Roy lost badly in the race but eventually was appointed to the federal bench, where he served with distinction.[19] Roy was a successful man of the law. Mike, the war hero, seemed trapped in a cage of mediocrity amidst feelings of unfulfilled promise.

Causes Greater than Self

Kitzingen, Germany, August 1982.

In the midst of the deep hostility between the Reagan administration and the Soviet Union, Daly received an invitation from Lt. Col. Jared "Jerry" Bates, the young commander of the 1st Battalion, 15th Infantry, 3rd Division, to visit his old outfit, which was stationed in Kitzingen, Germany, near Würzberg, not far from Nuremberg. He hoped Daly's visit would "boost morale" among soldiers who would be on the line if "the balloon went up." Daly accepted and returned to Germany for the first time since having left on a stretcher thirty-seven years before. "You brought me back," he later joked in a speech, "and on my feet." Arriving at the base, he stayed in the "Audie Murphy Suite," where he spent a fitful night barely sleeping as "faces came back to me." Before dawn he walked across the parade field to a small memorial park where boulders bore plaques. He stood there alone as the sun's rays began to lighten the sky, "remembering, fighting against forgetting, fearing that if the memories dimmed he would become a stranger to himself."

That evening he addressed an officer's banquet. At their request, he wore his Medal of Honor, something he normally would not do. He found this occasion different—special. He felt himself among people who would understand what he said. He noted that he had served with two divisions, the 1st and the 3rd, "both excellent—but," he added, "my heart belongs to the 3rd." His voice cracking at times with emotion, he spoke movingly about the infantry, "the Queen of Battle": "When things hang in the balance, it is the infantry that a country calls on. It falls on them to close with the enemy and decide the day." And he spoke of his men: "We lost some of our best people. . . . They were often men who took the most chances and without whom you could never win a battle. They came from every walk of life—they represented the very best of my generation. You would have been proud to serve with them. As a platoon leader and company commander they sustained me then just as they sustain me now."

No speech had meant so much to him. Perhaps no moment since the end of the war had proved so cathartic for him. He employed the podium as his "bully pulpit" to preach the "gospel according to Daly." The human spirit cries for more, he declared, than self-interest and self-aggrandizement. "Every man deserves a cause greater than himself." To the soldiers in front of him he said: "All of us here are privileged people, for we have been called to defend the most noble experiment the world has ever known—that man can but seek his destiny while living in freedom." America's purpose was to "hold high the torch of liberty . . . to every freedom-loving person. . . . The bedrock of our values is our belief in the importance and sanctity of the individual." To that end he firmly insisted that true American soldiers abide by a code consistent with American values: "We do not shoot prisoners of war . . . terrorize civilian populations . . . or threaten the defenseless. For us to win in a way that would jeopardize our values would mean that we had failed." (Years later, during the Iraq war, reports of US soldiers abusing and torturing prisoners at Abu Ghraib prison—a stark betrayal of the code he cherished—would shock, dismay, anger, and deeply hurt him.) He ended by quoting Joseph Addison: "Courage is the thing. Everything goes if courage goes." He added, "Without courage there is no protection for our other values. Every man loses his courage at times. All of us should pray every morning that God will give us the courage to do what is right. And remember when you pray that if you rise at all a better man—your prayer has been answered. Never underestimate the good that one man can do." The officers rose and applauded appreciatively. "Remember us," he said, "as long as you can. We will never forget you."[1]

For twelve years after the war, Mike struggled to find his path in life. Then, one Sunday in 1957, he found it. The Smith family paid their weekly Sunday visit to the Daly house for drinks. This time they had invited an attractive, petite, straightforward, humorous, and talented woman named Margaret "Maggie" Miller to accompany them. It was at this gathering that Mike met Maggie, though he had seen her and known of her before they were formally introduced. Born Margaret Wallace, Maggie was the great-granddaughter of Lewis "Lew" Wallace, the author of *Ben Hur: A Tale of the Christ*. Growing up, she attended a "progressive" school that emphasized the arts, and she became interested in musical theater. As a young woman of college age, she performed in summer stock, and in September 1942 she landed an ingénue part for six months in the Broadway musical *Janie*. In June 1943 she married William Sanford Miller, with whom she had two children, a boy, W. Sanford Miller Jr., born in 1944, and a girl, Blair Miller, born in 1945. Maggie and William divorced in 1951.

Maggie knew Mike's mother through mutual friends. All of them regularly went together to the Melbourne Park racetrack, and that was where Mike first noticed her. She was a single mother living with her two children

A new mission. *Courtesy St. Vincent's Hospital Foundation. St. Vincent's Hospital, Bridgeport, Connecticut.* Always happiest when working on behalf of others and in the service of a cause greater than self, Daly found a new sense of mission at St. Vincent's Hospital (now Medical Center) in Bridgeport, Connecticut. Known as "the conscience of the hospital," he devoted himself to serving the needs of the terminally ill, the poor, and the neglected. In 1964 he joined the lay advisory board of the hospital, and in 1973 began twenty-two years on its governance board. In addition, in 1978, while still serving on the board of the hospital, he helped spearhead the creation of the St. Vincent Hospital Foundation. During his twenty-year stint on its board, he served as chairman for almost eight years, helping to raise tens of millions of dollars.

in her mother's house. The breakup of her marriage had devastated Maggie emotionally, and she was a long time recovering. Maggie was four years older than Mike, who at age thirty-two was still single, "a somewhat dissolute, aimless bachelor with possibly a drinking problem," according to his brother-in-law, William N. Wallace. Another friend of Mike and Maggie quoted Mike as saying he "never would have made it without Maggie." The friend continued, "Both had a salutary effect on each other, one recovering from the war and the other from a failed marriage."[2]

Mike and Maggie went through a three-year courtship that included her baptism in the Roman Catholic Church and the protracted (twenty-month), expensive process of obtaining a church dissolution of Maggie's first marriage. (Canon law allows an unbaptized convert to Roman Catholicism the privilege of terminating an existing marriage to an unbaptized spouse in order to marry a Catholic.) Thus Mike and Maggie were able to wed with the blessing of the church, something Mike wanted both out of religious conviction and tradition and because he knew how much their marrying in the church meant to his parents. He did not want to disappoint them on that score.

Finally, when everything seemed in order (thanks in part to help Mike received from a Jesuit friend at Fairfield University who was also a canon lawyer), Mike read in a newspaper that Pope Pius XII had recently departed Rome for his summer vacation at Castel Gondolfo. He flippantly remarked to Maggie that he hoped the elderly pope didn't die before he had signed off on their petition. But Pius XII did die that weekend, which necessitated more months of waiting until the new pope granted the petition. Mike and Maggie finally married on January 31, 1959. Following their marriage, they spent a year-long honeymoon in Ireland, living in a cottage in Wicklow, near the Irish Sea, while a trusted friend tended to Mike's business back home. Their daughter, Deirdre, was born there.[3]

On their return from Ireland, Mike and Maggie purchased a piece of property from Mike's parents and built a house about one-half mile from the one in which Mike grew up. Marriage provided Mike with emotional stability. Unlike Audie Murphy, who went through unhappy marriages and numerous liaisons, Mike found happiness and fulfillment with his wife. He found her full of levity, spunk, and fun, and he admired and enjoyed her immensely. (She irreverently referred to Mike's parents' place, Belle Assis, as "Belle Asses.") Marriage and "instant family"—he reared his two stepchildren—gave Mike a greater sense of responsibility and purpose, a greater incentive to "do well in the commercial world." Echoing his description of himself in combat, Mike said, "Family concentrated my mind. When people depend on you, you are more motivated and concentrated. You can't afford to fail."

At the time of his marriage, Daly was not wealthy, and he was worried about his prospects. Abandoning notions of law school and politics, he focused on making a living. The challenge of meeting the needs of his family restored in Mike the sense of working for a purpose beyond himself, but even though he became successful as a salesman, he drew little satisfaction, fulfillment, or joy from his job. Indeed, to find relief from what he called the "sales routine," he turned to reading, an activity he had not particularly enjoyed as a youth. He became an avid fan of the great eighteenth-century English writer Samuel Johnson and an avid collector of aphorisms.

Put simply, the needs of his family took precedence over his lack of enthusiasm for his career. The birth of his son Michael Wallace "Mickey" Daly on December 22, 1960, proved both joyful and challenging to him and his family. A doctor at Yale Medical Center diagnosed Mickey as "severely retarded" as the result of a brain injury he suffered at birth. Predicting that Mickey would never be able to walk or talk, the doctor recommended institutionalizing him.

Both the diagnosis and the prognosis struck Mike and Maggie like a shot. But shocked and pained as they were, both bridled at the doctor's suggestion that they institutionalize their son, and they refused to accept his prognosis. Mike felt uncertain about how to handle the situation, but Maggie devoted herself to finding a treatment that would help Mickey become a functioning, reasonably independent person. To that end, she and Mickey spent two months per year for three years in Philadelphia at the Institute for the Advancement of Human Potential, whose staff stimulated neurological development through exercises and activities similar to those used with stroke victims. Maggie, Mike, and Mickey succeeded. Mickey learned to walk and talk, attended school, and, came to hold down a job. After being toasted by friends and family at one of his birthday celebrations, Mike responded quietly, "Mickey Daly is the bravest soldier I have ever known."[4]

Mickey fortunately found himself in a loving, cohesive family environment in which the children of Maggie's first marriage and of her second regarded each as full brother and sister. When asked about how Mike functioned as a stepfather, Sanford Miller replied, "There was never a better one." And he and his sister loved Mike's car! It was "an Olds convertible, gray, with a red leather interior and lots of chrome. We . . . would sit in it for hours. The car was unfortunately stolen from the railroad station (by someone we went to school with) and totaled. My Mother said Michael never owned a great car after that. She called all his subsequent cars, dentist cars."

But fancy car or not, Sanford developed a deep bond with his stepfather, even before he came to appreciate fully the significance of the Medal of Honor and the heroism it represented. Like Mike, Sanford bucked rules and had a rough time at boarding school. When he returned home to live and to attend local schools, he was deeply grateful for the "discipline of kindness" and understanding Mike showed to him. No doubt the two recognized similar qualities in each other, including Sanford's penchant for raising hell. Sanford's decorated service with the army in Vietnam between October 1969 and November 1970 added an even deeper level of connection between the two. "The bottom line," he wrote, "is Michael Daly . . . was a great father, stepfather and grandfather, no disappointments there. I think Michael also had a profound impact on his grandchildren."[5]

In his relationships, Daly displayed a genuine social egalitarianism, an attitude reinforced by his experiences during the war. He wrote a friend, "You would have been so proud of these American soldiers often from the bottom of the economic ladder." His friends included an army general, a bank president, an electrician, an African American gardener, a Polish mason, and the fire chief and firemen of Fairfield. He treated employees and former employees of his household or business and their families as members of his family. Kevin Sjodan, whose grandmother had worked as maid at the Daly home for years, and whose mother served as Mike's secretary, became a close friend and served as an usher at his funeral. Margaret Wolonski, the nanny who tended Mike and Maggie's children, was a beloved figure in the

Daly household and traveled with the family to Deirdre's graduation from Dartmouth College. Daly's stepson, observed: "I think we all learned, or at least I did, that everyone is important, not just the rich, well educated, but people of character, who work hard. Michael Daly was a true egalitarian."

In February 1970, with Sanford fighting in Vietnam, and with the nation in social and racial turmoil, Daly used a newspaper interview, following naturalization ceremonies at which he had spoken, to turn the topic to black troops. He praised "the tremendous job the Negro soldiers are doing" in Vietnam. "It should be shouted from the roofs," Daly continued, calling it "the most positive thing that has happened in our race relations. Blacks are giving their lives for whites and vice versa. . . . The dedication of the black soldier has to be a great thing for the future of this country."[6]

Years later, in 1984, Capt. Jesse Pugh became the first African American to command "Daly Company." He had read the file on Daly, and one day during a gunnery exercise he picked up a pen and wrote him a letter. Daly replied, and that Christmas the men of the company sent Daly a Christmas card. Mike responded by sending Pugh a check for $200 and asking him to buy a drink for every man in the unit. When Pugh returned to the United States, the two men stayed in touch through letters and phone calls. And when Pugh returned from Operation Desert Storm in 1991, he said that, other than immediate family, "Mike Daly was the first person I wanted to make contact with. I guess it was the warrior spirit. I wanted him to know that I was here doing that job." They met for dinner, both men embracing as old friends and fellow comrades in arms, and did more talking than eating. When Pugh was promoted to the rank of lieutenant colonel in 1992, he invited Daly to the ceremony and Daly attended. Pugh had told Maj. Gen. John M. Pickler, the officer presiding at the ceremony, about his relationship with Daly. In a sign of respect, Pickler generously invited Daly to stand in the reception line with the general officers, where he received an outpouring of esteem from officers and enlisted men alike.[7]

Although his marriage and family proved rewarding for him, Daly still felt the gnawing absence of a "cause greater than self" in his life outside his family. He had always been happiest in the role of rescuer—the knight coming to the aid of those in distress. In 1964 he found such a role at St. Vincent's Hospital in nearby Bridgeport, Connecticut, then a bustling industrial center. St. Vincent's, which had opened in 1905, was sponsored and run by the Daughters of Charity of Saint Louis, a Roman Catholic order of sisters known for their work in hospitals, schools, and orphanages. There, at St. Vincent's, Daly found a new mission that would become his passion and his avocation. For thirty-four years, through his volunteer service to St. Vincent's, Daly would

Exorcising ghosts. *Courtesy Daly Family Photos.* With some of the men of "Daly"
Company. In 1982, in an emotional and cathartic visit to Able ("Daly") Company in
Germany, and in an address to the officers of the battalion, Daly exorcised some of
the "ghosts" of the war. On his return to the United States, he sent the company
commander money to buy each member of the company a drink.

come to the rescue of the "wounded," this time in a hospital setting rather
than on the battlefield. Perhaps his work in the hospital also served both as a
symbolic way of ministering to all those wounded men he had seen during the
war and as expiation for the German lives he had taken in combat. St. Vincent's gave Daly a greater sense of purpose in his life, something that, sadly,
eluded the hero-turned-actor Audie Murphy, who wrestled with personal
demons until his untimely death at age forty-six in a plane crash.

Daly's involvement with St. Vincent's began in 1964, when the Daughters of Charity were making decisions about a new hospital then under construction and scheduled to open in 1966. Alexander "Bud" Hawley, a non-
Catholic friend of Daly's who headed People's Bank in a part of Fairfield
known as Southport, approached him and asked him to consider serving on
a lay advisory board for the hospital. Given his personal history, Mike puck-
ishly responded, "I thought hospitals were places to stay out of!" Daly also
felt reluctant because of the press of his own business and family obligations,
but "something" told him he should do it.

Daly's interest in medical care stretched back to his experiences both during and after the war. Medical care, after all, had saved his life and mended
his wounds. But there was more. The heroic selflessness, care, and compassion that army chaplains and medics had shown in the field, which he had
both witnessed and experienced personally, impressed him deeply. In particu-

lar, he remembered the medic who stayed with Pvt. Joseph Daly throughout that freezing night in Alsace, as the young man slowly died of his wounds. Daly remembered his own feelings of helplessness at being unable to mitigate Private Daly's pain, or that of so many others whom he had seen wounded. He hated to see people suffer. Now, through St. Vincent's, he could help those suffering from injury and illness. He could put his Catholic faith's social teachings into action on behalf of those who needed rescuing, who needed healing.

Daly accepted the sisters' invitation. With each year, he became ever more involved in the hospital. In 1973 he became a member of the hospital's governance board, and he served in that capacity until 1995. Bony, tall, slightly stooped out of deference to his height, with high forehead, balding pate, graying, wispy hair, and prominent nose, Daly became a common figure at St. Vincent's. As he became more familiar with the hospital and its board and staff, he spent an increasing amount of time there. He took a personal interest in the institution and its people, walking the corridors, getting to know the nurses and staff. He told his son-in-law that if one really wanted to learn what was going on in a hospital, one needed to talk to nurses more than doctors. He was gentle, thoughtful, a good listener, and a quiet but tenacious advocate for patients.

Known for his dedication to improving patient care, he exercised the "due diligence" of a board member. Quietly, gently, and insistently he sought to promote improvements in the quality of hospital personnel, services, and programs. On one occasion, when the board had moved to finalize hospital privileges for a physician who had been cleared for credentialing by the hospital administration, Daly courteously but insistently objected. He knew of an incident involving the doctor and one of his patients in which the doctor had not acted in the patient's best interest, placing the patient at some risk. Daly stood firm in his opposition to the physician, and the board decided to deny privileges to the doctor. As was so characteristic of him, Daly sought to protect others. He would say, "The hospital gets better [for patients], or it gets worse. It never stands still." Clearly he wanted it to get better. But while he took a keen interest in physician credentialing and other quality-assurance measures, he became best known as a compassionate champion of the indigent, the elderly, and the terminally ill. Ronald J. Bianchi, vice-president of the St. Vincent's Foundation and vice-president for marketing and public relations of St. Vincent's, called him the "the conscience of the hospital."

He might well have added something about Daly's "Midas touch." Daly's expertise lay not so much in administration or finance as in institutional advancement through fund-raising. He and two other board members helped spearhead the hospital board's authorization of the St. Vincent's Hospital

Foundation. The foundation aimed to raise an endowment to protect, preserve, and advance the mission-driven services of the hospital that benefited
the community. In 1978, while still serving on the hospital board, Daly also
joined the board of the newly formed St. Vincent's Foundation. In 1986 he
became chair of its board, a position he filled for almost eight years. He re-
tired from the board of the Foundation in 1998.

His local celebrity as a war hero and his family's social prominence and
connections gave Daly entrée to the political and business elite in the area—
all potential major donors or influential with potential donors. His winning
personality, charm, sincerity, and commitment to the cause did the rest. He
was, after all, a pretty successful salesman by profession.[8]

Daly played a vital role in helping the St. Vincent's Foundation get off the
ground by garnering the support of two men from Fairfield, First Selectman
John J. Sullivan, and Bud Hawley, the president of People's Bank. Both men
feared that the headquarters of the Daughters of Charity might decide to use
money donated for St. Vincent's to fund other institutions or activities run by
the order. Daly effectively dispelled their misconceptions by assuring them of
the independent status of the foundation, which had its own board and act of
incorporation, separate from those of the hospital. And he personally pledged
that the money would stay at St. Vincent's. Daly enjoyed such standing and
credibility in the community that both men agreed to contribute. Their willingness to do so, according to a longtime member of the St. Vincent's Hospital Foundation, represented a great victory for Daly in that he eliminated
what had stood as a great stumbling block to expanded giving. In 1992, when
Daly stepped down as chairman of the board of St. Vincent's Foundation, he
received the Connecticut Hospital Association Award in recognition of his
service. By 2005 the endowment Daly had played such a key role in starting
and building had reached more than $100 million.[9]

As Daly focused on his growing family, business, and board responsibilities at St. Vincent's, his mother and father remained in close proximity, just
up the street. With the years the elder Daly's limp from his wound became
more pronounced. He rode horses until he was no longer able. Then, using his walker, he went to the pasture to watch his grandchildren ride. On
June 10, 1974, the man who had played such a prominent role in Michael's
life died in his home at the age of eighty-two. When the hearse containing his
body moved down the driveway, Mike, his siblings, and the household staff
all saluted. A faithful attendee of annual reunions of his beloved WWI 18th
Regiment, Paul Daly was laid out in his living room in full uniform in a flag-
draped coffin. During the three-day wake, veterans, neighbors, politicians,
and horsemen told stories, ate and drank, and paid their final respects to "the

Colonel." He was the very model of an officer and a gentleman. His lofty standards had spurred Mike to great heights of heroism but had also left him, despite his Medal of Honor and success in business, with a lingering sense of never having quite measured up. Memorabilia of his soldier-father hung above Mike's desk in his office at Daly and Associates. Two were framed photographs of Paul Daly in uniform: one, a head shot placed such that the father appeared to be gazing down at the son; the other, an elongated photo of him receiving the Distinguished Service Cross in front of drawn-up ranks on his return to the United States in 1919. An oversized French poster from World War I decorated the wall to the side of his desk.[10]

For almost thirty years after the war, Daly spoke little about his wartime exploits or his Medal of Honor. A family friend observed that Daly turned any and every conversation around to the other person: "I don't think I ever heard any interior revelations other than quotes or aphorisms about a general condition. He was simply not wired constitutionally to talk about himself. He seemed [predisposed] to talk in global, not personal, terms."

Daly touched base with Audie Murphy, who struggled with post-traumatic stress disorder and who bemoaned his troubles with ex-wives and girlfriends. And he attended some gatherings of the Medal of Honor Society. Although Daly avoided publicity about his wartime exploits, in a 1970 interview he acknowledged that the medal had helped some recipients and hurt others. "Some people blame their misfortunes on it," he said. With characteristic modesty and self-deprecation, he added, "It must be put in perspective. It is a purely personal thing. Your country does not owe you anything because you received this medal. After all, it was my [good] fortune that somebody wasn't shooting straight." In another, much later, interview, he reflected, "You've got to be careful. You can become a professional hero. There's an awful sadness with that. You spend your life going from ceremony to ceremony. You have to move on. Life is a long-distance race. If too much of your life is centered on things you did early—there's a sadness. You can only stand up and hear what you did a few times. It's something you did at one time. There is also an embarrassment about the killing aspect. You don't want to be known for killing."

Daly did not speak explicitly about it until the last days of his life, but his having killed German soldiers weighed on his conscience. Indeed, from the day he left Europe, Daly had been waging another war—one within. He touched on it in a letter written to a friend in 2003: "War and the knowledge of the terrible massive cruelties of our lifetime can lead to a certain pessimism—a tendency towards misanthropy. You have to fight that and be of good cheer." Daly's "good cheer" was very much an act of faith and will.[11]

The fortieth anniversary of "D-Day," in 1984, with its many ceremonies capped by President Reagan's eloquent speech in Normandy evoking the memory of "the boys of Pointe du Hoc," helped reignite interest in World War II. The nation "rediscovered" what Tom Brokaw dubbed "the greatest generation" in his influential book by the same title, and historian Stephen Ambrose among others turned out numerous books and articles highlighting the experiences of America's citizen soldiers. Several books about Medal of Honor recipients included accounts of Daly's action at Nuremberg. He was also the subject of an excellent article in the May 1983 issue of *Yankee* magazine. But Mike found the attention embarrassing and shied away from it. He regarded himself not as a hero but as someone who was at the right time and place. "Anyone," he once told William Wallace, "would have done what I did. Luck is important in life, but in combat it is crucial. The bravest things are often done with God the only witness." When the Fairfield Historical Society wanted to create an exhibit about his World War II service and awards, he demurred.[12]

The demons of war lingered in Daly's mind and soul. His otherwise lively eyes hinted at a pensive sadness; they bespoke, besides a buoyant, almost boyish spirit, deep pain. The aching memories of American men lost and the moral burden of German soldiers killed weighed upon him. But as one family friend observed, "The gentility, the responsibility he felt to the dead formed a hard shell over his insides. In the end, he was always a soldier." When he did bring up his wartime experiences, usually it was to share its comic aspects. Even when Sanford returned from Vietnam, the two men rarely discussed or compared their experiences.

A deeply sensitive person, Daly would sink into dark depressions, especially around Christmas and Memorial Day. According to Maggie and Sanford, he spent the better part of most Memorial Days alone, in mourning. Once when he spoke on Memorial Day in Weston, Connecticut, Harry Reasoner, who lived in nearby Westport, quoted him on his CBS nightly newscast. That would be Daly's last Memorial Day speech. On subsequent Memorial days he went to Mass, attended the town parade, and listened to others give speeches. Then, getting into his car, he drove along Long Island Sound and northward through small towns or down to West Point. At the Academy he walked the plain and visited the cemetery. He would return home after dark. "Certain memories make my bones shiver," he once told a writer, "You would think that that emotion would dampen with the years. Yet, strangely, it grows stronger."

In 1980 Daly's daughter, Deirdre, who was spending a semester abroad studying at Edinburgh University, attempted to understand better the part of her father's life that she did not know—the part that, as one writer said, he kept hidden away within himself, just as he kept his and his father's medals out of sight in a velvet-lined case. She crossed the English Channel to visit Omaha Beach. On viewing the seemingly endless rows of white crosses at the American cemetery above the beach, Deirdre thought of her father's solitary drives on Memorial Day and envisioned "an animal tearing at its own wound in an attempt to destroy the pain." When she returned, she and her father talked. He told her: "I used to wonder why my father looked back so much, even more as he got older. Now I understand. It's probably the one time in life when you are willing to sacrifice everything for the guy alongside of you. You never have that again. You forget the carnage and the sadness and you remember one thing—you had a cause greater than yourself." He had tried to impart that insight to the soldiers of "Daly Company" when he visited them in Germany in 1982.[13]

One result of renewed public interest in the war proved especially embarrassing to Daly. The Connecticut state legislature passed a law requiring that the Motor Vehicle Association issue special license plates to the six Medal of Honor holders in the state. According to William Wallace, Daly "felt horrified" when fancy red-white-and-blue license plates arrived at the Daly home. The one numeral—"3"—was embossed and was accompanied by wreaths, garlands, and the Medal of Honor. Daly now faced a dilemma. He did not want to appear ungracious or to cause adverse publicity by seeming to spurn the honor. Maggie came up with the solution. "Give me the damn things," she said. "I'll put them on my truck." (She had her own landscaping business.) "And people will say, 'There goes that crazy Maggie Daly with those things on her truck.'" In 2003, Maggie could drive with her Medal of Honor tags on the "Captain Michael J. Daly Highway," the segment of Interstate Route 95 from Bridgeport to Westport designated as such by the Connecticut General Assembly.[14]

Daly was pleased, however, by the resurgence of interest in the war itself, and he found it especially gratifying that many long-separated veterans began to reconnect and to share their stories with the public and the younger generations. One day, as Daly was sitting in his office, in walked Dr. Jesse Fisher, the sergeant who had saved his life in Nuremberg. They had not seen each other since the day Fisher scooped blood out of his throat. When Daly did not recognize him, Fisher introduced himself. Mike offered to take him out to lunch to catch up, but Fisher had other business and had to decline. When Mike thanked him for saving his life, Fisher replied that he just wanted to see him, say "hello," and thank his old captain for having risked his life so many times on his behalf and that of the rest of the company.[15]

In 1995 Daly had a similar experience with another former member of Able Company. Troy Cox, who lived in Rienzi, Mississippi, outside Tupelo, happened to see a short article about Daly in the *Purple Heart* magazine. He thought Daly was as great a hero as Audie Murphy—Able Company's answer to Baker Company. For years he had wanted to find Daly "to thank him for what he did for all of us." Obtaining Daly's address and phone number from the magazine editor, he wrote Daly a letter. But unable to wait for the reply, he picked up the phone and called. "I told him that I was one of his boys from World War II." He thanked Daly for everything he had done and told him that he was "the best leader we ever had." Deflecting the praise, Daly responded, "Troy, good men always made leadership easier."

Daly visited Troy at his home in 2000. Having toured the Shiloh battlefield, Mike, Sanford, brother-in-law Phil Drake, and close friend Jock Hannum drove to Rienzi. It was an emotional reunion: "Flags and family members lined the driveway and saluted as the van pulled in. Mike emerged, and the two men hugged, tears streaming down their faces. The group then enjoyed great southern hospitality in Troy's home. One of Troy's sons told Mike that it was a great honor to meet him because for years his father had told him that Mike was "the bravest man he had ever known." Mike repaid the compliment by saying at dinner that, although people argued about which side had won at Shiloh, he knew that "southern sergeants won World War II.[16]

In October 2002, in the wake of 9/11, the United States Military Academy decided to bestow on "The American Soldier" its Sylvanus Thayer Award, given annually "to an outstanding citizen of the United States whose service and accomplishments in the national interest exemplify personal devotion to the ideals expressed in the West Point motto, "Duty, Honor, Country." The Academy invited Daly and nine other Medal of Honor recipients to represent "The American Soldier" at the award ceremony. On September 30, 2002, before traveling to West Point, Daly penned a special request to Lt. Gen. William J. Lennox, superintendent of the Academy. After thanking the general for his invitation, Daly added disarmingly, "Some sixty years ago I spent plebe year at the Academy. Regrettably, I was a failure as a cadet spending just about all free time walking the area." He then requested an amnesty on punishment tours for cadets in honor of the visit of the Medal of Honor recipients. Aware that that the Academy normally observed that practice only when royalty and heads of state visited, he added that such an amnesty "would close an important circle for this ancient soldier."

On October 9, Brig. Gen. Leo A. Brooks Jr., responded graciously, thanking Daly for participating in the Thayer Award Review and noting that Daly and the other Medal of Honor recipients "represent all that we are trying to instill in our young men and women here at the Academy. You truly represent the ideals of the American soldier." Turning to the matter of amnesty, he took care to note that he respected "the request of one of our nation's greatest heroes" but said that in the interest of consistency in the Point's discipline program, the granting of amnesty would remain reserved only for heads of state.

After sixty years and his country's highest military honor, Michael Daly found himself still jousting with the Academy over discipline—and still losing! "I had to take a shot at amnesty or never forgive myself," he wrote to a friend. On October 3, standing in a light, cold drizzle on the parade ground as the cadets marched by, Daly felt what he called "the old ambivalence— thoughts of ancient values, sacrifice, what our country stands for at her best, but knowing . . . I was a fish out of water up there." He told students at Fairfield High School: "At the end of my plebe year I left and was glad to leave. But there is something about the place that sticks to your ribs. You can go up there now in your winter years—walk alone above the parade ground in the evening and something stirs in your soul—all that history and dedication that has held our country in such good stead"[17] Sixty years after his ill-fated matriculation, West Point still seemed to represent some "unfinished business" for the old hero.

Eight years earlier, in 1994, Daly finished some other business, retiring from and essentially closing down Daly and Associates, the firm he had founded forty years earlier. He retained its name and continued to do some consulting along with his hospital work. Trim of body and lively in mind and spirit into his eighties, Daly, whose voice became more nasal, weaker, and less distinct as a result of the old wound to his palate, joked about "the artillery of time taking its toll" on his body. Even so, every day he dressed in coat and tie and went faithfully to his small office overlooking Long Island Sound in Southport. He remained active in the affairs of the hospital, and many days found him taking a plant or other small gift to a shut-in or sharing lunch with someone suffering from a terminal illness. He had an abiding sympathy for the outcast, for the down-and-out, especially veterans, and often would give money to strangers in need, bring them home at night for supper, or invite them for Thanksgiving dinner. He drove veterans to the hospital for chemotherapy treatments and sat with them in the waiting room. Displaying that playful sense of humor that never left him, he would say, "Now watch, the nurse will come and grab me instead of you." Sure enough she would, assuming that the tall, somewhat gaunt, dignified man seated in front of her was the patient! Ever the courtly soldier, when he walked friends or visitors to their car after a visit, no matter how inconsequential, he would step back, stand straight and tall, and salute as a mark of courtesy.[18]

Showing respect and affording dignity to others was a central imperative in Daly's life. Increasingly in his later years he focused on respect and dignity for those in the final stages of life. Daly mobilized his family to create the "Daly Fund" at St. Vincent's Hospital, which helped make possible a palliative-care program for the terminally ill that would, in Daly's words, "protect and enhance human dignity no less than human health." Joseph Daly's death in Alsace had planted the seeds of Daly's commitment to the cause of palliative care. According to Ron Bianchi, Daly's persistence, resilience, flexibility, and inspirational leadership—qualities he had shown on the battlefield—proved crucial in accomplishing his goal of creating an endowment for the palliative-care program and in winning acceptance of it from the board and the physicians at St. Vincent's.

Establishing the program was not easy. Because physicians understandably were reluctant to let go of patients and admit that they would not survive, it was not surprising that some doctors reacted skeptically to a proposal to direct resources to palliative care. In Daly's mind, however, nothing more naturally reflected the mission of the church's medical institutions than to be with people at the end of life, to make their final journey as peaceful, dignified, and pain free as possible. (Father Thornton had been there for him on the battlefield in Nuremberg when he had lingered at death's door.) And he succeeded. Pvt. Joseph Daly, forever young and forever present in Mike Daly's memory, must surely have smiled down appreciatively on his fellow Irish-American when the St. Vincent's board of trustees approved the Palliative Care Program under its first director, Dr. Daniel E. Woolman.[19]

On May 24, 2006, Fairfield University, recognizing Daly's contributions to country and community, awarded him an honorary doctorate. Part of the citation read, "For a lifetime of generous service, to his country, his community and those in it who suffer, the President and the Board of Trustees of Fairfield University hereby proclaim: Michael Joseph Daly, Doctor of Laws, *honoris causa*." Echoing Sergeant Lebowitz sixty years earlier, Ron Bianchi described Daly, as quite simply, "the finest man I've ever known." In 2007, the Connecticut Veterans Hall of Fame inducted Michael Daly into its ranks. Daly had a much less elevated view of himself. Writing in 2004, he said he was a "peddler, patriot, potential philanthropist—but in truth an average man of average accomplishments straining to overcome his own human frailties." In another letter he added, "In truth there is nothing extraordinary in what I did—what is extraordinary are the opportunities I had."[20]

World War II compelled millions of young Americans during their formative late teens and early twenties to undergo a searing rite of passage. Daly did so at Omaha Beach, in the Norman countryside, in Belgium, and in eastern France and southern Germany. In those places this independent, free-spirited, daring, cocky, privileged "bad boy" found his best self, serving first as an enlisted man in the 18th Infantry Regiment and then as an officer in the 15th. In the midst of war he matured beyond his years, emerged as an extraordinary leader in a high risk environment, and found a mission that came to animate him. He realized that he could harness his leadership, daring, physical courage, athleticism, and, yes, his budding wisdom and altruism in the service of causes greater than himself: the defeat of Nazism and the welfare of the men under his command. In a real sense, his father's tutelage had prepared him for this role—not that of a bloodthirsty killing machine but that of a knight, a protector, willing to risk his life and use deadly force to defend and rescue others. Both as an enlisted man and as an officer, he embraced this role, which subsequently became the template for the rest of his life. As an officer he accepted the ultimate responsibility of a leader: making life-and-death decisions amid the chaos of war. He employed his leadership and fighting abilities to motivate his men to accomplish their mission, and to protect them as best he could.

In the Gospel of Saint John in the Christian scriptures, Jesus says, "Greater love hath no man than this, that a man lay down his life for his friends." During his service in World War II, Michael Daly lived those words on a daily basis, repeatedly placing himself in harm's way to shield and protect others. No doubt his heroism was buttressed by a teenager's natural optimism, feelings of invincibility, and love of adventure. But on stepping off the LCI(L) into the surf off Omaha Beach, Daly saw the romanticism of war dissolve. On that day and on many terrible days and months thereafter, he witnessed young men like himself killed and dreadfully wounded. But he did not succumb to blind rage, cynicism, hopelessness, fatigue, or despair. Something else sustained him. Author Larry Smith identifies it in his book *Medal of Honor Winners in Their Own Voices*. He writes that every one of the Medal of Honor recipients he studied "was the kind of guy who thinks of somebody else before he thinks of himself." Recent empirical studies of heroic leaders, including Medal of Honor recipients, bear out that observation.[21]

In the cauldron of war, Daly displayed heroic leadership: courage, adaptability, daring, initiative, integrity, and the wisdom of Oliver—selfless devotion to his men. That selfless devotion, reclaimed after a period of drift following the war, would give meaning and purpose to Michael Daly for the rest of his life. One of Daly's closest friends observed, "The death surrounding him during World War II encouraged him to see the humanity in everyone, leading him to care deeply for his men during the war, and eventually for the patients of St. Vincent's Hospital thereafter." On a snowy, forbidding night in 1945 he had been unable to provide proper medical care to relieve the suffering of young Pvt. Joseph Daly, but through his work at St. Vincent's Hospital he would ensure that the most vulnerable in society would receive the care they needed and that those facing death would find comfort, dignity, and peace. The newly constructed emergency center at St. Vincent's Hospital—the Michael J. Daly Center for Emergency and Trauma Care—is a fitting memorial to a man who so often tried to rescue others. A Portuguese proverb reads, "God writes straight with crooked lines." Out of war Michael Daly drew inspiration for a life of service.

In the spring of 2008, Daly was diagnosed with advanced pancreatic cancer. He reacted serenely and philosophically: "I've led a charmed life. I should have died at that wall forty-three years ago." He continued to go to his office daily. In late June, as he grew thinner and weaker, he slipped and injured his leg. The next morning, though he was unable to drive his car to the office, he was up and about his house using a walker. With a glimmer in his eye, he told his daughter Deirdre, "I am easy to wound, but hard to kill!"[22] Humor, courage, and indomitable spirit in the face of trial—the stuff of heroes. In the words of one of his grateful former comrades in arms (who had grown old because decades earlier a young Michael Daly had pledged his life to bringing him and others like him home safely) he was "the genuine article."

On July 24, 2008, Michael Daly received the last rites of his church—for the second time. Back in 1945, suffering from what appeared to be a fatal wound, Mike had smiled with relief when he saw the priest approach to administer what then was called the sacrament of extreme unction (now the Sacrament of the Anointing of the Sick). Sixty-three years later he smiled again when his friend and spiritual advisor, the Reverend Samuel Scott, entered his room in his home in Fairfield to do the same. When Scott finished and rose to leave, Daly extended his long, thin, bony hand to Scott's, grasped it firmly, and shook it. Then Daly saluted the priest from his bed—the parting gesture of the old soldier. He had told the priest: "The world needs peacemakers. Anyone can shoot a gun."[23] But once again Daly was too self-effacing, for as combat studies of World War II showed, just "anyone" could not shoot a gun. In his willingness to do so, and to accept the personal burden it entailed, Daly, the warrior, paradoxically served as a peacemaker. He helped rid the world of Nazism, thereby rescuing a continent from tyranny. Then, taking the lessons learned from that experience, he devoted much of his adult life to caring for the sick and dying.

On July 25, 2008, Michael Daly passed away at his home in Fairfield surrounded by a loving family and numerous devoted friends. At the wake, sitting atop the American flag that draped the casket, lay a smaller, tightly

Michael J. Daly, September 15, 1924–
July 25, 2008. *Courtesy Daly Family
Photos.* Margaret "Maggie" Daly,
Michael's wife of forty-nine years,
accepts the flag that had draped his
coffin. The sergeant from the 10th
Mountain Division presented it to her
"from a grateful nation."

wrapped one: the Medal of Honor flag. Light blue with gold trim and a field
of thirteen white five-pointed stars arranged in the form of a three-bar chev-
ron, the flag replicated the Medal of Honor ribbon. During the moving and
beautiful funeral service at a packed Saint Pius X Church, two West Point cadets served as color guard. At the cemetery a contingent from the 10th Mountain Division, one of the most frequently deployed US Army divisions during
the wars in Iraq and Afghanistan, rendered military honors. During the final
service at the Daly family burial plot—designated by a large cross bearing
the family name with rectangular flat slabs of inscribed marble marking individual graves—a lone hawk circled silently above the large gathering. It all
seemed to have come full circle—father, church, West Point, army, family
and friends, the Fairfield Fire Department, close associates from St. Vincent's
Hospital—the sum of a man's life, a hero's life. Three volleys rang across the
cemetery, sending the hawk off on another course, next the haunting beauty
of "Taps," and then a flyover by a modern "hawk"—an army Black Hawk
helicopter. Awed silence followed, signaling a collective, unspoken, profound
recognition that, as Gen. Brent Scowcroft, former national-security advisor to
President George H. Bush, had written to Michael Daly's close friend, Hobart
"Hobey" Gardiner: "So long as we can call on and count on such people, the
Republic will be safe."[24]

Michael Daly had shown the fierceness of Roland and the wisdom of Oliver as learned on his father's knee. In the process he had borne away the prize

for valor. Beneath his photograph in the funeral program appeared a line from his 1982 speech to the men of Daly Company in Würzberg: "It is something we pray for—that God will give us the courage to do what is right." It was a fitting epitaph. Time and again, Michael Daly had shown such courage in the service of others.[25]

Appendix

ACT OF JULY 9, 1918, MEDAL OF HONOR

"That the President is authorized to present, in the name of the Congress, a medal of honor only to each person who, while an officer or enlisted man of the Army, shall hereafter, in action involving actual conflict with an enemy, distinguish himself conspicuously by gallantry and intrepidity at the risk of his life above and beyond the call of duty."

Source: Congressional Medal of Honor Society, The Medal, History: URL: http://www.cmohs.org/medal-history.php

UNITED STATES ARMED FORCES: SELECTED DECORATIONS

The Medal of Honor was awarded by the President, in the name of Congress, to a person who, while a member of the Army, distinguished himself conspicuously by gallantry and intrepidity at the risk of his life above and beyond the call of duty while engaged in action against an enemy of the United States. The deed performed must have been one of personal bravery or self-sacrifice so conspicuous as to clearly distinguish the individual above his or her comrades and must have involved risk of life. Incontestable proof of the performance of the service was exacted and each recommendation for the award of the decoration was considered on the standard of extraordinary merit.

Description: A gold five-pointed star, each point tipped with trefoils, 1½ inches wide, surrounded by a green laurel wreath and suspended from a gold bar inscribed "Valor," surmounted by an eagle. In the center of the star, Minerva's head surrounded by the words "United States of America." On each ray of the star is a green oak leaf. On the reverse is a bar engraved "The Congress To" with a space for engraving the name of the recipient.

Ribbon: The medal is suspended by a neck ribbon, 1⅜ inches wide, Bluebird (67117). A shield of the same color ribbon with thirteen White (67101) stars, arranged in the form of three chevrons is above the medal. The service ribbon is 1⅜ inches wide with five White stars in the form of a "M."

The Distinguished Service Cross was awarded for extraordinary heroism not justifying the award of a Medal of Honor. The act or acts of heroism must have been so notable and have involved risk of life so extraordinary as to set the individual apart from his comrades.

Description: A cross of bronze, 2 inches in height and 1¹³⁄₁₆ inches in width with an eagle on the center and a scroll below the eagle bearing the inscription "For Valor." On the reverse side, the center of the cross is circled by a wreath with a space for engraving the name of the recipient.

Ribbon: The ribbon is 1⅜ inches wide and consists of the following stripes: ⅛ inch Old Glory Red (67156); ¹⁄₁₆ inch White (67101); 1 inch Imperial Blue (67175); 1¹⁄₁₆ inch White; and ⅛ inch Old Glory Red.

The Silver Star was awarded to a person who, while serving in any capacity with the US Army, was cited for gallantry in action. The required gallantry, while of a lesser degree than that required for award of the Distinguished Service Cross, must nevertheless have been performed with marked distinction.

Description: A Gold star, 1½ inches in circumscribing diameter with a laurel wreath encircling rays from the center and a ³⁄₁₆-inch-diameter silver star superimposed in the center. The pendant is suspended from a rectangular shaped metal loop with rounded corners. The reverse has the inscription "For Gallantry in Action."

Ribbon: The ribbon is 1⅜ inches wide and consists of the following stripes: ³⁄₃₂ inch Ultramarine Blue (67118); ³⁄₆₄ inch White (67101); ⁷⁄₃₂ inch Ultramarine Blue; ⁷⁄₃₂ inch White; ⁷⁄₃₂ inch Old Glory Red (67156) (center stripe); ⁷⁄₃₂ inch White; ⁷⁄₃₂ inch Ultramarine Blue; ³⁄₆₄ inch White; and ³⁄₃₂ inch Ultramarine Blue.

The Legion of Merit was awarded . . . for exceptionally meritorious conduct in the performance of outstanding services and achievements. The performance must have been such as to merit recognition of key individuals for service rendered in a clearly exceptional manner. Performance of duties normal to the grade, branch, specialty or assignment, and experience of an individual was not an adequate basis for this award. Justification of the award might accrue by virtue of exceptionally meritorious service in a succession of important positions.

The **Bronze Star Medal** was awarded for heroic or meritorious achievement or service. Awards could be made for acts of heroism of lesser degree than that required for the award of the Silver Star. If awarded for valor in combat, a *V* device, signifying valor, was attached to the ribbon.

> *Description:* A bronze star 1½ inches in circumscribing diameter. In the center thereof is a ³⁄₁₆-inch-diameter superimposed bronze star, the center line of all rays of both stars coinciding. The reverse has the inscription "Heroic or Meritorious Achievement" and a space for the name of the recipient to be engraved. The star is suspended from the ribbon by a rectangular shaped metal.

> *Ribbon:* The ribbon is 1⅜ inches wide and consists of the following stripes: ¹⁄₃₂ inch white (67101); ⁹⁄₁₆ inch scarlet (67111); ¹⁄₃₂ inch white; center stripe ⅛ inch ultramarine blue (67118); ¹⁄₃₂ inch white; ⁹⁄₁₆ inch scarlet; and ¹⁄₃₂ inch white. loop with the corners rounded.

The **Purple Heart** was awarded in the name of the President of the United States to any member of the Armed Forces who, while serving in the armed forces, was wounded or killed by weapon fire, or who died after being wounded, regardless of the fire causing the wound

> *Description:* A Purple heart within a Gold border, 1⅜ inches wide, containing a profile of General George Washington. Above the heart appears a shield of the Washington Coat of Arms (a White shield with two Red bars and three Red stars in chief) between sprays of Green leaves. The reverse consists of a raised Bronze heart with the words "For Military Merit" below the coat of arms and leaves.

> *Ribbon:* The ribbon is 1⅜ inches wide and consists of the following stripes: ⅛ inch White (67101); 1⅛ inches Purple (67115); and ⅛ inch White (67101).[1]

Acknowledgments

I have taught at Georgetown Preparatory School, Michael Daly's high school *alma mater*, and the nation's oldest Jesuit high school, for thirty-four years. Saint Ignatius Loyola, the founder of the Jesuits, valued two virtues above all others: gratitude and generosity. I would like to express the former to those who, during the course of researching and writing this book, have shown me so much of the latter.

Over the years, the administration of Georgetown Preparatory School has been wonderfully supportive of my research and writing. For this book I would especially like to thank presidents William L. George, SJ, and Michael J. Marco, SJ, and headmasters James P. Power, the late Edward M. Kowalchick, and Jeffrey L. Jones. Through the Lawler Family Endowed Chair of History, Peter C. Lawler, Ms. Mickey Lawler, Ms. Anne Logan, and Gregory E. Lawler gave important encouragement and support to this project. Robert C. Barry first posed to me the question that led to this book, and Michael J. Horsey and Daniel E. Paro provided invaluable help in planning my first trips to Europe to trace Michael Daly's route; Thomas F. Conlan, Brian J. Gilbert, Bonita M. Hanes, Lawrence E. Rocca, Benjamin D. Williams, and John P. Williams graciously gave of their time and expertise in reading and editing the manuscript at various stages of development. I hope that this book justifies their efforts on my behalf. Trevor Bonat, Gary L. Daum, and Brian A. Gnatt came to my aid with their expertise in computer graphics and photography. When faced with translating documents written in German, I turned to Marialouise S. Collins, Peter C. Hughes Sr., Peter C. Hughes Jr., and Gisela Hughes-Allen. Their help was invaluable. So also was that given me by Teresa A. Gormley and the staff of the Office of Institutional Development for access to their collection of school publications and for help in tracking down alumni. Carol Freeman, School Registrar, a marvel of efficiency, helped with details large and small. Tammy Alvarez's excitement about the book and her efforts to find a publisher buoyed me at a time when I needed it, as did a memorable first visit to Omaha Beach with Dr. Albert F. and Marianne "Mimi" Fleury and their son, Christopher. This occurred after a very informative conversation over dinner at their home with Lt. Cmdr. Joseph P.

Vaghi Jr., USNR (ret.), the youngest "beachmaster" on Omaha Beach (Easy Red Sector) on June 6, 1944. Col. G. Thomas Cosentino arranged for a tour of West Point and shared with me his insights on things military. My eleventh-grade US history students continue to enliven and enrich my life. Each year, they are introduced to Michael Daly in a case study. Their questions and observations about him and their reaction to his story deepened my understanding of him and strengthened my resolve to share his story with others.

I owe a special debt to Professor Dennis E. Showalter, former president of the Society of Military History, for his willingness to read the unsolicited manuscript of a stranger and for his encouragement to submit the manuscript to Texas A&M University Press.

Dr. William J. Bennett took time from his hectic schedule to critique the manuscript and also graciously provided a segment on his national radio show to mark Michael Daly's passing. Keith W. Olson, my mentor from the University of Maryland, read and expertly commented on the manuscript, as he has done so generously with each of my books.

I wish to thank all those whose names are listed in the bibliography, who graciously submitted to interviews and/or allowed me use of family correspondence. A special thanks to relatives of deceased interviewees who gave me permission to use their loved ones' interviews. I would also like to acknowledge the members of the Daly family, especially Margaret "Maggie" Daly, Deirdre Daly Pavlis, and W. Sanford Miller for their encouragement and help in this project. Sanford carefully reviewed the manuscript and saved me from numerous errors. William N. Wallace, brother of Maggie Daly, and longtime Daly family friends Andrew A. and Timothy H. Smith, provided valuable information and insights. The Reverend Samuel V. Scott of Saint John Fisher Seminary, Bridgeport, Connecticut, graciously shared a copy of the homily he delivered at Michael Daly's funeral.

All authors benefit from the kindness of strangers, but I was especially graced with help from people who seemed to appear out of nowhere at the most unexpected but opportune moments: Louis Appleton, Registrar, Portsmouth Abbey School; Robert Asahina, author of *Just Americans; How Japanese Americans Won a War at Home and Abroad: The Story of the 100th Battalion/442nd Regimental Combat Team in World War II;* Lt. Gen. Jared L. Bates (ret.); Patrick Baumann, local historian, Riedwihr, France; Mayor Didier Belliard, Saint-Loup-du-Gast, France; Dr. Ludwig Benkert, Bad Neustadt an der Saale, Germany; Mechthild "Meggy" C. Benkert, Attorney/Advisor, Seventh (Army) Joint Multinational Training Command, Würzberg, Germany; Friedrich Braun, historian, Heroldsberg, Germany; Harald Braun, Munich, Germany; Carol Cepregi, Congressional Medal of Honor Society; Margaux Dietrich, Colmar, France; Jean-Paul Fleith, Maison Rouge, France; Jean-

Marie Gosselin, Big Red One Assault Museum, Colleville-sur-Mer, France; Susanne Kaiser, Guest Service, Tourist Information Center, Bad Neustadt an der Saale, Germany; Pius Kehl, Grossheubach, Germany; Dr. Karl Kunze, Nuremberg, Germany; Susan Lintelmann, Manuscripts Curator, Special Collections, United States Military Academy; Walter W. Meeks III, Curator, Fort Stewart Museum, Fort Stewart, Georgia; Henri-Pierre and Marie-Pierre Lemessier, Bayeux, France, and René A. Moreau, Herve, Belgium; Ulrich Müller, Heidelbingerhof, Zweibrücken, Germany; Lt. Col. Suzanne Nielsen, Social Sciences Department, United States Military Academy; Thomas Noll, Treasurer of the Municipality of Rothenbuch, Germany; Seth Paridon, The National World War II Museum; Annick Pineau, Saint-Loup-du-Gast; Roger Portier, founder of the Cobra Memorial, Marigny, France; Charles S. Porucznik, Valparaiso, Indiana; Christian Schmitt, Laudenbach, Germany; Marcel and Mathilde Schmetz, Remember Museum, Thimister-Clermont, Belgium; Hubert Simon, State Archivist for Lampertheim, Germany; Sally Slenczka, Nuremberg, Germany; Lt. Col. Timothy R. Stoy, Historian of the Society of the 3rd Infantry Division, United States Army, as well as President and Historian of the 15th Infantry Regiment Association; Jeff Danby, author of *Day of the* Panzer; Chaisson Sylvain, Ferme du Lieu Béziers, Ville La Vacquerie, France; Vanessa van Atten, Département Philosophie, Histoire, Sciences de l'Homme, Bibliothèque nationale de France; Geert van den Bogaert, Battle of Normandy Memorial Museum, Bayeux, France; Father Isaac Veronica, visiting priest, Grossheubach, Germany; Remy Wehrle, Strasbourg, France; Andrew E. Woods, Research Historian, Robert R. McCormick Research Center, Cantigny First Division Foundation, Wheaton, Illinois; Pia and Karl Wünsch, Rothenbuch, Germany; Gerard Zoeller, Hawthorne, New York; the staff of the Musée du Memorial des Combats de la Poche de Colmar, Turckheim, France; the staff of the Seeley G. Mudd Manuscript Library, Princeton University; the staffs of Modern Military Records, and the Textual, Cartographic and Architectural, Library, Motion Picture, Sound and Video, and Still Picture research rooms of the National Archives and Records Administration, College Park, Maryland; and the staff of the US Army Heritage and Education Center, Carlisle, Pennsylvania.

The staff at Mapping Specialists Ltd., especially Marketing Manager Steve Davies, Project Manager Don Larsen, and Senior Cartographer Paul Lobue, were extremely professional, friendly, and responsive. This book is enriched by their meticulous work.

I owe a great debt of gratitude to the staff at Texas A&M University Press who have been unfailingly supportive and enthusiastic about this project. A heartfelt thanks to Editor-in-Chief Mary Lenn Dixon, her assistant, Diana L. Vance, and Thom Lemmons, Managing Editor. A special word of appreciation goes to John P. Drayton, the copy editor, whose careful reading of the manuscript improved it substantially and saved me from some embarrassing gaffes. I must take responsibility for any inadequacies that remain. After all, John is a superb copy editor, not a miracle worker!

Finally, the two special women in my life, Phyllis Linda Ouellette, and Meghan Elizabeth Ochs, my wife and daughter, remain what they have always been, the loves of my life.

Notes

INTRODUCTION

1. Telephone interview with Michael Daly, August 25, 2005. A paraphrase of a famous line often attributed to George Orwell but actually belonging to Winston Churchill: "We sleep safe in our beds because rough men stand ready in the night to visit violence on those who would do us harm."

PROLOGUE

1. For a thorough description of the Medal of Honor, see the Appendix.

2. This was the largest mass presentation of the Medal of Honor in history. *Washington Daily News*, August 23, 1945, final edition; *New York Times*, August 23, 1945. Daly's was one of the last Medals of Honor awarded for action in the European theater. On February 26, 1946, Pvt. Joseph Frederick Merrell was awarded the Medal of Honor posthumously for heroism near Lohe, Germany, on April 18, 1945, the same day as Daly's action in Nuremberg. In 2000, Daniel K. Inouye (later US senator from Hawaii) and Joe Hayashi were awarded Medals of Honor—Hayashi's posthumously—for their actions on April 21 and 22, 1945, respectively, while serving with the 442nd Regimental Combat Team in Italy. E-mail, Carol Cepregi, Congressional Medal of Honor Society, to author, June 5, 2009.

3. Telephone interview with Michael Daly, July 18, 2002; *New York Times*, August 19, 1945; August 23, 1945.

4. Congressional Medal of Honor Society, History, http://www.cmohs.org/medal-history.php; Larry Smith, *Beyond Glory: Medal of Honor Winners in Their Own Words* (New York: W. W. Norton, 2003), xiv–xv; "Introduction by Mike Wallace," in Allen Mikaelian, *Medal of Honor: Profiles of America's Military Heroes from the Civil War to the Present* (New York, 2002), ix–xv; David F. Burrelli, "Medal of Honor: History and Issues," Library of Congress, Congressional Research Service, Foreign Affairs, and National Defense Division, http://www.mishalov.com/Medal_Honor_History_Issues.html; list of Medal of Honor Recipients in Archives of Congressional Medal of Honor Society, Mt. Pleasant, SC, attached to e-mail from Carol Cepregi, Congressional Medal of Honor Society, to author, June 5, 2009; fact sheets attached to e-mail, Carol Cepregi, Congressional Medal of Honor Society, to author, March 31, 2011.

1. Joseph Dorst Patch, *A Soldier's War: The First Infantry Division, AEF (1917–1918)* (Corpus Christi, TX: Mission Press, 1966), 85–90.

2. Larry Smith, *Beyond Glory: Medal of Honor Winners in Their Own Voices* (New York: W. W. Norton, 2003), xvii; 1870 Federal Census, Ward 19, District 17, New York City; "A Very Lively Primary," *New York Times,* October 2, 1893; "In Mr. Stillings's District," *New York Times,* September 1893; "Surrogate Notices," *New York Times,* July 26, 1894; "In the Real Estate Field," *New York Times,* March 29, 1894; and "A Catholic Club Reception," *New York Times,* January 9, 1896; Information Sheet filled out by Paul Gerard Daly, United States Military Academy Special Collections and Archives, United States Military Academy Library; telephone interview with Michael Daly (hereafter TID), August 20, 2002; William K. Wyant, *Sandy Patch: A Biography of Lt. General Alexander M. Patch* (New York: Praeger Publishers, 1991), 26–28.

3. Transcript of Paul Gerard Daly, Class of 1912 and excerpts from the *Princeton Alumni Weekly,* Princeton Undergraduate File, Princeton University Archives (PUA), Seeley G. Mudd Manuscript Library, Princeton University.

4. "West Point in the making of America," http://americanhistory.si.edu/westpoint/history_6b.html; "Official Register of the Officers and Cadets of the United States Military Academy [1913, 1914, 1915]"; "Regulations for the United States Military Academy," and "Abstract of Delinquencies," United States Military Academy Special Collections and Archives; "Major Paul Daly Receives DSC for Heroic Acts," newspaper clipping, n.d., Daly Family Papers (hereafter DFP).

5. Donald M. Kington, "The Plattsburg Movement and its Legacy," *Relevance: The Quarterly Journal of the Great War Society* 6, no. 4 (1997): 4, http://ww.worldwar1.com/tgws/re1011.htm; War Records, Paul G. Daly, Princeton Undergraduate File, PUA, Seeley G. Mudd Manuscript Library, Princeton University; Frank Parker, Brigadier General, USA, to Major Paul Daly, Commanding 3rd Battalion, 18th Infantry: Subject: Record in the 18th Regiment, n.d., DFP.

6. Patch, *A Soldier's Story,* 66, 79–81; handwritten copy of original words written by Gen. Frank Parker for proposed Medal of Honor citation for Paul G. Daly, attached to letter from Parker to Paul Daly, March 23, 1923, DFP.

7. Consolidated Index Card, Organization Records, 1st Division, Subject Index and Cross Reference to Doc. File, 6603–6980, Box 138, Record Group (hereafter RG) 120, Records of the American Expeditionary Forces, National Archives and Records Administration II (hereafter NARA II); Ordre Du Corps D'Armée No. 41 [Pierre Georges], Duport, Le Général Commandant, 6th Corps d'Armée, copy DFP; General Orders No. 20, 1st Division Headquarters, May 17, 1918, Sector, World War Records, First Division, AEF, Regular, Citations First Division, vol. 23, copy in Museum and Collections, The First Division Museum and Library at Cantigny, McCormick Research Center, Wheaton IL; the Citation Star, Act of Congress on July 9, 1918 (65th Congress, Sess. II, chap. 143, p. 873), and War Department Bulletin 43 (1918). On July 9, 1932, Congress replaced the Citation Star with the Silver Star. See Institute of heraldry, http://www.tioh.hqda.pentagon.mil/Awards/silver_star.aspx; Gen. Pierre

Georges DuPort represented France at the ceremonies surrounding the transportation and interment of the Unknown Soldier in Arlington National Cemetery, October 23–November 11, 1921. See "Unknown Soldier chosen in France," *New York Times,* October 25, 1921; "The Unknown Soldier Comes Home, 1921," EyeWitness to History, www.eyewitnesstohistory.com.

8. Richard W. Stewart, ed., *American Military History,* vol. 2, *The United States Army in a Global Era, 1917–2003* (Washington, DC: United States Army Center of Military History, 2005), 37–38, http://www.army.mil/cmh-pg/books/AMH-V2/AMH%20V2/index.htm#html; "Three Years Ago Today, *Flushing Daily Times,* n.d., clipping in DFP; "The Memorial to the 1st Division at Buzancy," http://www.webmatters.net/france/ww1_buzancy_usa.htm.

9. Patch, *A Soldier's Story,* 79, 155–58; Paul G. Daly, *Croix de Guerre* File, World War I, Organization Records, 1st Division, Headquarters, Dec. File 220.5, Record Group 120, Records of the American Expeditionary Forces, NARA II; "Major Paul Daly Receives DSC For Heroic Acts," *New York Herald Tribune,* February 4, 1919; Order 20,460, "D" Extract, General Headquarters of the French Armies of the East, July 16, 1919, The Marshal of France, Commander-in-Chief of the French Armies of the East, [Henri-Philippe] Petain, and listing of Paul G. Daly's assignments, promotions, and injuries, Paul G. Daly, Princeton War Records Committee, Princeton Undergraduate File, PUA, Seeley G. Mudd Manuscript Library, Princeton University.

10. Consolidated Index Card, Organization Records, 1st Division, Subject Index and Cross Reference to Doc. File, 6603–6980, Boxes 138, 140, 152, 154, 156, Record Group 120, NARA II; Patch, *A Soldier's War,* 79; Frank Parker to Paul Daly, March 31, 1923, and July 2, 1945; Charles S. Coulter, Major (ret.), US Army to Paul Daly, April 9, 1946, DFP; e-mail, W. Sanford Miller Jr. to author, August 21, 2008.

11. James Scott Wheeler, *The Big Red One: America's Legendary 1st Infantry Division from World War I to Desert Storm* (Lawrence, KS: University Press of Kansas, 2007), 92, 81–109.

12. Consolidated Index Card, Organization Records, 1st Division, Subject Index and Cross Reference to Doc. File, 6603–6980, Boxes 138, 140, 152, 154, 156, in Record Group 120, NARA II; Patch, *A Soldier's War,* 79; Frank Parker to Paul Daly, March 31, 1923, and July 2, 1945; Charles S. Coulter, Major (ret.), US Army to Paul Daly, April 9, 1946, DFP.

13. Photograph in Patch, *A Soldier's War,* 165; Wheeler, *The Big Red One,* 99–105.

14. Brig. Gen. Frank Parker, Hqtrs. 1st Inf. Brigade, AEF, Wirges, Germany, to Major Paul G. Daly, January 25, 1919, DFP; Patch, *A Soldier's War,* dedication page.

15. Consolidated Index Card, Organization Records, 1st Division, Subject Index and Cross Reference to Doc. File, 6603–6980, Box 138, Record Group 120, NARA II; "Col. P. G. Daly, 83, Dies; Recipient of War Medals," obituary, *Bridgeport Post,* June 11, 1974; "Great Crowd Sees 27th's Heroes Get Awards for Valor," *New York Times,* March 24, 1919; see, also *New York Times,* March 30, 1919, and "Obituary Notes," *New York Times,* March 18, 1919, and March 20, 1919.

16. "Miss M. Mulqueen Weds Paul G. Daly," *New York Times,* December 28, 1920; telephone interview with Julia Ann Patch Diehl, August 10, 2002.

17. *New York Times,* September 29, 1920, December 28, 1920, and May 27, 1921. Daly did not graduate from Columbia Law School but passed the New York Bar Exam.

18. Obituary, Col. Paul G. Daly, *The Fairfield Citizen-News,* June 12, 1974, and "Paul Gerard Daly '12," *Princeton Alumni Weekly,* July 2, 1974, copy in Princeton Undergraduate File, PUA, Seeley G. Mudd Manuscript Library, Princeton University; TID, July 3, 2002.

19. Wyant, *Sandy Patch,* 26, 28, 40; TID, July 3, 2002; "Daly Double," *The American Legion Magazine* (December 1945): 50; Mel Allen, "Only Afraid to Show Fear: Portrait of a Hero," *Yankee* (May 1983): 79; Obituary, Col. Paul G. Daly, *Fairfield Citizen-News,* June 12, 1974; e-mail, W. Sanford Miller Jr. to author, August 21, 2008; telephone interview with W. Sanford Miller, Jr., August 31, 2008; telephone interview with Andrew A. Smith, July 21, 2008; e-mail, Andrew A. Smith to author, August 25, 2008; e-mail, Timothy H. Smith to author, August 25, 2008; TID, July 3, 2002, and December 20, 2005; Allen," Only Afraid to Show Fear," 77. Paul and Madeleine Daly had four sons (Michael, Thomas, who went by his middle name: Gilroy "Roy," Daniel, and Dermot) and three daughters (Madeleine, the eldest of the siblings, Alison, and Bevin). See "Obituary, Col. Paul G. Daly," *Fairfield Citizen-News,* June 12, 1974, and "Paul Gerard Daly '12," *Princeton Alumni Weekly,* July 2, 1974, copy in Princeton Undergraduate File, PUA, Seeley G. Mudd Manuscript Library, Princeton University.

CHAPTER 2

1. Mel Allen, "Only Afraid to Show Fear: Portrait of a Hero," *Yankee* (May 1983): 79; interview, William Wyant with Madge Daly Potter, July 24, 1984, typescript copy in possession of author; telephone interview with Michael Daly (hereafter TID), June 15, 2006, June 8, 2004; newspaper clipping, n.d., containing an oval photo of Mike Daly and his sister Madge, clipping in author's possession; "Daly Double," *American Legion Magazine* (December 1945): 50; TID, July 3, 2002, and June 15, 2006.

2. TID, August 20, 2002, June 15, 2006, June 8, 2004, and July 2, 2007; letter, Michael J. Daly to author, June 6, 2002; "Daly Double," 50; *The Song of Roland,* translated by Dorothy L. Sayres quoted in William K. Wyant, *Sandy Patch: A Biography of Lt. General Alexander M. Patch* (New York: Praeger Publishers, 1991), 70, 79.

3. TID, July 3, 2003, and June 15, 2006.

4. Letter, Michael J. Daly to author, June 6, 2002; TID, December 30, 2002, and July 8, 2004; letter, Alison D. Gerard to author, July, 15, 2010; telephone interview with Alison D. Gerard, March 29, 2005.

5. TID, July 3, 2002, August 8, 2002, June 7, 2005, and July 16, 2005; Mel Allen, "Only Afraid to Show Fear," 79; TID, August 20, 2002, July 16, 2006, August 2, 2004, and August 1, 2007; obituary, Paul G. Daly, *Bridgeport Telegram,* June 12, 1974; e-mail, W. Sanford Miller Jr. to author, August 21, 2008; e-mail, Andrew A. Smith to author, August 29 and 30, 2008; telephone interview with Andrew A. Smith, July 21, 2008.

6. TID, March 18, 2003, July 10, 2003, August 20, 2002, March 18, 2003, August 11, 2005, and December 20, 2005; e-mail, W. Sanford Miller Jr. to author,

August 21, 2008; telephone interview with Phillip Drake, July 5, 2006; School Ledger, 1941, Georgetown Preparatory School Archives, North Bethesda, MD.

7. Stephen J. Ochs, *Academy on the "Patowmack": Georgetown Preparatory School, 1789–1927* (Rockville, MD: Georgetown Preparatory School, 1989), 53–66; William S. Abell, *Fifty Years at Garrett Park: Georgetown Preparatory School, 1919–1969* (Baltimore, MD: Private printing, 1970), 157. Ironically, the first residents of this oldest boys' Catholic high school in the country were women. They had come to Washington, DC, to work in government service during World War I. Because of a severe housing shortage, the federal government requested that Georgetown University lease the building to the government for a year. The university did so, and women resided in the newly finished main building during 1918.

8. Georgetown Preparatory School Catalogues, 1938–42, Office of Institutional Advancement, Georgetown Preparatory School, North Bethesda, MD; "Notes of House Consultation," typed and appended to a letter, Rev. William A. Ryan, SJ, to Rev. John LaFarge, SJ, February 2, 1953, and Notes of House Consultation, February 16, 1937, House Consultors' Minutes Books, Jesuit Cloister, Georgetown Preparatory School, North Bethesda, MD. Preserving and enhancing the school's elitist reputation explained in part why, during Mike Daly's freshman year, the Reverend Henry Wiesel, rector-president of the institution, rejected a request from the Washington Redskins professional football team to use the school's facilities for preseason training camp between August 4 and September 17, 1938. Wiesel and his Jesuit advisors (consultors) at the school decided against the proposition because they felt it inconsistent with the school's mission. First, conducting the training camp on campus not only would make it difficult to prepare the campus facilities for the opening of school (scheduled for September 19) but also might damage the playing fields from overuse, rendering them unusable by the boys. In addition, Wiesel and his consultors feared that the presence of "thirty football warriors" on campus—the image of the pro football player in the 1930s differed significantly from what it became later—would harm Prep's reputation as a "select school." Had Mike Daly and many of his classmates known of the confidential Redskins proposal, they no doubt would have looked on it far more positively than had the Jesuits! See, Stephen J. Ochs, "When Prep said 'No' to the Redskins," *Alumnews,* (Fall 2002): 8–11.

9. Georgetown Preparatory School Catalogues, 1938–42.

10. Telephone interview with Robert L. Barrett, Georgetown Preparatory School Class of 1941, July 6, 2002; TID, August 20, 2002, July 8, 2002, and July 2, 2004; Georgetown Preparatory School Catalogues, 1938–42.

11. Secondary School Record of Michael J. Daly; Robert S. Arthur, SJ, Headmaster, to Paul G. Daly, July 3, 1941, letter in Georgetown Preparatory School Archives; TID, July 3, 2002, and July 2, 2004.

12. Telephone interviews with Robert L. Barrett, July 7, 2002, and John L. Brunett, SJ, Georgetown Preparatory School Class of 1941, June 27, 2003; TID, July 3, 2003, June 13, 2004 and July 18, 2005; telephone interview with Gerard F. Kunkel (Georgetown Preparatory School Class of 1942), August 23, 2002; *Cupola, 1941* (Georgetown Preparatory School yearbook); *Little Hoya* (Georgetown Preparatory School student newspaper), November 4, 1937, 4; October 24, 1938, 4; October 31, 1939, 2; *Cupola, 1941,* Office of Institutional Advancement, Georgetown Preparatory School.

13. Telephone interview with Robert L. Barrett, July 6, 2002; *Little Hoya,* November 22, 1939, 4. TID, July 3, and July 18, 2002; *Cupola,* 1941; *Little Hoya,* Summer 1941.

14. Collin R. Payne, Brian Wansink, and Koert Van Ittersum, "Profiling the Heroic Leader: Empirical Lessons from Combat-Decorated Veterans of World War II," *The Leadership Quarterly* 19, no. 5 (October 2008): 547–55; Thomas A. Kolditz, *In Extremis Leadership* (San Francisco, CA, 2007); Cadet Rom Iammartino, "Characteristics of Medal of Honor Recipients and Combat Experienced Soldiers," typescript copy, May 2003, Research Project for Course PL498 in the Department of Behavioral Sciences and Leadership, original in Department of Behavioral Sciences and Leadership, United States Military Academy; TID, July 10, 2003; telephone interview with Alison D. Gerard, March 29, 2005.

15. Telephone interview with Robert L. Barrett, July 6, 2002; TID, July 3, 2002 and August 11 and 24, 2005.

16. *Little Hoya,* October 12, 1939; telephone interview with Alison D. Gerard, March 29, 2005; *Cupola,* 1941; Daly quoted in Allen, "Only Afraid to Show Fear: Portrait of a Hero," 134; TID, July 3, 2002; Telephone Interview with Robert L. Barrett, July 6, 2002.

17. TID, July 18, 2002, August 20, 2002, July 17, 2003, December 23, 2003, and July 2, 2004; Hoya Saxa.Com, http://www.hoyasaxa.com/sports/histo6.htm; W. C. Heinz, "Tackles Offer No Comparison," *New York Sun,* 1946, clipping in author's possession.

18. "Prep Spirit," *Little Hoya,* October 31, 1939; letter, Michael Daly to author, March 6, 2003.

19. Secondary School Record of Michael J. Daly; letter, Robert S. Arthur, SJ, Headmaster, to Paul G. Daly, July 3, 1941, Georgetown Preparatory School Archives; TID, July 3, 2002.

CHAPTER 3

1. William K. Wyant, *Sandy Patch: A Biography of Lt. General Alexander M. Patch* (New York: Praeger Publishers, 1991), 85; telephone interview with Michael Daly (hereafter TID), August 20, 2002, July 3, and July 8, 2003, and August 20, 2003.

2. "Results of the Prep Poll," *Little Hoya,* October 31, 1939; "Prep Poll," *Little Hoya,* November 22, 1939; TID, July 8, 2002.

3. Since 1969 the former Portsmouth Priory School has been known as Portsmouth Abbey School.

4. TID, July 3, 2002; Portsmouth Abbey School, Office of the Registrar, Report of Michael J. Daly's Grades, 1941–42, Louis Appleton, Registrar, to author, August 23, 2002, and Portsmouth Priory Football team photograph, 1941; telephone interview with Andrew A. Smith, July 21, 2008.

5. Interview, William Wyant with Madeleine "Madge" Daly Potter, copy of typescript, July 24, 1984; Timothy H. Smith e-mail to author, August 26, 2008; Jeffrey J. Clarke and Robert Ross Smith, *Riviera to the Rhine* (Washington, DC: Center of Military History, US Army, 1993), 33; Wyant, *Sandy Patch,* 12, 27.

6. William Wyant interview with Madge Daly Potter. July 24, 1984; Charles

Whiting, *America's Forgotten Army: The True Story of the US Seventh Army in World War II* (New York: St. Martin's Press, 1999), 54; quoted in Wyant, *Sandy Patch*, 40.

7. "South Pacific Veteran Home, Col. P. G. Daly," *Fairfield News*, June 11, 1943; TID, August 24, 2005, and July 8, 2004;

8. TID, July 3, 2002.

9. "The Americal Division History," http://www.americal.org/ambook.shtm; Wyant, *Sandy Patch*, 57. Paul Daly found that he didn't much like Australian troops in New Caledonia: their accent, what he regarded as their poor work habits, and their seeming inability to make a martini the way he liked it.

10. TID, August 24, 2005, and July 8, 2004; Paul G. Daly to Princeton Alumni Association, Class of 1912, February 21, 1961, Paul G. Daly File, Princeton University Undergraduate Files, Princeton University Archives, Seeley G. Mudd Manuscript Library, Princeton University; "Col. Daly Honored," *The Tacoma Tribune*, September 25, 1943; untitled and undated speech delivered in January, 1943, by Colonel Paul G. Daly to his platoon leaders on the eve of combat on Guadalcanal Island, typed copy furnished to the author by Lt. Gen. (ret.) Jared L. Bates, October 19, 2008.

11. TID, August 20, 2002, July 3, 2002, January 20, 2003, August 24, 2005, July 8, 2003, August 24, 2005, and August 28, 2007; photographs, Company H-2 (company and individual) in United States Military Academy Special Collections and Archives, United States Military Academy Library, and Cadet Service Record, Michael Joseph Daly, Class of 1945, Office of the Registrar, United States Military Academy.

12. Letter, Michael J. Daly to author, June 6, 2002; TID, July 3, August 8 and 28, 2002, July 1, 2003, January 31, 2005, and August 5, 2006.

13. Telephone interview with James E. "Ed" Shilstone, January 31, 2005; two e-mails, James E. Shilstone to author, February 2, 2005; "The Cadet Chapel," http://www.usma.edu/chaplain/cadetchapel.htm; Gen. Donald V. Bennett (ret.), with William R. Forstchen, *Untarnished Honor: A West Point Graduate's Memoir of World War II* (New York, 2003), 36–37; "The Catholic Chapel," http://www.usma.edu/Chaplain/catholicchapel.htm; TID, August 28, 2002 and July 1, 2003; letter, Michael J. Daly to author, January 17, 2005.

14. TID, August 20, 2002, August 20, 2003, and August 5, 2006.

15. Wyant, *Sandy Patch* (New York, 1991), 85; TID, August 20, 2002, July 3, and July 8, 2003, and August 20, 2003.

16. TID, July 3, 2003, August 20, 2002, March 18, 2003, January 2, 2004, and July 9, 2007.

17. TID, June 15, 2006.

18. TID, March 18, 2003; Edward G. Miller, *Nothing Less Than Full Victory: Americans at War in Europe, 1944–1945* (Annapolis, MD: Naval Institute Press, 2007), 15; Robert R. Palmer, "The Procurement of Enlisted Personnel: The Problem of Quality," in William R. Keast, Robert R. Palmer, and Bell Irvin Wiley, *The Procurement and Training of Ground Combat Troops* (Washington, DC: Center of Military History, US Army, 2003), 2–4; Max Hastings quote, in Max Hastings, *Armageddon: The Battle for Germany, 1944–1945* (New York: Knopf, 2004), 186; Robert S. Rush, *Hell in the Hürtgen Forest: The Ordeal and Triumph of an American Infantry Regiment* (Lawrence, KS: University Press of Kansas, 2001), 69, fn. 17. According to the

1940 US Census, vol. 6, 36 percent of white males had an eighth-grade education, 24 percent had some high school, 25 percent had graduated high school, and 14 percent had some college.

19. Letter, Paul G. Daly to Michael J. Daly, September 4, 1943, Daly Family Papers (DFP).

20. Paul Daly to Michael Daly, Michaelmas [September 29] 1943.

21. TID, July 3, 2002; William R. Keast, *Provision of Enlisted Replacements,* Army Ground Forces Study 7 (Washington, DC, 1946), 1, http://www.history.army .mil/books/agf/agf007/index.htm; William R. Keast, Robert R. Palmer, and Bell Irvin Wiley, *The Procurement and Training of Ground Combat Troops,* 405, http:// www.archive.org/stream/procurementtrainoopalm/procurementtrainoopalm_djvu.txt; William R. Keast, *Provision of Enlisted* Replacements, Army Ground Forces Study 7 (Washington, DC, 1946), 1, 17, http://www.history.army.mil/books/agf/agf007/ index.htm.

22. TID, July 3, 2002; Keast, *Provision of Enlisted Replacements,* 1, 17, http:// www.history.army.mil/books/agf/agf007/index.htm; John Sloan Brown, *Draftee Division: The 88th Infantry Division in World War II* (Lexington: University Press of Kentucky, 1986), 42–43; TID, December 23, 2003; "Daly Double," *The American Legion Magazine,* (December 1945): 51.

23. Wyant, *Sandy Patch,* 85–86; Paul G. Daly to the Princeton Alumni Association, February 21, 1961, Princeton Undergraduate File, PUA; *Tacoma News Tribune,* September 25, 1943, clipping, copy in author's possession; "Japs Tough and Tricky but Americans Better Fighters Says Col. Daly Back from Guadalcanal," *Bridgeport Sunday Post,* June 6, 1943. Gathered together in Palm Springs for Christmas, the Daly and Patch families could put the war aside for a brief time. Led by the "tuneless trio" of Patch, Paul Daly, and Daly's daughter, Madge, the group sang Christmas carols, after which they lounged around the kidney-shaped pool. Both Paul Daly and Patch wore long Australian shorts when they went swimming. Mary Martin, the singer/ actress, saw the slightly built Patch shirtless and in his shorts and exclaimed, "Good Lord, it's Mahatma Gandhi!" See Wyant, *Sandy Patch,* 86.

24. Letter, Michael Daly to author, June 6, 2002; Rush, *Hell in the Hürtgen Forest,* 90; TID, July 3, 2002, July 18, 2002, July 28, 2002, and July 10, 2003; Military Record and Report of Separation, Certificate of Service for Michael J. Daly, copy in author's possession. Michael Daly obtained this certificate, along with other documents, from the National Personnel Records Center, St. Louis, MO, prior to the 1973 fire that destroyed both his and his father's files.

CHAPTER 4

1. Unit Journal, 3rd Battalion, 18th Infantry (hereafter 3rd Battalion Unit Journal), June 2, 1944, Box 5951, Entry 427: WWII Operations Reports, 1st Inf. Division, 301 Inf (18) 7–0.3 to 301 Inf (18) 7–3.9, June to October, 1944, Record Group 407: Records of the Adjutant General's Office, 1905–81, National Archives and Records Administration II, College Park, MD; photograph, June 4, 1944, SC#190504, Photograph Collection, Museum and Collections, Robert R. McCormick Research Center, First Division Museum at Cantigny (hereafter FDMC), Wheaton, IL.

2. Roland G. Ruppenthal, *US Army in World War II, Logistical Support of the Armies,* vol. 1, *May 1941–September 1944* (Washington, DC: Department of the Army, 1995), 232, http://www.archive.org/details/logisticalsuppor11rupp. Between May 1943, and May 1944, 1.6 million US troops and 5.5 million measurement tons of supplies arrived in Great Britain. See Barry J. Dysart, *"Materialschlact:* The 'Matériel Battle' in the European Theater," in Alan L. Gropman, *The Big 'L': American Logistics in World War* II (Washington, DC: National Defense University, 1997), 351; letter, Michael J. Daly to the author, June 6, 2002; telephone interview with Michael Daly (hereafter TID), June 19, 2003; e-mail, Andrew A. Smith to author, July 21, 2008.

3. "Col. Paul Daly dies at 83," obituary, *Fairfield Citizen-Times,* June 12, 1974; "Daly Double," *American Legion Magazine,* (December 1945): 53; Paul G. Daly to Princeton Alumni Association, Class of 1912, February 21, 1961, Paul G. Daly File, Princeton University Undergraduate Files, Princeton University Archives, Seeley G. Mudd Manuscript Library, Princeton University; TID, June 21, 2007; William K. Wyant, *Sandy Patch: A Biography of Lt. General Alexander M. Patch* (New York: Praeger Publishers, 1991), 87–89, 91, 93–98; Rick Atkinson, *The Day of Battle: The War in Sicily and Italy, 1943–1944* (New York: Henry Holt and Co., 2007), 147–49, 170–73, and 295–96; Michael Daly saw the letter after his return from the war, TID, June 21, 2007; see also telephone interview with Alison D. Gerard, March 29, 2005.

4. Letter from Daly to author, June 6, 2002; TID, July 3, 2003, June 21, 2007, and July 9, 2007.

5. Dennis E. Showalter, "Introduction to the History Book Club Edition," in Charles B. MacDonald, *Company Commander* (New York: History Book Club, 2006), xi–xii; Max Hastings, *Armageddon: The Battle for Germany, 1944–1945* (New York, 2004), 73–74.

6. TID, June 21, 2007, June 6 and 19, July 3, and July 18, 2002; James Scott Wheeler, *The Big Red One: America's Legendary 1st Infantry Division from World War I to Desert Storm* (Lawrence, KS: University Press of Kansas, 2007), 265; "Commemorative History of the Eighteenth Infantry Regiment, First Infantry Division, US Army, 1812–1944," typescript, November 8, 1944, in Quinton F. Reams Papers, Box 1, Folder 5, US Army Military History Institute at the Army Heritage and History Center, Carlisle, PA; Showalter, "Introduction to the History Book Club Edition," in Charles B. MacDonald, *Company Commander,* x.

7. Third Battalion Unit Journal, June 1, 1944; Wheeler, *The Big Red One,* 265; H. R. Knickerbocker et al., *Danger Forward: The Story of the First Division in World War II* (Washington, DC: Society of the First Division, 1947), 181; letter, Daly to author, June 15, 2003; Army Field Manual FM 100–5, "Operations," 15 June 1944, 5, in Flint Whitlock, *The Fighting First: The Untold Story of the Big Red One on D-Day* (Boulder, CO: Westview Press, 2004), 62.

8. Interview, Robert F. Stringer, Hopkins, Minnesota, 2nd Lt., Company I, 18th Infantry regiment, Veterans Project, p. 6, American Folk Life Center, Library of Congress, Washington, DC.

9. Franklyn A. Johnson, *One More Hill* (New York, 1949), 138; TID, July 3, 2002; Eisenhower quoted in Johnson, *One More Hill,* 140.

10. "Neptune," CT 18—Assault Group o–3, Ship, "List of Assault Ships," First Division Museum; "LCIL, Landing Craft Infantry, Large," and "LCVP, Landing Craft

Vehicle, Personnel" (more commonly known as a Higgins Boat), http://en.wikipedia
.org/wiki/Landing_Craft_Infantry and http://en.wikipedia.org/wiki/LCVP.

11. Oral History, Lewis C. Smith, I Company, Oral History Collection, p. 4,
FDMC; letter, Daly to author, June 6, 2002; TID, July 3 and 18, 2002, and November 21 and June 21, 2007. On the importance of veteran small-unit leaders for unit
success and for the successful integration of replacements, see Robert S. Rush, *Hell
in the Hürtgen Forest: The Ordeal and Triumph of an American Infantry Regiment*
(Lawrence, KS: University Press of Kansas, 2004), 342–44. Saint Maurice was a senior
officer of an all-Christian unit of a Roman army in the third century. When he and his
men refused an order to sacrifice to the Roman gods, they were killed.

Prayer to Saint Michael the Archangel:
Saint Michael the Archangel,
defend us in battle.
Be our protection against the wickedness and snares of the devil.
May God rebuke him, we humbly pray;
and do Thou, O Prince of the Heavenly Host —
by the Divine Power of God —
cast into hell, Satan and all the evil spirits,
who roam throughout the world seeking the ruin of souls. Amen.

12. Letter, Daly to author, June 6, 2002; TID, July 3, 2003; Robert F. Stringer,
2nd Lt., Company I, 18th Regiment, transcript, Oral History Collection, p. 5, FDMC.

13. Lewis C. Smith, I Company, 18th Regiment, transcript in Oral History
Collection, p. 5, FDMC.

14. Robert W. Baumer with Mark J. Reardon, *American Iliad: The 18th Infantry Regiment in World War II* (Bedford, PA: Aberjona Press, 2004), 196.

15. Raymond Stott, transcript in Oral History Collection, p. 9, FDMC; letter,
Daly to author, June 6, 2002;

16. Letter, Daly to author, June 6, 2002; TID, July 3 and July 18, 2002; Raymond Stott, transcript, p. 9, copy in FDMC.

17. Lewis C. Smith, transcript in Oral History Collection, p. 5, FDMC; TID,
June 6 and 19, 2002, July 3, July 18, and December 30, 2002.

18. Baumer, *American Iliad*, 196.

19. TID, July 3, 2002; Baumer, *American Iliad*, 196; 3rd Battalion Unit Journal,
June 6, 1944.

20. TID, June 6 and 19, July 3 and July 18, 2002; e-mail, Andrew E. Woods,
FDMC, to author, June 23, 2009; William Hale Jr., clipping, File 38719, Veterans
Project, American Folk Life Center, Library of Congress, Washington, DC.

21. Lewis C. Smith quoted in Whitlock, *The Fighting First,* 198; Lewis C. Smith,
Service Survey Questionnaire, Veterans Collection, 1st Infantry Division, 18th Regiment, Army Military Institute, Army Heritage and History Center; e-mail, Andrew E.
Smith to author, July 21, 2008; TID, June 6 and 19, July 3 and 18, December 30, 2002.

22. Letters, Daly to author, June 6 and 19, July 3 and 18, 2002; TID, June 16,
2008; Johnson, *One More Hill,* 141; Joseph Balkoski, *Omaha Beach: D-Day, June 6,
1944* (Mechanicsburg, PA: Stackpole Books, 2004), 307–308.

23. Letter, Daly to author, June 6, 2002.

24. Letter, Daly to author, June 6, 2002; Baumer, *American Iliad,* 198; Jean-Pierre Benamou, *Omaha Beach, Normandy, 1944* (Album Souvenir, Bilingual Edition, Cully, France: OREP Editions, 2004); TID, July 3, and July 18, 2002; typescript copy of speech written by Michael J. Daly, November, 1996, in author's possession.

25. Telephone interview with Willie W. Sutherland and Michael Davis, June 23, 2009; telephone interview with Lewis C. Smith, July 21, 2010; Whitlock, *The Fighting First,* 203–204; TID, July 3, 2002.

26. Baumer, *American Iliad,* 225.

27. Quoted in Whitlock, *The Fighting First,* 205; TID, June 6 and 19, July 1, 3 and 18, and December 30, 2002.

28. TID, July 3, 11, and 18, 2002; Edward G. Miller, *Nothing Less than Full Victory: Americans at War in Europe, 1944–1945* (Annapolis, MD: US Naval Institute Press, 2007), 77; "Omaha Beachhead (6 June–13 June, 1944)," American Forces in Action Series, Historical Division, War Department, Facsimile Reprint, 1984–89–94, United States Army Center of Military History, Washington, DC, 82–85, http://www.army.mil/cmh-pg/books/wwii/100–11/100–11.htm.

CHAPTER 5

1. Telephone interview with Michael Daly (hereafter TID), June 27, 2007.

2. TID, December 20, 2002.

3. Robert W. Baumer with Mark J. Reardon, *American Iliad: The 18th Infantry Regiment in World War II* (Bedford, PA: Aberjona Press, 2004), 227–31; TID, July 29, 2002.

4. Baumer, *American Iliad,* 231; Peter R. Mansoor, *The GI Offensive in Europe: The Triumph of American Infantry Divisions, 1941–1945* (Lawrence, KS: University Press of Kansas, 1999), 270; Stephen Ambrose, *Citizen Soldiers: The US Army from the Normandy Beaches to the Bulge to the Surrender of Germany, June 7, 1944–May 7, 1945* (New York: G.P. Putnam's, 1997), 18–19; Franklyn A. Johnson, *One More Hill* (New York: Funk and Wagnalls, 1949), 146; Joseph Balkoski, *Beyond the Beachhead* (Mechanicsburg, PA: Stackpole Books, 1999), 86–89, and 93; TID, July 3 and 8, 2002, and June 24, 2005.

5. TID, July 3 and 8, 2002; Unit History, 18th Infantry Regiment, June 30, 1944, for Period 1–30 June, 1944, Box 5938, Entry 427: WWII Operations Reports, 1st Inf. Division, 301 Inf (18) 7–0.3, August 43–September 46, Record Group 407: Records of the Adjutant General's Office, 1905–81; National Archives and Records Administration II, College Park, MD (hereafter NARA II).

6. Max Hastings, *Armageddon: The Battle for Germany, 1944–1945* (New York: Knopf, 2004), *Armageddon,* 73; Flint Whitlock, *The Fighting First: The Untold Story of the Big Red One on D-Day* (Boulder, CO: Westview Press, 2004), 242; Joseph R. Balkoski, *Beyond the Beachhead,* 231–32; TID, July 3 and 8, 2002; 3rd Battalion Journal, Box 5951, Entry 427: WWII Operations Reports, 1st Inf. Division, 301 Inf (18) 7–0.3 to 301 Inf (18) 7–3.9, June to October, 1944, Record Group 407: Records of the Adjutant General's Office, 1905–81, NARA II; Johnson, *One More Hill,* 140.

7. Johnson, *One More Hill,* 152.

8. Johnson, *One More Hill,* 152–53; Lewis C. Smith, Oral History Collection, Robert R. McCormick Research Center, First Division Museum Cantigny, Wheaton IL.

9. Lewis C. Smith, Oral History Collection, p. 8, telephone interview with Lewis C. Smith, July 20, 2010.

10. Third Battalion Journal, June 7–12, 1944; Baumer, *American Iliad,* 236–37; Johnson, *One More Hill,* 140; interview with Bernard and Claude Marie, July 12, 2005, Le Ferme Béziers, Ville La Vacquerie, France.

11. Interview, Geert van den Bogaert with Dean Weissert (member of 1st Battalion Hqtrs., 18th Infantry Regiment during World War II), Eustice Nebraska, June, 2004, original in possession of Geert van den Bogaert, Caen, France; Baumer, *American Iliad,* 238–39.

12. Statement by Robert C. Hess Jr., Captain, 18th Infantry, Commanding, Co. "I," to [name obscured], Secretary, General Staff, Hq. Seventh Army, 3 December 1944, copy in author's possession. Michael Daly procured this letter and other documents from his Military Personnel Records at the National Personnel Records Center, St. Louis, MO.

13. Third Battalion Unit Journal, June 7–12, 1944; "Silver Star," Citation in General Orders No. 68, 25 August 1944, Hqtrs. 1st US Inf. Division, Entry 427: WWII Operations Reports, Record Group 404, NARA II; "Daly Double," *American Legion Magazine* (December 1945): 53; Statement by Robert C. Hess Jr., 3 December 1944; Unit Journal, 3rd Battalion, 18th Infantry (hereafter 3rd Battalion Unit Journal), June 15, 1944; telephone interview with Lewis C. Smith, July 20, 2010;

14. Wheeler, *The Big Red One,* 294–96.

15. 3rd Battalion Unit Journal, July 20, 1944, June–October 1944.

16. Martin Blumenson, *Breakout and Pursuit.* (Washington, DC: Center of Military History, US Army, 2005), 219–222, at URL: http://www.archive.org/details/breakoutpursuitooblum; Wheeler, *The Big Red One,* 302–303.

17. Sam Carter quoted in Baumer, *American Iliad,* 245; Wheeler, *The Big Red One,* 302; Blumenson, *Breakout and Pursuit,* 234–236, at URL: http://www.archive.org/details/breakoutpursuitooblum; TID, June 24, 2005.

18. 3rd Battalion Unit Journal, July 26, 1944, June–October 1944. [date?]

19. "Action of the 3rd Battalion at Marigny, 26–27–28 July," Entry 427: WW II Operations Reports, 1st Division.18th Infantry Regiment, Combat Interviews, Box 24011, Record Group 407: Records of the Adjutant General's Office, 1905–81, NARA II; TID, July 18, 2002, August 24, 2006, and June 27, 2007; Bill Mauldin, *Up Front* (New York: Henry Holt and Co., 1945; 2000), 93.

20. "Action of the 3rd Battalion at Marigny, 26–27–28 July"; Major Henry V. Middleworth quoted in Baumer, *American Iliad,* 253–54.

21. Wheeler, *The Big Red One,* 309.

22. Baumer, *American Iliad,* 254–57; Wheeler, 309; 3rd Battalion Unit Journal, August 1, 1944.

23. TID, July 31, 2007.

24. Telephone Interview with Lewis C. Smith, July 20, 2010.

25. Interview with Victor Le Rai, Georges Bréteau, Fernand Thuault and Alfred

Monsallier, four citizens of Saint-Loup-du-Gast, France, August 4, 2007; quote from Victor Le Rai.

26. "Handwritten Notes de M. l'abbé Louis Lévêque curé de Saint-Loup-du-Gast (December 22, 1940–October 1, 1980), "Guerre 1939–40 Contre Allemagne et Bataille de Saint-Loup-Du-[Gast] 5 AU 13 Août, 1944," Municipal Archives of Saint-Loup-du-Gast, copy given to author in Saint-Loup-du-Gast, August 4, 2007; William I. Hitchcock, *The Bitter Road to Freedom: The Human Cost of Allied Victory in World War II Europe* (New York: Free Press, 2009), 27–28.

27. "Handwritten Notes de M. l'abbé Louis Lévêque curé de Saint-Loup-du-Gast.

28. "Handwritten Notes de M. l'abbé Louis Lévêque curé de Saint-Loup-du-Gast.

29. Battalion Unit Journal, August 9, 1944; Statement by Robert C. Hess Jr., Captain, 18th Infantry, Commanding, Co. "I; "Handwritten Notes de M. l'Abbé Louis Lévêque, curé de Saint-Loup-du Gast."

30. Baumer, *American Iliad*, 257; 3rd Battalion Unit Journal, August 18, 1944.

31. Baumer, *American Iliad*, 257–59; 3rd Battalion Unit Journal, September 10 and 11, 1944; "Commemorative History of the Eighteenth Infantry Regiment, First Infantry Division, US Army, 1812–1944," typescript, November 8, 1944, Quinton F. Reams Papers, Box 1, Folder 5, US Army Military History Institute at the Army Heritage and History Center Carlisle, Pennsylvania.

32. Letter, Michael J. Daly to author, June 6, 2002; TID, June 19, 2003 and July 3, 2002; Baumer, *American Iliad*, 258.

33. TID, July 3, 2002, July 18, 2002, January 2, 2004, and June 24, 2005.

34. Max Hastings, *Armageddon*, 6, 12–17; Wheeler, *The Big Red One*, 312; "Daly Double," *American Legion Magazine* (December 1945), 53; TID, June 21, 2007.

35. 3rd Battalion Unit Journal, September 10–11, 1944; TID, July 18, 2002; Troy D. Cox quoted in Troy D. Cox, *An Infantryman's Memories of World War II* (Booneville, MS: Brown Line Printing, 2003), 157; "Daly Double," 53; Charles B. MacDonald, *Company Commander* (New York History Book Club, 2006), 285; Office of the Adjutant General, *Army Battle Casualties and Non-battle Deaths in World War II: Final Report 7 December 1941–31 December 1946*, Statistical and Accounting Branch, Office of the Adjutant General under Direction of Program Review and Analysis Division, Office of the Comptroller of the Army (Washington, DC, Department of the Army, 1953), 92.

36. Lt. Gen. Alexander "Sandy" M. Patch to Julia Adrienne Littell Patch, November 6, 1944; William K. Wyant, *Sandy Patch: A Biography of Lt. General Alexander M. Patch* (New York: Praeger Publishers, 1991), 144–49.

CHAPTER 6

1. Headquarters 100th Infantry Division, Office of the Commanding General, General Orders No. 17: Award of Silver Star to Paul G. Daly, Colonel, 15 January 1945, copy in author's possession; William K. Wyant, *Sandy Patch: A Biography of Lt. General Alexander M. Patch* (New York: Praeger Publishers, 1991), 159; W. B. Martin Jr. to Col. Paul Daly, November 29, 1945, and Major General Burress to Col.

Paul G. Daly, December 23, 1944, Daly Family Papers (hereafter DFP); telephone interview with Michael Daly (hereafter TID) June 16, 2006, August 20, 2002, and June 21, 2007; "Daly Double," *American Legion Magazine* (December 1945): 53.

2. Wyant, *Sandy Patch*, 2–5, 12, 22, 36; One story, recounted by Bill Mauldin, the cartoonist, spread through the army. Whether true or simply apocryphal, it illustrated the positive reputation that Patch enjoyed among the GIs in the 3rd Infantry Division who called themselves, "Dogfaces." The story involved the policy of declaring recently liberated towns in southern France "off limits" to GIs in order to minimize incidents of theft, rape, or misunderstandings between troops and civilians. According to the story, Patch picked up a hitchhiking paratrooper on the Riviera. The general asked the paratrooper his destination and the paratrooper replied, "Cannes." Patch told him that headquarters had designated it "off-limits," to which the paratrooper supposedly replied, "Hell, that's okay. I can sneak in and nobody will see me until I'm ready to leave." Mauldin writes, "Either the general wasn't wearing his stars on the jeep or the paratrooper didn't give a damn." In any case, the paratrooper's remarkable honesty so impressed Patch that he gave the paratrooper a pass. He wrote it out in longhand and instructed all the MPs of his command that the paratrooper was not to be arrested. Mauldin added, "It doesn't matter whether the story is true or not. If Patch had been a martinet, nobody would have bothered to repeat the yarn. You can learn a lot about a general by listening to the stories told about him by his combat men." See Bill Mauldin, *Up Front* (New York: Henry Holt and Co., 1945), 195–96.

3. Sergeant quoted in Charles Whiting, *America's Forgotten Army: The True Story of the US Seventh Army in WWII* (New York: St. Martin's Press, 1999), 81.

4. TID August 20, 2002; Jeffrey J. Clarke and Robert Ross Smith, *Riviera to the Rhine* (Washington, DC: Center of Military History, US Army, 1993), 81–82; Wyant, *Sandy Patch*, 2–3; TID July 3, 2003.

5. Wyant, *Sandy Patch*, 2–3; Sandy Patch to Julia Patch, November 6, 1944, Gen. Alexander McCarrell "Sandy" Patch Papers, USMASCA; Wyant, *Sandy Patch*, 154–55; TID July 3, 2003.

6. Wyant, *Patch*, 142. The friendship between Patch and Paul Daly led to an unusual dinner for Colonel Daly with American writer Gertrude Stein and her companion, Alice B. Toklas, who was a renowned cook. The two women resided in a little French railway town, Culoz, near the Swiss border. Elated at the American liberation of the area, in September, Stein invited General Patch to a chicken dinner. She closed her note with the words, "Long live the Americans." Patch politely accepted the invitation, saying that he looked forward to "meeting the lady whose literary works and humanitarian achievements I have long admired," though in fact he had never read any of her writing. He told his wife that "she puts together a lot of repetitions which have significance to only those whose minds are in a higher sphere than mine." When, two weeks later, heavy fighting in the Vosges Mountains prevented Patch from keeping his appointment for dinner, he found a way to play a joke on Paul by sending him in his place, knowing how much Daly disliked modern art and poetry. In typical fashion, however, Daly, who could be most charming and who enjoyed "the fine things of life," rose to the occasion and found Stein an excellent conversationalist and Toklas a great cook. He enjoyed himself so much that he overstayed his visit.

7. Edward G. Longacre, *War in the Ruins: The American Army's Final Battle*

against Nazi Germany (Yardley, PA: Westholme Publisher), 142–47; letter, Michael J. Daly to Franklin Gurley, military historian, February 16, 1993, copy in author's possession; copy of a speech given by Col. Paul G. Daly to junior officers, n.d., DFP; Will Alperin to Franklin Gurley, February 7, 1993, copy in author's possession; Wyant, *Sandy Patch*, 159.

8. Headquarters 100th Infantry Division, Office of the Commanding General, General Orders No. 17: Award of Silver Star to Paul G. Daly, Colonel, 15 January 1945, copy in DFP; Patch quoted in Wyant, *Sandy Patch*, 159; Michael D. Doubler, *Closing with the Enemy: How GIs Fought the War in Europe, 1944–1945* (Lawrence, KS: University Press of Kansas, 1994), 235, 237; W. B. Martin Jr. to Colonel Paul Daly, San Antonio, Texas, November 29, 1945, Major General Burress to Colonel Paul G. Daly, December 23, 1944, DFP; TID August 20, 2002, and June 21, 2007.

9. TID July 29, 2002, August 20, 2002, and June 21, 2007; Reports of the General Board, United States Forces, European Theater, General Board Reports, No. 6: "Appointments and Promotions in the European Theater of Operations," 8, Combined Arms Research Library, Fort Leavenworth, KS, http://www.cgsc.edu/carl/eto/eto.asp; Statement by Robert C. Hess Jr., Captain, 18th Infantry, Commanding, Co. "I," to [name obscured], Secretary, General Staff, Hq. Seventh Army, 3 December 1944, copy in author's possession.

10. TID July 18, July 30, and August 20, 2002, July 3 and 10, 2003, and June 21, 2007; Sandy Patch to Julia Adrienne Littell Patch, November 12, 1944, Patch Papers; Headquarters, 15th Infantry, Office of the Regimental Commander, 16 February 1945 to Commanding General, Hq. Seventh Army, APO 758, Battlefield Promotion, copy; " The Fifteenth Infantry Regiment Lineage and Historical Narrative," http://www.geocities.com/Eureka/Plaza/7750/15thinfo2.html.

11. Max Hastings, *Armageddon: The Battle for Germany, 1944–1945* (New York: Knopf, 2004), 141, 196; TID August 20, 2002, and June 21, 2007.

12. Headquarters 100th Infantry Division, Office of the Commanding General, General Orders No. 17: Award of Silver Star to Paul G. Daly, Colonel, 15 January 1945, copy in author's possession; Wyant, *Sandy Patch*, 159; W. B. Martin Jr. to Colonel Paul Daly, November 29, 1945, and Major General Burress to Colonel Paul G. Daly, December 23, 1944, both Daly Family Papers; TID June 16, 2006, August 20, 2002, and June 21, 2007; "Daly Double," 53.

CHAPTER 7

1. Telephone interview with Michael Daly (hereafter TID), August 28, 2002, and June 21, 2007; Kennard R. Wiggins Jr. (Brig. Gen. [ret.]), "Lieutenant General John Wilson (Iron Mike) O'Daniel, US Army," *Delaware Journal of Military History* 1, no. 1 (n.d.), http://militaryheritage.org/JrnlMilHistory.html; Fifteenth Regiment Operations Reports for the Month of January 1945, pp. 1–3, Entry 427: WWII Operations Reports, 3rd Infantry Division, 303 Inf (15)-0.3 to 303 Inf (15)-0.6, Box 6373, Jan–April, OP Reports, 15th Regiment, Box 6379, Record Group 407: Records of the Adjutant General's Office, 1905–81, National Archives and Records Administration II, College Park, MD (hereafter NARA II); TID, August 28, 2002, and June 21, 2007; copy of undated newspaper article (*Bridgeport Post* or *Bridgeport Telegram*) in author's possession.

2. Ted Ballard, *Rhineland* (Washington, D.C, United States Army Center of Military History, 1995), 21–24, http://www.army.mil/cmh/brochures/rhineland/rhineland.htm.

3. Jeffrey J. Clarke and Robert Ross Smith, *Riviera to the Rhine* (Washington, DC: Center of Military History, US Army, 1993), 81–82.

4. Robert C. McFarland, ed., *The History of the 15th Infantry Regiment in World War II* (Chelsea, MI: Society of the Third Division, 1990), 250–51.This is largely a transcription of an unpublished history of the 15th Regiment compiled in 1945 and found in the Regimental Papers of the 15th Infantry Regiment, Record Group 407, NARA II; TID, December 28, 2006.

5. Donald G. Taggart, ed., *History of the Third Infantry Division in World War II* (Washington, DC: Infantry Journal Press, 1947), 291; Memorandum 5, "Awards," Headquarters 15th Infantry, January 14, 1945, Unit Journal and File, 15th Inf. Regt.—European Campaign, Box 6379, Entry 427: WWII Operations Reports, 3rd Inf. Division, 303 Inf (15)-0.3 to 303 Inf 06, Record Group 407: Records of the Adjutant General's Office, 1905–81, NARA II. Division and Regimental headquarters constantly urged company commanders to submit the names of those who had earned recognition for bravery. The memorandum cited in the text ended with these words: "Give your men the awards they have earned. By order of Lt. Col. Hallett Edson."

By the end of World War II, sixteen members of the 15th Regiment had received the Medal of Honor. The regiment suffered 1,633 killed, 5,812 wounded, and 419 missing in action. Among the Medal of Honor recipients in the 1st Battalion were Audie Murphy of Baker Company and Michael J. Daly of Able Company. See "1st Battalion—15th Infantry Regiment," http://www.globalsecurity.org/military/agency/army/1-15in.htm; Lieutenant Colonel Ware remained in the army after the war and advanced to the rank of major general, one of the few draftees in army history to become a general officer. In March 1968 he assumed command of the 1st Infantry Division in South Vietnam. On September 13, 1968, he was killed when the helicopter from which he was directing a combat operation was downed by antiaircraft fire. The first army general officer to die in South Vietnam, he was posthumously awarded the Distinguished Service Cross.

6. McFarland, *History of the 15th Regiment,* 251–52; Taggart, ed., *History of the Third Infantry Division,* 290. Clarke and Smith, *Riviera to the Rhine,* 49, 511.

7. Telephone interview with Troy D. Cox (hereafter TIC), July 22, 2008; TID, June 15, 2006, and August 28, 2008.

8. TID, July 25, 2005, August 11, 2005,and June 15, 2006; Paul Daly quoted in William Wyant interview of Madge Daly Potter, July 24, 1984, copy of typescript in author's possession.

9. McFarland, *History of the 15th Regiment,* 251–52; Clarke and Smith, *Riviera to the Rhine,* 437, 533; Lt. Melvin J. Lasky, "La Maison Rouge: The Story of an Engagement," typescript, in Box 6373, Entry 427: World War II Operations Reports, 1940–48, 303 Inf (15)-0.6, Record Group 94, Record Group 407: Records of the Adjutant General's Office, 1905–81, NARA II.

10. Clarke and Smith, *Riviera to the Rhine,* 534, 539; Gen. Jean de Lattre de Tassigny quoted in McFarland, ed., *History of the 15th Infantry,* 251–52; Gen. Friedrich Wiese quoted in William K. Wyant, *Sandy Patch: A Biography of Lt. General Alexander M. Patch* (New York: Praeger Publishers, 1991), 170–71.

11. Hallett D. Edson, Lt. Col, 15th Inf, Commanding, "January 5, 1945, "Report of Operations for the Month of December, "Comments and Lessons Learned," p. 5, Entry 427: WWII Operations Reports, 3rd Inf. Division 303 Inf (15)-0.3 to 303 Inf (15)-0.6, Box 6373, Record Group 407: Records of the Adjutant General's Office, 1905–81, NARA II; McFarland, ed., *History of the 15th Infantry Regiment,* 251–52; Unit Journal, 15th Regiment, January 21, 1945, Box 6378, Entry 427: WWII Operations Reports, 3rd Inf. Division 303 Inf (15)-0.3 to 303 Inf (15)-0.6, Record Group 407: Records of the Adjutant General's Office, 1905–81; Maj. Hugh A. Scott, Headquarters, Third Infantry Division, G-2 Estimate, January 27, 1945, WWII Operations Reports, 3rd Inf. Division, 303–2.15, Record Group 407: Records of the Adjutant General's Office, 1905–81, NARA II.

12. Clarke and Smith, *Riviera to the Rhine,* 532–34, 536–46; Roger Cirillo, *Ardennes-Alsace* (Washington, DC, US Army Center of Military History, 1995), 51, http://www.45thdivision.org/CampaignsBattles/ardennes_alsace.htm; Lasky, "La Maison Rouge."

13. Audie Murphy, *To Hell and Back: The Classic Memoir of World War II by America's Most Decorated Soldier* (New York: Henry Holt and Company, 2002), 220, 223, 228–29; "In Brief," from *Intelligence Bulletin* 8 (April 1945): 3. http://www.lonesentry.com/articles/inbrief/index.html.

14. TID, November 21, 2002, June 22, 2006, and July 20, 2006; Audie Murphy, *To Hell and Back,* 220; Charles Whiting, *America's Forgotten Army: The True Story of the Seventh Army In WWII* (New York St. Martin's Press, 1999), 119, 144; Robert Asahina, *Just Americans: How Japanese Americans Won a War at Home and Abroad, The Story of the 100th Battalion/442nd Regimental Combat Team in World War II* (New York: Gotham, 2006), 184.

15. McFarland, *History of the 15th Infantry Regiment,* 253–55; Murphy, *To Hell and Back;* TID, November 21, 2002, December 30, 2002; e-mail, J. Leon Lebowitz to author, August 8, 2002. Lebowitz made copies of the company records for himself.

16. Troy D. Cox, *An Infantryman's Memories of World War II* (Booneville, MS: Brown Line Printing, 2003), 157.

17. McFarland, *History of the 15th Infantry Regiment,* 256–58; Citation, Record of Award of Decoration, Silver Star Medal, Second Lieutenant Michael J. Daly, January, 25, 1945, The Adjutant General's Office, Decorations and Awards Branch, Washington, DC, copy in author's possession; Lasky, "La Maison Rouge"; Interview with Gene Palumbo, July 1997, "Audie Murphy Research Foundation and Newsletter" (Winter 1998): 9, http://www.audiemurphy.com/newsletter_pdf/amrf_news3 .pdf; Cox, *An Infantryman's Memories,* 98.

18. Paul Fussell, *The Boys' Crusade: The American Infantry in Northwestern Europe, 1944–1945* (New York: Modern Library, 2003), 131;Taggart, *History of the Third Infantry Division,* 301; letter, Michael Daly to author, June 6, 2002; TID, August 28, 2002, November 21, 2002, December 30, 2002; copy of a speech given by Michael J. Daly, November, 1996, in author's possession.

19. Roland G. Ruppenthal, *US Army in World War II, Logistical Support of the Armies, September 1944 to May 1945,* vol. 2 (Washington, DC, 1995), 215–18, http://www.archive.org/details/logisticalsuppor02rupp.

20. Ruppenthal, *Logistical Support of the Armies,* vol. 2, 229–30.

21. Ruppenthal, *Logistical Support of the Armies,* vol. 2, 215–28.

22. General Board Report, United States Forces, European Theater, General Board Report 94, "Trench Foot (Cold Injury, Ground Type), 4, Combined Arms Research Library, Fort Leavenworth, KS, http://www.cgsc.edu/carl/eto/eto; General Board Report 91, "Combat Exhaustion," 3–4; Ruppenthal, *Logistical Support of the Armies,* vol. 2, 229 and 231; TID, December 30, 2002, and July 29, 2008; Richard E. Engler Jr., *The Final Crisis: Combat in Northern Alsace, January 1945* (Bedford, PA: Aberjona Press, 1999), 102.

23. Cox, *An Infantryman's Memories,* 99.

24. General Board Report 94: "Trench Foot," 10; Edward G. Miller, *Nothing Less Than Full Victory: Americans at War in Europe, 1944–1945* (Annapolis, MD: Naval Institute Press, 2007), 187; Max Hastings, *Armageddon: The Battle for Germany, 1944–1945* (New York: Knopf, 2004), 184–85; Asahina, *Just Americans,* 149–51; TID, December 30, 2002, and July 20, 2006; TID, February 8, 2010.

25. TIC, February 8, 2010. Morale also plunged among the tankers of the 756th Tank Battalion, which was attached to the 3rd Division. Writing in the "Commander's Narratives" for January 1945, the commander of the 756th noted that the enemy strongly resisted his tank attacks with all known antitank defenses and with his own armor, and continued his policy of counterattacking any advances. He pointed to the loss of seventeen Sherman medium tanks and one 2½-ton truck and to the accompanying loss of seven of nine medium-tank platoon leaders, one company commander, and many experienced enlisted tank commanders. All this seriously threatened the efficient employment of armor, he claimed. Continuous operation with companies at about 50 percent strength in tank personnel had seriously affected morale of "shaky" men and led, at times, to the scattering of tanks instead of keeping the platoon intact. Without officer supervision the tanks had not always performed as well as they could have. Finally the Commander bemoaned the forcible demonstration once again of the superiority of enemy tanks and self-propelled guns. "In *no* case did enemy armor piercing (AP) projectiles fail to penetrate our tanks, while one of our tanks bounced five shots off a German tank at close range. In some cases enemy projectiles passed completely through our tanks. The effect on the morale of our tank crews is obvious." See Cheryl Esposito, *The 756th Tank Battalion in the European Theater* (N.P.: Privately printed, 1999), x. Jeff Danby graciously provided the author with a copy of the book.

26. TIC, February 8, 2010; letter, James C. "Jimmy" Elling to "Cath," Katherine Irene Elling, May 10, 1945, original in possession of Jacqueline Elling-Cox of Tucson, Arizona, one of Mr. Elling's daughters.

27. Sandy Patch to Julia Patch, February 24, 1945, copy in Patch Papers, United States Military Academy Special Collections and Archives.

28. TID, December 30, 2002, and July 20, 2006; Cox, *An Infantryman's Memories,* 129–30.

29. Edwin K. Adam, comp., "A Little of the History of Company A, 1st BN, 15th Infantry Regiment, World War II [As told by the former members and taken from Morning Reports]," (Clarksville, IN: Fifteenth Infantry Regiment Association, November 1, 1996), 3–4; Hastings, *Armageddon,* 140; infantry veteran quoted in Stephen Ambrose's "Introduction," in Bill Mauldin, *Up Front,* viii–ix.

30. TID, June 15, 2006; Cox, *An Infantryman's Memories,* 100; Hastings, *Armageddon,* 142.

31. Cox, *An Infantryman's Memories,* 156–57.

32. Wyant, *Sandy Patch,* 172.

33. McFarland, *History of the 15th Infantry Regiment,* 262–64.

34. Kenneth B. Potter, Major, 15th Inf. Commanding, to Commanding Officer, 15th Infantry (APO 3), February 7, 1945, Subject: Promotion of Officer, copy in author's possession; McFarland, *History of the 15th Infantry Regiment,* 266–67.

35. Kenneth B. Potter, Major, 15th Inf. Commanding, to Commanding Officer, 15th Infantry (APO 3), February 7, 1945, copy in author's possession; McFarland, *History of the 15th Regiment,* 266–67; Charles B. MacDonald, *Company Commander* (New York: History Book Club, 2006), 297–98; Charles B. Macdonald, *The Mighty Endeavor: The American War in Europe* (New York: Quill, 1986), 460; Hastings, *Armageddon,* 73;Troy D. Cox quoted in Cox, *An Infantryman's Memories,* 158; interview with Gene Palumbo, July 1997, "Audie Murphy Research Foundation and Newsletter" (Winter 1998): 10–11, http://www.audiemurphy.com/newsletter_pdf/amrf_news3.pdf.

36. Cox, *An Infantryman's Memories,* 97.

37. Adams, "A Little of the History of Company A," 4; Hallett D. Edson, Lt. Col. 15th Inf. Commanding, 15th Regiment Operations Report for the Month of February 1945, "Comments and Lessons Learned," 3.

38. Taggart, ed., *History of the Third Infantry Division in World War II* (Washington, DC: Infantry Journal Press, 1947), 312; Hallett D. Edson, Lt. Col, 15th Inf. Commanding, 15th Regiment Operations Report for the Month of February 1945, "Comments and Lessons Learned," 1.

39. Robert Schertzinger, *Biesheim: Photographiquement Votre* (Biesheim, 2002), 10; Hallett D. Edson, Lt. Col, 15th Inf. Commanding, 15th Regiment Operations Report for the Month of February 1945, "Comments and Lessons Learned," 1.

40. *History of the 15th Regiment,* 269; Hallett D. Edson, Lt. Col, 15th Inf. Commanding, 15th Regiment, Operations Report for the Month of February 1945, "Comments and Lessons Learned," 1; Kenneth B. Potter, Major, 15th Inf. Commanding, to Commanding Officer, 15th Infantry (APO 3), February 7, 1945, subject: Promotion of Officer, copy in author's possession; Cox, *An Infantryman's Memories,* 100–101; historian quoted in Clarke and Smith, *Riviera to the Rhine,* 552. Contemporary US military doctrine viewed tanks as primarily anti-infantry weapons rather than antitank weapons. Tank destroyers had the task of engaging enemy tanks, American tanks dealt with enemy automatic weapons, and the infantry dealt with antitank gun crews. See Clarke and Smith, *Riviera to the Rhine,* 554; citation for third Silver Star for action on February 4, 1945, copy in author's possession from Daly's Military Personnel Records at The National Personnel Records Center; TID, July 16, 2007. In June 1945, after the war had ended in Europe, the European Theater of Operations established a general board of officers to analyze the strategy, tactics, and administration employed by US forces in the European Theater. The board concluded that many Silver Stars should have been Distinguished Service Crosses but that "to attempt to rectify the situation at this late date might only cause additional injustice." See, General Board Report 10: Awards and Decorations in the Theater of Operations," 8.

41. McFarland, *History of the 15th Infantry Regiment,* 269; Hallett D. Edson, Lt. Col. 15th Inf. Commanding, "Summary of Enemy Operations," 15th Regiment Operations Report for the Month of February 1945, 2; Cox, *An Infantryman's Memories,* 101–102.

42. Kenneth B. Potter, Major, 15th Inf. Commanding, to Commanding Officer, 15th Infantry (APO 3), February 7, 1945, subject: Promotion of Officer; TID, June 7, 2007, and August 14, 2007. After the war, when Daly was an auto-parts salesman, he ran into a former member of Able Company who operated a service station in Rochester, New York. The man, whose name escaped Daly, recounted Daly's yelling "Shoot the bastards"; e-mail, J. Leon Lebowitz to author, August 8, 2002. Troy Cox quotes and recollections in Cox, *An Infantryman's Memories,* 102–103.

43. McFarland, ed., *History of the 15th Regiment,* 269, 269–70; Wyant, *Sandy Patch,* 174; Murphy, *To Hell and Back,* 262, Taggart, *History of the Third Infantry Division,* 322 and 324.

44. TID, December 23, 2003; Robert S. Rush, *The US Infantryman in World War II* (Oxford, UK: Osprey Publishing, 2003), 30; Joseph Balkoski, *Beyond the Beachhead: The 29th Infantry Division in Normandy* (Mechanicsburg, PA: Stackpole Books, 2005), 91.

45. Kenneth B. Potter, Major, 15th Inf. Commanding, to Commanding Officer, 15th Infantry (APO 3), February 7, 1945, subject: Promotion of Officer, copy in author's possession; David "Spec" McClure, "How Audie Murphy Won His Medals, Part II," in *Audie Murphy Research Foundation Newsletter* 2 (Spring 1997): 14, http://www.audiemurphy.com/newsletter_pdf/amrf_news2.pdf.

46. TID, March 18, 2002, and March 29, 2008; John Fennelly, "In Memoriam Al Blozis," http://www.giantsfootballblog.com/2011/05/30/in-memoriam-al-blozis/, May 30, 2011, 8:23 pm: "When, in 1942, Blozis attempted to enlist in the US Army, he was rejected because of his 6'5" height. Turned down by the army, he then played three seasons of football with the New York Giants, earning All-Pro accolades. His greatest desire, however, was to enlist in the army. As a result of the manpower crunch of 1944, the army changed its earlier restrictions on height, and Blozis entered as a twenty-six year-old lieutenant. He was killed during his first patrol in the Vosges Mountains, only two weeks after he joined General Patton's 3rd Army; telephone interview with Andrew A. Smith, July 21, 2008; e-mail, W. Sanford Miller Jr. to author, August 4, 2008; Col. (ret.) John J. Tominac, "Recollections," *Audie Murphy Research Foundation Newsletter* 2 (Spring 1997): 10, http://www.audiemurphy.com/newsletter_pdf/amrf_news2.pdf.

47. E-mail, W. Sanford Miller Jr. to author, August 4, 2008; TID, July 3, 18, and 21, 2002, and June 7, 2007. Daly expressed embarrassment about having harbored hard feelings toward the Germans for so long after the war's end.

48. Hastings, *Armageddon,* 90–91, 148; S. L .A. Marshall, *Men against Fire: The Problem of Battle Command* (Norman, OK: University of Oklahoma Press, 2000), 117; Taggart, *History of the Third Division,* 329; Whiting, *America's Forgotten Army.*

49. Huggens, Captain, Inf. Headquarters, Third Infantry Division, Entry 427: WWII Operations Reports, G-2 Periodic Report, February 2, 1945, Annex A, p. 5, in "Report of Operations, Third Infantry Division In France, 1–28 February 1945, WWII Operations Reports 303 Inf (15)-0.3 to 303 Inf. (15)-0.6, Box 6111, Record

Group 407: Records of the Adjutant General's Office, 1905–81, NA; McFarland, *The History of the 15th Regiment*, 270–71; Pyle quoted in Ballard, *Rhineland*, 34, http://www.army.mil/cmh/brochures/rhineland/rhineland.htm. Murphy was awarded the Medal of Honor, the Distinguished Service Cross, two Silver Stars, the Legion of Merit, two Bronze Stars, three Purple Hearts, the French Legion of Honor, the French Croix de Guerre (plus Palm), and the Belgian Croix de Guerre 1940 Palm; Balkoski, *Beyond the Beachhead*, 91.

CHAPTER 8

1. Troy D. Cox quoted in Troy D. Cox, *An Infantryman's Memories of World War II* (Booneville, MS: Brown Line Printing, 2003), 118–19; Citation, Record of Award of Decoration, Bronze Star Medal, Michael J. Daly (1st Lt., Capt.) [for action taken as a 1st Lt.], August 27, 1945, Office of the Adjutant General, Decorations and Awards Branch, Washington, DC, copy in author's possession; telephone interview with Michael Daly (hereafter TID), July 18 and August 20, 2002, and June 25, 2003.

2. Dogface Soldiers: US Third Division WWII, a photographic journey of the US Third Division in WWII, The Rhineland Assault into Germany, slide 2, http://www.dogfacesoldiers.org/rhineland/xxxx-03.htm; Gen. Jean de Lattre de Tassigny quoted in William K. Wyant, *Sandy Patch: A Biography of Lt. General Alexander M. Patch* (New York: Praeger Publishers, 1991), 175; Audie Murphy, *To Hell and Back: The Classic Memoir of World War II by America's Most Decorated Soldier* (New York: Henry Holt and Co., 2002), 262–63.

3. Burton Barr quoted in Mel Allen, "Only Afraid to Show Fear: Portrait of a Hero," *Yankee* (May 1983): 138; Major General John W. O'Daniel, Major General, US Army Commanding, Headquarters Third Infantry Division, to Lieutenant General Alexander M. Patch, Commanding General, Seventh Army, March 2, 1945, copy in General Alexander McCarrell "Sandy" Patch Papers, United States Military Academy Special Collections and Archives (hereafter USMASCA), United States Military Academy Library (hereafter USMAL); Patch quoted in Mel Allen, "Only Afraid to Show Fear," 138; e-mail, W. Sanford Miller Jr. to author, August 23, 2008.

4. Biographical Sketch of Audie Leon Murphy at Audie L. Murphy Memorial, http://www.audiemurphy.com/biograph.htm; Audie Murphy Born 75 years Ago," *The Dragon* [15th Infantry Newsletter] (April 1999): 10, taken from Edward F. Murphy, *Heroes of World War II* (Novato, CA: Presidio Press, 1990).

5. TID, November 21, 2002, August 11, 2005, and June 11, 2007.

6. Headquarters 15th Infantry (APO 3), Report of Operations for the Month of March 1945, pp. 1–3, Entry 427: WWII Operations Reports, 3rd Infantry Division, 303 Inf (15)-0.3 to 303 Inf (15)-0.6, Box 6373, Jan-April, OP Reports, 15th Regiment, Record Group 407: Records of the Adjutant General's Office, 1905–81, National Archives and Records Administration II, College Park, MD (hereafter NARA II); "Report of Operations for the Month of March, 1945," p. 1; Hqtrs. 15th Regiment, Daily Bulletin Number 17, "Officer's Party," Entry 427: WWII Operations Reports, 3rd Inf. Division, Jan-May 1945, Unit Journal 15th Inf. Regt—European Campaign, WWII Operations Reports, 3rd Infantry Division, 303 Inf (15)-0.3 to 303 Inf (15)-0.6, Box 6379, Record Group 407: Records of the Adjutant General's Office, 1905–81, NARA II.

7. TID, August 28, 2002, June 19, 2003, and June 20, 2003; Charles Whiting, *America's Forgotten Army: The True Story of the Seventh Army in WWII* (New York: St. Martin's Press, 2001), 155. Napoleon changed the original design of the Madeleine church to that of a monument in the Greek style to memorialize French military prowess. After his defeat at Moscow in 1812, however, he returned to the original idea of a church.

8. Ted Ballard, *Rhineland,* (Washington, DC: Center of Military History, US Army, 1995), 2 and 7, http://www.army.mil/cmh/brochures/rhineland/rhineland.htm.

9. Wyant, *Sandy Patch,* 178–79; The Campaign For Germany," 15 March to 9 May, for 7th Army Historical Section, 1–2, 15th Infantry History, Entry 427: WWII Operations Reports, 3rd Infantry Division, 303 Inf (15)-0.3 to 303 Inf (15)-0.6, Box 6379, Record Group 407: Records of the Adjutant General's Office, 1905–81, NARA II.

10. Donald G. Taggart, ed., *History of the Third Infantry Division in World War II* (Washington, DC: Infantry Journal Press, 1947), 331; Robert C. McFarland, ed., *The History of the 15th Infantry Regiment in World War II* (Chelsea, MI: Society of the Third Division, 1990), 273–74; The Campaign For Germany," 15 March to 9 May, for 7th Army Historical Section, 1–2; telephone interview with Troy D. Cox (hereafter TIC), June 12, 2010. The retreating Germans hid time bombs with three-day timers in shops and houses on the main street of Hornbach. Several days later the bombs detonated, destroying the structures and killing a number of GIs. See Cheryl Esposito, ed., *The 756th Tank Battalion in The European Theater* (N.p.: Privately printed, 1999), 241.

11. Message included in Alexander M. Patch, Diaries (official), 10/01/44–2/6/45, Vol. 3, Dec. 1, 1944–Feb. 28, 1945 (2 June 1945–March 20, 1945), 611, Alexander McCarrell "Sandy" Patch Papers, United States Military Academy Special Collections and Archives and United States Military Academy Library.

12. "G-2 Estimate, Enemy Situation," Annex 1 to Field Order 2, March 12, 1945, in 303–2.15, G-2 Estimate, 3rd Infantry Division, Box 6373, Entry 427: WWII Operations Reports, 303 Inf (15)-0.3 to 303 Inf (15)-0.6, Record Group 407: Records of the Adjutant General's Office, 1905–81, NARA II; "Westwall, Springboard of 1940, Assumes Defensive Role" from *Tactical and Technical Trends* 51 (October 1944), http://www.lonesentry.com/articles/ttt/westwall-siegfried-line.html.

13. Wyant, *Sandy Patch,* 179.

14. "G-2 Estimate, Enemy Situation," Annex 1 to Field Order 2, March 12, 1945; Buchen-Busch Weld Attack: 44th Infantry, part 1, http://efour4ever.com/44thdivision/buchen.htm.

15. McFarland, *History of the 15th Infantry Regiment,* 274–75; Taggart, *History of the Third Infantry Division,* 334; Cox, *An Infantryman's Memories,* 116–17.

16. Topographic Map, Army Map Service, "WWII, Zweibrücken Area," M-864, European Theater, Deutschland, United States Army, Germany M841-Germany, Zweibrücken, 6710–11, 6810–11, Record Group 77: Records of the Office of the Chief of Engineers, NARA II; US Seventh Army, *Official Diary* (February 1, 1945–June 2, 1945), vol. 3, 605–606; "G-2 Estimate, Enemy Situation," Annex 1 to Field Order 2, March 12, 1945; Taggart, *History of the Third Infantry Division,* 334; McFarland, *History of the 15th Regiment,* 275; Cox, *An Infantryman's Memories,* 117.

17. TID, August 9, 2005; letter, Ed Adams to Capt. Michael Daly, June 4, 1989, in author's possession; TIC, July 5, 2002; Cox, *An Infantryman's Memories,* 116–20.

18. Edwin K. Adams, comp., "A Little of the History of Company A, 1st BN, 15th Infantry Regiment, 3rd Infantry Division, World War II [as told by the former members and taken from Morning Reports], The Fifteenth Infantry Regiment Association, Clarksville, IN (November 1, 1996), 4; McFarland, *History of the 15th Regiment,* 274–78; letter, Edwin K. Adams to Michael Daly, June 4, 1989, in author's possession.

19. TIC, August 24, 2006; telephone interview with Stanley A. Porucznik, July 26, 2002; Citation, Record of Award of Decoration, Bronze Star Medal, Michael J. Daly (1st Lt., Capt.) [for action taken as a 1st Lt.], August 27, 1945, Adjutant General's Office, Decorations and Awards Branch, Washington, DC, copy in author's possession.

20. McFarland, *History of the 15th Regiment,* 274–78; Cox, *An Infantryman's Memories,* 118–19; TID, July 18, 2002.

21. Cox, *An Infantryman's Memories,* 118–19; Citation, Record of Award of Decoration, Bronze Star Medal, Michael J. Daly; TID, July 18 and August 20, 2002, and June 25, 2003; William R. Keast, *Provision of Enlisted Replacements,* Study 7 (Washington, DC: Center of Military History, US Army, 1946), 32; Reports of the General Board, United States Forces, European Theater of Operations, General Board Report 91, "Combat Exhaustion," 2–3, 6, 32, Combined Arms Research Library, Fort Leavenworth, KS, http://www.cgsc.edu/carl/eto/eto.asp; Edward G. Miller, *Nothing Less Than Full Victory: Americans at War in Europe* (Annapolis, MD: Naval Institute Press, 2007), 189; John S. Brown, *Draftee Division: The 88th Infantry Division in World War II* (Lexington: University Press of Kentucky, 1986), 158.

22. McFarland, *History of the 15th Regiment,* 279, 281; Hastings, *Armageddon,* 184.

CHAPTER 9

1. Telephone interview with Michael Daly (hereafter TID), July 1 and December 23, 2003, and June 12 and 15, 2006; paraphrase of a line used by Joseph Balkoski in *Beyond the Beachhead: The 29th Infantry Division in Normandy* (Mechanicsburg, PA: Stackpole Books, 2005), 91.

2. Letter, Michael J. Daly to author, June 6, 2002; TID, July 3, 2002; S. L. A. Marshall, *Men against Fire: The Problem of Battle Command* (Norman, OK: University of Oklahoma Press, 2000), 117; Robert S. Rush, *Hell in the Hürtgen Forest: The Ordeal and Triumph of an American Infantry Regiment* (Lawrence, KS: University Press of Kansas), 328.

3. TID, July 3 and December 30, 2002, and August 11, 2005;

4. Mauldin, *Up Front* (New York: Henry Holt and Co., 1945), 16; Rush, *Hell in the Hürtgen Forest,* 94; telephone interview with Jack Kessinger, July 21, 2002; see, G.O. 371, 3rd Division, July 21, 2002, and August 2, 2004; telephone interview with Jacqueline Elling-Cox March 31, 2011; telephone interview with J. Leon Lebowitz, July 18, 2002; letters, Lebowitz to author, July 25, 2002, and August 8, 2002.

5. Telephone interviews with Jack Kessinger, July 21, 2002, and August 2,

2004; Rush, *Hell in the Hürtgen Forest,* 315; e-mail, J. Leon Lebowitz to author, August 8, 2002; telephone interview with J. Leon Lebowitz, July 18, 2002; Letter, Edwin K. Adams to "Capt. Michael Daly," June 4, 1989, in author's possession;

6. Telephone interview with J. Leon Lebowitz, July 18, 2002; TID, July 8 and August 20, 2002, July 1 and August 20, 2003, and August 11, 2005; copy of a speech given by Michael J. Daly, November 1996, in author's possession; Reports of the General Board, United States Forces, European Theater of Operations, General Board Report 91, "Combat Exhaustion," 5–7, Combined Arms Research Library, Fort Leavenworth, KS, http://www.cgsc.edu/carl/eto/eto.asp; Edward G. Miller, *Nothing Less Than Victory: Americans at War in Europe, 1944–1945* (Annapolis, MD: Naval Institute Press, 2007), 189.

7. Letter, Daly to author, June 6, 2002; TID, November 21, 2002, July 9, 2003; Rush, *Hell in the Hürtgen Forest,* 316; TID, August 22, 2003, June 12, 2006, June 27, 2007, and September 14, 2006; telephone interview with Richard Dettman, July 3 and 9, 2003; Patch quoted in Wyant, William K. *Sandy Patch: A Biography of Lt. General Alexander M. Patch* (New York: Praeger Publishers, 1991), 74; General Gavin quoted in Max Hastings, *Armageddon: The Battle for Germany, 1944–1945* (New York: Knopf, 2004), 74, 232–33.

8. Letter, Daly to author, June 6, 2002; quotation from *Army Talks* in Balkoski, *Beyond The Beachhead,* 80; Rush, *Hell in the Hürtgen Forest,* 334; TID, July 3, July 29, and August 28, 2002, March 18 and July 1, 3, and 9, 2003, June 12, 2006, and June 27 and August 14, 2007; telephone interview with Jacqueline Elling-Cox, March 31; e-mail, Jacqueline Elling-Cox to the author, April 4, 2011; Daly quote about Elling taken from Daly letter to Kathleen Elling Dobson offering condolence on the death of James C. Elling, May 21, 2003, copy in author's possession; General George C. Marshall quoted in Marshall, *Men Against Fire,* 42; telephone interview with J. Leon Lebowitz, July 18, 2002; telephone interview with Richard Dettman, July 3 and 9, 2003. The extent to which infantry riflemen fired their weapons on offense has sparked controversy. In his influential, *Men against Fire,* first published in 1946, Brig. Gen. S. L. A. Marshall, chief historian for the European Theater of Operations, claimed that his extensive post-action interviews with infantry rifle companies in the Pacific and Europe on the "ratio of fire" had revealed that only 15–25 percent actually discharged their weapons. Marshall's claim became the accepted wisdom of the US Army and of a number of well-received authors writing about World War II, including John Keegan and Max Hastings. Many veteran leaders, however, took issue with Marshall immediately after the war, scoffing at his assertions that ran so counter to their own experience and observations. In 1988, historian Roger J. Spiller challenged Marshall's ratio of fire claims on a number of fronts, including raising serious questions about the quality of Marshall's methodology—notably his failure to employ statistical evidence in support of his very specific claims, and his chief aide's inability, in post-action interviews, to recall Marshall's ever raising the issue. For Marshall's critics, see Roger J. Spiller, "S. L. A. Marshall and the Ratio of Fire," *RUSI Journal* (Winter 1988): 63–71, Frederic Smoler, "The Secret of the Soldiers Who Didn't Shoot," *American Heritage* 40, no. 2, (March 1989): 37–45. Daly's recollections of the ratio of fire in the platoon and the company he commanded tended to correspond with Marshall's figures.

9. TID, July 1 and December 23, 2003, and June 12 and 15, 2006; paraphrase of a line used by Balkowski in *Beyond the Beachhead*, 91.

10. TID, July 30, 2002 and January 2, 2004; Dennis E. Showalter, "Introduction to History Book Club Edition," in Charles B. MacDonald, *Company Commander* (New York: History Book Club, 2006), x; Richard E. Engler Jr., *The Final Crisis: Combat in Northern Alsace, January 1945* (Bedford, PA: Aberjona Press, 1999), 187; US Army Divisions in World War II, http://www.historyshots.com/usarmy/backstory .cfm; Hastings, *Armageddon,* 187; General Patch, addressing what he termed "the "present serious personnel shortages," askted that SHAEF authorize a special shipment of infantry replacements for his army. Sixth Army Group estimated that it needed 13,320, but the Seventh Army Diary noted that, for February SHAEF would allocate 5,234 infantry reinforcements to the Sixth Army Group. Alexander McCarrell "Sandy." Patch, Diaries (official), 10/01/44–2/6/45, Vol. 3, Dec. 1, 1944–Feb. 28, 1945 (2 June 1945), January 24, 1945, 533, Alexander M. Patch Papers, USMASCA; Fussell, *The Boys' Crusade: The American Infantry in Northwestern Europe* (New York: Modern Library, 2003), 95–96, 98; Roland G. Ruppenthal, *US Army in World War II, Logistical Support of the Armies, September 1944 to May 1945*, Vol. 2 (Washington, DC: Center of Military History, US Army, 1995), 339–42, http://www.archive .org/details/logisticalsuppor02rupp.

11. TID, July 29, 2002; Cox, *An Infantryman's* Memories, 95–97; Rush, *Hell in the Hürtgen Forest,* 311, 319, 321, 333, 335. Rush takes issue with S. L. A. Marshall's contention that the effectiveness of a squad in combat depends on the cohesion that grows from bonds developed outside combat. His study of the 22nd Infantry Regiment in the Hürtgen Forest suggests that so long as there remain some veteran junior leaders around whom replacements can coalesce, the squads, platoons, and companies of an infantry regiment can continue to fight effectively. "Only when those veteran junior leaders became casualties," he argues, "did the regiment grind to a halt."

12. TID, July 16, 2007, July 3 and 30, 2002.

13. TID, July 16, 2007.

14. Mauldin, *Up Front,* 38–39; TID, July 3, 2003, July 16, 2007, June 12, 2006, and Nov. 21, 2002.

15. Stephen Ambrose cites Bing West, *The Strongest Tribe: War, Politics, and the Endgame in Iraq* (New York, 2008), 37; Cox, *An Infantryman's Memories,* 145; TID, March 29, 2008.

16. TID, June 12, 2006; telephone interview with Jesse Fisher, July 6, 2002; TID, July 16, 2007.

17. Telephone interview with Jesse Fisher, July 6, 2002; TID, July 10, 2003, and June 27, 2007.

CHAPTER 10

1. Max Hastings, *Armageddon: The Battle for Germany, 1944–1945* (New York: Knopf, 2004), 32; telephone interview with Michael Daly (hereafter TID), July 31, 2006.

2. TID, June 27 and July 16, 2007; Alexander S. Patch, Diaries (official), 10/01/44–2/6/45, Vol. 3, Dec. 1, 1944–Feb. 28, 1945 (2 June 1945), March 25, 1945, 622,

Alexander "Sandy" McCarrell Patch Papers, United States Military Academy Special Collections and Archives and United States Military Academy Library; Hastings, *Armageddon*, 367–68.

3. Robert C. McFarland, ed., *The History of the 15th Infantry Regiment in World War II* (Chelsea, MI: Society of the Third Division, 1990), 285.

4. Audie Murphy, *To Hell and Back: The Classic Memoir of World War II by America's Most Decorated Soldier* (New York: Henry Holt and Co., 2002), 268.

5. Hastings, *Armageddon*, 22, 82–85; S-2 Report, April 2, 1945, Unit Reports, 15th Infantry, Entry 427: WWII Operations Reports, 3rd Infantry Division, 303 Inf (15)-0.3 to 303 Inf (15)-0.6, Box 6379, Record Group 407: Records of the Adjutant General's Office, 1905–81, National Archives and Records Administration II, College Park, MD (hereafter NARA II); TID, August 24, 2006; Charles B. MacDonald, *Company Commander* (New York: History Book Club, 2006), 307; TID, June 27, 2007.

6. McFarland, ed., *History of the 15th Infantry Regiment*, 281–82; telephone interview with Troy D. Cox, July 5, 2002, and July 22, 2008.

7. McFarland, *The History of the 15th Infantry Regiment*, 281–84, 287; Hastings, *Armageddon*, 82; interview with Halle and Herman Wind, August 7, 2007, Laudenbach, Germany; John Shirley, *I Remember: Stories of a Combat Infantryman in World War II* (Livermore, CA: J. B. Shirley, 1993), 67; Cox, *An Infantryman's Memories*, 127–28, 135–36.

8. William K. Wyant, *Sandy Patch: A Biography of Lt. General Alexander M. Patch* (New York: Praeger Publishers, 1991), 187; McFarland, *History of the 15th Infantry Regiment*, 285–86;

9. *Dokumentation uber das Kriegsende in Grossheubach [Documentation of the War's End in Grossheubach]: A Detailed Summary of the Exhibition of the Historical and Geographical Society in the Spring of 1995 and the Draft of the Record of Those Killed in Action in World War 2* (Grossheubach Historical and Geographical Society, 1995), 3–11; telephone interview with Gerard Zoeller, January 2, 2007.

10. McFarland, *A History of the 15th Infantry Regiment*, 286; obituary of James Elling, sent to the author by Michael Daly.

11. Telephone interviews with Gerard Zoeller, January 2, 2007, and August 21, 2008.

12. Hastings, *Armageddon*, 160, 285–86. Helmut Sünderman quoted in *Time,* September 18, 1944, http://www.time.com/time/magazine/article/0,9171,796696,00 .html?promoid=googlep

13. Hastings, *Armageddon*, 163; Franz Hofer quoted in *Time,* September 18, 1944, http://www.time.com/time/magazine/article/0,9171,796696,00 .html?promoid=googlep.

14. Hastings, *Armageddon*, 163, 169; Stephen G. Fritz, *Endkampf: Soldiers, Civilians, and the Death of the Third Reich* (Lexington: University Press of Kentucky, 2004), 11–14, 23–24; *Rüstzeug für die Propaganda in der Ortsgruppe* 2 (January 1945), 31, German Propaganda Archive, Calvin College, http://www.calvin.edu/academic/ cas/gpa/2choices.htm. This website provides the text from one side of a 16 x 23.5 cm leaflet provided to local propaganda leaders as an example of what they could use to keep people fighting. (The text on the other side focuses on the importance of keeping silent about matters interesting to the enemy.)

15. Telephone interviews with Gerard Zoeller, January 2, 2007 and August 21, 2008; TID, June 15, 2006.

16. McFarland, *History of the 15th Infantry Regiment,* 286–87.

17. Bobrowitz [Teacher], "Schilderung der Chronik Bobrowitz wohl der Pfarr-chronik folgend mit Ergänzung von Artur Pfeifer ["Description from The Chronicle of the Educational Establishment [Volksschule] Rothenbuch, with an addition by Artur Pfeifer," Teil, S. 33–34. Furnished to the author by Thomas Noll, Treasurer of the Municipality of Rothenbuch, Germany.

18. TID, August 10, 2006, and August 2, 2007; personal interviews with Karl Wunsch and Pia Wunsch in Rothenbuch, Germany, August 14, 2006; McFarland, *History of the 15th Infantry Regiment,* 288.

19. *Aus der Chronik der Erziehungsanstalt Rothenbuch [From the Chronicle of the Rothenbuch Educational Establishment 2]* II, Teil, S. 1–7, n.p., 1945. Furnished to the author by Thomas Noll, Treasurer of the Municipality of Rothenbuch, Germany.

20. McFarland, *History of the 15th Infantry Regiment,* 292; letter, Daly to author, February 17, 2007; e-mail, Charles S. Porucznik to author, August 24, 2010; Citation for S.Sgt. Stanley A. Porucznik, June 19, 1945, Headquarters Third Infantry Division, "Award of the Bronze Star Medal . . . for meritorious achievement in actual combat . . . 7 April 1945," copy furnished to the author by Charles S. Porucznik.

21. Interview with Dr. Ludwig Benkert, August 9, 2007, Bad Neustadt, Germany; Hallett D. Edson, "Report of Operations for the Month of April 1945, 2, Entry 427: WWII Operations Reports, 3rd Infantry Division, 303 Inf (15)-0.3 to 303 Inf (15)-0.3–0.6, Box 6373, Jan-April, OP Reports, 15th Regiment, Record Group 407: Records of the Adjutant General's Office, 1905–81, NARA II; telephone interview with Ludwig Benkert, translated by Susan Kaiser, Tourist Information, Kurverwaltung/Bad Nuestadt Gimbh, August 14, 2006, Bad Neustadt, Germany; Hastings, *Armageddon,* 422; Fritz, *Endkampf,* 190.

CHAPTER 11

1. Robert McFarland, ed., *The History of the 15th Infantry Regiment in World War II* (Chelsea, MI: Society of the Third Division, 1990), 286–92; "Study of the German National Redoubt," March 31, 1945, 3rd Infantry Division, Entry 427: WWII Operations Reports, 1940–48, 3rd Infantry Div., 303–2.10 to 303–2.18, in Box 6158, Record Group 407, Records of the Adjutant General's Office, 1917–85, National Archives and Records Administration II, College Park, MD (hereafter NARA II); S-2 Report, April 8, 1945, Unit Reports, 15th Infantry, Entry 427: WWII Operations Reports, 1940–48, 3rd Infantry Division, 303 Inf (15)-0.3–2.10 to 303–2.18-Inf (15)-0.6, Box 6158, Record Group 407: Records of the Adjutant General's Office, 1905–81, NARA II; Max Hastings, *Armageddon: The Battle for Germany, 1944–1945* (New York: Knopf, 2004), 422.

2. Richard J. Evans, *The Third Reich at War* (New York: Penguin Press, 2009), 698–99; Richard E. Engler Jr. and Theodore MacKechnie, *The Final Crisis: Combat in Northern Alsace, January 1945* (Bedford, PA: Aberjona Press, 1999), 342; interview with Friedrich Braun, Heroldsberg, Germany, August 8, 2007.

3. McFarland, *History of the 15th Infantry Regiment,* 292–94; photograph

from J. Leon Lebowitz's scrapbook, compiled by the company clerk during the war, copies of photographs in author's possession.

4. McFarland, *History of the 15th Infantry Regiment*, 292–94; Emil Trautman, "Recollection: Ike, Patton, and Me"; 7 Years with the 15th," *The Dragon* (October 2006): 21; Report of Operations for the Month of April 1945, Headquarters 15th Infantry, May 1, 1945, 2, 15th Infantry, Entry 427: WWII Operations Reports, 1940–48, 3rd Infantry Division, Box 6373, Record Group 407: Records of the Adjutant General's Office, 1905–81, NARA II.

5. Interview with Friedrich Braun, August 8, 2007. Mr. Braun, who lived on the outskirts of Nuremberg during the war, has studied and written extensively about the battles in and around Heroldsberg and Nuremberg. Mr. Braun and his son, Harald, graciously guided the author along the route traveled by Able Company. Mr. Braun identified the sites of combat and gave the author a detailed account of what happened. See Friedrich Braun, *Der 2. Weltkrieg in den nordöstlichen Vororten von Nürnberg* (Vienna: Selbstverlag [Self-published], 1999).

6. McFarland, *History of the 15th Infantry Regiment*, 292–94; interview with Friedrich Braun, August 8, 2007; telephone interview with Michael Daly (hereafter TID), August 14, 2007; Unit Journal of the 15th Regiment, April 16, 1945.

7. "Nuremberg: Battle for a Symbol," http://www.kriegsende.nuernberg.de/english/index.html; information on the website was provided by Karl Kunze, former Headmaster of Nuremberg College and contemporary witness and historian. He is the author of *Kriegsende in Franken und der Kampf um Nürnberg im April 1945* [*The End of the War in Franconia and the Battle for Nuremberg in April 1945*], Nuremberg, Germany: Selbstverlag [Self-published], 1995.) Dr. Kunze and Sally Slenczka graciously escorted the author on a tour of historic Nuremberg and of the battle sites around the old city wall.

8. Karl Holz quoted in "Chronology of the Last Battles," in "The End of the War in Nuremberg," and in Stephen G. Fritz, *Endkampf: Soldiers, Civilians, and the End of the Third Reich,* (Lexington: University Press of Kentucky, 2004), 203; Hitler's response is quoted in "The End of the War in Nuremberg," http://www.kriegsende.nuernberg.de/english/chronology/index.html; Unit Journal of the 15th Regiment, April 16 and18, 1945.

9. "Chronology of the Last Battles" in "The End of the War in Nuremberg."

10. McFarland, *History of the 15th Infantry Regiment*, 294; telephone interview with Troy D. Cox (hereafter TIC), August 24, 2006.

11. Holz quoted in William K. Wyant, *Sandy Patch: A Biography of Lt. General Alexander M. Patch* (New York: Praeger Publishers, 1991), 191.

12. Unit Journal of the 15th Regiment, April 18, 1945.

13. Troy D. Cox, *An Infantryman's Memories of World War II* (Booneville, MS: Brown Line Printing, 2003), 145.

14. A White House press release, August 23, 1945, contains the eyewitness accounts quoted above and also the Medal of Honor citation; a War Department press release, August 4, 1945, summarizes Daly's actions, quotes eyewitnesses, and includes the citation. Both press releases are found in Medal of Honor-US Army, 1946–48, No. 2, WWII Citations, Folder 3, Box 283, US Army Chief of Information, Public Information Division, Record Group 319: Records of the Army Staff, 1903–96,

NARA II; see also *New York Times,* August 15, 1945, Cox, *An Infantryman's Memories,"* 146, and TIC, February 8, 2010; Donald G. Taggart, ed., *History of the Third Infantry Division in World War II* (Washington, DC: Infantry Journal Press, 1947), 357–58 (Taggart had access to all files relevant to the award.); TID, July 31, 2006, and June 15, 2006; letter, Kathy Dodson to Michael Daly, May 29, 2003, in author's possession. Daly's actions on April 18, 1945, along with those of Pvt. Joseph Morrel near Lohe, Germany, on the outskirts of Nuremberg, were the last acts of heroism in the European Theater recognized by the awarding of the Medal of Honor until 2000. In that year Daniel K. Inouye and Joe Hayashi were awarded Medals of Honor (Hayashi posthumously) for their actions in Italy on April 21 and April 22, 1945, respectively. See e-mail entitled "Recipients by Place and Date of Action" from Carol Cepregi, Congressional Medal of Honor Society, to author, June 5, 2009.

15. TID, July 3, 2002, March 18, 2003, August 9, 2005, July 31, 2006, and August 14, 2007; TIC, February 8, 2010; William I. Hitchcock, *The Bitter Road to Freedom: The Human Cost of Allied Victory in World War II in Europe.* (New York: Free Press, 2008), 191; Daly quote recounted during TIC, February 8, 2010.

16. Copy of "Memo to C. G., subject: 'Phone call from Colonel Dean, Chief Surgeon, ET USA,'" Military Personnel Records at the National Personnel Records Center, St. Louis, MO; letter, Michael Daly to author, November 9, 2004; TID, July 3, 2002, June 25, 2003, August 9, 2005, July 31, 2006, and August 14, 2007; telephone interview with Jesse Fisher, July 6, 2002.

17. TID, July 3, 2002, and August 6, 2005; General Patch interviewed in *Bridgeport Telegram,* October 18, 1945.

18. Sandy Patch to Julia Patch, Kitzingen, Germany, April 23, 1945, General Alexander McCarrell "Sandy" Patch Papers, United States Military Academy Special Collections and Archives and United States Military Academy Library; Patch Papers, United States Military Academy Special Collections and Archives; "Daly Double," *American Legion Magazine* (December 1945), 52; Medical Report on Michael Daly, Maj. M. A. Cox, MC, and Maj. R. M. Ericson, MC, "Michael J. Daly, 01692630, 1st Lt., A, 15th Inf., 3rd Div., 10 Field Hospital, April 19–23, 1945," Michael J. Daly Military Personnel File, National Personnel Records Center, St. Louis, MO; Office of the Adjutant General, *Army Battle Casualties and Non-battle Deaths in World War II: Final Report 7 December 1941–31,* December 1946, Statistical and Accounting Branch, Office of the Adjutant General under Direction of Program Review and Analysis Division, Office of the Comptroller of the Army (Washington, DC: Department of the Army, 1953), 6.

19. Charles B. McDonald, *The Last Offensive* (Washington, DC: Office of the Chief of Military History, US Army, 1973), 422–25; an account provided by Colonel Richard Wolf to the director of the *Stadt Archiv Nürnberg* in 1955, contained in an e-mail, Friedrich Braun to author, December 4, 2011. Wolf knew that in disobeying orders from the High Command he had committed a crime punishable by death. Early in the morning of April 20, 1945, therefore, he fled the command bunker via a secret passage. He was apprehended by US soldiers that same day. Friedrich Braun, *Der 2. Weltkrieg in den nordöstlichen Vororten von Nürnberg* [World War II in the Northeastern Suburbs of Nuremberg] (Vienna: Selbstverlag [Self-published], 1999), 305.

20. Fritz, Stephen G. *Endkampf,* 174–75, 191–92, 203; Wyant, *Sandy Patch,*

191; "The End of the War in Nuremberg." One report from the 45th Infantry Division noted cryptically that two hundred Germans had been "liquidated" in Nuremburg.

21. J. Leon Lebowitz, photographs from scrapbook, copies in author's possession; interview with Maj. Timothy A. Stoy, Historian of the 15th Regiment, June 21, 2007.

CHAPTER 12

1. Medical Report on Michael Daly, Maj. M. A. Cox, MC, and Maj. R. M. Ericson, MC, "Michael J. Daly, 01692630, 1st Lt., A, 15th Inf., 3rd Div., 10 Field Hospital, April 19–23, 1945," Michael J. Daly Military Personnel Records, National Personnel Records Center, St. Louis, MO; copies of photographs from J. Leon Lebowitz scrapbook; telephone interview with Michael Daly (hereafter TID), November 21, 2002, July 18, 2003, and June 7 and 24, 2005.

2. TID, November 21, 2002; Mel Allen, "Only Afraid to Show Fear: Portrait of a Hero." *Yankee* (May 1983): 77–79, 134–44; "Daly Double," *American Legion Magazine* (December 1945): 50.

3. TID, July 16, 2007.

4. During WWII, members of the 1st Infantry Division won sixteen Medals of Honor, the second-highest total among all army divisions. See "3rd Infantry Division in World War II," *Army Magazine* (November 2003): http://www3.ausa.org/webint/DeptArmyMagazine.nsf/byid/CCRN-6CCSAV

5. Caption under photo of Truman bestowing the Medal; "Out Going Classified Message, Re: Award of Medal of Honor to 1st Lieutenant Michael J. Daly and T/Sgt. Francis J. Clark, July 12, 1945," Army AG, Classified Decimal File, 1943–45, 200.6 (March 1, 1945) to (July 21, 1945), Record Group 404: Records of the Adjutant General's Office, 1917–58, NARA II; War Department, Classified Message Center, Decorations and Awards Branch, Military Personnel Division, The Adjutant General's Office, "The Liberation of Fortress Europe" (unpublished typescript), US Army, Chief of Information, Public Information Division, News Branch, Medal of Honor, US Army No. 11, Documents and Preliminary Monograph, Box 292, Record Group 319: Records of the Army Staff, National Archives and Records Administration II, College Park, MD (hereafter NARA II); *Bridgeport Sunday Herald,* August 26, 1945.

6. Letter, Ned Morrill to Madeleine and Paul [Daly], New York City, August 7, 1945, Daly Family Papers (hereafter DFP). The medal Daly received from Truman's hands on that rainy summer day is described in the Appendix.

7. "Hero's Welcome Accorded Capt. Daly in Fairfield," *Bridgeport Post,* August 25, 1945; "Fairfield Gives Capt. Daly Hero's Welcome; 'It's Sweller Than Getting Medal,' He Says," *Bridgeport Telegram,* August 25, 1945; "Fairfield Hails Hero Capt. Mike Daly, CMH," *Bridgeport Sunday Herald,* August 26, 1945; "Daly Double," 51; "A True Pioneer: WASP Ann [Kirk] Shaw Carter (44-W-10) aka Whirly Girl 2," http://www.wingsacrossamerica.us/web/carter_ann_2.htm; telephone interview with Mrs. Ann Kirk Shaw Carter, August 1, 2005.

8. "Thousands Take Part in Victory Party," *Fairfield News,* September 7, 1945; "10,000 See V-J Day Parade in Fairfield, Hear Capt. Daly," undated (but most likely September 7, 1945) press clipping, in author's possession.

9. *Cupola 1946*, p. 40; telephone interview with Reed P. Clark III [Georgetown Preparatory School class of 1947], August 20, 2008; *GPrep Alumnews*, October 1945; "Vincent X. Flaherty—Congressional Medal for Hoya Prep Star," *Washington Times Herald*, August 8, 1945; "Daly Double," 50–54.

10. Allen, "Only Afraid to Show Fear," 77; TID, August 24, 2005; "Daly Double," 51.

11. William K. Wyant, *Sandy Patch: A Biography of Lt. General Alexander M. Patch*. (New York: Praeger Publishers, 1991), 214–15; "Gen. Patch Urges Peacetime Draft, Unified Command" and "Famed Leader of Seventh Army Visits Col. Daly in Fairfield," *Bridgeport Telegram*, October 18, 1945; William Wyant interview with Madge Daly Potter, July 24, 1984, copy of typescript in possession of author. While on the flight to Bridgeport, Patch's pilot and aide, Major Anderson, turned over the flying to Madge, who had taken flying lessons. She even landed the plane on its return flight. A week later she received an order, forwarded by Patch, prohibiting any civilian from flying a military plane.

12. Wyant, *Sandy Patch*, 214–15; "Gen Patch Urges Peacetime Draft, Unified Command," and "Famed Leader of Seventh Army Visits Col. Daly in Fairfield," *Bridgeport Telegram*, October 18, 1945; Wyant interview with Madge Daly Potter, July 24, 1984, transcript in author's possession.

13. TID, June 24, 2005; letter, Daly to author, January 26, 2006. Army bureaucrats eventually caught up with Hughes while he was still at Cushing Hospital, but they dropped the case because they had no experience in dealing with a soldier who had left his unit without permission in order to get into combat rather than to avoid it. E-mail, W. Sanford Miller Jr. to author, August 27, 2008; e-mail, Andrew A. Smith to author confirming his brother Timothy's recollections, August 30, 2008; TID, June 24, 2005.

14. "A True Pioneer: WASP Ann [Kirk] Shaw Carter"; telephone Interview with Ann Kirk Shaw Carter, August 1, 2005.

15. TID, August 20, 2002, and June 7, 2005; Parnell E. Bach to Mel Allen, senior editor, *Yankee*, October 11, 1983, DFP.

16. TID, November 21, 2002, July 17, 2003, and March 28, June 7, August 11, 2005; telephone interview with Jack Ringel, August 3, 2008; letter, Frank J. Parker to Paul Daly, August 2, 1945, DFP.

17. TID, July 3, 2002, July 17, 2003, and August 11, 2005; Allen, "Only Afraid to Show Fear," 141; e-mail, William N. Wallace to author, July 18, 2008. Hobart "Hobey" Gardiner, a Yale University graduate and former executive for Exxon Oil, said Daly was "the best self-educated person" he knew—that he read between the lines of books and obtained more from his reading than most—a tribute to his inquisitiveness, intelligence, and Jesuit education. See e-mail, W. Sanford Miller Jr. to author, August 21, 2008.

18. TID, December 30, 2002, July 17, 2003, June 7 and July 16, 2005; e-mails, Andrew Smith to author, July 21 and August 25, 26, and 29, 2008; e-mail, Timothy Smith to author August 31, 2008.

19. TID, December 30, 2002, January 20, 2003, August 13, 2004, June 7, 2005, and July 31, 2007. For an excellent treatment of the difficulties of readjustment experienced by many returning GIs, see Thomas Childers, *Soldiers from the War Re-*

turning: The Greatest Generation's Troubled Homecoming, (Boston: Houghton Mifflin Harcourt, 2009). Law Student's Qualifying Certificate 33337, Michael Joseph Daly, May 1956, copy in possession of the author; e-mail, Andrew Smith to author, July 21, 2008; Caitlin Moore, "1959 Fairfield Town Election: The Factors allowing Democratic Leaders to Accomplish a Democratic Revolution," n.d., unpublished ms., Account no. 2002.5, copy in Fairfield Historical Society, Fairfield, CT.

EPILOGUE

1. Mel Allen, "Only Afraid to Show Fear: Portrait of a Hero," *Yankee* (May 1983): 143–44. Colonel Bates would go on to become the fifty-eighth inspector general of the army, retire as a lieutenant general, and remain a friend of Daly until his death; handwritten copy of Daly's speech in author's possession. Daly strongly opposed the war in Iraq.

2. Telephone interview with W. Sanford Miller Jr., August 31, 2008; Internet Broadway Database, http://www.ibdb.com/production.php?id=1214; telephone interview with Michael Daly (hereafter TID), July 18, 2002; e-mails, William N. Wallace to author, July 18 and August 26 and 27, 2008; e-mail, W. Sanford Miller Jr. to author, August 28, 2008; TID, July 16, 2005; e-mail, Hobart "Hobey" Gardiner to author, June 28, 2006.

3. TID, September 27, 2002, July 10, 2003, and July 16, 2005; telephone interview with W. Sanford Miller Jr., August 31, 2008. Maggie was received into the Catholic church at the Abbey of Regina Laudis in Bethlehem, CT, a religious community of contemplative Benedictine nuns that included as one of its members, Mother Margaret Georgina Patton, granddaughter of General George S. Patton and daughter of Mike's West Point classmate George S. Patton IV.

4. TID, December 30, 2002, June 9 and August 13, 2004, and July 3 and August 1, 2007. While Mike and Maggie were dating, and even after their marriage, whenever Mike called Maggie on the telephone he would begin, "Hello, this is Mike Daly," a formal mannerism that, according to a friend, "drove her crazy!" e-mail, Timothy H. Smith to author, August 30, 2008; e-mails, W. Sanford Miller Jr. to author, August 21 and 28, 2008; e-mail, Hobart "Hobey" Gardiner to author, June 27, 2006; e-mail, William N. Wallace to author, July 18, 2008; e-mail, W. Sanford Miller Jr. to author, July 1, 2009.

5. TID, June 9, 2004; e-mails, W. Sanford Miller Jr. to author August 21 and 28 and September 6, 2008.

6. E-mails, W. Sanford Miller Jr. to author, August 28 and September 6, 2008; letter, Michael Daly to author, March 6, 2003; "World War II Hero Praises Negro Soldiers in Vietnam," *Norwich* [CT] *Bulletin,* February 19, 1970. Daly supported Nixon's policy of Vietnamization while also defending the right of dissent for opponents of the war. He expressed disappointment with the length of time it was taking the South Vietnamese to improve their strength to the point that they could defend their own country. "When they are able to do that," he said, "we should accelerate the pullouts."

7. Telephone interview with Jesse Pugh, August 7, 2006.

8. TID, December 30, 2002, June 13, 2003, August 13, 2004, July 6, 2005,

August 11, 2005, and June 12, 2006; Autobiographical Sketch of Audie Leon Murphy, at Audie L. Murphy Memorial Website, http://www.audiemurphy.com/biograph.htm, and Max Hastings, "Hollywood Hero," in *Warriors: Portraits from the Battlefield* (New York Knopf, 2005), 219–35; telephone interview with W. Sanford Miller Jr., August 31, 2008; telephone interview with John Barry, July 21, 2008; e-mail, Andrew A. Smith to author, July 21, 2008; e-mail, telephone, and personal interviews with Ronald J. Bianchi, June 12, 2003, July 22, 2008, July 1, 2009, and November 23, 2011; TID, August 13, 2004.

9. TID, June 6, 2006; "The Connecticut Hospital Association 83rd Annual Meeting," Wednesday, June 13, 2001: 2001 Connecticut Hospital Association Awards, copy in author's possession; telephone interview with John Barry, July 21, 2008.

10. Allen, "Only Afraid to Show Fear," 143; TID, July 10, 2003; telephone interview with W. Sanford Miller Jr. August 31, 2008; photograph of Michael Daly's office in Allen, "Only Afraid to Show Fear," 77.

11. Andrew Sullivan to author, September 1, 2008 (e-mail); TID, September 27, 2002, June 7, 2005, and August 11, 2005; e-mail, Andrew Smith to author, July 27, 2008; letter, Michael Daly to author, March 6, 2003.

12. Allen, "Only Afraid to Show Fear"; William N. Wallace to author, July 18, 2008 (e-mail) ; "WWII Hero Earned Medal of Honor for Protecting his Men," obituary, *Los Angeles Times*, July 29, 2008.

13. Allen, "Only Afraid to Show Fear," 77; TID, June 7, 2005; Andrew Smith e-mails to author, July 27 and September 1, 2008; telephone interview with Andrew Smith, July 21, 2008; Daly to author, March 6, 2003; e-mail, W. Sanford Miller Jr. to author, July 1, 2009; letter, Michael Daly to author, August 13, 2004; Deirdre Daly to Family, October 7, 1979, copy in author's possession; Daly quoted in Allen, "Only Afraid to Show Fear" 142.

14. E-mail, Hobey Gardner to author, September 23, 2006; e-mail, William Wallace to author July 18, 2008.

15. Telephone interview with Jesse Fisher, July 6, 2002.

16. Telephone interview with Troy D. Cox July 5, 2002; Troy D. Cox, *An Infantryman's Memories of World War II* (Booneville, MS: Brown Line Printing, 2003), 230–31; e-mail, W. Sanford Miller Jr. to author, September 1, 2008.

17. TID, August 12, 2006; letter, Michael Daly to Lt. Gen. William J. Lennox, superintendent United States Military Academy, September 30, 2002, letter, Brig. Gen. Leo A. Brooks to Daly, October 9, 2002, and letter, Michael Daly to author, October 24, 2002, all in author's possession; handwritten copy of remarks made to students, 1996, in author's possession; letter, Daly to author June 6, 2002; "Michael Daly, 83, Dies; Won Medal of Honor," obituary, *New York Times*, July 29, 2008.

18. TID, December 30, 2008; telephone interview with Timothy Smith, July 21, 2008; e-mail, Timothy Smith to author, September 1, 2008.

19. Letter, Daly to author, March 28, 2005; TID, June 12, 2006; Ronald J. Bianchi to Michael, J. Daly, March 28 and September 13, 2005, letters in possession of author; telephone interview with John Barry, July 21, 2002; telephone interview with Ronald J. Bianchi, July 22, 2008;

20. *Fairfield Citizen-News,* May 24, 2006; Program, Fifty-Sixth Commencement of Fairfield University, May 21, 2006; telephone interview with Ronald J.

Bianchi, June 12, 2003; letters, Michael Daly to author, June 6, 2002, September 14, 2004, and May 30, 2006.

21. Larry Smith, *Beyond Glory: Medal of Honor Winners in Their Own Voices* (New York: W. W. Norton, 2003), xvii. See also Collin R Payne, Brian Wansink, and Koert van Ittersum, "Profiling the Heroic Leader: Empirical Lessons from Combat-Decorated Veterans of World War II," *Leadership Quarterly* 19, no. 5 (October 2008): 547–55; Thomas A. Kolditz, *In Extremis Leadership: Leading As If Your Life Depended on It* (San Francisco: Jossey-Bass, 2007), x-xi, pp. 37–39, 85, 103, 203–205.; Cadet Rom Iammartino, "Characteristics of Medal of Honor Recipients and Combat Experienced Soldiers" (typescript copy, May 2003), Research Project for Course PL498 in the Department of Behavioral Sciences and Leadership, original in Department of Behavioral Sciences and Leadership, United States Military Academy.

22. E-mail, W. Sanford Miller Jr. to author, July 17, 2008; telephone interview with Andrew Smith, July 21, 2008.

23. Homily delivered by Rev. Samuel Scott at the funeral of Michael J. Daly, July 29, 2008, Saint Pius X Church, Fairfield, Connecticut, typescript copy in author's possession.

24. This account is based on the author's personal observations at the funeral and burial service. On October 23, 2002, Congress passed Pub. L. 107–248, authorizing the presentation of a Medal of Honor Flag to recipients of the decoration. See "Designation of the Medal of Honor Flag." 36 USC § 903: US Code, http://codes .lp.findlaw.com/uscode/36/I/A/9/903/notes; "Medal of Honor Flag," The Institute of Heraldry, US Army. Archived from the original on September 11, 2006, http://web .archive.org/web/20060911012812/http://www.tioh.hqda.pentagon.mil/Flags_Guidons/ MedalOfHonorFlag.htm; Brent Scowcroft to Hobart Gardiner, November 2, 2005, in author's possession.

25. Program of the Mass of Christian Burial for Michael J. Daly, Saint Pius X Church, Fairfield, Connecticut, July 25, 2008.

APPENDIX

1. The Institute of Heraldry, Office of the Administrative Assistant to the Secretary of the Army, http://www.tioh.hqda.pentagon.mil/Awards/decorations.aspx

Glossary

UNITED STATES ARMY MILITARY UNITS, WORLD WAR II

For administrative and tactical purposes, military forces are organized in units of various sizes. Army personnel may be grouped in the following manner:

Army. Two or more corps, commanded by a lieutenant general.

Army Group. Several field armies, usually commanded by a full general.

Battalion. Three or more companies, commanded by a lieutenant colonel. (As of July 15, 1943, battalions had an authorized force of 860; as of January 24, 1945, 871.)

Company. Basic combat unit consisting of three rifle platoons, a weapons platoon, and a headquarters company, commanded by a captain. (As of July 15, 1944, infantry companies had an authorized strength of 187 men and 6 officers.)

Corps. Two or (usually) three divisions, commanded by a major general.

Division. The command units for large formations of three or more infantry regiments with various supporting troops, commanded by a major general. (An infantry division was authorized 14,300 soldiers.)

Regiment. Large unit formation consisting of three or more battalions, commanded by a colonel. (As of July 15, 1943, regiments had an authorized strength of 3,118; as of January 24, 1945, 3,068.)

Rifle Platoon. Three squads with a five-man headquarters, commanded by a lieutenant.

Rifle Squad. Twelve men led by a sergeant.

Source: Dennis W. Showalter, "Introduction to the History Book Club Edition," in Charles B. MacDonald, *Company Commander* (New York, 2006), xii-xiii; Robert S. Rush, *The U.S. Infantryman in World War II* (Oxford, 2003), 20–30.

Selected Bibliography

MANUSCRIPTS AND ARCHIVES

Big Red One Museum, Colleville-sur-Mer, Normandy, France.

"Order of Battle of the United States Army, World War II, European Theater of Operations: Divisions." Paris, France: Office of the Theater Historian, 1945. http://www.history.army.mil/documents/eto-ob/etoob-toc.htm.

Daly Family Papers. Copies in author's possession.

Fairfield Historical Society, Fairfield, Connecticut.

Federal Census, 1870. Ward 19, District 17, New York City.

Fort Stewart Museum, Fort Stewart, GA.

Georgetown Preparatory School
    Georgetown Preparatory School Archives, North Bethesda, MD.
        Blue and Gray, 1937–41 [student literary magazine]. In Office of Admissions.
        Cupola, 1937–41 [yearbook]. In Office of Institutional Advancement.
        Georgetown Preparatory School Catalogue, 1938–42. In Office of Institutional Advancement.
        Jesuit House Consultors' Minutes Books. In Jesuit Cloister.

Library of Congress. Washington, DC
    Veterans Project. American Folk Life Center.

Robert McCormick Research Center. First Division Museum at Cantigny, Wheaton, IL
    Oral History Collection.
    Photographs.
    World War Records. First Division, AEF Regular, Citations First Division. Vol. 22. Copy in Museum and Collections.

Le Mémorial Cobra de Marigny. Marigny, France.

Musée Memorial des Combats de la Poche de Colmar. Turkheim, France.

Portsmouth Priory [now Abbey] School Archives and Office of the Registrar, Portsmouth, NH.

Princeton University Undergraduate Files, Paul G. Daly. Princeton University Archives, Seeley G. Mudd Manuscript Library, Princeton University.

Quinton F. Reams Papers, US Army Military History Institute, Army Heritage and History Center, Carlisle, PA.

Saint-Loup-du-Gast Municipal Archives. Saint Loup-Du-Gast, Mayenne, France.
    "Handwritten Notes de M. l'abbe Louis Lévêque curé de Saint-Loup-du-Gast," December 22, 1940–October 1, 1980.

"Guerre 1939–1940 Contre Allemagne et Bataille de Saint-Loup DU [Gast] 5 AU 13 Août, 1944."

United States Military Academy, West Point, NY

Special Collections Department

"Official Register of the Officers and Cadets of the United States Military Academy," 1913, 1914, 1915.

"Regulations for the United States Military Academy, and Abstract of Delinquencies."

Cadet Service Record, Michael Joseph Daly, Class of 1945, and Office of the Registrar.

General Alexander McCarrell "Sandy" Patch Papers.

US Army Military History Institute, Army Heritage and History Center, Carlisle, PA

Quinton F. Reams Papers.

Lewis C. Smith, Danville, VA, Oral History Collection.

US Government Archives Relating to the Military

National Archives and Records Administration II, College Park, MD

Record Group 77: Records of the Office of the Chief of Engineers. 77.12.3 General Records of the Army Map Service and its Successors.

Record Group 94: Records of the Adjutant General's Office, 1917- Army AG, Classified Decimal File, 1943–45

Record Group 111: Office of the Chief Signal Officer, 1860–1982 Still Pictures, 1860–1982.

Signal Corps Photographs of the United States Army in World War II, especially the 1st and 3rd Divisions and in particular the 18th and 15th Infantry Regiments.

WWII French Invasion, Beach Heads, Omaha, Utah, Books 1–4.

WWII France, Invasion of Normandy, Omaha and Utah Beaches. Boxes 1302–1303.

Motion Pictures, 1917–63 (WWII training and combat films ["Army Depository Copy {hereafter ADC} Film"])

1st Infantry Division

"US Infantry in Normandy, France, July 11, 1944." ADC- 1382.

"US Infantry in Normandy, France, July 11, 1944." ADC-1410.

"Marigny, July 27, 1944." ADC-1667.

"Marigny: US Troops (18th Regiment) take Marigny, France, July 27, 1944." ADC-1993.

"Cerisy Forêt: No. 1 Enemy in Normandy: Hedgerows, July 21, 1944. ADC-1665.

3rd Infantry Division

"Shells landing on Dragon's Teeth, near Zweibrücken, Germany, March 18, 1945." ADC-3858.

"15th Regiment of 3rd Division Crosses the Rhine
River, March 26, 1945." ADC-3858
"15th Regiment in Germany, April 20, 1945."
ADC-4215.
"Wrecked City and Burning Buildings, April 20,
1945." ADC-4211.
Record Group 120. Records of the American Expeditionary Forces
(World War I)
Organization Records, 1st Division, Subject Index and Cross
Reference to Doc. File, 6603–6980, Box 138.
Record Group 319: US Army Chief of Information, Public Information
Division, New Branch.
Medal of Honor-US Army, 1946–48, No. 2, WWII Citations
Record Group 407: Adjutant General's Office, 1917–
Entry 427: WW II Operational Reports, 1940–48: Military unit files
among these records consist mostly of historical reports, after
action reports, unit journals, and general orders.
1st Infantry Division
3rd Infantry Division
18th Infantry Regiment
15th Infantry Regiment
National Personnel Records Center, Military Personnel Records (NPRC-MPR), in
Saint Louis, Missouri.

AUTHOR INTERVIEWS (IN PERSON AND BY TELEPHONE),
CORRESPONDENCE (MAIL AND E-MAIL), AND ORAL-HISTORY
TRANSCRIPTS

Mel Allen (Editor, *Yankee* magazine; author of an insightful article on Michael
Daly)
Robert L. Barrett (Classmate of Michael Daly at Georgetown Preparatory School)
John Barry (Member of the board of St. Vincent's Hospital Foundation)
Jared L. Bates (Lieutenant General [ret.]) (As a lieutenant colonel in 1982, Bates
invited Michael Daly to visit his old outfit stationed in Kitzingen, Germany,
near Würzberg.
Patrick Baumann (Local historian, Riedwihr, France)
Ludwig Benkert (Physician; resident of Bad Neustadt an der Saale, Germany, in
1945)
Ronald J. Bianchi (Vice-president for Marketing and Public Relations, St. Vincent's
Hospital, Bridgeport, Connecticut; President/Chief Executive Officer, St. Vin-
cent's Medical Center Foundation)
Friedrich Braun (Resident, Heroldsberg, Germany; historian of Battle of Nuremberg)
Harrold Braun (Son of Friedrich Braun)
John L. Brunett, SJ (Classmate of Michael Daly at Georgetown Preparatory School)
Jacqueline Elling-Cox (Daughter of James C. Elling)

Carol Cepregi (Deputy Director of Operations, Congressional Medal of Honor Society)

Reed P. Clark III (Student at Georgetown Preparatory School, 1945–49)

Troy D. Cox (private and sergeant, Able Company, 15th Regiment; reunited with Michael Daly in 1990s)

Michael Joseph Daly

Paul Gerard Daly (Michael Daly's father)

Richard Dettman (Member, Able Company)

Julia Ann Patch Diehl (Daughter of General Alexander Patch)

Katherine Dea Elling-Dodson (Daughter of James C. Elling)

Phillip Drake (Brother-in-law of Michael Daly)

Jesse Fisher (Dentist; sergeant in Able Company who saved Michael Daly's life in Nuremberg)

Hobart "Hobey" Gardiner (Neighbor and close friend of Michael Daly in his later years)

Alison D. Gerard (Sister of Michael Daly)

Jack D. Kessinger (Private and scout in Able Company, 15th Regiment; recipient of Silver Star in 1945.

Gerard F. Kunkel (Georgetown Preparatory School Class of 1942)

Karl Kunze, Ph.D. (Historian, author, former headmaster of the Nuremberg College; resident of Nuremberg during World War II)

Julian Leon Leibowitz (Company clerk, Able Company, 15th Regiment)

Bernard Marie and Claude Marie (Brothers living in La Maugeraye, France, who as young boys lived near where Michael Daly's company was encamped)

W. Sanford Miller Jr. (Stepson of Michael J. Daly)

Alexander M. "Sandy" Patch (Lieutenant General, US Army; friend of Daly family)

Madge Daly Potter (Sister of Michael Daly [transcript of interview by William Wyant, July 24, 1984; copy in author's possession])

Roger Portier (Fourteen years old at time of Battle of Marigny; founder and director of Cobra Memorial, in Marigny, France)

Charles S. Porucznik (Son of Stanley A. Porucznik)

Stanley A. Porucznik (Staff sergeant, Able Company)

Jesse Pugh (Company commander, Able Company, Germany, 1984)

Victor Le Rai, George Bréteau, Fernand Thuault, and Alfred Monsallier (four citizens of Saint-Loup-du-Gast, France, August 4, 2007)

Jack Ringel (Resident of Fairfield, Connecticut; longtime friend of Michael Daly)

André and Valérie Rosselot (residents of Biesheim, France; lived in the village when US forces liberated it)

Robert Schertzinger (lifelong resident, Biesheim, France; close friend of Rosselots; town historian and author of history of Biesheim during war)

Marcel and Mathilda Schmetz (Founders, Remember Museum, Thimister-Clermont, Belgium)

James E. "Ed" Shilstone (Classmate of Michael Daly at West Point)

Andrew A. and Timothy H. Smith (Brothers; friends of Daly family)

Lewis C. Smith (Private, 3rd Platoon, I Company, 3rd Battalion, 18th Regiment [transcript in Oral History Collection, McCormick Research Center, 1st Division Library and Museum])

Timothy H. Smith (Daly family friend)
Lt. Col. Timothy R. Stoy (historian for Society of the 3rd Infantry Div. and the 15th Regiment Assoc.)
Robert F. Stringer (Resident of Minnesota; 2nd lieutenant, Company I, 18th Regiment [transcript, p. 5, Oral History Collection, McCormick Research Center at Cantigny, Wheaton, IL; typescript, Veterans Project, American Folk Life Center, Library of Congress, Washington, DC])
Willie W. Sutherland (Last surviving member of I Company, 18th Regiment, at time of telephone interview, June 23, 2009)
Geert van den Bogaert, Bayeux, France (Tour guide, Normandy invasion sites)
William N. Wallace (Brother of Maggie Daly; brother-in-law of Michael Daly)
Dean Weissert (Resident of Eustice, Nebraska; member of Company H, 18th Regiment [transcript of interview with Geert van den Bogaert, June, 2004])
Karl Wunsch (Longtime resident of Rothenbuch, Germany)
Pia Wunch (Daughter of Karl Wunch; resident of Rothenbuch, Germany)
Halle and Herman Wind (Longtime residents of Laudenbach, Germany)
Gerard Zoeller (Ten-year-old resident of Grossheubach, Germany, in 1945; later served in 3rd Division and became American citizen)

NEWSPAPERS

Bridgeport Post, August 25, 1945
Bridgeport Sunday Herald, August 26, 1945
Bridgeport Sunday Post, June 6, 1943
Bridgeport Telegram, June 12, 1974; August 25, 1945, October 18, 1945
Fairfield News, June 11, 1943, 4-A
Fairfield Citizen-News, June 12, 1974, May 24, 2006
Fairfield Citizen-Times, June 12, 1974
Little Hoya (Georgetown Preparatory School newspaper), 1937–41
Los Angeles Times, July 29, 2008
New York Times, 1893; 1894; 1896; March 24 and March 30, 1919; August 23, 1945; and July 29, 2008. See also "Obituary Notes," March 18, 1919, March 20, 1919, September 29, 1920, December 28, 1920, and May 27, 1921.
Norwich [Ct.] *Bulletin,* February 19, 1970,
Tacoma Tribune, September 25, 1943
Washington Daily News, August 23, 1945
Washington Times Herald, August 8, 1945

GOVERNMENT PUBLICATIONS

Army Battle Casualties and Nonbattle Deaths in World War II: Final Report 7 December 1941–31 December 1946. Washington, DC: Program Review and Analysis Division, Office of the Comptroller of the Army, 1953. http://www.ibiblio.org/hyperwar/USA/ref/Casualties/index.html
Ballard, Ted. *Rhineland.* Washington, DC: Center of Military History, US Army, 1995. http://www.army.mil/cmh/brochures/rhineland/rhineland.htm

Blumenson, Martin. *Breakout and Pursuit*. Washington, DC: Center of Military History, US Army, 2005. http://www.archive.org/details/breakoutpursuitooblum

Cirillo, Roger. *Ardennes Alsace*. Washington, DC: Center of Military History, US Army, 1995. http://www.45thdivision.org/CampaignsBattles/ardennes_alsace.htm

Clarke, Jeffrey J., and Robert Ross Smith. *Riviera to the Rhine*. Washington, DC: Center of Military History, US Army, 1993. http://www.archive.org/details/rivieratorhineooclar

Gropman, Alan L., ed. *The Big "L": American Logistics in World War II*. Washington, DC: National Defense University Press, 1997.

Harrison, Gordon A. *Cross Channel Attack*. Washington, DC: Center of Military History, US Army, 2002. http://warchronicle.com/16th_infantry/historiantales_wwii/crosschannel_easyred.htm

"Honor System and SOP." USCC Pamphlet 632–1. West Point, NY: Department of the Army, United States Corps of Cadets. 1999. http://www.west-point.org/publications/honorsys/honorsys.html

"In Brief." *Intelligence Bulletin* 3, no. 8 (April 1945). http://www.lonesentry.com/articles/inbrief/index.html

Keast, William R. *Provision of Enlisted Replacements*, Army Ground Forces Studies No. 7. Washington, DC: Center of Military History, US Army, 1946. http://www.history.army.mil/books/agf/AGF007/index.htm

Keast, William R., Robert R. Palmer, and Bell Irvin Wiley. *The Procurement and Training of Ground Combat Troops*. Washington, DC: Center of Military History, US Army, 2003. http://www.archive.org/stream/procurementtrainoopalm/procurementtrainoopalm_djvu.txt.

Kington, Donald M. "The Plattsburg Movement and Its Legacy," *Relevance: The Quarterly Journal of the Great War Society* 6, no. 4 (Autumn 1997): 4. http://www.worldwar1.com/tgws/re1011.htm

MacDonald, Charles B. *The Last Offensive*. Washington, DC: Office of the Chief of Military History, US Army, 1973. http://www.history.army.mil/html/books/007/7-9-1/index.html

———. *The Siegfried Line Campaign*. Washington, DC: Office of the Chief of Military History, US Army, 1963. http://www.history.army.mil/books/wwii/Siegfried/Siegfried%20Line/siegfried-fm.htm

Omaha Beachhead (6 June–13 June 1944). Washington, DC: War Department, Historical Division, 1945. http://www.history.army.mil/books/wwii/100-11/100-11.HTM

Palmer, Robert R. *The Mobilization of the Ground Army*. Washington, DC: Historical Section, Army Ground Forces, 1946. http://www.history.army.mil/books/agf/AGF004/index.htm

Service Survey Questionnaire. Veterans Collection, 1st Infantry Division, 18th Regiment. Carlisle Barracks, PA: Army Heritage and Education Center. http://www.carlisle.army.mil/ahec/VEC/historical.cfm

Stewart, Richard W., ed. *American Military History*. Vol. 2, *The United States Army in a Global Era, 1917–2003*. Washington, DC: Center of Military History, US Army, 2005. http://www.history.army.mil/books/AMH-V2/AMH%20V2/index.htm

West Point Alumni Foundation. *Register of Graduates and Former Cadets, United States Military Academy.* West Point, NY: United States Military Academy, 1998.

BOOKS

Abell, William S. *Fifty Years at Garrett Park: Georgetown Preparatory School, 1919–1969.* Baltimore, MD: Private printing, 1970.

Adam, Edwin K., comp. "A Little of the History of Company A, 1st BN, 15th Infantry Regiment, 3rd Infantry Division, World War II (as told by the former members and taken from Morning Reports)." Clarksville, IN: The Fifteenth Infantry Regiment Association, 1996.

Ambrose, Stephen E. *D-Day, June 6, 1944: The Climactic Battle of World War II.* New York: Simon and Schuster, 1994.

———. *Citizen Soldiers: The US Army from the Normandy Beaches to the Bulge to the Surrender of Germany, June 7, 1944–May 7, 1945.* New York: Simon and Schuster, 1997.

———. *Band of Brothers: E Company, 506th Regiment, 101st Airborne, from Normandy to Hitler's Eagle's Nest.* New York, Simon and Schuster, 2001.

———. *Duty, Honor, Country: A History of West Point.* Baltimore: Johns Hopkins University Press, 1966.

Ambrose, Stephen E., Cowley Robert, et al. *No End Save Victory: Perspectives on World War II.* New York: G.P. Putnam's, 2001.

Asahina, Robert. *Just Americans; How Japanese Americans Won a War at Home and Abroad: The Story of the 100th battalion/442nd Regimental Combat Team in World War II.* New York: Gotham, 2006.

Atkinson, Rick. *The Day of Battle: The War in Italy and Sicily, 1943–1944.* New York: Henry Holt and Co., 2007.

———. *An Army at Dawn: The War in North Africa, 1942–1943.* New York: Henry Holt & Co., 2002.

Aus der Chronik der Erziehungsanstalt Rothenbuch II [The Chronicle of Rothenbuch Educational Establishment 2]. Teil, S. 1–7. N.p., 1945. Furnished by Thomas Noll, treasurer of the Municipality of Rothenbuch, Germany.

Balkoski, Joseph. *Beyond the Beachhead: The 29th Infantry Division in Normandy.* Mechanicsburg, PA: Stackpole Books, 1999.

———. *Omaha Beach: D-Day, June 6, 1944.* Mechanicsburg, PA: Stackpole Books, 2004.

Baumer, Robert W., with Mark J. Reardon. *American Iliad: The 18th Infantry Regiment in World War II.* Bedford, PA: Aberjona Press, 2004.

Benamou, Jean-Pierre. *Omaha Beach, Normandy, 1944.* Bilingual Edition. Cully, France: ORÉP Edition and Communication, 2004.

Bennett, Donald V., with William R. Forstchen. *Honor Untarnished: A West Point Graduate's Memoir of World War II.* New York: Forge, 2003.

Bonn, Keith E. *When the Odds Were Even: The Vosges Mountain Campaign, October 1944–January 1945.* Novato, CA: Presidio Press, 2006.

Braun, Friedrich. *Der 2. Weltkrieg in den nordöstlichen Vororten von Nürnberg*

[World War II in the Northeastern Suburbs of Nuremberg]. Vienna: Selbstverlag [Self-published], 1999.

Brooks, Victor. *The Normandy Campaign: From D-Day to the Liberation of Paris.*
Cambridge, MA: Da Capo Press, 2002.

Brown, John Sloan. *Draftee Division: The 88th Infantry Division in World War II.*
Lexington: University Press of Kentucky, 1986.

Carafano, James Jay. *After D-Day: Operation Cobra and the Normandy Breakout.*
Boulder, CO: Lynne Rienner Publishers, 2000.

Champagne, Daniel R. *Dogface Soldiers: The Story of B Company, 15th regiment,
3rd Infantry Division.* Bennington, VT: Merriam Press, 2003.

Childers, Thomas. *Soldiers from the War Returning: The Greatest Generation's
Troubled Homecoming.* Boston: Houghton Mifflin Harcourt, 2009.

Clifford, John Gary. *The Citizen Soldiers: The Plattsburg Training Camp Movement,
1913–1920.* Lexington: University Press of Kentucky, 1972.

Collier, Peter, and Nick Del Calzo. *Medal of Honor: Portraits of Valor Beyond the
call of Duty.* Congressional Medal of Honor Foundation. New York: Artisan,
2003.

Cox, Troy D. *An Infantryman's Memories of World War II.* Booneville, MS: Brown
Line Printing, 2003.

De Lattre de Tassigny, Jean. *The History of the French 1st Army.* London, 1952.

*Dokumentation uber das Kriegsende in Grossheubach [Documentation of the War's
End in Grossheubach.* A detailed summary of the exhibition of the Historical
and Geographical Society in the spring of 1995 and the draft of the record of
those killed in action in World War 2]. Grossheubach, Germany: Grossheubach Historical and Geographical Society, 1995.

Doubler, Michael D. *Closing with the Enemy: How GIs Fought the War in Europe,
1944–1945.* Lawrence, KS: University Press of Kansas, 1994.

Engler Jr., Richard E., and Theodore MacKechnie. *The Final Crisis: Combat in
Northern Alsace, January 1945.* Bedford, PA: Aberjona Press, 1999.

Esposito, Cheryl. *The 756th Tank Battalion in the European Theater.* N.p.: Privately
Printed, 1999.

Evans, Richard J. *The Third Reich at War.* New York: Penguin Press, 2009.

Fritz, Stephen G. *Endkampf: Soldiers, Civilians, and the Death of the Third Reich*
Lexington: University Press of Kentucky, 2004.

Fussell, Paul. *The Boys' Crusade: The American Infantry in Northwestern Europe.*
New York: Modern Library, 2003.

———. *Doing Battle: The Making of a Skeptic.* Boston: Little Brown and Co., 1996.

———. *Wartime: Understanding and Behavior in the Second World War.* New York:
Oxford University Press, 1989.

Goddard, William B., ed. *The Seventh United States Army: In France and Germany,
1944–1945.* 3 vols. Heidelberg, Germany: Heidelberg Gutenberg Printing,
1946. http://wwiiarchives.net/servlet/document/index/107/0

Graham, Don. *No Name on the Bullet: A Biography of Audie Murphy.* New York,
Viking, 1989.

Halter, Alphonse, and Gilbert Meyer. *Dictionnaire biographique des maréchaux et* généraux alsaciens et des maréchaux et généraux morts en Alsace: de l'Ancien Régime à nos jours. Colmar, France: Editions d'Alsace, 1994.

Hastings, Max. Armageddon: The Battle for Germany, 1944–1945. New York: Knopf, 2004.

———. Overlord: D-Day and the Battle for Normandy. New York: Simon and Schuster, 1984.

———. Warriors: Portraits from the Battlefield. New York: Knopf, 2005.

Heidenheimer, Arnold J. Vanguard to Victory: History of the 18th Infantry. Aschaffenburg, Germany: Main-Echo Verlag, 1954.

Hitchcock, William I. The Bitter Road to Freedom: The Human Cost of Allied Victory in World War II in Europe. New York: Free Press, 2009.

Huebner, Andrew J. The Warrior Image: Soldiers in American Culture from the Second World War to the Vietnam Era. Chapel Hill: University of North Carolina Press, 2008.

Johnson, Franklyn A. One More Hill. New York: Funk and Wagnalls, 1949.

Joiner, Ann Livingston. A Myth in Action : The Heroic Life of Audie Murphy. Baltimore: Publish America, 2006.

Knickerbocker, H. R., et al. Danger Forward: The Story of the First Division in World War II. Washington, DC: Society of the First Division, 1947.

Kolditz, Thomas A. In Extremis Leadership: Leading As If Your Life Depended on It. San Francisco: Jossey-Bass, 2007.

Kotlowitz, Robert. Before Their Time: A Memoir. New York: Knopf, 1997.

Kunze, Karl. Kriegsende in Franken und der Kampf um Nürnberg im April 1945 [The End of the War in Franconia and the Battle for Nuremberg in April 1945]. Vienna, Austria: Selbstverlag [Self-published], 1995.

Longacre, Edward G. War in the Ruins: The American Army's Last Battle with Nazi Germany. Yardley, PA: Westholme Publisher, 2010.

MacDonald, Charles B. Company Commander. Introduction by Dennis E. Showalter. New York: History Book Club, 2006.

———. The Mighty Endeavor: The American War in Europe. New York, Quill, 1986.

Mansoor, Peter R. The GI Offensive in Europe: The Triumph of American Infantry Divisions, 1941–1945. Lawrence, KS: University Press of Kansas, 1999.

Marshall, S. L. A. Men against Fire: The Problem of Battle Command. Norman, OK: University of Oklahoma Press, 2000.

Mauldin, Bill. Up Front. New York: Henry Holt and Co., 1945.

McCaulay, Philip Martin. World War II Medal of Honor Recipients. Raleigh, NC, 2010.

McFarland, Robert, C., ed. The History of the 15th Regiment in World War II. Chelsea, MI: Society of the Third Infantry Division, 1990.

McManus, John C. The Americans at D-Day: The American Experience at the Normandy Invasion. New York: Forge, 2004.

Mikaelian, Allen. Medal of Honor: Profiles of America's Military Heroes from the Civil War to the Present. Introduction by Mike Wallace. New York: Hyperion, 2002.

Miller, Edward G. *Nothing Less Than Full Victory: Americans at War in Europe, 1944–1945.* Annapolis, MD: Naval Institute Press, 2007.

Murphy, Audie. *To Hell and Back: The Classic Memoir of World War II by America's Most Decorated Soldier.* New York, Henry Holt and Co., 2002.

Murphy, Edward F. *Heroes of World War II.* Novato, CA: Presidio Press, 1990.

Ochs, Stephen J. *Academy on the "Patowmack": Georgetown Preparatory School, 1789–1927.* Rockville, MD: Georgetown Preparatory School, 1989.

Patch, Joseph Dorst. *A Soldier's War: The First Infantry Division, AEF (1917–1918).* Corpus Christi, TX: Mission Press, 1966.

Proft, R. J. *United States of America's Congressional Medal of Honor Recipients and their Official Citations.* Columbia Heights, MN: Highland House II, 2002.

Pyle, Ernie. *Brave Men.* New York, 1944.

Ruppenthal, Roland G. *Logistical Support of the Armies.* Vol. 1: *May 1941–September 1944.* Washington, DC: Department of the Army. 1953. http://www.archive.org/details/logisticalsuppor11rupp

———. *Logistical Support of the Armies.* Vol. 2: *September 1944–May 1945.* Washington, DC: Department of the Army. 1959. http://www.archive.org/details/logisticalsuppor11rupp

Rush, Robert S. *GI: The US Infantryman in World War II.* Oxford, UK: Osprey Publishing, 2003.

———. *Hell in Hürtgen Forest: The Ordeal and Triumph of an American Infantry Regiment.* Lawrence, KS: University Press of Kansas, 2004.

Schertzinger, Robert. *Biesheim: Photographiquement Votre.* Biesheim, France, 2002.

Schilderung der Chronik Bobrowitz wohl der Pfarrchronik folgend mit Ergänzung von Artur Pfeifer, ebd., S. 33–34. Furnished to author by Thomas Noll, Treasurer of the Municipality of Rothenbuch, Germany

Seidel, Franz. *Lost Battalions.* Novato CA: Presidio Press, 2007.

Shirley, John. *I Remember: Stories of a Combat Infantryman in World War II.* Livermore, CA: J. B. Shirley, 1993.

Short, Neil. *Germany's West Wall: The Siegfried Line.* Illustrated by Chris Taylor. Oxford, UK: Osprey Publishing, 2004.

Simpson, Harold B. *Audie Murphy, American Soldier.* Hillsboro, TX: Hill College Press, 1999.

Sinton, Starr, Robert Hargis, and Ramiro Bujeiro. *World War II Medal of Honor Recipients.* Vol. 2, *Army and Air Corps.* Oxford, UK: Osprey Publishing, 2003.

Slaughter, John Robert. *Omaha Beach and Beyond: The Long March of Sergeant Bob Slaughter.* Minneapolis, MN: Zenith Press, 2007.

Sloat, Warren. *The Battle for the Soul of New York.* New York, 2002.

Smith, Larry. *Beyond Glory: Medal of Honor Winners in Their Own Voices.* New York: W. W. Norton, 2003.

Taggart, Donald G., ed. *History of the Third Infantry Division in World War II.* Washington, DC: Infantry Journal Press, 1947.

Thompson, Jack, Jack Belden, and Don Whitehead. *Danger Forward: The Story of the First Division in World War I.* Washington, DC: Society of the First Division, 1947.

Weigley, Russell F. *Eisenhower's Lieutenants: The Campaigns of France and Germany, 1944–1945.* 2 vols. Bloomington: Indiana University Press, 1981.

West, Bing. *The Strongest Tribe: War, Politics, and the Endgame in Iraq.* New York: Random House, 2008.

Wheeler, James Scott. *The Big Red One: America's Legendary 1st Infantry Division from World War I to Desert Storm.* Lawrence, KS: University Press of Kansas, 2007.

Whiting, Charles. *American Hero: The Life and Death of Audie Murphy.* Long Preston, UK: Magna Large Print Books, 2003.

———. *America's Forgotten Army: The True Story of the US Seventh Army in WWII — and an Unknown Battle That Changed History.* New York: St. Martin's Press, 2001.

Whitlock, Flint. *The Fighting First: The Untold Story of the Big Red One on D-Day* Boulder, CO: Westview Press, 2004.

Williams, Clark. *The Story of a Grateful Citizen.* New York: privately printed, 1934.

Williams, Mary H., comp. *Chronology: 1941–1945.* Washington, DC: Office of the Chief of Military History, Department of the Army, 1960. http://www .history.army.mil/html/books/011/11-1/index.html

Wyant, William K. *Sandy Patch: A Biography of Lt. Gen. Alexander M. Patch.* New York: Praeger Publishers, 1991.

Yeide, Harry, and Mark Stout. *First to the Rhine: The 6th Army Group in World War II.* Minneapolis, MN: Zenith Press, 2007.

Zoepf, Wolf T. *Seven Days in January: With the 6th SS-Mountain Division in Operation Nordwind,* Bedford, PA: Aberjona Press, 2001.

ARTICLES

Adam, Edwin K., comp. *A Little of the History of Company A, 1st BN, 15th Infantry Regiment, Infantry Division, World War II (as told by former members and taken from "Morning Reports).* The Dragon (Fifteenth Infantry Regiment Association Newsletter). Clarksville, IN: The 15th Infantry Regiment Association, 1996.

Allen, Mel. "Only Afraid to Show Fear: Portrait of a Hero." *Yankee* (May 1983): 77–79, 134–44.

"Alumnus of the Year." [Georgetown Preparatory School] *Alumnews,* October 1945.

"Audie Murphy Born Seventy-Five Years Ago." *The Dragon* [15th Infantry Regiment Association newsletter] (April 1999): 10–13.

Broadwater, Robert. "The 3rd Infantry Division in World War II." *Army Magazine* 53, no. 11 (November 2003): 34–40. http://www3.ausa.org/webint/ DeptArmyMagazine.nsf/byid/CCRN-6CCSAV

"Daly Double." *American Legion Magazine* (December 1945): 50–54.

"Excerpts from July 1997 interview with Gene Palumbo." *Audie Murphy Research*

Foundation Newsletter 3 (Winter 1998): 8–12. www.audiemurphy.com/amrf/
amrf_news3.pdf

"Fighting in Normandy." *Combat Lessons* 4 (1944): 5–19. http://www.lonesentry
.com/normandy lessons/index.html

"Germany: Gott mit Uns." *Time,* September 18, 1944. http://www.time.com/time/
magazine/article/0,9171,796696,00.html?promoid=googlep

Ginn Jr., L. Holmes, W. E. Wilkinson, and Edward J. Whiteley. "Combat Exhaustion." Reports of the General Board, United States Forces, European Theater,
no. 91. http://www.cgsc.edu/carl/eto/eto.asp

Ginn Jr., L. Holmes, Edward J. Whiteley. and W. E. Wilkinson. "Trench Foot (Cold
Injury, Ground Type)." Reports of the General Board, United States Forces,
European Theater, no. 94. http://www.cgsc.edu/carl/eto/eto.asp

Guelzo, Allen C. "Hero Standing." *Imprimis* 38, no. 5/6 (May/June 2009): 4–7.

Iammartino, Rom. "Characteristics of Medal of Honor Recipients and Combat
Experienced Soldiers." Typescript, May 2003. Original in Department of
Behavioral Sciences and Leadership, United States Military Academy, West
Point, NY.

Mataxis, Ted. "7th Army's Operations during Nordwind, Hitler's Last Offensive."
Paper presented at 1998 meeting of Society of Military History. http://www
.trailblazersww2.org/history_nordwind_mataxis.htm

Moore, Caitlin. "1959 Fairfield Town Election: The Factors Allowing Democratic
Leaders to Accomplish a Democratic Revolution." n.d. Acc. no. 2002.5. Copy
in Fairfield Historical Society, Fairfield, CN.

Ochs, Stephen J. "Gallantry above and Beyond: The Story of Michael Daly '41,
Prep's [Georgetown Preparatory School's] Medal of Honor Recipient," *Alumnews* (Fall 2003): 2–11.

———. "When Prep [Georgetown Preparatory School] Said 'No' to the Redskins."
Alumnews (Fall 2002): 8–11.

Payne, Collin R, Brian Wansink, and Koert van Ittersum. "Profiling the Heroic
Leader: Empirical Lessons from Combat-Decorated Veterans of World
War II." *Leadership Quarterly* 19, no. 5 (October 2008): 547–55.

Smoler, Frederic. "The Secret of the Soldiers Who Didn't Shoot." *American Heritage*
40, no. 2 (March 1989): 37–45.

Spiller, Roger J. "S. L. A. Marshall and the Ratio of Fire." *RUSI Journal* 133, no. 4
(Winter 1988): 63–71.

"There Are Two Possibilities." *Rüstzeug für die Propaganda in der Ortsgruppe* 2
(January 1945): 31. German Propaganda Archive. http://www.calvin.edu/
academic/cas/gpa/2choices.htm. Accessed November 25, 2011.

Trautman, Emil. "Ike, Patton, and Me: Seven Years with the 15th," *The Dragon*
[15th Infantry Regiment Association newsletter], October 2006: 15–22.

Van Way, Charles W., Cooper B. Rhodes, and Ben P. Stratton. "Appointments and
Promotions in the European Theater of Operations." Report no. 6. General
Board, United States Forces, European Theater of Operations. Combined
Arms Research Library, Fort Leavenworth, Kansas. http://www.cgsc.edu/carl/
eto/eto.asp

Van Way, Charles W., John I. Ladd, and Charles W. Daly. "Award and Decorations in a European Theater of Operations." Report no. 10. General Board, United States Forces, European Theater of Operations, Combined Arms Research Library, Fort Leavenworth, KS. http://www.cgsc.edu/carl/eto/eto-010.pdf

"West Wall, Springboard of 1940, Assumes Defensive Role." *Tactical and Technical Trends* 51 (October 1944). http://www.lonesentry.com/articles/ttt/westwall-siegfried-line.html. Last Accessed December 5, 2011.

Wiggins Jr., Kennard R. (Brigadier General [ret.]). "Lieutenant General John Wilson (Iron Mike) O'Daniel, US Army." *Delaware Journal of Military History* 1, no. 1. N.d. http://militaryheritage.org/JrnlMilHistory.html. Last accessed November 30, 2011.

INTERNET SOURCES

"The AMERICAL Division History." http://www.lonesentry.com/usdivisions/history/infantry/division/pacific/americal_infantry_division.html. Last accessed December 5, 2011.

Audie Murphy Research Foundation. http://www.audiemurphy.com/amrf.htm. Last accessed December 5, 2011.

Buchen-Busch Weld Attack: 44th Infantry Part I. http://efour4ever.com/44thdivision/buchen.htm. Last accessed December 5, 2011.

Burrelli, David F. "Medal of Honor: History and Issues," Library of Congress, Congressional Research Service, Foreign Affairs and National Defense Division. http://www.mishalov.com/Medal_Honor_History_Issues.html Last accessed December 5, 2011.

Cobra Memorial, Marigny, France. http://www.normandie-tourisme.fr/Cobra-Memorial—Memorial-Cobra/PCU/MARIGNY/fiche-PCUNOR 050FS00085–2.html. Last accessed November 25, 2011.

"Colmar Pocket." *Wikipedia.* http://en.wikipedia.org/wiki/Colmar_Pocket. Last accessed December 5, 2011.

Dogface Soldiers: US Third Division, World War II. http://www.dogfacesoldiers.org. Last accessed December 5, 2011.

The Dragon (Fifteenth Infantry Regiment Association Newsletter). http://www.15thinfantry.org/DragonIssues.htm. Last accessed December 5, 2011.

Eighteenth Infantry Regiment Association. http://www.18inf.org. Accessed November 25, 2011.

The End of the War in Nuremberg. http://www.kriegsende.nuernberg.de/english/index.html. Accessed November 25, 2011.

"Fifteenth Infantry Regiment Lineage and Historical Narrative." http://www.oocities.org/eureka/plaza/7750/15thinfo2.html. Last accessed December 5, 2011.

"First Battalion—15th Infantry Regiment." http://www.stewart.army.mil/units/3BCT/unit115INF/history.asp. Last accessed November 25, 2011.

"History," Congressional Medal of Honor Society. http://www.homeofheroes.com/moh/history/society_history.html Last accessed December 5, 2011.

Internet Broadway Database (IBDB): The Official Source for Broadway Information. http://www.ibdb.com/production.php?id=1214. Last accessed December 5, 2011.

"Medal of Honor Flag." The Institute of Heraldry, US Army. Archived September 11, 2006. http://www.tioh.hqda.pentagon.mil/UniformedServices/Flags/ Medal_of_Honor_Flag.aspx. Accessed November 25, 2011.

"The Memorial to the US 1st Division at Buzancy." http://www.webmatters.net/ france/ww1_buzancy_usa.htm. Accessed November 25, 2011.

"Military Medals." http://usmilitary.about.com/od/armymedals/ss/moh.htm. Last accessed December 5, 2011.

National Order of Battlefield Commissions. http://en.wikipedia.org/wiki/ Battlefield_promotion. Last accessed December 5, 2011.

"Operation Cobra: The Breakout." Normandie 1944 Espace Historique. http://www .normandiememoire.com/NM60Anglais/2_histo4/histo4_p07_gb.htm. Accessed November 25, 2011.

Remember Museum, Thimister-Clermont, Belgium. http://remembermuseum.com/ en/?Remember_Museum. Accessed November 25, 2011.

756 Tank Battalion Association. http://www.756tank.com/index.html. Last accessed December 5, 2011.

Society of the First Infantry Division. http://www.1stid.org. Accessed November 25, 2011.

Society of the Third Infantry Division, US Army. http://www.warfoto.com/3rdiv .htm. Last accessed December 5, 2011.

"The Unknown Soldier Comes Home, 1921." http://www.eyewitnesstohistory.com/ unknown.htm. Last accessed December 5, 2011.

US Armed Forces Award. http://www.tioh.hqda.pentagon.mil/Awards/ order_of_precedence.aspx. Last accessed December 5, 2011.

US Army Divisions in World War II. http://www.historyshots.com/usarmy/ backstory.cfm. Last accessed December 5, 2011.

"West Point in the Making of America." http://americanhistory.si.edu/westpoint/ history_6b.html. Last accessed December 5, 2011.

AUDIOVISUALS

"Ringel Family Memories." 16mm color film of 1946 Memorial Day parade in Fairfield, Connecticut. Courtesy Jack Ringel, Fairfield, Connecticut.

The Best Years of Our Lives. Samuel Goldwyn, 1946.

Index

Note: Page numbers in *italics* indicate photographs and illustrations.

panzerfäuste: and Allied invasion of Germany, 144–45, 152–54; and Battle of Normandy, 72; and Battle of Nuremberg, 157, 160, 164; and Colmar Pocket campaign, 96, 117; and German *Kampfgruppe,* 144–45; and *Hitlerjugend* battalions, 157

Panzer IV tanks, 99, 117

parades honoring Daly, 170–71, *171,* 174

Paris, France, 120–21

Parker, Frank, 7, 8–9, 179

Patch, Alexander McCarrell "Mac," III, 45, 81, 84–86, 88–89, 116

Patch, Alexander "Sandy," *89;* on American front-line troops, 135; and Ardennes offensive, 92; and assault on the Siegfried Line, 122; assigned to Seventh Army, 45; background, 82–83; and chain of command, *132;* and Colmar Pocket campaign, 85, 93; and command changes, 86–87; commission of Mike Daly, 82, 88–89; illness and death, 176–77; and invasion of Germany, 143; leadership style, 83–85, 86–87; loss of son, 85–86; and Operation Anvil, 82–83; and Pacific theater service, 28–31; relationship with Daly family, 16, 41, 81–82, 85–89, 167–68, 174, 176–77, 218n23; reputation among GIs, 224n2; and strain of war, 107

Patch, Joseph "Dorst," 5, 8–10, 16, 28

Patton, George, IV, 27, 36

Patton, George S., Jr.: and Battle of Normandy, 71, 74; and invasion of Germany, 147; and invasion of southern France, 85; Patch on, 86; replaced by Paul Daly, 45

Payne, Deland, 114

Pearl Harbor, 28, 120

Peckham, Elijah, 72

Périers-Saint-Lô highway, 69

Pickler, John M., 188

pillboxes, 121, 124. *See also* Siegfried Line (West Wall)

Pius XII, 186

Plattsburg Training Camp, 7

political affiliation of the Daly family, 15, 182

Portsmouth Priory School, 4, 28, 29, 177

Porucznik, Stanley A. "Proz," *135,* 136, 153

Potter, Kenneth, 116

Preh, Walter Jacob, 153, 154

"Prep Spirit" (Daly), 21, 25

Presidential Unit Citation, 117

Princeton Alumni Weekly, 6

prisoners of war: and Allied advance into Belgium, 80; and Battle of Normandy, 60, 63, 66, 78, 79; and Battle of Nuremberg, 159, 162–63, 169; and Colmar Pocket campaign, 108, 114; treatment of, 141–42, 162–63; used as labor by Germans, 147

propaganda, 147, 149, 160

psychological stress of war, 105–6, 109, 130, 131, 138

public opinion on the war, 80

Pugh, Jesse, 188

Purple Heart magazine, 195

Purple Hearts: awarded to Michael Daly, xviii, 4, 93; awarded to Murphy, 231n49; awarded to Paul Daly, 6, 8; origin and design of, 204

Pyle, Ernie, 79, 117

race relations, 188

Rasp, Siegfried, 97

ratio-of-fire studies, 234n8

Ratio Studiorum, 19

Ray, Brian, xiii

Reagan, Ronald, 193

Reasoner, Harry, 193

Regimental Combat Teams, 49, 51, 54

Reich Labor Service, 160

Repp, Walter, 148

Rhine-Rhone Canal, 110